Books are to be returned on or before
the last date below.

SOCIOLOGISTS AND MUSIC

SOCIOLOGISTS AND MUSIC

AN INTRODUCTION TO THE STUDY OF MUSIC AND SOCIETY

SECOND EDITION

PAUL HONIGSHEIM

Edited, with a new Preface and
Bibliographic Update by

K. PETER ETZKORN

Transaction Publishers
New Brunswick (U.S.A.) and London (U.K.)

New material this edition copyright © 1989 by Transaction Publishers, New Brunswick, New Jersey 08903
Originally published in 1973 by John Wiley and Sons

Library of Congress Catalog Number: 88-13830
ISBN: 0-88738-281-9
Printed in the United States of America

Library of Congress Cataloging-in-Publication Data

Honigsheim, Paul, 1885–1963.
    Sociologists and music : an introduction to the study of music and society through the later writings of Paul Honigsheim / edited, with a new preface and bibliographic update, by K. Peter Etzkorn.—2nd ed.
      p.   cm.
    Rev. ed. of: Music and society. 1973.
    Includes bibliographies and indexes.
    ISBN 0-88738-281-9
    1. Music and society.   I. Etzkorn, K. Peter.   II. Honigsheim, Paul, 1885–1963. Music and society.   III. Title.
ML3795.H745   1989
306'.484—dc19   88-13830
                                        CIP

For Kyle Peter, Lars Peter and
Hildegard, to whom I owe
more than they will ever know.

CONTENTS

On Forms of Music and Forms of Society   215

BIBLIOGRAPHIES

TRANSACTION PREFACE

Sociologists have always been fascinated with music. In one way or another they have encountered music as an important social force in its own right, as an accompaniment or byproduct of phenomena they studied (such as youth culture or the drug scene), or as a means for obtaining social compliance (as in religious ceremonies or in the military). Few, however, have paid systematic attention to how social science can use data from musical life to shed light on a better understanding of musical institutions, the social and artistic conditions of musicians, or the refinement of sociological methods and theory. As the world is metaphorically shrinking as a result of the communication revolution, cultural barriers are simultaneously being erected in furtherance of public policy. And, while the wealth accumulated from the distribution of rock and roll music may be considered a validation of teachings of the Protestant ethic, elsewhere this phenomenon is viewed as the work of the devil. It is evident that opportunities for sociological inquiry and clarification abound.

This book goes one step toward remedying this situation by culling the existing literature for building blocks toward introducing sociological synthesis and by presenting the English version of the extensive writings on music and society by Paul Honigsheim.

A major portion of Honigsheim's unpublished work on the sociology of music can be presented again to sociologists, social anthropologists, ethnomusicologists, and other interested readers. While Honigsheim was not able to complete his own life's work and see it through to publication, he left behind in manuscript drafts of chapters, numerous outlines, and handwritten notes. Few sociologists spent an entire life studying social aspects of music, collecting data by reading widely, excerpting sources, and synthesizing this wealth of information under broad-ranging rubrics that encompass religion and politics, economics, philosophy, and of course, sociology. Honigsheim's annotated bibliography suggests the breadth of his scholarly involvement with music; it also suggests that the full benefit of his scholarship and erudition will never be harvested by us.

To provide readers with some background on the intellectual history of the sociology of music, the introductory essay reviews major contributions and developments. Some of these antedate Paul Honigsheim, others are contemporary. Because a number of scholars have written on the subject, an attempt is made to present the variety of approaches to the sociology of music contained in their writings and to suggest directions the field should be exploring. Somewhat more extensive summaries are provided for the works of those not likely to be readily accessible in library collections.

The sections dealing with Paul Honigsheim are largely reconstructed from his notes. They follow the original texts as closely as possible. Hence, while a considerable amount of editing, translating, and polishing of the Honigsheim drafts is evident when these versions are compared with the originals, neither the basic structure of the exposition nor the manner of illustration was fundamentally changed. These discussions—of the nature and social function of music; of occasions for the use of music; of the specific social dimensions of the status and role of musicians and the interdependencies with other occupational roles; of the social structure of musical audiences; of religious, class, and economic dimensions of musical activities; of political and nationalistic aspects of music; and of forms of music and forms of society—can be viewed as faithful reconstructions of Paul Honigsheim. The decision was deliberately made not to round out or fill in gaps of documentation in the Honigsheim drafts from the results of my own research. It is felt that this decision is consistent with his attitude toward scholarly life, which he portrayed as the five tragedies of the sociologist (Honigsheim, 1961). These may be summed up by his observation that the resolution of social issues cannot be attained through a "final revolution" or an ultimate battle (*allerletzte Schlacht*). Instead Honigsheim believed that only a readiness for "eternal revolution" is sociologically and ethically defensible (Ibid:33). He indicated that sociologists are obligated to be permanently willing to reject, in light of new evidence, that which they seem to have established as fact, as well as guard as best they can against the rigidification through conventions imposed by social institutions of individual modes of inquiry (Ibid). It is hoped that the reader will not be disappointed by the incomplete nature of Honigsheim's later writings but will find in them a guide and starting point for reflection and further inquiry.

In making this collection once more available, I accord foremost appreciation to J. Allan Beegle and William H. Form, Honigsheim's former colleagues and literary executors, who initially encouraged me to prepare the Honigsheim notes for publication. I wish to acknowledge their early and generous assistance in numerous ways but also their and the continued efforts of Erwin Scheuch and Alphons Silbermann to keep interest in Honigsheim's scholarship alive; to the librarian of Michigan State University under whose auspices research in the Honigsheim collection was facilitated; to the State College Foundation of California State University, Northridge, for major assistance with the typing of numerous initial drafts; to Chris Haake-Pfaender and Rainer Koehne, who helped with deciphering, verifying, and translating the entries in the bibliography; and to René König, Gottfried Eisermann, Johannes Winkelmann, and Karl Troost, who were generous in sharing with me memories of Paul Honigsheim's years in Germany, thus helping me to gain a fuller picture of the manifold talents and interests of this comparative scholar. To Christine Valentine and Marte Steele I owe special notes of thanks for their unstinting efforts to keep jargon at a minimum and to help me translate Honigsheim's notes into English.

The permission of B. G. Teubner Verlagsgesellschaft to translate passages from Franz Pöggeler, ed., *Im Dienste der Erwachsenenbildung* is gratefully acknowledged.

A NOTE ON THE BIBLIOGRAPHIES

The three bibliographies form an integral part of this introduction to the sociological study of music. The first bibliography, Titles Selected and Annotated by Paul Honigsheim, was prepared from his handwritten notes. Because it was frequently impossible to decipher details of spelling and bibliographic reference, the entire bibliography was checked against the following standard reference works:

"Biblio," 1934–, *Cataloque des ouvrages parus en langue française dans le monde entier*. Paris: Service bibliographique des messageries Hachette. Reprint. Liechtenstein: Kraus, 1968.

Bibliographie der deutschen Zeitschriftenliteratur, 1901–, by F. Dietrich. Reprint. Liechtenstein: Kraus, 1961.

British Museum General Catalogue of Printed Books to 1955. New York: Readex Microprint, 1967.

A Catalogue of Books Represented by Library of Congress Printed Cards, by Association of Research Libraries. New York: Rowman and Littlefield, 1967.

Catálogo general de la Librería Española, 1931–1950. Madrid: Instituto Nacional del Libro, 1957.

Catálogo general de la Librería Española e Hispano-Americana. Madrid: Cámeras Officiales del Libro, 1901–1930.

Catalogue Général de la Librairie Française, 1840–1946. Reprint. Liechtenstein: Kraus, 1967.

The Cumulative Book Index. New York: H.W. Wilson, 1912–.

Deutsches Bücherverzeichnis. Leipzig: Börsenverein, 1911–.

Jahres-Verzeichnis der deutschen Hochschulschriften, 1885–. Reprint. Vaduz: Kraus, 1965.

The National Union Catalog, by Library of Congress. London and Chicago: Mansell, 1968.

In spite of diligent labor, numerous entries could not be verified. These are identified by the following notations: XX, the entire entry could not be verified; XA, the bibliographic information for the main entry could be verified but the accuracy of the specific title, such as an article in a journal, could not be checked separately.

The second and third bibliographies "Bibliographic Entries for Sociologists" and "Music and Bibliographic Update" contain references for the introductory essay and update the literature on the sociology of music.

K. Peter Etzkorn
St. Louis, Missouri

MUSIC AND SOCIETY

THE LATER WRITINGS OF
PAUL HONIGSHEIM

INTRODUCTION

BY

K. PETER ETZKORN

SOCIOLOGISTS AND MUSIC

The nineteenth century formally gave birth to sociology. Its founder, Auguste Comte (1798–1857), had included the treatment of the arts and of aesthetic matters in his analyses of the historical development of society and in his plans for a better world. But it was Wilhelm Dilthey (1833–1911) who more directly adumbrated the work on art and music of succeeding sociologists. The theoretical interests of some of these tend to retain the emphasis on the general themes and comprehensive research approaches advocated by this thinker. Other publications in particular the more recent ones, by sociologists dealing with music and society (Faulkner, 1968; Nanry, 1972; Stebbins, 1964) tend to focus on more substantive topics.

As an introduction to Paul Honigsheim's later edited writings we offer summaries of representative sociological publications preceding his work. We hope that these can also provide the reader with an introduction to the history of ideas in which the studies of Honigsheim are embedded. These studies combine a philosopher's concern for fundamental methodological issues of social science with a searching examination of historical details in the musicological literature for their contributions to a generalized conception of music and society. The sociologist's reflections on data conventionally associated with historical writing and their incorporation in his effort at generalization are of interest to both the music historian and the social scientist.

THE INFLUENCE OF WILHELM DILTHEY

Although never particularly known for being sympathetic to sociology, Dilthey also stimulated sociological discourse in other contexts, such as in the extensive debate on the role of Verstehen in historical and sociological analysis. Moreover, his overall efforts in explicating methodological foundations for human sciences, which he worked out systematically so that they would benefit from the methodological accomplishments of the natural sciences, are recognized as having had wide influence in several disciplines. H. Stewart Hughes circumscribes Dilthey's importance in the social sciences in the following words: "One may state Dilthey's significance in most general fashion by characterizing his work as the first thoroughgoing and sophisticated confrontation of history with positivism and natural science" (Hughes, 1958:194). In the following discussion we will be primarily interested in Dilthey's ideas on the social study of music.

It is in the context of the various methods and objects of humanistic studies that Dilthey develops his theory on music. In a section he calls "The Musical Understanding," he argues that, of all arts, music is most bound by technical rules, yet it is also the freest in calling forth emotional responses. Series of tones arranged in rhythmic patterns frequently have meanings that are not manifestly contained within them. For Dilthey,

> This is not a psychological relationship between emotional states and their representation in fantasy. . . . It is a relationship between an objective musical work and its parts, as a creation of fantasy, and the work's meaning in every melody, that is, what it tells the listener about the emotional feeling which results from the relations between rhythm, melody, harmony, and the motions expressed thereby. Not psychological but musical relationships form the subject of inquiry for the study of musical genius, work, and theory. . . . The relationship between a musical work and what it expresses to the listener and what, therefore, is speaking through it, is definite, capable of comprehension and demonstration. (Dilthey, 1927:222)

While the musical composition is, therefore, held to communicate definite meanings, the roles of the composer and performing artist in this communication process are oblique. Dilthey seems to feel that the intrinsic relation between the interactions of the performance and the emotional state—the influence of the emotional state conveyed by the music upon the performance—is not open for empirical demonstration. The process is internal to the musician, and not even subject to his own analysis.

Unwittingly, in the darkness of the soul it is moving, and only in the musical composition is the dynamical relationship that sprang from these depths expressed. . . . That, exactly, is the value of music, that it is an expression of the feelings (*Gemüt*) of the artist, and that it makes them objective. This complex consisting of quality, duration, form of movement, and content is to be analyzed in the musical composition and to be brought into distinct awareness as relation between rhythm, tonal sequence, and harmony, a relationship between beauty of sound and musical expression. (Dilthey, 1927:223)

In Dilthey's view, experiences in life are expressed through musical forms and, consequently, a link between the theory of music and the biography of composers ought to be established.

An application of this theory can be gleaned from Dilthey's studies of the German national character. In a section on the great German music of the eighteenth century, Dilthey searches in the "objective" characteristics of music for the meaning it expresses. This meaning is then related back to "German" characteristics. For example, Bach's *Pastoral Symphony* "is one of the deepest inventions of Bach, which sprang from the depths of Germanic fantasy, including all future presentations of our national feelings" (1933:237). His methodological precepts for humanistic studies call for the scientific analysis of various analytic aspects of entire cultures. He argues, for instance, that "the meaning of 'nation' can only be expressed analytically" (1923:41). Concepts such as soul of a people (*Volksseele*), nation, or spirit of a people are as futile in humanistic studies as is "force of life" for physiology. Therefore, the real understanding of a nation's life has to be sought through scientific analysis of the grammar, rhetoric, logic, aesthetics, ethics, jurisprudence, political theory, and music of a particular people.

If one were to derive from Dilthey's study of music in Germany his underlying model of analysis, a threefold program for research would be revealed. The essential aspects of Dilthey's program would be concern with the technical rules governing the musical expressions and forms of a people's music—as it were, rules directly applicable to the music; concern with the cultural and psychological values (emotions) that are expressed in a given social setting through appropriate (musical) communication; and concern with the mutual interaction among musical elements, musicians, and social setting or structure. Dilthey's program would require that equal emphasis be given to these three analytic dimensions. Subsequent work by other students in the sociology of music and ethnomusicology has frequently tended to emphasize one or the other dimension at the expense of a more integrated view.

This brief sketch of Dilthey's observations concerning the role of music in German culture provides both a reminder of the essentially idealistic tradition of nineteenth century German social science and philosophy, and also a yardstick, a benchmark as it were, by which to view the later developments of a sociological approach to music. Questions that occupy the attention of later students of music and society, such as the problem of the relationship between musical expressions and cultural representation, are clearly initiated in Dilthey's thoughtful discussions. For Dilthey, the composer translates his fantasies into music. Its formal aspects manifest the composer's conception of content or meaning, which inspired his composition. The performer's personal emotional disposition will be responsible for his articulating or not grasping the composition's total emotive content. It would appear, then, that for Dilthey a proper performance can only come about if performer and creator share their emotive attitudes, or better, are united in one person. How the composer or performer channels his emotional feelings into musical creations remains, therefore, a major empirical question. Dilthey, however, does not show us the intrinsic links between the technical rules of music and the emotive states of the musicians. Nor does he help us in exploring the social foundation of these rules. Dilthey's nominalistic orientation prevented him from formulating a more sociological approach to music—for him, music is an individual expression.

SOME BLINDSPOTS

There can be no doubt that studies on the complex relationships between music and society would be advanced by rigorous conceptualizations spelling out key variables and expected relationships. Informed by such methodological discussions, the collection of data could become more useful to scholars than were the random reports in the journals of travelers telling of exotic peoples and places. When Georg Simmel (1858–1919) focused his attention to a study of the ethnological and psychological foundations of music (Simmel, 1882), for example, the research literature available to him was rather inconclusive. Simmel could nevertheless be nominated as one of the pioneers in the sociology of music and in comparative musicology as well, since his study was published prior to the works of other scholars who are credited with having established musicology. Bruno Nettl, a leading contemporary ethnomusicologist, reminds us of the rather recent history of this discipline by referring to the difference of opinion concerning its true founder. He writes that some would give this honor to Carl Stumpf (1848–1936), who published a study on the Bella Coola Indians in 1886, while Jaap Kunst (1959:2–3) would place A. J. Ellis (1814–1890) in this spot. "Whichever of these scholars is considered the real founder of our field, its beginnings belong properly in the 1880's, the time in which historical musicology also began" (Nettl, 1964:14–15). It is of course true that the last decades of the nineteenth-century saw the rise of many of the specialties now assigned separate departments within our universities; they also provided the incentive for ongoing debates about how to divide scholarly activities between humanistic and social sciences.

This debate affected the question as to whether the study of music was to be part of the humanities or the social sciences. Alan P. Merriam laid this issue to rest by suggesting that ethnomusicology partakes of both science and the humanities: "its approach and its goals are more scientific than humanistic, while its subject matter is more humanistic than scientific" (1964:25). And somewhat earlier he said: "The ethnomusicologist is, in effect, sciencing about music" (1964:25). More recent writing suggests that this long-standing debate was, indeed, rather meaningless. Jean Piaget's remark sums up what is becoming a consensus among scientists: "We shall confine ourselves here to pointing out that no distinction can be drawn between the disciplines frequently referred to as the 'social sciences' and those known as the 'human sciences,' since social phenomena clearly depend upon all human characteristics, including psychophysiological processes, while reciprocally the human sciences are all social, viewed from one angle or another" (Piaget, 1970:1). It may well be a sign of the increasing maturity of the various disciplines dealing with man and his works that scholarly cooperation is becoming increasingly oriented by substantive questions rather than by the departmental affiliation of the researchers. In the study of music in society, the rise of interdisciplinary cooperation going beyond sociology and anthropology is more noticeable precisely because of the conventional assignment of the study of music to the humanities. Although certain music historians did not appear to be overly handicapped by their loyalties to the humanities, they frequently paid homage to principal colleagues by academic games of one-upmanship, as when Serauky called sociology a *Hilfswissenschaft* to musicology (Serauky, 1934), a call repeated by Hans Mersmann as late as 1953 (Mersmann, 1953).

MUSICOLOGICAL SOCIOLOGY

Dilthey's methodological points on the analysis of music and the interdependence between music as a cultural manifestation of interacting members of social collectivities and the social conventions governing the making of particular musics no doubt was known to Honigsheim, as must have been many of the studies that follow. A number of studies of music in social systems by musicologists and music historians have been less directly concerned with postulating relationships between elements of analysis and scientific generalization. For example, Arnold Schering (1877–1941), one of the most influential scholars in this context, distinguishes between musical types by referring to the institutional setting in which the music is generally performed or for which it is intended by its composer (Schering, 1931). On this basis he suggests that in the history of the Western world, music has three main functions. It is used originally in connection with religious cults. At a later stage it is employed also for the benefit of the secular community. And last, it primarily serves the aesthetic gratification of the listeners. He proposes that different types of social organization are characteristically correlated with these musical types, and that consequently there are also different patterns of social relationships that are correlated with the performance of these types of music. The tasks for sociology are, according to Schering, to give an historical account of the changing functions of music in society in various periods by stressing the analysis of the relationship between music and society and the various forms of society in which music is performed.

Gerhard Pinthus—like Schering, a trained musicologist—approaches the sociological study of music from the formal analysis of musical styles (Pinthus, 1932). He searches for an explanation of different stylistic phenomena in the varying structures of the performer-audience relationship. By paying special attention to the structure of the audiences, he presents a coherent history of changing musical styles in Western music as they are paralleled by changes in the audiences. Pinthus's sources show that stylistic changes are introduced when the social structures of the performance situation change. For this reason he believes that it can be shown that each musical style is addressed to an audience of distinct social characteristics, and that when a society becomes increasingly differentiated, appreciation of the arts and of musical styles differs according to social subclasses. Although Pinthus's original approach is motivated by tradition musicological concerns, he transcends these boundaries and proposes a social-structural hypothesis that is still in need of systematic test. His study also illustrates that sociological analyses are of value to traditional musicology, and that the materials and categories of the professional student of music are a source of important hypotheses for the sociologist.

Another contributor to the sociology of music, Walter Serauky (1903–1959), proposes a research program that conceives of sociology as secondary (*Hilfswissenschaft*) to musicology. Sociology can help to tighten up general music theory by including sociological considerations of the historical influences on primarily musical elements and forms. The principal task of the sociology of music, then, becomes the discovery of the "typical and cultural conditions under which music comes into existence" (Serauky, 1934). Sociology should make "intelligible for us why a certain style may have emerged in the social and cultural structure of a given period, and thus clarify the sociological pre-requisites and conditions involved." Compared to Schering or Pinthus, Serauky's interest in the sociology of music is more limited. Serauky's concerns are those of the historically oriented musicologist who, as a matter of course, refers to the inevitable "social conditions," which have something to do with the course of human events. His proposal for a sociology of music is designed more to serve the social history of musical styles than to advance sociology as a generalizing study of man, society, and music.

A number of studies by American sociologists on social aspects of music, on the other hand, utilize musical data to illustrate, or even empirically test, scientific propositions from the rich corpus of the diverse traditions of sociological theory. Of American sociologists the names of John H. Mueller (1895–1965), Karl Schuessler (1915–   ), Howard S. Becker (1928–   ), Max Kaplan (1911–   ), Dennison Nash (1924–   ), and Seymour Leventman (1930–   ) stand out among those who have contributed empirically-oriented studies that reveal knowledge of and sensitivity to issues in the musicological literature. None of these authors, however, seem to have intended to offer overarching schemes setting forth programs of study for the sociology of music. Hence scholars who have treated the sociology of music with different objectives are found in a number of disciplines, and their publications have appeared sporadically. Furthermore, some of them have based their theses on dogmatic ideological stances. For these reasons the following summaries do not give evidence of much cumulative work in the sociology of music. They will, however, provide an introduction to the important issues as raised by key figures roughly corresponding to the time of Paul Honigsheim's life.

MARXIAN APPROACHES TO THE SOCIOLOGY OF MUSIC

ERNST HERMANN MEYER

A rather different approach to the problem area of music in society is taken by the music historian Ernst H. Meyer (1905–   ). Indebted to the

Marxian literature, he regards both music and the other arts as "reflections of the social conditions of their times" (Meyer, 1952:232). Music in
its content and form represents significant aspects of social reality and is
"an important means for the information of consciousness . . . a form of
the cognition of reality" (1952:10). In Meyer's analyses most examples of
contemporary music turn into *Kitsch*. They are said to be stagnant, decadent, repetitive, conservative, capitalistic, and not adequate for the
progressive elements of the working classes.[1]

At the time the work from which these quotes are taken was published,
Professor Meyer occupied the sociology of music chair at the University
of Berlin (East Germany). Even though some earlier studies deal with
specific topics in music history (Meyer, 1946, 1934), his current preoccupation appears to be with an application of Marxian terminology to
musicology. In this endeavor, the substructure of his concern, to borrow
a term from his Marxian vocabulary, shows close affinities to traditional
music aesthetics. He expounds, for example, on the problem of the relative adequacy of content and form of musical styles. The superstructure,
however, appears to be of a more direct political nature.

There is also an interesting shift of his views within the context of his
book. Initially he argues that the function of music is to mirror social
reality. Yet as the book progresses this descriptive function of music
(that is, what music *does*) is changed into a normative state: Music attains
the *obligation* of representing the progressive elements within society.

Judging from Meyer's critiques of contemporary music, he does not
seem to offer an independent set of musical criteria by which to assess the
adequacy of music's representational function. The only measure of adequacy would appear to be the degree to which the music pleases the
mood of its critics. It seems that in order to be consistent Meyer must
now negate his earlier position concerning the descriptive function of
music. He must now imply that the creation of musical forms and styles
can be relatively independent of immediate social determinants, while at
the same time the interpretation of these very musical creations would
be viewed as being subjected to social influences. This is, of course, quite
different from his initial musical mirror thesis. Consistent with this later
version, the evaluation of musical styles can then proceed by using any
suitable aesthetic theory (including some Marxian version), or the evaluation could even be wholly arbitrary according to the demands of the
moment. At any rate, musical creations can then be criticized. This
would seem to be logically impossible if one adheres to the mirror thesis,

[1] These epithets are extracted from various contexts in which Meyer deals with contemporary music.

under which only the social conditions responsible for the music can be criticized. By criticizing the music, however, Meyer has reopened the possibility of an analysis of the position of music within society and thus paved the way for the scientific rather than ideological analysis of music. Sociology of music in East Germany, when judged by this early publication, appears to have struggled toward combining the politically expedient with the scholarly desirable.

The Czech School

A rather different perspective is conveyed in a Czechoslovakian publication on the sociology of music (Fukač, 1967). This brochure introduces the Western reader to empirical work carried on prior to the 1968 invasion and to the theoretical conceptions behind these efforts. It also supplies an interesting historical discourse on the tradition of sociological concerns with music in Czechoslovakia. The historical section outlines a series of sociological studies on art and music, beginning with the published work of Otakar Hostinský (1847–1910), the founder of the first Czech school of musicology. Theoretical ideas were refined through laboratory tests, especially by his student Zich (1879–1934). Other students helped create a scholarly climate, which led to the founding of the Prague school of the sociology of music of the 1930s. The Prague school produced publications such as *Music as Means of Propaganda* (Vučkovič, 1932), *Ideology and Music* (Stanislav, 1936), and *Musical Culture, Art, and Life* (Stanislav, 1940). This first period of the Prague school ended with the German 1938 occupation and the stormy postwar years. Sociological topics were also dealt with in Moravia through the work of Helfert (1886–1945) and his students. Fukač's brochure refers, for example, to a study by Karel Vetterl *On the Sociology of Radio Music* (1938), which is said to employ modern methods of sociology.

With the end of World War II, sociological concerns with music re-emerged in Czechoslovakia. Empirical studies on musical education (Šamko, 1947), theoretical interests on *The Social Functions of Music* (Kresáneks, 1961), and studies on musical taste (Karbusicky and Kasan, 1964) are cited as examples of postwar publications.

It is Fukač's opinion that the majority of Czech specialists in the sociology of music adhere to a theoretical position that accepts the social character of music and strives toward its most encompassing explication. For this approach, problems of methodology rather than of substantive nature become predominant. One of the methodological issues emphasized in this study is the problem with the *Destruktion der Pseudokon-*

kretheit (the need of phenomenological analysis of pseudofacts). It is argued, for example, that "it is impossible to examine the musical interests of social groups *per se*" (30) without questioning the meaning of the answers (facts) obtained through merely empirical study. Sociologists, it is demanded, must transcend vulgar sociologisms, must specify their methods of research in keeping with their objectives, and must, among other caveats, not fall into the trap of thinking that by having given a new name to a phenomenon it has already been explained (45). The degree of methodological sophistication conveyed in this Prague brochure is, without question, of great promise for sociological work.

GEORG SIMMEL

Many of the problems raised by writers on the sociology of music discussed in the preceding pages already formed the central task of Georg Simmel's *Psychological and Ethnological Studies on Music* (Simmel, 1882; Etzkorn, 1964, 1968). Simmel never surpassed the sociological perspective and sensitivity for the subject of this relatively early work.

Simmel's early study of music is motivated by the scientific inadequacy and incompleteness of the Darwinian theory concerning the sexually-stimulated origin of music. As a replacement he proposes an explanation that accounts for the practice of music as a complement to the development of speech. Music, for him, has its basis in speech, and speech is already a manifestation of social relations: "It seems most likely to me that the source of vocal music is the spoken word, which is exaggerated by emotion in the direction of rhythm and modulation" (Etzkorn 1968: 100). Hence, Simmel accounts for the transformation of speech into music (rhythm and modulation) by the psychological search for adequate expressions. Sudden fright and pain can only produce shrieking or shouting. However, there will be emotions in which "the excitement at any given moment is probably too strong to be expressed in simple words, and therefore takes refuge in musical exaggeration" (102).

For Simmel, then, music begins with the rhythmic organization of speech sounds and the concurrent variation of pitch, that is, the use of different registers or pitches for contrastive effects. Although at this stage of development music is clearly differentiated from ordinary speech, it needs another impulse to develop into an art, an impulse that is not part of these first origins. Art music for Simmel is characterized by a certain independence from emotions. Art music obtains objectivity. This does not mean that feelings disappeared altogether from music—music is still agitated and inspired by them. But art music and its performance should not result directly from the release of emotional tensions. By the establishment of the rules of polyphonic setting, for example, the spontaneous process of creating art was intercepted. Music now depends on complicated rules. On the basis of differential application of complicated rules to the setting and creation of music, Simmel goes on to differentiate between types of music and typical social settings.

Once he has located it as one of the diversified activities of man, Simmel studies music along with other cultural expressions. Even art music, as we have seen, is distinguished from "original" music not by anything intrinsically aesthetic, but by the system of rules that govern its production and reception, and which are held to be extensions of rational actions into the realm of music. Of course this secular attitude toward music is consistent with Simmel's general analytic position toward social phenomena, which he views, unlike Dilthey, through an interactionalist perspective. Music is a social-psychological and not a psychic expression. Through the process of socialization, individuals become familiarized with the approved pattern of musical expression of their groups. Different social forms will have different histories of socialization and, consequently, different modes of musical expression. In Simmel's analysis, then, music must be viewed as an intimate part of social reality: It is socially conditioned and conditions the social groups involved in it. Hence, to state his case, Simmel searches the ethnographic literature for crosscultural data to supplement information on musical practices in the Western world. The task of the sociologist cannot be confined to explaining the musical culture of European fine art music; instead he must show that music is a human expression with forms appropriate to various social settings.

In this early study, Simmel did not employ the distinction between purely objective features of music and their meaning—that is, their social interpretation. This distinction, which is characteristically employed in his later works (K. H. Wolff, 1950:17), is also frequently encountered in the work of other early sociologists. Indeed, Simmel employs it for the purpose of separating sociology from other social analytical sciences. In this early study, music is treated as an integral feature of its respective social setting. As in the German idealistic tradition, the *Wesen* (essence) of music and society is treated as one unit. The meaning of music is implicated in the meaning of society. Consistent with this assertation, Simmel avers that the artist who creates music is so strongly integrated in his society that his musical creations are true expressions of the essence of his country. In refuting Darwin's origin theory of music, Simmel is thus preoccupied with showing that music cannot be explained as a primarily organic response to certain biological drives. Rather, music is a highly developed articulation of social processes, which can best be apprehended when viewed as simultaneous expressions of the unifying *Wesen* of a society.

The problems of social analysis that derive from this conceptualization for the study of music in society are manifold. Perhaps foremost of these problems is the concern with the proper empirical referent for the concepts *Wesen* and *Volksseele,* which play such an important role in this early paper. Yet, as we have shown elsewhere, Simmel offered many promising leads, which were independently confirmed by several American sociologists studying musical socialization and the role of taste groups (Etzkorn, 1964).

MAX WEBER

Simmel's early study does not appear to have become a source of stimulation for subsequent scholarship. The same cannot be said of Max Weber's (1864–1920) published writing on the *Rational and Social Foundations of Music* (1921). Although this essay was published posthumously and probably would not have been released by Weber in its present form (Baumgarten, 1964:482), direct links to the works of Paul Honigsheim, Kurt Blaukopf, and several others can be drawn. Like Simmel, Max Weber directs some attention to establishing the legitimacy of social scientific inquiry in matters musical and cultural. While Simmel devotes considerable effort to demonstrating the total integration of music into the societal fabric, and indeed manages to integrate his analysis of music with that of certain forms of heightened societal experiences, Weber appears to view music more as a resultant of particular social emanations than as an intrinsic nexus of all. Much of the published fragment of his essay is devoted to a demonstration that contemporary music is more rational than music known from earlier times and other places (Silbermann, 1963). For Weber, rationalization in music means that there is a trend toward the smoothest utilization of the tonal material in terms of avoiding possible disharmonious interferences of the music overtones amongst each other; hence his study is predominantly suggestive of an acoustical analysis of the various tonal systems. The decision to perform the musical compositions in one voice or in a number of voices becomes a major analytical tool. The latter performance always requires a more rational music than purely melodic performances. Tonal systems of purely melodic music are less rationalized than those employed by harmonic music.

Although Weber does not utilize the concept in his discussion of tonal materials, his argument is so typically Weberian that one may be permitted to apply his heuristic device of the "ideal type" to his own discussion. If we postulate contemporary Western music to be the ideal type of all music, or more precisely, if the tonal material of contemporary harmonic Western music is taken as an ideal type of harmonically rationalized music, Weber's discussion of other tonal systems as not being fully rationalized becomes more understandable. The tonal material of primitive tribes, for example that of the Vedda, extends over a rather limited range as compared with Western music; its range is considerably smaller than an octave. In general, says Weber, tonal materials that recognize the interval distance of an octave and beyond are not the most primitive, and are to a certain degree already rationalized. "The pentatonic system presupposes at least the octave and its division into parts of some order, that is a partial rationalization; and it is, therefore, not really primitive" (1921:14). The Vedda's scale, however, does not extend to the octave, and thus is not even partially rationalized. Nevertheless, says Weber, "one should be careful not to think of primitive music as a chaos of unregulated arbitrariness" (25). The case of the Vedda illustrates Weber's procedure. His major emphasis is on the study of the suitability of tonal systems for the harmonic music of the late Vienna School period. He examines the development of tonal systems, which by progressive technological rationalizations culminates in the contemporary system which uses the equal temperament. Thus, technological developments affect the rationalization of tonal systems, as they also affect other spheres of social life. The impact of piano and organ manufacture and the earlier perfection of the techniques of musical notation are related by Weber to various stages in the history of the occidental tonal system.

In this fragmentary study, Weber never discusses musical phenomena apart from their physical sound properties. Thus his analysis is devoted to the social correlates of the sound structures of music, which is somewhat analogous to the study of the morphemic structure of language practiced by structural linguistics. In contrast to Simmel, Weber first investigates musical phenomena by applying a fully developed analytical system, namely that of acoustics, to the musical phenomenon. The sociological task, in this preparatory study, seems to rest in the discovery of social-structural categories that are significantly related to the categories of the acoustical system. With his study Weber wished to demonstrate that sociological analysis could be *wertfrei* (value-free, rational) and still contribute to the enhancement of our knowledge of culture, even in such value-loaded realms as the musical arts.

KURT BLAUKOPF

The most conspicuous sign of the incomplete nature of Weber's study is the absence of definitions for his concepts. In order to carry on with Weber's analysis of tonal systems, Kurt Blaukopf (1914–   ) published his *Musiksoziologie* (1950), which, so far as I could discover, is the first book-length study bearing this title. For Blaukopf the primary objective of the sociology of music is "to conceive of the production and reproduction of music within the context of the historical and developmental process of human society" (1950:8). He feels that musicology is in need of this sociological corrective, which is "a transitory science whose task will be completed once musicology takes care of this work systematically within its own domain" (1955:342). Thus he shares with Serauky and Mersmann the conviction that sociology is a *Hilfswissenschaft* to the theoretical branches of professional musicology.

What contributions of sociology to musicology does Blaukopf envisage, and where does his work connect with Max Weber's? In his judgment, music historians have neglected the impact of social forces on the development of music history; social forces, he feels, always enter into the dialectic relationship between the content and form of artistic creations. The form follows immanent laws, while the content is assigned to the form of social processes. Blaukopf feels that an overemphasis on the study of structural limitations has blinded much of musicology to the proper consideration of the social forces that select and utilize the structurally limited materials (1950:50). Even though I do not believe that Blaukopf's position toward immanent laws of music has been demonstrated (or for that matter is even scientifically tenable), his further discussion of the social aspects of music requires our attention here.

Changes in musical style, he suggests, are incomprehensible if the history of musical styles is treated independently of social history. The same holds for changes in aesthetic attitudes, which must be viewed as embedded in social, political, and economic dimensions. "The untangling of these relationships is indeed the contribution of the sociology of music. . . . The sociology of music starts from the realization that these social, political, and economic conditions do not influence and color the praxis of music only from the outside, but determine its innermost essence" (Blaukopf, 1950:14).

In an extensive treatment of the development of tonal systems, which is patterned after Yasser's *A Theory of Evolving Tonality* (1932), Blaukopf picks up Max Weber's study of thirty years ago. "An art form like that of the Renaissance, which postulated in such a strong fashion naturalness, individuality, and pleasantness, necessarily had to search for a technical system which was capable of presenting the third dimension in music as well as painting" (1950:87–88). When he encounters conflicts between his and Yasser's discussion of the transition from the subinfra-diatonic to the supradiatonic tonal systems, he excludes evidence of tonal systems that cannot be subsumed under these idealistic schemes. Blaukopf argues: "We will have to talk only about those tonal systems which are of more than regional importance" (1950:44–45). Thus he truncates Weber's problem by extrascientific criteria. As in Meyer's book, arguments from Marxian social criticism are advanced to carry the responsibility for this extrascientific concern. Indeed, the introductory chapter to his *Musikoziologie* praises the Marxian interpretation of history as an example of a realistic world-view, yet he fails to apply his detailed exposition of Plechanow's economic factors to a demonstration of the hypothesized necessary dependence of musical phenomena on these economic determinants. The first book calling itself a sociology of music tends to be more interesting to the sociologist for its ideological rather than for its sociological content.

In this context it must also be noted that the musical changes in which Blaukopf is evidently interested are restricted to those in the tonal material. (They are always in the direction of progressive differentiation of the octave.) This might further indicate that Blaukopf's sociology is oriented more toward a philosophy of musical history than science. His stipulation of an "immanent law of musical progress" would support such an interpretation, and it would also account for his distaste of accounting for those empirical cases that do not conform with his postulated doctrine. Further support for this interpretation of Blaukopf's conception of the role of sociology can be found in his call for its assistance in the elimination of social obstacles which, he claims, fetter the path of musical development. He does not provide any empirical evidence of the "fettering" process. As a consequence one may conclude that his assertion of social factors determining musical changes is not based on systematic accomplishments of sociological analysis, but rather on his ideological commitment to social criticism.

Blaukopf criticizes those historians who look for correspondence between artistic developments and the sociopolitical realm, by saying that whenever the "relationship between the aesthetic facts and the aesthetic-economic-political facts cannot be concretely presented, one will always have to take refuge in the auxiliary concept *Zeitgeist*. Thereby the explanation of these relationships, which is demanded by sociology, is replaced by an interpretation in the sense of idealistic aesthetics" (1950:9). It is difficult to see how Blaukopf escaped the realization that the criticism he applied to the historians of the arts applied to his own *Musikso-*

ziologie. While Blaukopf understood Weber's attempt to extend his analysis of rationalization to the arena of music, he neither extended Weber's empirical work, nor did he carry on Weber's tradition of separating politics from sociology.

Whether politics and sociology can and should be separated is, of course, a question not to be dismissed lightly; it is worthy of explicit treatment and must not be treated obliquely or disguised in dogmatic pronouncements. The following summary also deals with contributions to the sociology of music that tend to be more ideological than sociological.

THEODOR WIESENGRUND ADORNO

Theodor W. Adorno (1903–1969), widely known to American sociologists as director of the Los Angeles Research Project on Social Discrimination and coauthor of *The Authoritarian Personality*, also made various contributions to musical scholarship under the broad confines of social philosophy. His publications, which were not limited to the social sciences, testify to the versatility of this thinker. By including Adorno in this overview, our attention will be directed to a somewhat special orientation in German social science, which was centered largely around the old and new *Frankfurter Institut für Sozialforschung*.[2] This orientation can perhaps best be distinguished from other sociological approaches by its self-conscious attempt to fuse critical social theory with methods for ascertaining empirical reality critically. In so doing, it applied critical judgments about this reality as derived from the theory.

During his association with this school and as one of its later spokesman Adorno, a trained musicologist, contributed widely to the sociology of music. His writings on this subject date back to the early 1930s. Some of these studies were conducted in the United States; the majority were written in German. Unfortunately, a few studies published in Austrian and Czechoslovakian journals could not be obtained for this analysis.

Adorno's first long study dealing with the relationships between music and society was published in 1932. This study attempts to isolate the social factors in Western society that give music the characteristics of merchandise rather than of art. Even though Adorno's terminology in his later writing camouflages his earlier Marxist rhetoric, he does not materially alter the points of view developed in this first study. And even though Adorno initially uses a great deal of Marxian terminology, a close

---

[2] For a brief history of the Institut, see Jay (n.d.) .

inspection of his contributions reveals that they express a bourgeois rather than a proletarian bias.

Adorno's concern with the changing role of (art) music in contemporary mass society, as compared with the past, is the central focus in all his work on music. His analyses of art music and its composers, of popular music, of radio and television music, always provide him with an opportunity to search for the negative influences of the social institutions of mass society on music.

Although the "objectivisation" of music as an art had been dependent on its rationalization (in Max Weber's sense), and on its detachment from mere utility, the very rationalization as carried through under the capitalistic economic order introduced a perfect alienation between music and men. "It [music] no longer serves the immediate needs, but obeys in company with all other products the laws of the marketplace operating on abstract goods. Music subordinates its use value, whenever there is any left, to the compulsion of exchange (*Tauschzwang*)" (Adorno, 1932: 103). In this process the very forces that brought music into existence as an art took genuine music away again from mankind, leaving only the mere appearance (*Schein*) of music behind. Adorno argues that unless it yielded to the demands of production for a market, music would be deprived of its social support, alienated and emptied of its contents under capitalist society. But in so doing, music as art becomes negated. "It is from here that every consideration of the social position of music must start if it wishes to avoid those deceptions which today so largely dominate discussion [of culture], deceptions partly in order to disguise reality, partly because of the mediating apology of music which is economically threatened" (1932:104). Music, while conscious of its alienation, lacks the knowledge of the social processes responsible for its condition. Instead of accusing the social situation, music considered itself the guilty party. "Instead of this [way of judging the situation], it must be understood that the social alienation of music . . . is itself a social fact; it is itself socially produced. Therefore, it cannot be corrected intramusically but only by changing society" (1932:104).

For Adorno, the social features that can be connected to the social alienation of music must form the subject of social analysis. He restricts this analysis on the whole, however, to the sphere of the composer-audience relationship in his various studies, though in a more general way he includes in his treatment of music other segments of society not directly concerned with music. This is necessary, of course, since his basic argument tends to be dominated by assertions about economic production relationships and concurrent alienation under the conditions of a capitalistic market. Since he restricts his detailed analyses to the musical sphere, he is able to address himself to a unified audience, which he assumes takes the values of music for granted. It is only among those who do not rigorously concern themselves with music that subjective tastes predominate. "As soon as one enters the field of [the study of] musical techniques and structure, the arbitrariness of evaluation vanishes and we are faced with decisions about right and wrong, and true and false" (1950:315).

Materialgerechtigkeit (doing right with the material) is one of the recurring themes in Adorno's *Philosophie der neuen Musik* (1949). Although he emphasizes that his philosophical analyses of music are as clearly differentiated from a sociological account as from an a priori system of aesthetics, his methodological preoccupation with the intramusical side of the mutual relationship between music and society again is underscored.

The production and appreciation (consumption) of music is analyzed as falling into two separate classes: Music that accepts *Warencharakter* (characteristics of merchandise), and follows the demands of the market; and music that on principle declines to yield to the market. For Adorno, then, the conventional distinction between serious and popular music is inadequate, since serious music often follows the demands of the market. His study *On Popular Music* (1941) illustrates how Adorno applies his concepts to an empirical situation. He shows how the composer works with a set of standardized rules and how the market receives the individual pieces of popular music, one undifferentiated from the other. The publisher of such music, Adorno shows, is faced with a real problem. If he wants a song to become a success, he must see to it that it is not too different from the standard format; yet it must be different enough to be distinguishable from other pieces. Thus, popular music not only accepts the characteristics of merchandise, it actually is merchandised as a commodity of the market.[3]

Adorno's study "Über den Fetischcharakter und die Regression des Hörens (1939) deals with aspects of the musical appreciation of serious music. As in the case of popular music, the market plays an important role in limiting musical production. Only a small amount of serious contemporary music reaches an audience. Audiences, which Adorno calls consumers, are described as exhibiting a docile, passive acceptance of the repetition and imitation of pregiven patterns; they bitterly resent any-

---

[3] For different analyses of the popular music industry in the United States, see Etzkorn (1966, 1969); Petersen (1971).

thing abnormal. It is primarily the "normal" style of serious compositions that reaches the audience.

Adorno distinguishes four types of serious music that are somewhat less subservient to the demands of the market:

1. Music which looks to itself for the solution of its problems and "like Leibniz's Monad presents not a preestablished harmony but an historically produced dissonance" (1932:108). Schoenberg is a representative composer of this type of music.

2. "Music . . . which acknowledges the fact of alienation as isolation and individualization and brings it into consciousness . . . which tries to negate it by taking recourse to past stylistic forms without realizing that they cannot be reproduced again in a completely changed society and with completely different musical materials" (1932:108). This music endeavors to "quote" a nonexistent objective *Gesellschaft* which, however, is a *Gemeinschaft* in its intentions. This type is represented by neoclassicism in late-capitalistic–industrial societies and by folklore in underdeveloped countries. It is called *objectivism*.

3. Like objectivism, the third type of surrealism also is based on the recognition of alienation. It is most consistently exemplified in the work of Kurt Weill and his librettist, Bertolt Brecht. "By breaking up the aesthetically immanent forms (*Formimmanenz*), this type tends toward the literary" (1932:109). It quotes eclectically from the styles characteristic of the bourgeois musical culture of the nineteenth century, as well as from those of contemporary *Verbrauchsmusik* (consumers' music).

4. Adorno's fourth type overcomes its alienation all by itself, even at the cost of its own immanent Gestalt, its very nature. This music is usually called *Gebrauchsmusik*, and may be produced by special commissioning. In that case it begins to approximate ordinary music in its subservience to the demands of the market.

With the exception of these four types, Adorno argues that music must be conceptually treated as a commodity: "*today the commodity character of music tends radically to alter it*. Bach in his day was considered, and considered himself, an artisan, although his music functioned as art. Today music is considered ethereal and sublime, although it actually functions as a commodity" (1950:311). The utilization of music by the public is related by Adorno to social sources, as is the emergence of the consumer. He argues that under capitalism the dominant goal in life is the achievement of success through work. From this total dedication of man to his work resulted a social evaluation of free time that is not conducive to the cultivation of the arts. The fate of contemporary serious music is directly attributed to this phenomenon. During his leisure hours, man expects distraction from his routine work. Yet even the organization of leisure time has to be utilized for the positive end of preparing him for new work, lest he fall victim to boredom. Adorno argues that these two goals are difficult to achieve, since to escape boredom and at the same time avoid any efforts are incompatible. As a way out of this dilemma, modern man turns to stimulants, including music, and pursues distractive activities when not at work at a routinized job. Adorno suggests that the mechanized process of labor "engenders fears and anxiety about unemployment, loss of income, war, [and] has its "nonproductive" correlate in entertainment; that is, relaxation that does not involve the effort of concentration at all" (1941:32).

Standardization, especially as practiced in popular music, reduces the demands on the listener's attention to a minimum. Listeners do not even have to be able to respond to the music as a vehicle of communication, as a language. The less music is a language sui generis, the more does it "serve as a receptacle for their [the people's] institutionalized wants. . . . The autonomy of music is replaced by a mere social-psychological function. Music today is largely a social cement . . . a means by which they achieve some physical adjustment to the mechanisms of present day life" (1941:39). This "adjustment" either is of the "rhythmically obedient" type characteristically associated with the radio culture of the young, or it is of the "emotional" type. But if music is to be appreciated as art, it cannot be merely taken as a means of "adjustment," as entertainment. Music has to be understood.

For Adorno, music as an art comes into its own right through its progressive liberation from functionally conditioned employment in social processes. This process of liberation is somewhat enigmatic, for while music is said by Adorno to be autonomous, having its own laws for its material, there is also man who determines its form. Thus, in Adorno's view, music can be mistreated if its laws are not obeyed by man and if the composer forges the musical material according to his own whim. These laws are accessible to man; they can be understood. Thus the analyst is able to judge man's manipulation of music as either conforming to the musical laws, or as disregarding them. If society does not obey these laws and rejects music that conforms to them, then the fault lies in society and not in music: Society will have to be reformed.

For the sociology of music serious problems of a scientific nature arise from Adorno's position. If we assert with Adorno that music has objective laws of its own, all that a scientist can do is to discover these immanent laws and see how they correspond with the actual development of music in the social realm. Unless we permit that different societies can have different musics with different intrinsic laws, such a theory is untenable on empirical grounds. Adorno does not cover other musics, however, but restricts his discussions to the tradition of Western art music; the music of China (which incidentally includes twelve tones in the system, like Western music) would not be considered musical art under his "sociology" because it is mostly "functional music." Any music based on different tonal materials would have to be excluded as well.

Adorno approaches the sociology of music with an implicit program in mind. We venture to suggest that it is not to study music and its relation to man in an objective manner, but to pronounce a system of values; and to find substantiation for these values is the aim of his sociology. These values are that reason and not emotion should rule man's actions, and that the rationalization of life is contrary to reason in that it denies the fulfillment of the progressive liberation of reason from the affairs of daily life.

What was said earlier in introducing his works—that Adorno's employment of Marxian terminology in his treatment of music seemed to hide his rather bourgeois bias—may now be pointed out easily. Adorno deplores the fate of music in mass society. The changes initiated through Calvin's conception of the proper way to salvation, the rising bourgeoisie, the coming of the proletariat, mass production, and commercialization of life have all taken hold of music. Music is a commodity like all other objects. Whereas the cultivation of music in the precommodity days was reserved to people who understood their music, the development of music has become dependent on the market situation, which is largely determined by consumers who do not understand the language of music. It is not music that is to be molded according to the times, therefore, but the social conditions that alienated music from its audience that must be corrected. The position of the middle class as the bearer of culture is becoming weaker and weaker, as the commercialization of life increases. One might conclude that Adorno represents the old guard of the bourgeois who, rather than welcoming it to the New World, tries to take "Custer's last stand" against the barbarism of the New Age.

PITIRIM A. SOROKIN

Before turning our attention more fully to Paul Honigsheim, we have yet to introduce the reader to the work of Pitirim A. Sorokin and Alphons Silbermann, both of whose contributions are more in keeping with contemporary views on sociology—that is, they are less dogmatic and more empirical in orientation.

The substance of Pitirim Sorokin's (1889–1968) concern with the study of music in its relationship with other aspects of the social scene is to be found in the first volume of his monumental *Social and Cultural Dynamics* (1937). Chapter 12, entitled "Fluctuations of Ideational, Sensate, and Mixed Forms of Music," is concerned with the definition of these forms of music and the fluctuation of the main styles in time and space. The closing section of this chapter is devoted to an analysis of concurrence of musical changes with fluctuation in other art forms. For this reason, Sorokin's study of music cannot be considered self-contained, since in the larger context of artistic developments music becomes just one other aspect of the broader concerns of Sorokin's study.

The larger concern of Sorokin's study is a study of the change and fluctuation of "Ideational," "Idealistic," and "Sensate" cultures. "It is not, however, a *history* of these cultures, but a *sociology of the their change*" (1937:9–10). Since most larger sociological works contain elements of a philosophy of history, and since most historical works contain sociological elements, Sorokin does not object to his *Cultural Dynamics* being classified with the philosophy of history. The border between these fields has not yet been satisfactorily delimited; as we have seen, scholars are focusing more on the substantive issues than on whether their work should be called philosophy or sociology. Only from a consideration of what Sorokin *does* with the fluctuations of musical styles can we infer the extent to which his contributions are of value to the sociology of music.

Sorokin approvingly quotes Boethius' Latin definition of music, which reads in translation: "Human music is that which is understood by everyone who descends into himself" [*in se ipsum descendit*]. This definition, says Sorokin, coincides with what he considers "Ideational" or symbolic, in contradistinction to the sensately audible forms in music: "in Ideational music the main thing is not how it sounds—pleasant or unpleasant —but what is hidden behind the sounds for which they are mere signs or symbols" (1937:532). Thus he defines types of music by the attitude exhibited by the listeners toward the sound stimuli. "These two forms of music represent two different mentalities, two different attitudes toward the world of sound and the world of reality" (1937:533). In order to respond similarly to the same musical stimuli, say, to recognize beauty in Ideational music, the audience has to have "a highly identical mentality, and a similar education in the interpretation of sound symbols (conditioned stimuli)" (1937:532n). Here Sorokin evidently agrees with Simmel, who stipulated the same conditions for musical greatness.

Sorokin's attitudinal definition of types of music might be called *nominalistically oriented,* since it is through the definition of the beholder that certain aspects in the stimulus are assigned to the respective category of Ideational or Sensate. His distinction between these types on musical-technical grounds could be termed *realistic*. Especially in his discussion of contemporary art music, Sorokin illustrates how theatricalism, quantitative colossalism, the complication of the texture of music and the deliberate creation of technical difficulties, the substitution of technique for genius and the amazing technical virtuosity of the performers characterize Sensate music (1937:580–84).

This dual definition of musical types raises interesting problems for analysis, since in one case Sorokin bases the category on "how it sounds" and in the other on "what it means." In order to be consistent throughout, both definitions would have to be applicable simultaneously. But as everyone who is familiar with some particular phase of music history knows, and as Sorokin incidentally explicitly acknowledges, the interpretation of the meaning of musical pieces is just as likely to be influenced by the social function of the piece as by its technical structure. That is, there is generally only a low-order correlation between the strictly formal aspects of music and its meaning. When studying sixteenth century music, Sorokin noted that "it is impossible to secure even relatively complete data about most works; even in regard to many that are known, it is impossible to decide whether they are religious or secular" (1937:574). Since "religious" and "secular" are categories that express the meaning of a musical composition, they are also closely related to the categories Ideational and Sensate: "as a rule religious music is more closely associated with the Ideational and secular with the Sensate" (1937:573). Sorokin admits that clear decisions as to the assignment of a given composition to one or the other category are difficult to make. He suggests that it is difficult even for specialists in music to assign exclusively to the religious category such compositions as J. S. Bach's *Mass* and *Magnificat*, the *St. John* and *St. Matthew Passions*, some of Palestrina's, Vittoria's and especially Orlando di Lasso's religious works, Beethoven's *Missa Solemnis*, Mozart's *Requiem*, Berlioz's *Tuba Mirum*, not to mention work such as Verdi's *Requiem*, Brahms's *Requiem*, or Stravinsky's *Symphony of Psalms*. These compositions "were at best religious only in part" (1937:577).

In applying them to a particular research problem, then, Sorokin does not consistently employ either one of his definitions, which is, perhaps, the major weakness of his presentation. He assigns the majority of the music of a given period to one rather than the other category, readily admitting that some musical compositions of the same period belong in a residual class. Thus, all periods are neither fully Ideational nor fully Sensate: "both forms are found in practically all cultures at all stages" (1937:564). How Sorokin assigned a musical composition to a given category, the criteria he used, is knowledge necessary for anyone who wishes to replicate his study. This problem is further compounded by the total exclusion of any type of folk music from Sorokin's study. Since folk music does not belong to "grand music," it therefore does "not stamp the integrated period of that culture," but is influenced by the domination of Ideational or Sensate forms of music (1937:570). Up to the most recent past, Sorokin is obviously generalizing beyond his data, which do not exist for his analysis, as far as folk music is concerned. And in the contemporary scene, there is some evidence that folk music (jazz) influenced grand music.

Generalizing from the presented evidence, Sorokin's definitions of musical styles present serious problems for replicative scholarship. Nevertheless, there are other suggestions in his study that are of relevance to our brief survey.

First, there is his recognition of the importance of social processes in the formation of musical tastes and practices. His insistence on the homogeneity of socialization patterns as a condition for the shared cultivation of Ideational music is matched by an incisive discussion of the social organizational arrangements that correspond to and support Sensate music appreciation. In this connection the rise of the institution of criticism is of particular interest. For Sorokin, the critic (he calls him "art lawyer") must mediate the tastes and standards of the multiple publics, since in Sensate periods there are no grand works of art equally convincing to all groups. Moreover, in the light of the great diversity of sensual stimulation provided in this period, intellectuals promulgate numerous theories by which to argue for one or the other preference. These theories "tend to justify the specific taste of their authors and the groups or factions of which they are representatives. Hence the necessity of the development of aesthetic criticism, theorizing, professional critics, 'reviewers,' 'estimators,' in the period of Sensate music" (1937:545). The professional critic, music educator, theoretician—the art lawyers—become important intermediaries between the artist and various publics by providing verbal rationales through which the Sensate music can be interpreted, if not commonly understood.

Second, there is the reference to the common universe of musical symbolism, which characterizes the entire musical experience of Ideational periods or the given substrata of a social system (the multiple publics) in Sensate periods. The symbols that express the dominant musical idiom, and that are chosen to convey these patterns "are usually pre-existing in the social milieu and precede the individual creators of such music . . . these creators usually accept them and only purify and modify them, without radical alteration" (1937:544). This emphasis on the social creation of symbolism is of course related to Durkheim's *conscience collective*, among other sociological concepts.

Third, Sorokin emphasized the interdependence of social processes with musical forms. Not only the critic, but the performer and composers as well are singled out by Sorokin for special attention. Different patterns of interaction between musicians and with their audiences are noted and brought into characteristic relationships with the dominant musical styles. In the Ideational period creative activities are more or less collective, so that neither the composer nor the performer is given an exposed role. In the Sensate period, however, the "professionalization and individualism of the music composer" is outstanding: "Everybody wants to attach his name to his work. . . . Collective creation, be it folk song or just a tune, has practically disappeared. Instead the last 'hit' of the crooner or of a successful song writer is broadcast over the country" (1937:585). Without showing by detailed musical illustrations the particular musical characteristics of Ideational and Sensate styles of music, Sorokin avers that these differences can be demonstrated. It is, of course, possible to show stark musical differences between, to quote Sorokin's extreme examples, Gregorian chant and the "hit" of the crooner (which he considers the musical equivalent to chewing gum). Yet the strength of Sorokin's analysis rests more convincingly in his exposition of social processes that parallel these musical differences than in his musical analysis.

With Sorokin's systematic concern with music, a landmark in sociological study has been reached. To our knowledge, he is the first sociologist who explicitly included music in a systematic, multivolume analysis of the sociological problems of societal and cultural integration. Previous investigations, including those of Dilthey, had been focused on the analysis of selected interrelationships between musical and social aspects. While the German idealist tradition of social analysis was also concerned with the integration of cultural phenomena in a total societal context, Dilthey nevertheless focused his analysis on the meaning of cultural manifestations for the individuals who experience them. Sorokin, however, is concerned with the logical-meaningful integration of social systems. He concerns himself with problems of the analysis of the cultural and social integration of social systems and is not satisfied with placing music into relationships with other concomitant phenomena. Sorokin examines music and the other arts by functional-causal and logical-meaningful analyses in order to discover the degree of integration of the human population in which they are found. Even taking its limitations under consideration—not all of Sorokin's analyses pass every rigorous scientific critique, and his methodological restriction to the cultural product of the "important segments of a population" raises problems concerning the validity of some of his particular generalizations—his study could set the direction of future sociological research in music.

ALPHONS SILBERMANN

An example of a quite different approach is the work of Alphons Silbermann, which has appeared in English, French, and German. His *The Sociology of Music* (1963) is based on *Wovon lebt die Musik* (1957), which in turn is derived from *Introduction à une Sociologie de la Musique* (1955). While the progressive editions do not greatly differ in coverage, they signal that Silbermann finds the study of the sociology of music challenging enough to stay with the field, as indeed he has through the present. In this respect, as in several others, his work is thus distinguished from the occasional or sporadic attention paid to music by some of the scholars discussed earlier (Silbermann, 1966, 1968). Insofar as his book offers a flexible definition of the sociology of music (1963:62), it can also be viewed as its author's prolegomenon to subsequent work. He offers a body of principles explicitly designed for the sociological study of contemporary music, taking as a starting point for analysis the unanalyzed musical phenomenon. The musical experience is viewed within a social context; musical events are studied wherever they occur—as elements of the mass entertainment media, the movies, television, and radio—and the response of audiences is ascertained. As Director of the Institute for Research in Mass Communications at the University of Lausanne he initiated empirical studies in these areas. Through his many years of teaching and research at the University of Cologne (where he also directs a research institute) he has influenced many students, so that one may speak of a Cologne school of the sociology of music. Some indication of the extent of Silbermann's influence can be gained from a glance at the special issue of the *Kölner Zeitschrift für Soziologie und Sozialpsychologie*, vol. 21, no. 3, which contains contributions by students and colleagues honoring him on his sixtieth birthday.

Silbermann's significance to the field consists less in his having provided a system of pronouncements concerning stipulated relationships between music and society than in his pursuit of questions about the social practices of musical life, and in his insistence that these questions be asked through the employment and refinement of methods borrowed from other sociological approaches to the study of cultural manifestations. Some of these techniques may lead to rather pedestrian conclusions, but this is true of many labors. It is precisely through the determination of the factual basis of musical phenomena that certain questions of value can be brought into proper perspective. It may, indeed, be of significance to know whether some fishermen listen to Schubert's *Trout Quintet* or which Australian chicken farmers aspire to find opportunities to hear or study Haydn's *The Hen Symphony,* how often, and under what conditions. Hence we fail to share Tibor Kneif's disdain for empirical sociological research on music (Kneif, 1971:33).

COMPARATIVE ETHNOMUSICOLOGY

Silbermann's insistence on empirical studies may also be considered representative of ongoing comparative research by ethnomusicologists who, rather than cogitating on whether the music of South India is more beautiful than that of North India, go into the field and record the music and appropriate social data. Under the influence of Mantle Hood, students at the University of California, Los Angeles during the 1950s began to gain empirical experience with foreign musics not only by describing the social practices in which musicians and audiences engage, but also by learning how to perform foreign musics on native instruments. By immersing themselves in the technical detail of studying foreign musics, students of ethnomusicology become especially sensitized to varying dimensons of the social learning process necessary for musical mastery. That music is fully embedded in social practices becomes even more obvious to these students, who study with native teachers. That teachers of music work within social traditions, that they may be threatened by passing on musical (esoteric) knowledge to foreigners, that foreign introduction of electronic gadgetry influences their own traditional roles, that politics influence music—these and other empirical realities become immediate foci of scholarly attention for these students, along with their recording of musical examples (Hood, 1971).

Empirical work in studying music in social contexts surely offers great promise. It will benefit from careful attention to detail and from a vision of a grand concept that fuses social institutions with musical accomplishments. The sociology of music should be centrally involved in this effort, since the tradition of sociology offers both technical expertise and theoretical grandeur.

THE WORK OF PAUL HONIGSHEIM

One sociologist combined a pursuit for detail with the hope of consolidating his effort in a magnum opus on the sociology of music. At the time of his death, Paul Honigsheim (1885–1963) was beginning to write up the results of his long-standing sociological studies on music. His bibliography testifies to this extended scholarly concern; papers on musical subjects date as far back as 1920 and continue through 1933, the year he went into exile in France.

A manuscript page found in his belongings, apparently intended to summarize his competencies in music and musicology, indicates that he also had extensive practical musical experience. He was in charge of social and intellectual activities of French and Belgian prisoners during World War I where he supervised, among other things, an amateur theater and a symphony orchestra. But this is not our only evidence of his practical experience in organizing and directing musical activities in responsible positions. As Director of the People's University of the City of Cologne from 1921 to 1933 he founded and directed a school for choral and community singing, eurythmic courses for beginners and advanced students, amateur theater courses and groups, public speech courses, and speech-chorus courses and groups. As a member of the Board of Popular Education of the city of Cologne from 1924 to 1928 he organized, among other things, popular concerts, and as a member of the Guiding Committee of the West German Radio (1928–1933) he supervised and made decisions on the appointment of conductors and instrumental musicians. In a humorous passage in a festschrift for a former associate he says of this period:

> I suddenly discovered what powers I had. I am, of course, musical and was trained as a singer, though I only sang my high baritone for my very best friends even when I was in the best of voice. But it is less important what one can do, than what others think one can. And there was the saying about me that I was very critical in matters musical. Now there were quite a few full-time singers, instrumentalists, and conductors who were appointed on annual contracts and who were quite concerned whether their contracts would be renewed. This applied especially to one of the conductors and every time when I attended a full rehearsal he would run up to me afterwards and ask whether he had taken the right tempi or whether I thought that he should have taken them faster. Others told me that he trembled for fear of me—he was probably the only person who has ever been afraid of as shy a young man as I. [Honigsheim, 1961:11]

He was also a member of the Moving Picture Committee of the Rhineland, and thus was involved with the problems of music in the early days of talking pictures.

During all these years he also taught seminars on the sociology of music at the University of Cologne, and lectured widely on the sociological and social-psychological background of the radio, movies, and sound recordings. He reminisces about these university activities: "We derived special satisfaction from the courses [*Übungen*] on approaches to popular musical culture. In some respect they were precursors of my sociology of music. Sporadically I lectured again on this subject after my retirement [from Michigan State University] when I was visiting professor in Oregon" (1961:9). And it was also during these later years that he once again began to publish papers on the sociology of music (1955,1958). No doubt the exigencies of his refugee existence in Paris, where he directed the French branch of the Frankfurt Institute of Sozialforschung from 1933–1936, did not permit him to continue working on the sociology of music. Feeling threatened by the Gestapo, he left Paris for Panama in 1936. From there he came to Michigan State University in 1938, where he joined the Department of Sociology, retiring from it in 1950. Yet, as his annotated bibliography indicates, he continued reading widely on his favorite subject during these years of movement. On coming to the United States, he had to find his way through the local conventions of academia. But as his friends at Michigan State and elsewhere are only too willing to tell, he was soon equally highly respected for his immense learning and for his warm and witty personality.

While his scholarly record on the sociology of music is already impressive, to round out the stature of this scholar requires that one refer also to his more than eighty publications on the sociology of culture, religion, and knowledge; to additional major articles on sociological methods, on the history of ideas, on social and economic history; to his more than eighty-five articles on pedagogy; and to his numerous book reviews. In addition to these scholarly publications are his continual contributions to the international peace movement. His biographers write: "Another subject dear to him was pacifism. On this subject he wrote with deep conviction and sincere interest in ideas of peace. A man like Honigsheim, who from his earliest years stood between different cultures, or more precisely was bridging them and united them happily in his person, simply had to contribute to the peace movement" (Beegle and Schulze, 1963:4).

What might Honigsheim's magnum opus on the sociology of music have included? Some idea can be gained from the working outlines he prepared for his seminars on the sociology of art. These are oriented "to give the students a knowledge of the relationships between the arts and social structure, the sociological background of the diverse attitudes towards arts in general and the various kinds of arts especially, as well as the social factors affecting the form and styles of arts" (Honigsheim, 1962:Preface). Sections have such titles as: "Meaning and Aims of Arts in the Various Social Structures"; "The Art-Producer"; "Groups of Artists"; "Degree of Esteem of the Artist"; "The Art Public and Customers"; "Attitudes of Primarily Religiously Oriented Groups Toward Arts"; "Attitudes of Groups and Institutions of Not Primarily Religious Character Toward Arts"; "Continuity, Transference, and Spread of Arts"; "The Economic Aspect of the Arts"; "The National Aspects of the Arts'; "The Racial Aspect of Arts"; "Kinds of Arts and Their Interrelationship with Social Structure"; and "Conclusion: Styles of Art, Mental Attitudes, and Society." Under each of these headings Honigsheim specifies various aspects or kinds of information that need to be examined for their bearing on the topic. For example, "The Art-Producer" opens with the question: "Who is involved in the process of art production?" From there he proceeds to Section A: "Societies in which little if any distinction exists between art producers and art consumers." For this section, Honigsheim outlines twenty-one subsections for investigation, ranging from "the artist as sorcerer" to "professionals connected with the commercial aspect of art." In his outline he provides some specific illustration for every subsection, and the reader is stimulated to search for analogous data in appropriate social contexts. While one might at first be of the opinion that Honigsheim's cataloguing of types and subtypes under each heading was an exercise of naming possible logical distinctions and then matching them with a contrived illustration, a look at Honigsheim's working bibliography, and even more so at his *Zettelkasten* (collection of handwritten notes) supports a different view. Honigsheim, no doubt, refined his outline through the challenge of his varied empirical-historical data, which needed to be theoretically housed.

Another source of what might have been Honigsheim's final version is his published work on forms of music and their relationship with social structures. For the investigation of this problem area, he set up five major categories or classes of analysis (Honigsheim, 1955). These categories with their respective subcategories follow a formal definition, according to which any sequence of tones intentionally produced either by one or by several human beings, distinguished from mere noise, and worthy of its emission will be called music. The five categories for investigation are: The Intended Meaning of Music, The Cultural Evaluation of Music, The Socioeconomic Position of the Musician, The Social Structure of the Audience, and Social Forms and Musical Forms. Under each heading Honigsheim offers ideal-typical subcategories, which are derived from certain counterparts in the musical and social history. In their present form, Honigsheim treats these ideal-typical categories as limited generalizations from previous experience and as hypotheses for further elaboration and investigation in concrete musicosocial situations.

On the basis of his published examples and analytical scheme we may suggest that he saw two important tasks for the sociology of music. The first is the systematic analysis of the processes related to the imputation of meaning to the musical phenomena. This task branches out into the analysis of the relationships between the intended meaning and the imputed meaning, and further into an analysis of the social conditions that are characteristically associated with differences between these meanings, and with their correspondence. The second task concerns the analysis of the social processes that co-determine the formal aspects of music: Given the social location of the phenomenon music, which are the processes (if any) that are determinate of particular manifestations in the musical phenomena? In Honigsheim's programmatic approach, the role of music in and for society varies with different societal structures, which are characterized by varying degrees of complexity. These, in turn, must be examined for their relationship to an explanation of differences in the social role, the type and meaning of musical performance, and the social position of musicians. Honigsheim's emphasis on interactional and structural categories brings his program closer to traditional concerns of sociology than to music history.

Another indication of Honigsheim's objectives for the sociology of music is, of course, contained in the various essays on music and sociology offered in this collection. These statements are selected and edited from a far larger collection of Honigsheim's original notes, some of which may have led to chapters in his own final version. Much of the material had to be translated into English, or entirely rewritten. The arrangement of the material was changed in many instances so as to provide a more coherent and less repetitive organization. In a number of cases, illustrations were eliminated when they were exact duplications used elsewhere in support of another point. On the whole, a concerted effort was made to present the material in a manner as faithful to Honigsheim as could be ascertained. While these essays cannot be said to represent what would have been Honigsheim's own final statement on the subject of sociology and music, we are confident that they represent elements that were considered crucial by Honigsheim, and also that they treat subjects that must be regarded as genuine elements of any sociology of music.

While a search of Honigsheim's *Zettelkasten* would produce the footnote material needed to document the numerous illustrations, the immense chore of searching and correlating the boxes full of notes with the edited version of the essays could not be shouldered by the editor. However, the reader should keep in mind that at least two half-sheets of note paper exist for any illustration used by Honigsheim, since he filed all his information in both an author file and in numerous subject files. While reading, he must have produced a flow of notes, which he then filed away in his many boxes. Whenever he began working on a given subject, he seems to have consulted his subject files, arranged the notes, and then written up the materials making frequent references to his notes. Honigsheim's author file on music is appended as his bibliography. That many titles did not find their way into these essays must be considered a disappointment by many readers. This applies particularly to his omission of data from many crosscultural studies; hence, his almost exclusive reliance on illustrations drawn from the fine-arts music of Western Europe and North America. A sociology of music would, naturally, have to be of a comparative nature. That Honigsheim considered sociology to be comparative and to be applicable to the study of non-Western society is evident in his published studies on anthropology and in his series of lectures on American Indians broadcast by RIAS-Berlin (Honigsheim, 1929;1930; 1937;1941;1957). The absence in these essays of more data on musical practices among non-Western peoples, as well as more systematic concern with "lowbrow," popular, youth, folk, or ethnic music, is to be regretted. But these omissions must be attributed to the fact that they represent preliminary versions, not to any limitation of the sociology of music to a concern solely with art music, a limitation Adorno and others explicitly practiced.

To argue for a crosscultural, comparative concept of sociology does not belittle the effort of those scholars who focus their attention on highly particular musical phenomena of Western society. There are ample problems connected with art music for sociologists to study. But it should be clear that both art and popular (or primitive, non-Western, etc.) music involve social dimensions, convey and create meanings, call forth societal responses, and are thus open to sociological study. Those who try to learn what it is that gives music a place in human society different from that of other activities find they have questions in common. By learning what are the specific social concomitants of music, and how they are related to other aspects of social life, students of society and of music may look forward to the day when their findings can become part of a general theory of sociology.

Honigsheim's approach to the sociology of music implies his healthy respect for the potential insight that intramusical attention to details of musical expression can produce. This is one phase of his work in which a close connection to Max Weber's published fragments on music is rather obvious. Honigsheim's indebtedness to Weber goes further, however. He wrote: "To some extent the author is indebted to ideas of Max Weber, and insofar as the essence of some religious groups is concerned, to some ideas found in the writings of Troeltsch" (1962:Preface). And from a partial transcript of one of Paul Honigsheim's lectures on the subject of the sociology of music we learn more.

[Max Weber] was himself tremendously musically minded. As in regards to so many other things, I did not always agree with his musical judgments, so that we often ended up arguing intensely. Anyway, he was fully familiar with musical theory, mastering the theory and structure of the instruments of all human history and knowing what they sounded like. He died too early to be able to publish on it. It may well be that I am the only one who knows about some of his ideas, because he nevertheless told them to me. He pointed in this direction: Christianity is almost the only culture that has produced purely instrumental compositions of such large scale and importance. In other cultures instrumental music is somehow less important, more of an introduction to something else. But it is the Christian world that has produced symphonies and similar things. Is there some connection to the structure of Christianity? . . . And Max Weber pointed also in this direction: If one looks at the great religions of the world one will discover that they, even against the original spirit of their founders, institutionalized the use of the body within religious ritual. But, asked Max Weber, where in Christianity do we have the use of the body within the worship ritual? Nowhere. There exist very few empirical exceptions, such as the coptic church of Ethiopia. . . . And you have similar things in some districts of southern Spain, where within the Catholic Church, special boys in special vestments dance around the altar. But these examples represent absolute exceptions, which moreover, can be traced to non-Christian influences, in the Ethiopian case even to pre-Moslem times. At any rate there is very little use of the body in Christian ritual. There remains only the fact that the celebrating priest accomplishes inclinations of three different kinds with the body. Yet frequently, when a priest celebrates service in a hurry, he does not take much care to give an exact performance. Needless to say that in the Protestant religion, especially when it is near to the Calvinist traditions, the body is considered as something connected with sex, and with original sin, and so on, and consequently is even less tolerated as a means to glorify God.

Max Weber's ideas on this are: Since Christianity eliminated the use of the body and of body rhythm which is so essential in other religious worship, it was able to give greater emphasis to other aspects. Accordingly, since it was not bound to the body and to body rhythm, it then developed an interest in instrumental music as a value in itself. Moreover [Weber suggested] you must keep in mind that there developed a strong interest in mathematics in the Christian world, even stronger than in the Islamic world of the later middle ages. That means, of course, that the interest in something abstract could then also become the cause of the development of physics and acoustics, and of physically and acoustically structured musical instruments. These are Weber's lines of reasoning on the causes and the development of what he calls *abstract music*, which, has nothing to do any more with man's nature, with the body, or with the human voice. [Honigsheim, n.d.]

Other glimpses of the highly stimulating discussions on artistic topics that went on in the circle of Max Weber's friends, who also included

Georg Lukács and Karl Mannheim, can be seen in Honigsheim's essay "Max Weber in Heidelberg" (1963,1968), in references in Marianne Weber's biography (1925), and particularly in the documents assembled in Baumgarten's magnificent compendium on Max Weber's work and person (1964). What becomes eminently clear from these sources is that the Max Weber known to us from his published work, giant though he appears, is only part of his genius. His range of interests, his personal influence on those in contact must have been immense. Being near him meant that one was exposed to a continuous flow of probing questions and hypotheses, none of them purely speculative, all of them based on some theory of another's, or some fact or bit of evidence. Weber would pursue a topic mercilessly, directing his biting wit at those present. At the same he would fire forth questions of how these facts could be connected with corroborating evidence, and what they, in turn, would mean.

The following essays illustrate how Honigsheim was fascinated by the Weber thesis on links between religious proscriptions concerning the use of the human body and the intellectualization (Freud might have called it sublimation) of social life. We find him returning to examples drawn from religious contexts in every essay, as well as exploring implications of the development of dance, of stage movement, of other physical activities for music. The same lecture that contains Honigsheim's recollections of Weber's hypotheses on the implications of the religious restriction of body use on the development of abstract music also offers a direct illustration of Weber's influence on Honigsheim's style of comparative scholarship. The latter told his audience:

> The problem, of course, is not only whether it is true what Weber says about Christianity, but whether it is also true about the other developed complex religions. There is one question especially that I cannot handle yet, but that in purely hypothetical terms can be posed. Zoroastrianism, in its 1200 years as the dominant religion of Persia developed, at least during certain periods, a metaphysical dualism which makes a sharp distinction between mind, God, and religion on the one hand and with nature, to which the body belongs, on the other. If Max Weber is right then the Zoroastrian culture should also have developed abstract music because of its strong dislike for the body and its elimination from worship ritual. [Honigsheim, n.d.]

Honigsheim proceeded to tell the students that in order to test this hypothesis he needed to study Persian music as well as gain more knowledge of Zoroastrianism and its long history. In particular he said that unfortunately he did not know whether this dualism between mind and body had really been as extreme as has occasionally been asserted.

As can be seen, Max Weber's spirit of inquiry was shared by Honigsheim, leading him into examining many ideas before reaching to conclusions. Let this careful attitude also guide future work in the sociology of music.

FUTURE PROSPECTS

One significant difference between these past studies and future studies on sociology and music can be anticipated. A far more explicit attack on questions of musical definitions and analytic method should be undertaken. We can understand why relatively little attention was paid to these issues during the formative years of study, when much effort and space in the published work was necessarily devoted to bolstering the claims that the study of sociology and music could and must be joined. This issue has now been settled. Moreover, the role of philosophy as methodological conscience of scientific efforts has gradually declined in most disciplines. Sociologists dealing with the arts must become self-conscious about the epistemological implications of their methodological posture, and cannot afford to wait for the criticism of other disciplines. Fortunately there are positive signs in this direction in current work on the sociology of the arts.

Some years ago, Jean Duvignaud submitted the thesis that the sociology of theater suffered from extreme mediocrity because its practicioners were satisfied with claiming that they had established parallels between a rigidified society and a dead theater. He chastised them for not realizing that they were dealing only with "two abstractions" (Duvignaud, 1965:37). He could, of course, have pointed out that any scientific concept functions as an abstraction of something else, and that what differentiates sterile and productive approaches is the degree to which concepts are interrelated and brought into correspondence with the world "out there." It is, therefore, not so much a question of whether one is defining the theater as an abstraction that handicaps sociological study, but what the researcher is doing with the concept. As I have proposed elsewhere, sociology must turn more of its methodological attention to defining the specific attributes in the arts and in music that account for their cultural meaning in concrete (rather than abstract) settings. In this view, art is considered to have a sphere of maximum impact, which is defined by sociohistorical parameters; moreover, the meaning of specific forms of artistic expression is characterized by their universal invalidity, rather than by universal validity. Relative to other media of interpersonal expression such as the language of chemical formulas, mathematics, or even conventional speech, the arts tend to communicate little of a pragmatic nature (Etzkorn, 1966). Simmel had of course already directed our attention to this issue when he suggested that art music expressed emotions in a diffuse manner (Etzkorn,

1964). The task for the sociologist would then be to discover the special characteristics of the arts that do communicate, even though only limited specific meanings, within defined social circles, may be communicated.

One of the special problems of the sociology of music, then, would consist in examining how the social action system of music is built upon such meager pragmatic bases. This is the problem Max Weber began to address himself to in his study of the building blocks of music, the social definition of appropriate tonal systems. But far more will need to be done. One may wish to ask, for example, if and to what extent the coterie around some prominent musician is based on a common capacity to "understand" significant details of the artistic communication, or on other nonmusical reasons. In the popular sphere, one might wish to explore which musical attributes differentiate the reception of rock music from other electronically amplified dance music—what is being recognized in the music, or in the setting, or in the musical socialization of artists and audiences, that leads to a shared definition of a musical (or perhaps social) situation? Or, more generally, one will need to study the various nature of social conditions for different forms of musical expression, in view of their specialized musical syntax and semantics, by focusing on the technical and structural communication problems implied through them (Etzkorn, 1972).

Steps toward aiding social analysis through musical analysis have been advocated sporadically in the programs of Dilthey, Weber, Blaukopf, and Adorno. More recently, partly under the influence of Lévi-Strauss (1958; 1963; 1964) and the work of ethnomusicologists, there has been an increase in the recognition of the centrality of music in the lives of all peoples and times. Sociology can rise to this challenge by developing methods germane to the study of this human universal, methods that not only define the social dimensions of music adequately to differentiate them from others, but that also contain specifications of its technical musical qualities.

Greater attention to the technical musical attributes of musical situations will sensitize the researcher to focus on the social dimensions most characteristically related to the musical phenomenon. For example, in a comparative study of the popular and serious music businesses it was possible to eliminate various organizational characteristics of music merchandizing as explanatory variables and, instead, to focus on the musical socialization of composers and performers, once technical differences between the compositional rules, the musical grammar, and performance traditions of popular and serious music had been examined. In particular, the absence of a technical vocabulary through which popular musicians could communicate critically with one another was noted. This absence contrasted sharply with the rather elaborate technical language and competence of musicians working with advanced serious music, with computers, and with rather explicit musical logics. Facility of manipulating musical skills, rather than the size of recording companies, their vertical integration in the music business, or covert or overt practices of plugging, turned out to be far more significant variables in accounting for song-writing in the popular music field (Etzkorn, 1963).

Attention to the technical dimensions of musical life will also help direct analysis to the emergence of "new" social roles and statuses in the contemporary musical scene. The close interdependence between the state of technology and musical practice, discussed by Weber, may be even more prominent today. Technologies of sound production (and reproduction) have provided a range of sounds for aesthetic manipulation that frequently requires broad electronic knowledge in addition to, or instead of, musical competence. The recording engineer with his assistants, the operator of the tape recorder at mixed media performances, the computer programmer, the supplier of amplification and sound modulation equipment, and many other "musical" specialists require sociological attention, especially when the traditional musicians' roles are shared or even dominated by them. This "new" electronic music, moreover, has the potential of challenging traditional notions of the social nature of music by becoming "private" music—the listener with quadrasonic earphones transforms the cavities of his cranium into the reverberation chambers of a most exclusive sound studio. That traditional notions concerning the structure of the entire composer-performer-audience relationship require reexamination in light of the technical differences and capacities of the new musical technologies becomes rather obvious. What is not so clear, however, is that traditional physical barriers between audience and performing musicians are also being removed, such as when during rock performances audiences climb onto the stage.

Here again, attention to the musical aspects of rock music may shed light on the social versus musical conditions for some of the more pronounced manifestations of communal musical experiences that have become associated with rock performances. Such musical analyses can offer rather refreshing insights, such as when Hood compares the recorded repertory of the Beatles with the widely held popular notion that compares the music's beat to the heartbeat or to the drive of an orgasm. Hood reports that "the measurement of tempo from beginning to end of piece revealed that it consistently slows down—a feature not readily comparable to 'the drive of an orgasm'" (Hood, 1971:18). Could it be that the reception accorded various rock groups is more related to managerial skills and packaging than to their music as music?

Sociologists are aware of this need of looking at the musical dimensions of these musical activities that provide the nexus for special types of social interaction (Horowitz, 1972), but they do not (yet) know how to handle them. In order to make progress toward this objective, what has been characterized as the "social problems" and "social indicator" approach to the sociology of art (Dees, 1972)—the tendency to look for art as an indicator or a reflection of the spirit of the age—may fruitfully be replaced with a more directly sociological definition and study of music as musically defined social activity. Paul Honigsheim's later writings, although set down over a decade ago, should contribute to this development in several ways. Incomplete statements as they are, they nevertheless provide an introduction to the breadth of musical materials that are subsumed under this subject; moreover, they offer us the fruits of a life's scholarly labors and preoccupations with the sociological study of the arts. Future students of this subject can derive substantive and theoretical hypotheses from the sample of comparative information on musically based social interaction situations as brought together by Honigsheim.

MAJOR THEMES AND VARIATIONS

GROWING INTEREST IN CULTURAL SOCIOLOGY

A glance at the "Bibliographic Update: 1972–1988" validates Robert N. Wilson's observation that interest in the sociology of culture is growing (1975). Indeed the updated bibliography was pared from a longer list of studies that incidentally added references to music to those that focused exclusively on music. Additional evidence of the growing interest in the sociology of culture and the arts is the establishment of a formal research committee by the International Sociological Association and by round-tables and paper sessions devoted exclusively to the sociology of the arts, which is recurrently featured at regional, national, and international conferences. Scholars have begun to recognize that sociology of the arts is more than a specialized sociology, for instance that the sociology of music "makes a very important contribution to sociological theory, . . . a fundamental approach to communication, to the whole scope of group formation, to social solidarity, and to integration (Zimmerman, 1975).

Most of the studies on music continue to extend Honigsheim's sample of comparative information on musically based social interaction situations. Many of these are concerned with musical aesthetics and semiotics. The majority of new studies, however, deal with musical interaction situations within delimited musical communities. In addition to methodological and theoretical studies, a small though important number of studies pay attention to emerging "new" social roles and statuses in the contemporary musical scene as adumbrated in Future Prospects in "Sociologists and Music" (see above). A brief review of major themes of sociological concern with music since the early 1970s shows the continued relevance of Honigsheim's opus for current sociology. As before in "Sociologists and Music," I will primarily provide summaries of contributions not (yet) available in English.

EMPIRICAL AND EVALUATIVE STUDIES

At the 1985 celebration of Honigsheim's 100th birthday, sponsored by the University of Cologne, Alphons Silbermann lauded Honigsheim for generating not philosophical but sociological approaches to understanding arts, music, and literature. And even though for many Adorno epigones, Adorno's relentless attacks on empirical sociology offered appealing rationales for regarding representatives of empirical study as uninvited disturbers of aesthetic contemplation, Silbermann showed that the sustained strength of Honigsheim's empirical approach was "that he hardly needed to devote a single word to respond to observations of social life or cultural phenomena made from levels of freefloating philosophic clouds, which, by their very nature would be fleeting by" (Silbermann, 1987:83).

Kurt Blaukopf and Alphons Silbermann, who, after Max Weber, are the current pillars and "senior scholars" of the sociology of music (Blomster, 1976:101) in Europe, join Honigsheim in his call to emulate the Max Weber tradition. Yet they admonish their followers to regard Honigsheim's writings as adding to Weber's program. For them it is not sufficient to say, "If you've read Weber you won't need to study Honigsheim" (Blaukopf, 1982:324; Silbermann, 1987:72). Although his writings require close reading, as several reviewers of *Music and Society* (Etzkorn, 1973) noted, the harvest is rich for those who undertake the effort (Hesbacher, 1975:110; Federico, 1975:657; Blacking, 1976:144). Silbermann ascribes some of these difficulties to Honigsheim's self-conscious *Notariatstil*, a style of writing that is "remote from evaluations, controversies and polemics [and] only obliquely points to conclusions" (Silbermann, 1985:69).

Equally responsible for the reluctance of musicologists and some sociologists to refer to Honigsheim's writings is Honigsheim's dedication to the task of clarifying relationships between human beings and human beings. As the sociology of religion cannot treat religious experiences accessible only to the person perceiving them, so Honigsheim's sociology of music can only deal with *social* or intersubjective musical phenomena. For Honigsheim, "an artfully constructed composition that remained in a desk drawer and has never been performed is not of any sociological relevance" (Ibid:78). However, for many musicologists the preoccupation with precisely such questions as the identification, nature, and autonomy of "the work of musical art" as embodied in the "intent" of the composer and given symbolic representation on paper, disk, or tape, remains a principal calling (Etzkorn, 1988:43; Lissa, 1975:17). In this context, the fate of Honigsheim's reception is not distinct from the empirical sociology of the arts—a fate, however, that is undergoing rapid transformations in the age of new technologies and media.

GENERAL SOCIOLOGICAL APPROACHES

Books by Karbusicky (1975), Kneif (1975), Rummenhöller (1978), Haselauer (1980), Blaukopf (1982), DaSilva (1984), Kaden (1985), Supicic (1987) and Destreri (1988) were published with "sociology of music" in their titles. These also attest to the increase in interest in the sociology of culture. Moreover, these "sociology" books are supplemented by edited volumes and doctoral dissertations with principal focus on the sociology of music such as Becker (1982), Bontinck (1974), Durga (1984), Kamerman (1983), Layton (1981), Levy (1979), Mark (1981), Martorella (1982), Menger (1983), Ostleitner (1987), Silbermann (1973, 1977, 1979, 1986), Wilson (1986), and others to be found in the bibliographic sections on Aesthetics, Media and Music or in Music and Communities such as Frith (1981) or Titon (1984).

After his emigration to West Germany, Karbusicky's "Empirical Sociology of Music" (1975) continues the tradition of the Czech school. He offers eight case studies that provide him with the vehicle to extol the virtues of scientific analysis as instrumental in the search for the truth about musical relationships in society. Questions of the aesthetics of "easy-listening" and "serious" music, of separating biopsychological constants from social conditioning of music perception, and of musical socialization and education represent starting points. Karbusicky employs empirical methods to find answers. For him the empirical search for answers represents what sociological work should be and not the exposition of some systematic exegesis. In so doing Karbusicky specifically invites Marxist sociologists in the West to overcome "their erroneous shyness of praxis" (p. 18) and all sociologists to study conditions of musical life with an attitude that accepts change as a constant. Since moving to the Federal Republic of Germany, Karbusicky continues conducting empirical studies on a broad range of topics which find reflection in numerous publications included in the bibliography. In the next section we will revisit another sociologist whose earlier work we already introduced in the preceding chapter, Sociologists and Music.

Blaukopf's *Foundation for the Sociology of Music* (1982) published more than thirty years after *Sociology of Music* (1950) offers twenty-nine chapters that examine music in many ways: as resulting from musical scales and from composing activities, as a means of expression of specific social strata dependent on technological aspects of sound reproduction or on financial support structures, instrumental and vocal music, and music played in modern concert halls or within tribal or ethnic settings. His text presents a scientific foundation for the analysis of music as an embodiment of social activities. Since musical life takes place within societal relations that are characterized by social change, Blaukopf carefully examines the sociological instruments made available by contemporary sociological theory for their applicability to the study of changes in music.

Blaukopf's experience of thirty years of empirical sociological research is condensed in this book, which does not even list in the bibliography his book on tonal scales (written in the late 1930s but not published until the early 1950s because of wartime persecutions), the principal source for our preceding analysis of Blaukopf. His 1982 book and his many research reports from the intervening years illustrate the power of empirical sociology and its ability to incorporate theoretical insights derived from an analysis of changing circumstances. Like Émile Durkheim, who throughout his sociological career refined his theories, Blaukopf is at peace to demonstrate that changes in music, in technological and media relations, need to be approached through empirical methods if they are to be made intelligible and are not to be ideologically "interpreted" through masks of prescribed clichés or formulae. He is perfectly at ease to apply these strictures to his own writings by revisiting and revising earlier findings in the light of new evidence.

Kaden, in *Sociology of Music* (1985), examines "what sociology of music should be" along with "social structures of musical communication." In addition he offers summaries of various case studies on social determinants of listener responses, musical notation, and composition. To provide a context for his data he mines the social scientific literature for insights that will help musicology to change its focus from a descriptive to an explanatory focus, from *Geisteswissenschaft* to *Gesellschaftswissenschaft*. Kaden's familiarity with and extensive use of literature in Slavic languages, infrequently cited in Western publications, makes this volume invaluable. Moreover, his judicious exposition of studies based on applications of historical materialism allows him to point to limitations of this approach when he concludes that they permit sociology to contribute only necessary but not sufficiently specific findings. This accomplishment Kaden confines to rigorous empirical inquiry of the study of music within a context of social reality. His book is a fine example of such work.

The works of Kneif and Haselauer aim less at providing full-fledged programs for sociological study than offering resources and suggestions for other researchers and students. Kneif's *Book of Readings in the Sociology of Music* (1975) makes accessible texts of sociological classics. Haselauer's *Handbook* (1980) provides definitions and occasionally offers extensive excursions on key terms from the sociological arsenal of concepts, methods, and research tools. Written in German, this book offers an efficient overview of sociological concerns with music. Related to these publications on "sociology proper" are those that take sociological aesthetics as their point of departure.

SOCIOLOGICAL AESTHETICS

As the bibliography reveals, much attention is still devoted to the exegesis of the intellectual legacy of Adorno. Many of these entries are European sources. This is consistent with the differences in sociological traditions between the United States and Europe (Etzkorn, 1975:45), which formed part of the stimulus for Blomster's essay "Sociology of Music: Adorno and Beyond" (Blomster, 1976:83).

In the American sociomusicological community it was observed that Adorno's writings and analyses on musical topics suffered from social-scientific defects. American sociology follows a model of science that seeks to produce findings with general applicability to all comparable social situations. Conclusions of sociological study are evaluated to the degree to which they approximate this scientific goal. Findings should either make claims to "universal validity" or, if they are meant to be only of particularistic relevance, they should explain their empirical limitations.

Adorno's writings tend to claim unlimited and unqualified validity, although their methodology allows only particularistic findings. For example, Adorno's study "On Popular Music" extrapolated experiences he collected in the metropolitan region of New York City (Adorno, 1941). These experiential data excluded musical genres (such as bluegrass, hillbilly, soul and blues) that were widely *popular* in other regions of North America. Consequently, Adorno's generalized conclusion that popular music attained the characteristics of goods and followed the demands of the consumer market might possibly have been applied to "popular music" distributed from the Brill Building in New York City, but without further methodological qualification had only limited if any applicability to other music that was "popular" in the regional and ethnic cultures of the times.

Further, sociomusicology found difficulties with Adorno's uncritical adoption of the musicological axiom of the *Eigengesetzlichkeit* of music. Sociologists noted that if one were to act on Adorno's premise that music must follow autonomous laws then it would become a principal task of sociology to uncover these immanent rules and to describe the extent to which musical life obeyed them. Since Adorno's writing did not allow that "other" societies might practice "other" types of music with "other" sets of musical laws—Adorno treated as his single ideal only musical developments in European art music in the direction of Schönberg: a rather restricted selection of music, even in European music—sociomusicology and ethnomusicology found that Adorno's writing was widely open to empirical contradictions beginning with his starting assumptions. Because of this different attitude toward scientific research, it was hardly possible for American social science to find a common scientific denominator for joining Adorno's pronouncements with the careful empirical studies of local researchers, much as individual scholars may have shared in his personal value judgments and aesthetic preferences. Similarly, among European sociologists working in the Weber tradition, neither Honigsheim, Blaukopf, nor Silbermann would mistake Adorno's aesthetic dicta for conclusions of empirical sociology.

Partly influenced by the dialogue between Walter Benjamin and Adorno concerning the aura of works of art (Etzkorn, 1974:336), and partly continuing the musicological tradition of focusing almost exclusively on the analysis of musical scores and documents at the expense of questions of musical realization and performance (Harrison, 1963:79–80), various authors addressed the aesthetic question to discover the proper definition of a musical work of art. Should sociologists be dealing with musical reproduction in addition to or at the exclusion of musical production, or should they be principally dealing with musical composition (production)? Should a recorded piece of music be called a work of art, or because of its loss of uniqueness, be treated as another instance of popular culture? Much of this discussion can be looked at as instances of two basic postures: only what is truly unique should form the subject of the sociology of art (i.e., an application of the conventional aesthetic perspective); and mass-produced objects, such as recorded musical performances disseminated in multiple copies, which lose their aura of exclusivity, should become objects of common or mass consumption (i.e., an adaptation of the conventional elitist perspective). Neither of these views adds much enlightenment to the sociological understanding of music. It must be questioned first, empirically whether the axiom of uniqueness can ever be applied to musical sound that is inseparable from performance of execution. How could one conceive of any sounded musical work as not dependent at some phase on performance for its realization, that is to say *existing* without a social context that implicates the roles of composer, performer, and audience? But if the reality of musical realization implies social circumstances of performance and *appreciation* (perception), then there are individual variations contained in them, as in Durkheim's conception of the *représentations individuelles* within the *conscience collective*. As a social fact, however, a musical work cannot be, by definition, unique. Second, individuals can find (aesthetic) satisfaction in any object, whether it is a single edition or mass-produced. Empirically there is no basis for claiming that only unique works of art can call forth aesthetic satisfaction, nor for the evaluative claim that the aesthetic satisfaction derived from a mass-produced work can only be less than that derived from a single work.

These aesthetically instigated discussions fail to raise more appropriate sociological questions such as how to bring empirical focus to the arguments by discerning what are the special qualities of social relations or interaction situations that are concatenated by a work of musical sound (Etzkorn, 1976:16–19). In order to bring sociological insights into musical life the question should not be whether music distributed on records and played through loudspeakers is any less of an artistic expression than live performances of music; instead sociologists need to ask whether the set of social relations involved in the sound of records is different, and how it is different, from that connected with live music performance.

SOCIOLOGY AND THE NEW MEDIA

I already anticipated that the sociological encounter of electronic technology would begin to challenge traditional notions of the social nature of music, since through the electronic creation and reception of sound it can become an almost "private" matter. The composition and playback of musical sound through a personal computer and through earphones can eliminate the involvement of other musicians or listeners. In light of these developments, I called for the reexamination of traditional notions concerning the structure of the entire composer-performer-audience relationship as they derived from the technical differences and capacities of the new musical technologies (see p. 39). Today loudspeakers and their smaller cousins the earphones have become the principal sources of musical sound heard by the majority of listeners most anywhere in the world. This mediamorphosis from live to loudspeaker music and its sociological consequences cannot be overlooked any longer. I have repeatedly noted that more specific attention needs to be paid to the phenomenological differences between objectified sound emitted from loudspeakers and performed, live music.

The electronic mediamorphosis continues to bring sound into the lives of people at an unprecedented scale. The sheer number of people exposed to loudspeaker music through radio, film, television, cable TV, video, hotel music, muzak, and music in the dentist's chair at any one moment is simply enormous. Phenomenologically and in terms of social relationships, loudspeaker music clearly refers to a different social reality from live music making. It is *objectified* sound, brought into being through the medium of compact disk, tape, a long-playing record, a pair of loudspeakers, or earphones. Moreover it can be manufactured, packaged, commercialized, merchandized, marketed, distributed, sold, bought, used, and stored. Even though there are only a few notions on which sociologists will readily agree, all would subscribe to the premise that they need to differentiate between the study of interpersonal relations and that of relations between persons and material objects.

From the foregoing it follows that the sociology of music will need to distinguish between situations in which musical sounds are the direct result of immediate music making (live performance in a concert hall, church, tavern, or living room) and situations in which musical sounds are reproduced through loudspeakers from a storage medium (LP, cassette, CD, etc.) on which they were registered at a prior time. In the former, performers translate notes or performance instructions into audible music by executing learned corporeal responses. Such performances, however, do not reflect an exact *mapping* of the musical script or composition. The performers' actions give significance to the signs (Hosokawa, 1987:536–55). On the other hand, in the reproduction from a storage medium, there is as exact a mapping of the once-sounded example as technology permits, capable of exact reproduction *ad infinitum*, without any new projection of a performer's subjective self.

Applied consequences for musical praxis from the music reproduced through New Media are particularly found in the fields of music education (Etzkorn, 1988). The current literature in this area addresses questions connected with mass-marketing, distribution, and political control over the import and use of foreign prerecorded tapes and disks.

Serious dialogue with the question of the phenomenological aspects of mediated music, however, is not entirely neglected; for instance, studies on the fate of contemporary composers explore its dependency on the shrinking demand for live music (Bontinck, 1984).

MUSIC EDUCATION AND AGE GROUPS

Youth and old age, along with teacher education and the utilization of New Media in music instruction, continue to inspire sociological studies. At both ends of the age spectrum, the subject of how computers can be used formed the basis for study. Other studies focus on the structure of teacher preparation, that of curricula, the organization of musical instruction on the tertiary level, and music programs in institutions for the elderly. Inquiry is also directed toward the impact of specific musical styles (rock and roll) on socialization and on stylistically specific induction in musical occupations. In these studies the sound of music, whether performed live or loudspeaker generated, is the *raison d'être* for implicating bystanders into social relations and interdependencies. And it is questions of social organization that typically dominate the discourse.

MUSICAL COMMUNITIES

The number of dissertations that in recent years have focused on musical communities indicates the direction scholarship is taking. Coming from different perspectives and pursuing disparate goals, they nevertheless share an attempt to explain the musical subject as resulting from its social or cultural setting. Whether the concern is changes in the organization of major orchestras in Europe or the United States, adaptation of musical practice to political directives, the use of music as an instrument of policy, or musical and social perception in tribal society, music is not disembodied from music making and is not viewed as a musical "work of art" (*Kunstwerk*) that, once fixed in notation, already possesses aesthetic value with or without social realization.

These studies recognize that musical creations, at the time of their coming into existence as spontaneous outbursts or as carefully crafted compositions on paper (to point to the end-points of a theoretical continuum), were influenced, if not conditioned, by the dominant and possibly governing cultural milieus of their "creators." Composers, performers, and their audiences are implicated in the same basic conventions of their social community which limit what is available to them for the making of music via instrumental or sound technology (including voice-production preferences) and the musical tones appropriately selected from the sound spectrum. These studies also show that any new live realization of a previously conceived composition cannot be an exact replication if the communal conditions have changed only so slightly. Indeed, attempts at realizing compositions or musical *Kunstwerke* under different social circumstances must, by necessity, introduce changes to avoid becoming an exact replication of their original edition. The "original" is *falsified* at every subsequent reproductive turn. One only needs to reflect on such factors responsible for changes in musical reproduction as (maintaining) the tuning of instruments, the sound properties of different instruments of the same instrument family, variations in playing technique (touch, vibrato, attack), or changes in the acoustics of performance locations.

Studies on music in communal or group settings regard as their province musicians and their audiences on all levels of the social order. They differ from conventional musicology, which for so many years considered the study of musical *monuments*, that is, the accumulation of editions of music in the library (which frequently were not even suited for realization through performance), as an important attribute of scholarship (Harrison, 1963:79–80).

POST-ADORNO SOCIOMUSICOLOGY IN THE UNITED STATES

In the concluding sections I will attempt to provide a synopsis of recent trends in American and European sociology of music and will comment on some of these developments by focusing on individuals and/or centers of research and teaching.

Howard S. Becker (1982) (Northwestern University) along with students writing dissertations under him continued to be guided by the theoretical posture of collective behavior. The associated methodological approach typically employs some variation of participant observation, or the extrapolation of data from case studies to more general significance. Becker's earlier studies focused on the social situation of jazz, but more recently (along with excursions into photography, fine arts, arts policy, and drama) he turned to studies of modern music and to the work of John Cage. These studies throw light on the interaction networks between occupants of social roles (composers, publishers, concert managers, publicists, etc.), social positions, and the status of musical life.

Richard Petersen (1975) (Vanderbilt University) along with his colleagues has been working on the subject of social control of music and cultural productions. He focuses on questions concerning how new artistic creations are socially controlled and manipulated, through which institutional mechanisms, and in the service of which interest groups.

R. Serge Denisoff (1987) (Bowling Green University) studies relations between the (musical?) content of popular music, music videos, and specific factors in the changing social environment. He initially conducted studies on the music industry and its business. Refining some of this earlier work, he has turned to the study of newer technologies and media.

John Shepherd (1986) (McGill University, Canada) has been engaged in some longitudinal studies that aim to develop theoretical explanations of taste and consumption patterns in popular music as a specific case of a more general sociomusicological model.

Max Kaplan (1980) and Robert Stebbins (1978) (University of Alberta) are engaged in joint studies of music as leisure pursuit. Kaplan continues his studies on how music education ties in with active musical life.

In my own studies I am concerned with societal and musical consequences for musical life occasioned by the introduction of the computer and loudspeaker music. These are far-reaching and include themes and variations on composing and composers, changes in notational systems and notating technology, the printing/publishing of music, sound production, reproduction and preservation, changes in the sound-scape, and changes in musical occupations and education.

And, at the various centers of ethnomusicology (Ann Arbor, Austin, Berkeley, Brown, Columbia, Illinois, Indiana, Maryland, Los Angeles, New York, Washington, Weslyan, and Wisconsin) the range of studies on the relationship between musical and social-cultural change is extensive. For a representative picture of the great variety of work, glance at a program for an annual meeting of the Society for Ethnomusicology, which will be impressive. Included are studies dealing with the changing roles of musical socialization in all kinds of modernizing societies, the influence of new media on traditional musical practices, and the political manipulation of musical activities for the purposes of state propaganda.

This survey obviously suggests conclusions different from those reached by the British sociologist Janet Wolf who, in assessing American sociology of music, averred that "the ideology of autonomy still rules in the study of music" and that "music is strangely absent" in the sociological study of the arts (Wolf, 1987:9).

EUROPEAN TRENDS AND THEMES

Perhaps the theme most central in the eyes of European sociologists is the topic of mass media policies and the role sociomusicology may play in their formation. The studies by Blaukopf, Bontinck, Gardos, and Mark (1983), Destreri (1976), Heister (1974), Kneif (1977), Smudits (1987) and Ostleitner (1987) directly address this issue as did the entire Conference on Sociomusicology at Göteborg University in April 1988 (Ling, 1988). Careful empirical analyses of the penetration of official broadcast programs by music from foreign sources, the share of regional music in the sale of recordings, and the percentage of live musical programming versus loudspeaker music reproductions and similar data are combined into indexes of music availability for different nationality and musical taste groups. Sociologists not only compile such data for policymakers in government but also interpret them allowing themselves to construct alternative scenarios for the future of musical occupations and life. The work of Wallis (1984) is representative of these studies and already has become well-known in America, perhaps because it was originally published in English.

Related to these interests are sociological concerns with mediamorphosis, or the introduction of new media as they affect changes in music production, reproduction, and reception. Much of this work was pioneered by Blaukopf (1974, 1982, 1983) and Silbermann (1973, 1987) in Austria and West Germany. Its ramifications for music education were taken up by various conferences of the International Society for Music Education (ISME) (Mark, 1981; Etzkorn, ISME:1988).

More directly addressing topics of mass communication as they relate to the sociology of the arts are several publications by Silbermann and his colleagues at Cologne (1977, 1979, 1986). Changes in the institutional world of music become the specific focus of inquiry in the work of Bontinck (1974, 1975) on education, and Heister (1983) on symphony concerts.

FINIS

This brings me to my final observation on the promise of sociomusicology in the post-Adorno era. It seems to me that there is quality work being done in the empirical study of music in contemporary society, that the range of topics is considerable with relevance for music education, aesthetics, public policy, and, perhaps most importantly, for composers and creators of new sounds and sound technologies. It also seems to me that the approach taken by Honigsheim to the study of music in social life continues to stimulate additional work. The following pages of Honigsheim's later writings will best serve as starting points for additional work. They provide an orientation to the kinds of questions empirical sociology would raise in typical circumstances. They also paint in historical background factors, principally for musical situations connected with European art music, as a sociologist would use them. In reading them, one should remember that Honigsheim's pages were never meant to offer the final word on any of the subjects that they touch on. Even had Honigsheim been able to write his own version, his posture of scientific doubt for empirical sociology would have invited his readers to criticize his findings. If his work is regarded as possible anwers to be revisited either in the light of new evidence he overlooks or with different implications for the future, because of changing technological or societal circumstances, readers will be sociologically rewarded but also entertained. Even the annotations to his bibliography contain veritable nuggets of insight as when he notes, "Hitler could have written this" regarding Glasenapp's book *Siegfried Wagner* (Glasenapp, 1906).

THE LATER WRITINGS
OF PAUL HONIGSHEIM

ON THE USES OF MUSIC
IN SOCIETY

Throughout Western society, conventional conceptions of music customarily involve notions of personal enjoyment, or aesthetic ideas that music is a value in itself. Conventional as they are today, a study of history and of various cultures reveals that these extramusical and individualistic associations with the experience and practice of music have appeared infrequently. Music has usually been considered principally as a supportive tool with immediate use for collectivistic and social purposes. For example, music, as the other arts, has often been connected with religious and even more with primitive magical practices.

It has been argued that primitive man does not think in the logical fashion of the Western world. Reports from certain cultures suggest that, at times, primitive man acts as if he is firmly convinced that by producing noise he may be able to influence forces supposed to be superior to him, forces believed to be located somewhere within nature. This practice is called *conjuration,* and much of music has been performed for this purpose. According to their beliefs, primitive peoples may have greater success in hunting by producing strong noises. And it has been believed that it may even be possible to incorporate magic forces located in another man's body into one's own body by producing such loud noises.

While the modern listener hardly considers music to have conjurational powers, more specifically musical aspects of music making can also be shown to have varied their importance through time. For example, we have come to consider melody as essential to music. But our emphasis on melody is applicable only for relatively few traditions of musical practice. Especially in primitive music rhythm, not melody, is supposed to be essential. The magic character and power of the musical performance is dependent on maintaining the correct rhythm. If some error is committed, or if someone dances out of rhythm, then an entire performance may be considered of no value, and may even be expected to cause damage for the group. Frequently not only the musical rhythm, but also certain instruments are supposed to have magical power. Musical instruments were often made from parts of human bodies, and were supposed to produce magic effects. Flutes, for instance, were sometimes made from bones, and the skin of a drum is often a human skin. But even when parts of the human body were not incorporated, instruments were held to be of magical character and able to produce magical effects.

Next to correct rhythm and the use of magic instruments, the intervals or the *musical distance* between the sounds are supposed to be of magic importance. Examples abound among the cultures of American Indians, Koreans, Japanese, and Hindus, and also in ancient Egypt, Palestine, and Greece. The fact that the true maintenance of the correct intervals is endowed with the character and importance of magic may help explain why musical intervals have rarely changed.

Related to the attribution of magical character to musical performances is the fact that persons supposed to be descended from divinities or related to magical powers are often specially honored. Painting and sculptoring have frequently been used to display the greatness or power of a god or a monarch. Music has been used to create the same impression. Loud noises made by trumpets, shrill sounding oboes, and drums are made so that everyone hears the approach of the powerful monarch. Such glorification is almost always connected with the intent of indoctrinating and educating the masses to defer to their gods and to selected persons.

Among the aims of musical performance can also be counted social indoctrination and education. Many religions have elaborated systems of indoctrination, for which special forms of music or the prohibition of certain instruments are used. Under certain political conditions, the entire educational system is brought under government control. In these cases, special care is taken to cultivate selected kinds of music or to emphasize special instruments, which are supposed to influence the masses in whatever way the political powers consider essential. Ancient China after Confucius (551–479 B.C.), some of the states of classic Greece, Hitler's Germany, and Soviet Russia have all considered music an indispensable part of political education.

Music has also occasionally been used for negative indoctrination as well. Music can show how ridiculous or inferior a person or a minority group disdained by the dominant group is supposed to be. For example, when a society turns against a traditional religion, music has sometimes been used to place the exponents of that religion, such as priests or ministers, in a comic situation. During the Enlightenment and the French Revolution, comic operas depicted priests and monks in ridiculous situations. Political leadership was ridiculed during periods of the decline of monarchies and aristocracies by deflating king and members of the nobility in operas. In relatively recent times, Soviet artists have ridiculed members of the bourgeoisie in similar ways. Another example is the character of Alberich, in the *Nibelungenring,* used by Richard Wagner (1813–1883) as a vehicle of anti-Semitism.

Some recent composers have used music to portray their personal enemies in demeaning situations. The best-known example is in Wagner's *Die Meistersinger,* when the character of Beckmesser is reduced to a satire of Italian opera and of Eduard Hanslick (1825–1904), the outspoken adversary of Wagner's concept of opera.

These examples demonstrate that music has been used for extramusical purposes in primitive as well as in more complex cultures. Certainly, the more the technical means of making music developed, the more man has become able to concentrate on enjoying the musical sounds as such independent of (or in addition to) their extramusical contexts. Even so, the enjoyment of music per se becomes the principal aim of musical productions only in certain cultures. This restriction applies especially to the aesthetic appreciation of music as a value in its own right.

Very few cultures, and almost exclusively within the confines of the Western world, have appreciated music for its inherent aesthetic value. Examples include the later Greek culture, the culture of the Roman Empire, and the West since the Italian Renaissance. These cultures accepted the idea that music can be free from extramusical aims, and highly appreciated music as a value in itself precisely because it does not have any other connotation.

As they vary among peoples and cultures, conceptions of the aim of music must be examined if one wishes to gain more than a descriptive understanding of variations of musical practice. Without information about musical practice in different places at varying times, little sociological insight can be gained from a discussion of changing aesthetic views. In the following essays, attention will be paid to descriptive and historical data on musical practice before the discussion returns to a systematic examination of links between societal views of musical practice and forms of musical expressions.

ON VARIOUS OCCASIONS
FOR THE PERFORMANCE OF MUSIC

The conventional assumption—that music has usually been performed in order to provide enjoyment to the listener or performer, or to both—is, as we have shown, without historical foundation. It is equally incorrect to say that most musical performances take place on occasions that are essentially musical in nature. To the contrary, it might be shown that for most of history most music has been performed in situations connected with religious worship. But complex empirical problems are involved in this generalization. Not only music but a great many attitudes and practices at present considered to be rather secular have traditionally been connected with religion in primitive cultures and even in some more complex cultures. Thus, it is often difficult to determine the extent to which certain kinds of music should best be considered as religious or as secular music.

CEREMONIAL OCCASIONS

Throughout most of history, turning points in the lives of group members have been marked by specialized group religious expressions. Accordingly, such moments are enriched by music that is supposed to be of religious character. The ceremony of baptism in Christianity and similar ceremonies when a child is incorporated into other religious groups illustrate such an event. Even more than baptism of the young, puberty ceremonies are important events for musical performances. Even relatively simple societies celebrate puberty rituals in fairly complex ways. To our own day, religious and secular groups alike mark by special ceremonies the day when a young person is no longer considered a child, but is accepted into adult society.

Weddings and funerals are also occasions for religious rituals. Funerals frequently employ some form of musical expression. During epidemics of contagious diseases when a great many people die, special forms of prayer and rituals incorporating music and even dancing have been reported to develop.

When a society shifts from a primarily religious to a more secular character, the ceremonial use of music tends to glorify the group and its political leaders. Certainly, every new nation state establishes its state holidays, which are occasions for performing songs of victory and other patriotic music. When a state is governed by a monarch or dictator, the life of the chief of state offers additional opportunities for patriotic celebrations, such as birthdays, coronation days, and even festivities for the reception of other heads of state. Feudal society had many occasions for public celebration, among which were tournament days and the knighting of young men who were accepted into adult society by the ruling nobility. No doubt the Mohammedan rulers of Spain between the eighth and thirteenth centuries had their own versions of such ceremonies. Conceivably, the middle and working classes in industrial societies prefer not to lose income from too many days off from work, making for fewer ceremonial celebrations in modern times.

MUSIC FOR ENTERTAINMENT

Ceremonial events are important to us for two reasons—they provide opportunity for the performance of existing music and for the creation of new compositions. Yet we must remember that most music performed at such events was primarily intended to mark the importance of the day, rather than to bring aesthetic enjoyment to the listener.

There were, however, occasions in history when music was performed largely for the enjoyment of the audience, such as at various types of banquets. Many examples can be found from the times of the ancient Greeks, throughout the Middle Ages among Celtic-speaking peoples and the continental courts of Europe, and down to modern times. Musical examples of this type include many of the "Divertimentos" of Wolfgang

Amadeus Mozart (1756–1791), which were composed specifically for the banquets of the duke or bishop. Banquet music was often performed in the garden rather than in the house. Since music performed outdoors limited the use of the piano, this practice encouraged the composing of chamber music. Naturally this type of musical performance was emphasized in countries with moderate climates, and therefore also appeared relatively early in the colonies in South America.

Garden Music

Of music performed in the open air, two special kinds may be mentioned. The first is that performed in some resorts during the summer months, when many people promenade and enjoy the seashore or the mountain air. The other kind is the music performed in restaurant gardens, especially in European countries. Sometimes a military band played in beer gardens with the financial support of the restaurant owner in the hope that by doing so, he might attract a greater number of guests and thereby increase the food and beverage consumption to such an extent that the relatively high cost of such a band would be absorbed. Of course, restaurant music is not always played in the garden. Many climates make this impossible. Nevertheless, whether performed indoors or out, music associated with any type of restaurant plays an important role in musical life because of the economic, in addition to the aesthetic, impact it generates.

MUSIC FOR WORK

Another type of music accompanies people at their work, whether they are employed individually or in groups. At least two very different types of work music might be distinguished. First is the primarily rhythmical music performed in primitive societies. Classified with this is certain rhythmically pronounced music from more complex cultures. Examples of rhythmical music that usually accompanies physical labor are the musical patterns brought by the Negro slaves from Africa and introduced on New World plantations, and the many sea chanties and riverboat chants, such as those sung by the Volga boatmen. An entirely different sort of work music is that encountered as background music in today's offices and factories, where it is piped in from central locations. This method of distributing background music is also used for therapeutic purposes in mental hospitals.

HOUSE MUSIC

While the above-cited cases may contain some built-in limitations to the aesthetic enjoyment of music, a considerable body of musical composition and practice is designed exclusively for personal enjoyment and gratification. Such is the music composed for performance within the home. We have evidence that house music was common as early as the era of ancient Greek culture, through the latter part of the Middle Ages. The development of middle classes in cities has been an important factor in this field, as has modern occidental culture, particularly in the northern regions, which is largely centered in the home. House music has also contributed to the cultivation of keyboard instruments and of certain types of chamber music. As already mentioned, the majority of chamber music compositions of the Classic and Romantic periods were primarily conceived of as house music.

THEATER MUSIC

Like the history of music, the history of the theater in the majority of cultures and epochs has been intimately connected with religion and magic. Except for pre-Christian Greek times and modern occidental culture, theatrical productions have been used primarily as representations of collective group feeling. Theater among Hindus, in the classic age of Greece, and during the Christian Middle Ages was a way of indoctrinating the people by visualizing and acting out for them what they already knew and were supposed to believe—to whit, the greatness of their divinities and the necessity of leading their lives according to the ethical rules of the group.

Only in early Greece and in the modern West has the theater assumed a pronounced individualistic character. With the rise of individualism, people began attending the theater for the purpose of seeking out new experiences and hearing something they did not already know. Theater and opera became entertainment for its own sake, rather than a ceremonial expression of the group's ethos.

Nowithstanding the general tendency, there were limitations within music on the development of "art for art's sake." One will recall that the performance of Italian opera during the seventeenth and eighteenth centuries was largely a social event. The upper classes' habit of visiting back and forth during recitatives, and other illustrations of the "social" nature of musical events will be discussed in greater detail in another context.

Other limitations on artistic absolutism in more recent times are exemplified by the religio-philosophical attitudes embodied in the Wagnerian festivals in Bayreuth during the Hitler years, and the Soviet state's avowed political intentions of manifesting the collectivist spirit through musical performances.

CONCERT MUSIC

Far more than the theater, the organization of regular concerts has provided opportunities to enjoy music as a value in its own right. Contemporary forms of concert performances originated as recently as the eighteenth century, when the bourgeoisie in the cities became increasingly wealthy. Despite their affluence, they were not admitted to high society, and so could not partake of musical performances held at court. To compensate, amateur musicians would gather in restaurants or in the living rooms of the bourgeoisie to perform a symphony or other work. As these amateurs practiced more and more, they gradually assured the status of "professional" musicians. At this point a new concept was introduced by opening concerts to the public, and those who were able bought tickets for single performances or even for an entire season or series of concerts.

In another section we will deal with the extent to which traveling virtuosos became dependent on the musical aspirations of these amateur orchestras, and with the extent to which their repertoire and program content was influenced by them. In concluding this essay, we will only mention some musical phenomena which to this day continue to be linked with religion or politics in some manner.

ORATORIOS

Organized religion continues to offer opportunities for musical performances during regular worship services or on special occasions. Yet religion is possibly of less significance for music today than in previous periods. An important indication of the decline of the role of religion in music is the transfer of oratorio performances from churches to concert halls. With that move the oratorio lost the primarily religious character it had been given by Johann Sebastian Bach (1685–1750) and George Frideric Handel (1685–1759), and came to be regarded as more secular and primarily musical than religious. Consequently, oratorio music is looked upon more and more a form to be appreciated in the same way as symphonic and other nonreligious music.

In the majority of epochs and cultures, social events of primarily non-musical character became occasions for the performance of music. Yet in our own time, Western culture has created conditions in which music has been given intrinsic value. To understand how these changes came about we will have to explore the social phenomena of music more fully and examine in detail the relationships between various kinds of music and the distinctive societal settings in which they are found.

ON THE VARIETY OF PERSONS
AND ACTIVITIES
INVOLVED IN MAKING MUSIC

Although today the sounds of music can be heard almost everywhere in Western society, this has not always been so. The mechanical and electronic devices that give it wide distribution have also caused music to lose some of its more obvious interpersonal connections. That someone had to create the particular combination of sounds, that this creation process may have involved the cooperation of others, that aesthetic and even political issues may have surrounded the transition of the creator's idea of how a piece should sound to its final broadcast from a transistor radio in a remote valley—all that is easily forgotten when one turns on the switch to obliterate with music what is perceived as oppressive silence. In this essay we attempt to sketch the social position and attitudes of various types of persons involved in the process of musical production in various social settings and at various historical stages. To simplify this description, these persons are classified by the nature of their contributions to the social process of making music.

MUSICAL SPECIALISTS AND ACTIVITIES

Individuals who directly or indirectly participate in making music can be classified into four major types, which can be further divided into various subtypes. The relationship of some of the social types to music is so obvious that they need not be described in detail. The origin, development, and function of others, however, require a more elaborate description, particularly of the producers of music found only in certain musical cultures. Such details as the overall economic situation, restrictions concerning sex, age, or nationality, and relative social position and interrelationships between members of the same and of other groups are omitted for now, but will be discussed later in the essay. These sections will all follow the general sequence of types of persons outlined below.

Bearing these restrictions in mind, we find that the following types of persons as directly or indirectly involved in the production of music.

Persons Linked with Performance of Music

1. *The composer*. The composer is the creator of musical compositions. His activity does not require detailed description at this point; it is sufficient to say that the composer will remain indispensable as long as music is created and performed.

2. *The creator of the text for vocal music*. A large amount of today's music is only instrumental. Accordingly, the creator of texts is a less universal type than the composer. In more complex cultures, there also exist larger compositions for specific texts. In such cases the author of the text may be identified and called the *librettist*.

3. *The conductor*. In almost every culture someone indicates the beginning and rhythm of a performance. Various means have been employed for this purpose. In some preliterate or Asiatic societies the drum was used. In ancient Greece the sandals of men known as *Prodoctypos* performed this function. Oyster shells in the Roman Empire, and wooden castanets among certain Mohammedan peoples have also been used. After many intermediate stages the modern conductor emerged. He is as responsible for the cohesive playing of the musicians as he is for the structure of the orchestra and the size of special orchestral sections such as violin, cello, and woodwind.

4. *The instrumentalist*. Since antiquity there have been two types of instrumentalists: orchestra members and soloists. The existence of the latter in the absence of a developed melodic tradition presupposes an in-

creasing interest in polyphony, the availability either of at least one other accompanying instrument or of a polyphonic instrument such as the piano or its forerunners, the virginal and the harpsichord, or the harp and organ. The organ, a secular instrument in the Roman and Byzantine empires, was used primarily as a church instrument in the occidental world. Because of this function, the organist became, regarding his attitude toward the surrounding world, a type sociologically different from other instrumentalists. It will, therefore, be necessary to examine him separately.

5. *The singer.* Just as instrumentalists, vocalists perform as members of a group or as soloists. Choir singing can be monophonic or polyphonic. Soloists perform heroic epics and warrior, religious, and folk songs, as well as the kind of solo vocal music found in operas, oratorios, and other large-scale compositions.

6. *The dancer.* Among the earliest recorded evidence of music, we find dancing as one of the first expressions of religious or other emotions. In certain cultures, various reasons, such as religion, are offered for disliking the body. In these cases, dancing is limited or even prohibited. This fact has occasionally influenced a culture's whole attitude toward music. Other cultures, however, have tolerated or even emphasized dancing. Professional dancers were originally either soloists or members of groups, the latter performing ballet. Ballets often became the art of the court and upper classes. Court dances were increasingly imitated by the middle class. Eventually, dancing shifted from the original religious and upper-class form to that performed by the lower classes. Art and folk dance remained sharply separated until the beginning of the twentieth century, when a change took place. Folk dancing and eurhythmics, invented by Emile Jacques-Dalcroze (1865–1950), were rediscovered and began to play an increasing part in national life.

7. *The stage manager.* Beginning with the moment theatrical performances involving more than one person came into existence (that is, with the beginning of religio-magical dances within primitive groups), a leader has been responsible for the accuracy of the performance. He was the forerunner of the modern stage director. Although unnoticed by most (including the audience), he is a permanent figure in theatrical performances.

Persons Connected with the Planning of Music

1. *The theoretician.* The theoretician is a more recent phenomenon. The three factors that must exist if the theoretician is to play a significant role in a culture are: a cult that regards the correct performance of

music as essential; a somewhat complex society that displays not only some degree of specialization of labor, but also a differentiated group of intellectuals; and the use of complex musical instruments for playing together.

We know about the role of music theoreticians in Chinese Confucianism. However, musical theory played perhaps an even greater role among the Hindus. That is easy to understand: Hinduism had already developed many centuries before Christ, and it reveals a theoretically minded people. Their outstanding men dealt with abstract problems concerning time and space. Accordingly, logic and mathematics played a great role in their thinking. They originated not only relatively complex instruments but also a theory of music, at least part of which came to Europe. In Europe, it was the ancient Greeks especially who developed music theory. Aristotle (384–322 B.C.) elaborated a deductive system (containing elements of induction and empiricism) that echoes Plato (428–347 B.C.). Aristotle's system led to an interest in musical theory among his followers. An example of someone who was primarily a music theoretician is the Aristotelian of the fourth century B.C., Aristoxenus.

In the early Middle Ages, the culture of the Mohammedan Arabs produced similar types. Various factors coalesced to make the Arabs, more than contemporaneous Christians, a people for whom an interest in mathematics and natural science could originate and develop, independent of religion and theology. Whether these Mohammedans were influenced (especially concerning musical theory) by the Hindus, who soon came under Mohammedan control, is still problematic. No matter what country they lived in, Mohammedans remained in contact with one another. Consequently, Hindu instruments and theory may have come to the Mohammedans in North Africa (especially the Pyrenean peninsula), which largely remained under Mohammedan Arabic control up to the fifteenth century. However strong or weak this Hindu influence may have been up to the fifteenth century, music (performed with plucked instruments and combinations of bowed strings) and musical theory played a great role in Mohammedan cultures.

Many Mohammedan philosophers and natural scientists applied their basic theories to music. These theoreticians, who later strongly influenced Christian medieval culture, were not primarily musicians but scholasticists. We will use the term *scholasticism* to denote an intermediate attitude between simple faith and science. It considers what is essential (especially everything metaphysical), as known not primarily through pure reason, but rather by revelation, sacred books, or authorities. In contrast to simple faith, reason is nevertheless deemed capable of increasing human knowledge. Reason is therefore considered able to systematize the content of revelation, sacred books, and authoritative declaration, and to show that this content is not antithetical to reason.

In the Middle Ages, prior to contact with the Mohammedans, in the Christian culture only priests (mainly monks, and particularly Benedictines) dealt with musical theory. The monastery and the cathedral were the primary places of musical development. Similarly, the monk's cell was almost the only place where anyone dealt with musical theory. This was where the scholasticist mentioned above mainly worked. These circumstances changed completely starting with the decline of the Middle Ages and the beginning of the Italian Renaissance. For many reasons, the culture became secular and interest shifted from theology to mathematics and natural science. Music, too, became largely secular.

Out of the convergence of all these factors grew an interest in the development of new instruments. New combinations of timbres necessitated investigations in the field of musical theory. This development explains why the person dealing with musical theory (just as his forerunner among Mohammedan Arabs) is primarily a theoretician rather than a musician. But, in contrast to the Mohammedan and Christian medieval musicologist, he is not a scholasticist but a scientist. Unlike scholasticism, science is based on the assumption that man is able to obtain knowledge through systematic reasoning, independent of revelations, sacred books, and authorities.

2. *The music critic.* Even more than the musicologist, the music critic is a relatively recent phenomenon, usually found only in highly developed literary cultures. The reason is obvious: Wherever music had been largely sponsored by monarchs or others of high rank, criticism was usually not permitted. Exceptions are not found until the period of enlightened absolutism. Empress Maria Theresa of Austria (1717–1780) allowed some criticism of musical performances. In the nineteenth century, life in general, and consequently music, became more democratized. More and more middle-class urbanites went to concerts. When they did not trust their own judgment they wanted to be informed to what extent, and for what reason, the performance may have been good or bad. Consequently, more and more newspapers added a music critic to their regular staff.

3. *The radio (public) lecturer on musical topics.* His activity is largely intended for the broad dissemination of various theoretical and historical principles of musicology. This he does on a rather popular level.

Persons Involved in the Transfer of Music Traditions

1. *The music teacher.* Persons specializing in the teaching of music were found in primitive societies in which music was connected with

magicoreligious beliefs. The correctness of performance was considered important for the welfare of the whole tribe, and the musical tradition had to be passed on to the next generation. Training in the proper performance practice was not highly formalized: Old men introduced the accepted techniques to the younger generation. This informal method of teaching has been at least partially maintained up to the present. For example, Gypsies usually do not have any formal education in music, but are informally taught by certain members of the tribe. In many primitive, religiously based societies the clergy executed this function (up to the Italian Renaissance). Nevertheless, heightened specialization in modern society brought some changes. Various types of music teachers appeared. They can be classified under three principles: according to sponsorship, into private and public teachers; according to their pupils, a viewpoint that will be important for us later, but can be omitted here; and according to the main objective of their teaching. Classifying them by subject category we find the following subtypes: the instrument teacher, the voice teacher, the dance teacher, and the theory teacher. There are interesting differences in student-teacher relations between instrument and voice teachers, but some of them are obviously connected with the nature of the instruments and the typical teaching situation.

The dance teacher requires a more detailed description. For reasons already mentioned, the teaching of dance is important, although informal, in primitive societies. In folk cultures, the younger generation simply imitates the older. In the modern occidental world, the dance became extremely complicated. Monarchs and other members of the upper classes sometimes sponsored or even participated in ballet performances. Thus the role of the ballet instructor gained significance. The incorporation of a corps de ballet into almost all opera houses contributed to his importance. Trained dancers became a necessity. Furthermore, in the nineteenth century, augmented wealth enabled the urban industrial and commercial population to imitate the customs of the court and the nobility, including their dances. Under such circumstances, in major Central European cities, a possibility for making a living appeared for amateurs. Finally, a growing interest in body rhythm and folk dances at the turn of the nineteenth century produced instructors for those forms. This will have relevance again in subsequent essays.

The theory teacher is primarily a musicologist, and has existed only since the relatively late establishment of a scientific study of music. However, beginning with the Renaissance, we find him everywhere. In Europe, musical education remained outside the universities for a long time. However, the universities, notably the liberal arts schools, tended to enlarge themselves by incorporating new branches of learning, especially those of a theoretical nature. Thus the musicologist existed not only in the special schools for music training, but also entered the universities as a member of the school of liberal arts. Here he devoted most of his time to the teaching of theory and music history. The American development was somewhat different, since the European separation of university and college, and also the conservatory of music are rare in America. Consequently, the musicologist may teach both music and nonmusic students at the same American institution.

2. *The music student.* The music student can also be classified according to various principles. One would be the distinction between pupils of private and public institutions; another between amateurs and future professionals. Both viewpoints will be important to us later. For the present they will be bypassed for two other standards. First, we may classify students according to the main objectives of their studies; second, by the kinds of relations between students and teachers. Looking first at their principle topic of study, we find the same subtypes as those of the music teacher. There are instrumental students, voice students, dance students, and theory students.

A special note about theory students is essential. The young person who participates in theory classes often does not intend to later use these studies in his main profession. There are three such types. First, there is the regular music student in an institution, who majors in voice, dance, or an instrument. He takes some theory either because it interests him or because it is required by the school. Second, there is the student taking a liberal arts course in a European university, studying philosophy, history of literature, or fine arts, who feels the need for some knowledge in the field of theory and history of music. The third case is typified by the musician who has a job and wants to improve his position and increase his prestige. In many European countries no higher status exists than having an academic degree. An ambitious musician can realize this ambition by obtaining a Ph.D. with a printed dissertation; the closest field for him to do so is in music history.

Increasingly, anyone who wishes to receive training in the production of music must first become a formal student. That was not always so in the past. This brings us to the second set of principles for classifying music students: the kinds of relations between pupil and teacher. There clearly exist two types. In the past, the music student was frequently an apprentice, similar to other young men who may have wished to become shoemakers, tailors, or other craftsmen. He normally lived in the house of the master, forming a part of the household, perhaps participating in the domestic work, and was completely under the guidance of his master, especially regarding the religious and ethical aspects of his life. The relation between master and apprentice was often regulated by the church and even more frequently by guild rules. The number of years the boy was supposed to live in his master's house was exactly fixed. Sometimes the possibility of abbreviation existed, provided the young man was to marry the daughter of his master or even the elderly widow of another master. All that changed or even disappeared when requirements for apprentices began approximating the social type of the student, and changed even more rapidly as education became more formalized and under state control. Presently, the usual condition is that the young man does no longer live with his master, but leads an increasingly independent existence, going to the place where he is taught only for his lessons. Normally, his teachers are not considered responsible for his private life or his religious and ethical attitudes.

Persons Connected with Technical Dimensions of Music Performances

These occupations are somewhat more marginal as far as the making of music is concerned. Nevertheless they are indispensable within the whole process of music production, and must be enumerated. In this discussion we will omit various economic and political aspects of their activity, this being the topic of a later essay. With this in mind we can classify these technicians into nine groups.

1. *The Copiers and Printers of Musical Scores.* There were forerunners of these occupations in preliterate cultures, where old men and teachers orally transferred songs or heroic epics from one generation to another. When writing became important, the copyist, such as medieval monks and Benedictine priests emerged. The copyist survived the invention of printing by engraving or etching musical scores onto printing plates. These new techniques required handicraft masters, who worked with journeymen and apprentices. In at least some European countries further specialization produced two different types, linked with one another by complementary functions: the printer, who was a tradesman, and the owner of a printing house or a publisher, who was an entrepreneur.

2. *The Seller of Musical Scores.* He has existed, of course, only since modern techniques of engraving, etching, and printing have been applied to the multiplication of musical scores.

3. *The Instrument Maker.* In most cultures he performed manual work similar to that of other handicrafts. This was so from the inception of occidental modern times to the manufacture of modern string, wind, and keyboard instruments. A growing demand for large numbers of instruments caused the shift from handcrafted to mass-produced instruments.

4. *The Seller of Musical Instruments.* In preindustrial epochs, the instrument maker usually worked on consignment for a customer. In the nineteenth and twentieth centuries, due to growing mass production,

tradesmen were increasingly employed as intermediaries.

5. *The Manufacturer of Media of Musical Dissemination.* These are the makers of sound recording, radio, and television implements. Their specializations have become possible by the convergence of at least two factors: technological development, accompanied by changes in the structure and mentality of society. The essential change was that a large number of persons with similar cultural attitudes and interests came into existence. Thus, it was possible to mass produce the kind of goods that suited the common needs of millions of people.

6. *The Seller of the Media of Musical Dissemination.* Obviously, this type is needed only after the aforementioned conditions have been realized.

7. *Organized Instruction in Methods of Instrument Manufacture.* The development of this teaching specialty paralleled the development of instrument manufacture. Initially, a handicraft master taught apprentices. The renowned makers of string instruments, especially the violin makers Guarneri, Amati, and Stradivarius are good examples. The members of these famous families were originally apprentices. Later, when masters, they became shop teachers of future well-known makers of string instruments. The nineteenth century produced a change in connection with the industrialization of instrument making. The teaching of instrument manufacture also became systematized, and shifted from the work shop to special teaching institutions.

8. *Instruction in the Manufacture of the Electronic Media of Musical Dissemination.* This is exclusively a modern, industrial mode of production. Therefore, the teacher of this profession is found in technical schools, where the subject matter resembles that of the field of engineering.

9. *Instruction in How to Sell Instruments and the Modern Means of Diffusion of Music.* With heightened mass production, selling became an applied science. Utilizing advertising techniques, marketing is being taught in schools of business administration, universities, and colleges.

We have now come to the end of our first typology, which looks at the individual primarily from a music related viewpoint, and classifies the persons involved in the production of music according to the kind of activity they perform. We will now explore their personal relationships with one another and with others.

COMBINATIONS OF MUSICAL SPECIALIZATIONS

Many persons belonging primarily to one category do not perform that particular form of musical activity exclusively. Therefore, we should look at various characteristic combinations of different musical occupations. At first, combinations of musical with nonmusical occupations will be omitted. Note furthermore that among all kinds of musicians we find persons who attempt to improve thir financial situation by giving music lessons, either privately or in publicly supported schools. Our discussion will follow the sequence of the previous typologies.

Rarely will a *composer* be occupied exclusively by composition. In countless cases (especially in preliterate societies, as well as among the Provençal troubadours of the Middle Ages and the bards of the Celtic-speaking peoples) the composer was his own poet, producing both text and melody. During the seventeenth and eighteenth centuries the orchestra grew larger, and its music more complex. Currently, a composer often conducts his own works as well as those of others. Among Catholics and Lutherans the composer is often also a church organist. While composers frequently function as poets, conductors, or organists, few have been noted singers. Albert Lortzing (1801–1851), a mid-nineteenth century German composer of comic operas, is an exception. In a few very rare cases, a composer has also been a dancer. Lully (1632–1687), one such exception, lived at the French court where ballet was highly regarded. Several composers have been musicologists or critics; one famous example is the German Romanticist, Robert Schumann (1810–1856).

Infrequently, a composer may try to be a productive philosopher of music, such as the Italian, Ferrucio B. Busoni (1866–1924), who gained recognition as a philosopher. The case of Richard Wagner is more complicated. Intending to proselytize a new philosophy, he expressed his view of the world by writing tragedies. He added musical skills to his poetic skills, thereby intensifying his dramas. The inverse is true of many other composers, who regard themselves as primarily composers rather than librettists. Their salient focus is the musicality of opera. In both cases, one person is simultaneously the musical composer and the writer of the text.

At first in modern times, the role of *conductor* was assumed by the orchestra's harpsichordist, or (since the modern violin family with the vaulted back became dominant) by the first violinist. The latter role was later called *concertmaster*. During the latter part of the eighteenth century and especially during the nineteenth century, orchestra members no longer assumed the additional responsibility of conductor. This change was connected with the increasing complexity of the modern orchestra, which saw the addition of such new instruments as the English horn, the bass clarinet, and the bass tuba. Groups of identical instruments were also subdivided into two or three subsections—for example, the division of the violas into three sections in some of the operas of Richard Strauss (1864–1949). Such changes demanded special training for future conductors. Consequently, the profession of conductor became independent of that of the orchestral instrumentalist. Conductors could receive specialized instrumental training without ever professionally playing an instrument in an orchestra.

The *instrumentalist* was originally supposed to perform on several instruments. Even during the nineteenth century he was usually expected to be able to play related instruments, such as the violin and viola, or the bassoon and double-bassoon. In the twentieth century, the players of newer instruments specialize in their one particular skill.

Instrumentalists have at times contributed to the process of instrument making. Often dissatisfied with the structure of their own instruments, they discussed possible improvements with instrument makers. Such joint efforts produced changes with major consequences for symphonic compositions. Four examples can be cited. First, there is Friedrich Wilhelm Wieprecht (1802–1872), who had been a brass-wind player and then became a band conductor in the Prussian army. Around 1830 the army used bass ophicleides as bass instruments. He found them insufficient and invented the bass tuba. He had the new instrument built in proportions corresponding to those of the cornet, with a tube relatively wide compared to its length. The tuba is now widely used in bands as well as in symphony orchestras. Karl Almenräder (1786–1843) played the bassoon in the court orchestra in Wiesbaden. According to him, the bassoon could not produce sufficiently pure low sounds. For fifteen years he experimented with changing the location of certain holes and keys, developing the bass bassoon. Hermann Ritter (1849–1926) was a violist. As others before him, he disliked the sound of this instrument, considering it both too nasal and too weak. He regarded the proportion between body and length as one of the causes of the acoustical deficiency. Together with the German physicist Gustav Robert Kirchhof (1824–1887), he built a larger instrument, the Ritter viola. And last, Johann Schnellar originally a kettle drummer, later taught this instrument at the Imperial Academy of Music in Vienna. At the turn of the nineteenth century the kettle drum was extremely difficult to tune—six screws had to be turned in the process. Schnellar interconnected all six, so that by turning a single screw, the pitch of the kettle drum could easily be changed. The instrument was used in many orchestras in this form until the invention of the pedal kettle drum.

The professional singer has often been obliged to perform various parts during the same performance. This was often so in the beginning of Italian opera. Singers also performed as actors in comedies and tragedies in both itinerant and small companies, and in big court theaters at the turn of the eighteenth century. Only a few singers were also composers. However, certain musicians who became well known after their deaths, such as Jacopo Peri (1561–1633), Alessandro Stradella (1642–1682), and Johann Matheson (1681–1764), combined the two functions.

As for the *professional dancer,* we have little knowledge of his secondary occupations. We only know that he was occasionally required to be a singer as well.

The *stage director* also performed other artistic functions in nearly every culture, except the more recent. Possibly the most important or experienced actors took care of stage direction. Ever since the development of the modern theater, the stage director of the opera has usually been a former singer, often a bass buffo. He may have lost his voice over the years, but by being stage master he was able to continue functioning as part of the operatic production.

Beginning with the nineteenth century, stage masters received special training in the technique of directing the dramatic part of performances. Since the turn of the century, with increasing specialization everywhere, to be a *Regisseur,* as he was called in Germany, or a *metteur-en-scène* in France, has been a distinct career. He may never have performed in tragedy, comedy, or opera (especially in Europe). However, he did receive special training, which was supposed to have qualified him as a stage director. Here a complete separation of occupations formerly connected with one another has taken place.

Musicologists almost regularly performed another function. Specialization in this line has occurred only relatively recently. In German-speaking countries, Eduard Hanslick of Vienna was the first person to consider the teaching of musicology at the university as his main occupation. Moreover, he was a music critic for a Vienna newspaper. A musicologist teaching at a university was often expected to lead a student orchestra or glee club. Nevertheless, he has been more and more removed from the other functions and branches of musical life, with which the music theoretician in the Hindu, Moslem, and Renaissance cultures were connected.

The *critic,* too, frequently performs musical functions. Composers such as Schumann and Hector Berlioz (1803–1869) wrote music criticism for a livelihood. Many musicologists and music critics find part-time work delivering radio or television lectures.

Numerous instrument and voice *teachers* are members of orchestra or opera ensembles. Many have attempted to obtain permanent appointments as state or city officials for job security and pension privileges. However, success often brought limitations. Many countries that have established such official positions have restricted the right of members of a state- or city-supported orchestra or educational institution to teach privately.

Dancing teachers sometimes have held a government position while dancing in a ballet company. Sometimes he or she is a full-time dancer forced to reduce his or her dancing, due to age.

Since the instrument or voice *student* generally no longer lives in a master's house, he has frequently needed to supplement his income by participating in musical productions. Previously, in poorer districts, such as Lutheran Germany, he and his fellow students sometimes received alms from burghers for singing in the streets. Once opera had become more established, and religious opposition to it decreased, he could often earn something by singing in the chorus. Sometimes he also gave lessons to children whose parents did not want to pay a trained music teacher.

Of the *various specialists* engaged in the technical aspects of music production, both copyists and instrument makers were often instrument-playing monks. The performer often made his own instrument, as in the beginning of American jazz. Occasionally, older musicians supported themselves by selling instruments. Modern means of music diffusion—records, radio, movies, and television—are almost completely mechanized, relying little on the direct act of music production. As a result, combinations of musical and technical activities are rare, though these occupations affect the developing aesthetic traditions rather significantly.

In many less complex cultures, the *instructor of instrument making* was a performer as well. Increasing industrialization facilitated the development in special schools of the profession of teacher of instrument construction. Modern technical means of music reproduction, such as records and radio and television broadcasts, are mass produced. Their teaching belongs to applied engineering. In the past, young men learned to make instruments by helping in the shops of their masters. Since industrialization, future instrument makers, broadcast engineers, record salesman, and television advertisers, if they receive advanced training at all, are college students. Their lives are not essentially different from those of other students, and they may or may not participate in musical activities.

This survey of activities and specialties related to the main performing musical occupations reveals the following: composers, conductors, instrumentalists, singers, and stage directors do related work besides their main occupation far more than outstanding performing solo musicians. This generalization does not apply so much to the teacher. Trends toward job security, pensions, and institutionalization decrease the possibility of combining various musical occupations. The newer specialties, connected with the technical aspects of music production and reproduction, do not usually combine various musical activities. On the contrary, they are more closely related to the business world, so that they tend to emphasize commercial activities along with their marginal musical roles.

COMBINATIONS OF MUSICAL WITH NONMUSICAL OCCUPATIONS

Our concern here is not with musical amateurs who perform during their leisure time. Rather, we are dealing with those situations where the performance of music is either part of a primarily nonmusical profession, or where the musical aspects of nonmusical jobs form a profession. In the second case, individuals may either consider both occupations equally important, or regard one as their main profession.

1. *The clergy.* Clergymen are representative of persons who consider their musical activity as part of their main profession. With few exceptions, such as extreme Calvinism, religion is closely linked with music. In both Christian and oriental religions, the clergy compose church music and lyrics. Many oriental and Christian monasteries supply instrumentalists. In the early Middle Ages, Benedictines were frequently organists. Even up to the present time, the clergyman is often (in the case of Catholicism) a member of a monastic order, and if he is not a priest-monk he is at least a friar. Soloists and choir singers in both church and bishop's court performances were often members of the clergy.

Dancers may perhaps also have belonged to the Christian clergy, as they do in many oriental religions, such as the Mahayana and Hinayana Buddhist orders. Judaism and Islam also employ dancers in religious worship. Within the Islamic religion, dancing appears in connection with Sufi mysticism and is largely represented by the dancing dervish. Of all the more complex religions, Christianity most disapproved of the use of the body and physical rhythms in religious worship. However, in the ancient Ethiopian Christian church liturgy, the celebration of Mass was interrupted by the deacon playing a drum while the priest danced.

Many religious groups have their own theater glorifying their gods or saints, in which members of the clergy have also served as stage directors. The Jesuits, who introduced theater to their educational institutions for boys during the Counter Reformation, are a recent example. One of the priests would supervise the play and act as stage director.

In some cultures, the music theoretician has been a member of the clergy. During Medieval Catholicism, for example, he was frequently a Benedictine. Yet little is known about clergy who function as music critics, although their reviews sometimes appear in religious journals and magazines. Considering the strong relationship between the monastery and music it is not surprising that younger monks and nuns were often taught music and making of instruments by older monks or nuns. Even the dance teacher has sometimes been a member of the clergy, especially among oriental cultures; the monks and lamas of Tibetan Buddhism are a good example.

2. *Intellectuals.* Intellectuals other than clergymen often comprise another group whose members consider their musical activity part of their main profession. For example, the Chinese mandarin is a trained intellectual, rather than a clergyman in the occidental sense. The recipient of musical training, he is supposed to be familiar with music theory and the possibilities for using music in worship and education. In many cases he can and does play one of the Chinese instruments.

A consideration of the occidental intellectual who is an amateur musician is also in order. (The intellectual who, besides his main profession, works in the field of musicology, or asserts that he can or must have a command of both fields, could be considered an exception). In this respect, there are three main types of intellectuals. First is the modern *philosopher.* If he formulates an aesthetic system, he may incorporate a theory concerning the essence of music, as did Kant and Schopenhauer. Another variant of this type is a thinker who develops a philosophy of history. Normally, he will include a theory about music as a manifestation of the mentality of an epoch. He might also discuss whether the history of music is sequential, as did the Romantic philosophers Georg Hegel (1770–1831), Friedrich Schelling (1775–1854), and Karl Krause (1781–1832).

By doing so, the philosopher approximates our second type, the anthropologist and ethnologist. The latter may deal with the music of primitives. Finding the same type of musical instrument or style at more than one location produces a typical problem for discussion: Did the phenomenon originate independently through parallel development or did it spread from one place to another? The answer has been a major source of disagreement between European and Latin American schools of anthropology. Our purpose here is not to attempt to resolve the problem, but to utilize it as an example of a fusion of ethnology and musicology. In such a case, it is often difficult to decide whether an investigator should be called an anthropologist or a musicologist. Sometimes the best classification may be as an anthropologically trained musicologist or ethnomusicologist.

The third type is the fiction writer who not only gives musicians an essential role in his novels, but also contributes to music theory. E. T. A. Hoffmann (1776–1822) and Thomas Mann (1875–1955) are well-known representatives of this type.

Another variant of these mixed occupations is represented by the professional musician who may also be a governmental appointee holding a high position (usually entrusted to a trained intellectual) in another field. One of the most extreme cases is that of Karl von Dittersdorf (1739–

1799), a court composer and conductor in the eighteenth century. The bishop who protected him gave him a high position in the forestry administration. Undoubtedly, his intention was not only to let the musician enjoy a relatively high salary, but also to give him a rank that would entitle him to mingle with the well born. Thus he could perform with those members of the nobility who were amateur musicians.

3. *Students.* Even more than the occidental intellectual, students, generally, should be considered. In some periods, doing some musical work helped a student finance his university education. As already mentioned, very poor students in Lutheran universities during the sixteenth and seventeenth centuries sometimes sang in the streets. Participation in the choir of a small opera house or in house performances sponsored by the nobility (as in Mozart's time) provided other opportunities for earning income. Such students normally come from the middle class (the latter, of course, provides a great reservoir of amateurs and will be discussed later in this respect). But here we must take note.

4. *Members of the lower middle class.* Countless small-store owners, clerks, and other members of the lower middle class subsidize their income by regularly playing an instrument in a band or orchestra, or occasionally at processions and fairs, or at a special festival. They are also called upon when a regular city-supported orchestra needs to be enlarged for a performance of, say, a symphony of Richard Strauss.

5. *Slaves and serfs.* On a socially lower level, slaves, serfs, semidependent peasants, and valets were occasionally used by their masters in orchestra or chamber music ensembles. The literature refers to such situations in the period of German and Austrian Classicism. Travelers have reported orchestras, even complete theaters, on Russian feudal estates, where everyone from composer to drummer was a serf. These serfs usually had other duties as well. There are similar reports of musical achievement by Negro slaves in the American South.

6. *Beggars.* Beggars might also be mentioned here, since musical performance can be considered a part of their profession. It is a means of attracting attention, which thereby increases the chances of receiving alms. Interestingly, almost every culture has one or more instruments denoted by a term corresponding to our "beggar instruments" (Bettler Instrument). Since the playing of such instruments is supposedly beneath an honorable musician's dignity, churches and music organizations sometimes forbid their professional musicians from playing them. The blind, often beggars themselves, are similarly in a marginal position musically. However, in some oriental cultures they may, for magicoreligious reasons, enjoy certain privileges in the performance of music.

THE ITINERANT MUSICIAN

The social type of itinerant musician either does not want to or cannot find a regular job; in either case he is a transient. Consequently, his earnings and living conditions fluctuate. Seldom in the middle stratum of society with its "petit bourgeois" mentality and its wish for security, he is occasionally near the top, but generally on the bottom. For centuries the Gypsy, as well as the minstrel or jongleur and the *Fahrende* of the Middle Ages belonged to this category. But the highly honored itinerant artist also existed in certain feudal periods. At the court of Moslem rulers or Celtic landlords, he sang epic songs glorifying heroic knights of past ages. Although his type vanished as feudalism decreased, he appeared again after the breakdown of traditional social groups and values following the Italian Renaissance. Naturally, he is a sociologically detached type and specializes mainly as a singer, instrumental virtuoso, dancer, or conductor (the latter at the end of the nineteenth and beginning of the twentieth centuries).

Other musicians tend to be not as itinerant as these solo specialists. The church organist, although a soloist, is rarely an itinerant musician, being closely connected with his instrument and a regular audience. The same applies to the majority of musicologists, critics, instrument makers, music teachers, and everyone who performs one of the functions connected with radio, television, movies, and the recording industry. In the course of a career many move from one location to another, but that does not mean that they are itinerants. Indeed, students in many fields have not studied in one place only, but have tried to gain experience and to have different master teachers, even in various countries, since the eleventh century.

THE FOREIGN MUSICIAN

If we review our various categories from the standpoint of national origin, we find that musicians are often foreigners to the countries in which they perform. In modern times the *composer* has often been an Italian, German, or Austrian whose works are performed outside his native land. Similarly, for centuries the operatic *librettist* was often of Italian origin, due to the country's stress on opera. Pietro Metastasio (1698–1782) is a characteristic example. In the eighteenth century composers everywhere set music to his librettos, thereby securing his worldwide fame.

Italy lost its dominance in conducting when *conductors* began to specialize and stopped performing other musical functions. In the eighteenth, nineteenth, and twentieth centuries, German conductors began to appear in many countries, including the United States. Like composers and librettists, *instrument soloists* of Italian origin have been found in many places since the seventeenth century. Somewhat later, German soloists began appearing in other countries, such as Czarist Russia, England, and America. Under special circumstances, there have even been exceptions to the earlier trend of exporting Italy's talents. Occasionally, from the sixteenth to the eighteenth centuries, instrumentalists of Dutch, Flemish, or Spanish origin appeared in the papal court in Rome, since the Pope, as the universal symbol of Catholicism, was able to attract and hire the finest contemporary instrumentalists.

In contrast, the organist is rarely a foreigner, but rather a product of the locale and the congregation where he plays. Generally, he plays within the church (and more recently in the synagogue as well), which presupposes some familiarity with the local customs. The *singer,* however, is often a foreigner. As early as the eighteenth century, Italian high sopranos and tenors performed everywhere, even at the court of the Russian czar. Especially in the nineteenth century, the number of Germans singing outside their own country was second only to the number of Italians.

The increasingly universal inclusion of Wagnerian operas in the repertoire contributed to this trend. To perform Wagner's operas, special vocal training was needed, particularly for such tenor, baritone, and bass parts as Siegfried, Tristan, Wotan, Sachs, Fasolt, and Fafner. These operas also required for larger orchestras than classic Italian opera. The vocal preparation for a tenor, baritone, or bass to sing such operatic roles as Mozart's Belmonte, Count Almaviva, or Sarastro, for example, reflected the more traditional approach of Italian opera style. Vocal training suited as preparation for performing roles in the new Wagnerian operas was developed to some extent in Germany. To this day, many singers who specialize in these roles are either of German extraction or have studied voice with German teachers.

Italians have played a leading role in the field of the dance, as well as in the other musical specializations we have considered so far. For many centuries, most *dancers,* particularly soloists, were of Italian origin. Eventually the courts in other countries also sponsored local talent. With increasing interest and support of ballet at the French court, French dancers, for example, began to appear outside France in the eighteenth century prior to the French Revolution. After the revolution, dancers who had been closely associated with the court of Louis XVI found that they could no longer appear in public in Paris. Jean Noverre (1727–1810), whose style was identified with the court of the deposed king, escaped to

England, where his previous association with the French court would not prevent his attaining great popularity. We will return to an examination of political influences on musical life in a different context, but the case of the refugee dancer can be regarded as an example. Another example of the rise of ballet in other countries and the corresponding decline of Italy's preeminence in this field can be supplied. In imitation of other European courts, the Russian czar developed ballet with soloists for his court. This group incorporated national characteristics, and so came to develop a style of its own. It also began to appear outside Russia, generating wide interest because of its supposedly unique styles of performance.

The *stage director* has rarely been of foreign origin. As previously mentioned, he often was a singer in his group. His professional contribution was, until recently, not considered very important. It seemed unnecessary to secure a foreigner for his duties. Specialists appeared at the beginning of the twentieth century, especially in Germany. The German *Regisseur* was invited to foreign countries. The most noted personality of this kind was Max Reinhardt (1873–1943). After the rise of Hitler, he worked as a stage director, rather than as an actor, in many places, among them France and America. His case is another example of political events influencing artistic life.

Concerning music *theoreticians* and musicologists, much less is known about their role in foreign countries in comparison with information on singers, instrumentalists, and other musicians. The amount of investigation made in music theory and music history in the past by Germans is certainly much larger than that made by native scholars of other countries. This fact can be easily explained. In German academic circles, more so than elsewhere, practical interest in music and in the historical approach to cultural phenomena converged. For this reason, music history is a characteristically German topic, even though little is known concerning German musicologists and *critics* working in other countries. There are however some notable exceptions. Curt Sachs (1881–1959), a German musicologist who taught in New York, was perhaps the most eminent representative of a special school of thought within ethnomusicology, a school that emphasizes the role played in civilization generally and in music particularly by the diffusion of cultural goods and man's migrations throughout history. Since American anthropologists tended to explain the appearance of the same phenomenon at more than one place in terms of independent parallel development, Sachs was in opposition to the dominant scholarly attitude found in his new country.

Certain circumstances produce *music teachers* of foreign origin. For example, a missionary teaches the songs and ritualistic music of his faith to his converts. Greek Orthodox missionaries of Bulgarian origin did so in the Ukraine and in Kiev. There is evidence that they brought Greek Orthodox music to Russia. The most common music teacher of foreign origin came from Italy after the Renaissance and the Counter Reformation. Germans are the next most common, especially in Russia and the United States. Except for references to Italian instructors of ballet, the literature does not convey a preoccupation with the study of dance teachers of foreign origin.

Italy, with the greatest influence in music following the Renaissance, drew *students* form almost every land. But beginning with the nineteenth century, many North Americans, Japanese, and others who wanted their countries to assimilate occidental culture studied in Germany and France.

For a long time, *instrument makers* apparently did not travel widely. Certain Germans in colonial North America provide some of the few exceptions. A similar situation exists concerning the teacher of instrument making. Sometimes we find the Italian abroad, but more often the students came to him. In past centuries foreigners often traveled to Italy to learn how to make string instruments. They traveled to the German workshops of J. Denner, Stoelzel, or G. Streitwolf for wind instruments, or, in the nineteenth century, to Paris to study under Adolphe Sax (1814–1894), the perfector of the bass clarinet and inventor of the saxophone.

This discussion of the role of the foreigner in music may be completed by considering the influence of musicians of foreign extraction on their adopted country. *Composers* of foreign origin rarely lived, produced, and/or were recognized in Italy. Only when the papal court was so attractive that everyone with elite aspirations preferred to work there did this occur. Numerous Italian composers worked in Germany in the feudal period, but there have been few composers of other nationalities there since the beginning of modern times. The Czech, Jan Zach (1699–1773), who in the eighteenth century lived at the court of the bishop of Mainz, is one of the few exceptions. England and America, too, only occasionally invited foreign composers. In the nineteenth century, certain foreign composers were asked to compose oratorios, and perhaps to perform them themselves, for major festivals in the two countries.

The situation with respect to the export of librettos is, as we have already noted, somewhat different. Indeed, many German and Austrian opera composers purchased librettos abroad from Metastasio or other Italian *librettists,* although there is no record of their appearing in person at the performance of their librettos.

When *conductors* began to be regarded as outstanding personalities, many countries, especially affluent nations such as England and America, invited them to appear. Bruno Walter (1876–1962) and Otto Klemperer (1885–   ) are two good examples. Their status as refugees again points to relationships between political events and music.

Concerts by foreign solo *instrumentalists* are in greater demand, from Russia to Latin America, than any other kind of musical performance. But, as already noted, organists travel less than their fellow instrumentalists.

Almost every country has invited and admired foreign *vocalists*. This general trend has however fluctuated in various countries with the times, as testified by Nazi Germany or the United States during World War I. We will examine more fully the role of national feelings in the development of music in our essay on music and politics.

With regard to solo *dancing*, Italian, and more recently Russian ballet dancers have gained almost universal esteem. With few exceptions, such as in the United States, foreign *stage directors* are not invited to work abroad on a permanent basis. Nor are foreign *musicologists* or *critics* routinely invited to become permanent members of the musical community. While most countries, especially Czarist Russia and America, have used Italians and Germans as music *teachers,* not much attention is found in the literature on the question of predilection for foreign dance teachers.

The innovative function of the foreign music *student* is opposite that of the teacher. The former does not bring anything significantly new to the country where he studies, but rather introduces the foreign approach and style to his own country upon his return. For centuries young men of diverse national origins went to study in Italy. In the nineteenth century, Germany especially attracted North Americans and Japanese. Nothing can be stated about countries with special attractions for students of dancing. As for instrument makers, apparently only the United States has been extremely attractive to those born on foreign soil. Students of the art of making instruments also went to Italy, Germany, and France.

In this section we have classified musicians of foreign origin, first according to the countries from which they have come, and then according to the countries they have influenced. On the basis of these data we have seen that there is no complete reciprocity between countries of origin and destination in any of the various spheres of musical activity. We have also seen that the internal political situation of countries has had a major impact on the selected musical phenomena. In conclusion, our study permits us to offer the following historical generalization: Italy and Germany, in that order, have had the greatest influence on musical activities, especially in Russia, England, the United States, Japan, and Latin America.

THE AMATEUR MUSICIAN

Numerous people produce music neither as their main nor as their side occupation, but rather in their leisure time as amateurs. They will be discussed roughly by their respective social rank, noting the musical specialties associated with their status.

1. *Monarchs.* We know of one Byzantine emperor and of a few rulers of small states during the Italian Counterreformation and in nineteenth century Germany who were composers. Some monarchs have been instrumentalists and have participated in the performance of chamber and orchestral music, as did certain rulers of small states during the Italian Renaissance. Frederick the Great (1712–1786) was renowned for his mastery of the flute. Emperor Joseph II (1741–1790) of eighteenth century Austria is another good example, typifying the worship of music customary in the Vienna of those days: Those without musical knowledge were not regarded as complete individuals.

However, monarchs generally only played an instrument—none are known to have performed as singers on the operatic stage. Empress Maria Theresa once intended to, but was told by members of her court that it would be inappropriate. There are only a few examples of rulers of small German territories participating in the singing of their choirs, such as a prince of Lippe under the conductorship of Brahms, but several French kings, among them Louis XIV, reportedly danced in their court ballets. Royal relatives have taken a far more active part musically than monarchs. However, they too have been largely instrumentalists, except for a few princesses known to have been composers.

2. *The nobility.* Two kinds of specialists can be noted among the feudal aristocracy, who were primarily instrumentalists. Sometimes old-fashioned instruments continued to be used, specifically in remote districts. The feudal landlord, as the preserver of tradition, himself sometimes played an old national instrument. Characteristic past examples can be found in Celtic-speaking lands. The bagpipe and Irish harp, for instance, were reportedly often played by Celtic landlords.

The other type, of course, is the member of the nobility who plays one of the instruments fashionable in his epoch. Here the nobility who spent summers on their estates and winters in their city palaces, in Vienna, for example, can be cited. The nobles who protected and admired Haydn and Mozart played at least one of the chamber music instruments. This fact will be examined later under two considerations: First, to what extent does music sponsorship affect the kind of compositions produced? Second, how does music affect social differentiation? Members of the nobility in such societies were often also trained singers—generally solo-ists, seldom choir members, and almost never performers on the opera stage.

3. *The Clergy.* As previously stated, their musicianship is part of their professional duties. If they perform music outside their ministry, it is in their leisure time as members of secular society. A few clergymen have composed music for purposes other than the church service. Father Vog-ler (1749–1814), a Benedictine abbot during the period of Austro-German classicism, is an example.

4. *Intellectual.* Whereas the Chinese intellectual generally performs musically as part of his professional duties, the opposite is true of the occidental intellectual. His musical participation is more likely to be a leisure time activity. Usually, he is a member of the middle class. Espe-cially since the piano has come into common use, he may utilize his tal-ent by entertaining at social gatherings. Frequently the daughter of a middle-class family receives piano lessons and entertains friends of the family at house parties. Indeed, in France her prospects for marriage, if she is known to have an extensive repertoire, were considerably im-proved. This circumstance applies primarily to countries where climate requires activity to be mainly indoors. Conversely, in the Mediterranean and tropical regions, the piano is generally replaced by such outdoor in-struments as the Italian mandolin and the Spanish guitar. Consequently, the middle-class girl who can sing increases her chances for marriage.

5. *Lower social classes.* Serfs and slaves who performed music cannot be regarded as amateurs since they were often forced to perform by their masters. The performing proletarian is another matter. He frequently imitated higher social classes, reflecting a universal rule formulated by the French sociologist Gabriel Tarde (1843–1904). A group in opposition to a more privileged group tries to convince the latter and itself that it can do as well as the privileged group by trying to imitate the latter. As long as proletarians do more than imitate and conscientiously try to develop their own music, they achieve not as individuals but rather as an organized association of amateurs.

WOMEN AND MEN IN MUSIC

Some kinds of music are not equally performed by members of both sexes; certain performances may even be restricted to one sex. We know, for example, of *dances* restricted to females among very unsophisticated Melanesian tribes. Hindu sacred books, the Vedas, record religious dances performed exclusively by women. In the classical period of Korean culture, secular dances were performed by young girls in the palaces of the monarchs and the members of the nobility. In ancient Japan, very small girls were bought by entrepreneurs, trained in dancing, and sold to tearooms to perform for the amusement of the customers; this has been considered by some as a kind of prostitution. Even the male oriented cultures of Sparta and Thebes in ancient Greece provided for religious associations of girls who danced at religious festivals. In some folk cultures, such as the Scandinavian, some dances were performed only by girls. For three centuries the Italian and French ballets, among others, were performed almost exclusively by women. Even male roles were danced by girls attired as men. The male dancer appeared on the stage only relatively recently, in connection with the rise of naturalism, and especially expressionism.

Similarly, groups of girls often appear as *singers*. In the relatively simple culture of the Dajaks in Indonesia, funeral singing is the province of women. In Korea, groups of girls sing at upper-class parties. Even in such pronounced male cultures as pre-Mohammed Arabia, women from outside came to perform songs at functions such as wedding ceremonies. The Celts had similar situations.

A new situation regarding the female role in singing occurred with the Counter Reformation. At Italian episcopal courts, listening to women singing was frequently considered indecent. The problems created by this attitude are obvious when one considers the important role opera played there. One solution was the use of castrates. Dressed as women, they sang soprano and contralto parts. Nevertheless, eighteenth century female singers were successful in insisting that they themselves should perform these roles. They argued that if the castrate could sing female parts, why should women not perform male roles? Consequently, female singers wearing long pants played heroes and male lovers in opera for more than a century.

This development also applied to a lesser extent to drama. For instance, Felicita von Vestvali (1828–1880) sang young opera heroes as a contralto, and on stage she played Shakespeare's Petruchio and Hamlet. She was greatly admired for her dual talents in both Europe and in America. The French actress Sarah Bernhardt (1845–1923) was one of the last of this type, playing both Hamlet and the Duke of Rechstadt (the son of Napoleon) in France and Germany. The public came out of curiosity to see a seventy-year-old woman playing a boy of seventeen, wearing white silk pants over her artificial leg. Even Richard Wagner composed for this kind of performer, creating in *Rienzi,* an early work that seems most un-Wagnerian in the traditional sense, the role of Adriano for a contralto wearing men's attire.

Later, the "trouser girls" vanished with the traditional Italian grand opera style. At the beginning of the twentieth century, Richard Strauss created the mezzo-soprano role of *Rosenkavalier,* but he did so as he shifted away from his extremely impressionistic orchestra and program symphonies (such as *Till Eulenspiegel* and *Don Quixote*). He even went so far as to incorporate into his opera *Ariadne auf Naxos* the coloratura aria of Columbine in a pre-Mozartian style.

Women have performed less frequently as *instrumentalists* than as singers. Again, there are examples in simple cultures. In the Corroboree dances performed by an Australian tribe, women serve as percussionists while the men dance. Small groups of women played lutes in ancient Egypt, certain Mohammedan districts, and at the court of the Holy Roman Emperor Frederick II (1194–1250) in Palermo. As the modern orchestra developed, it tended not to use women as instrumentalists. Especially in the latter part of the eighteenth century and during the entire nineteenth century, big orchestras supported by a monarch, the state, or city, employed male musicians almost exclusively. Female harpists were among the few exceptions.

Later, at the turn of the nineteenth century, as economic conditions and public opinion changed, women began to enter various professions formerly closed to them. In Europe, and especially in the United States, women became both orchestra members and soloists. However, their opportunities were still limited. They appeared almost exclusively as piano, violin, and cello soloists, but were even opposed in the last-named capacity. The composer, pianist, and academy teacher Ernst Rudorff (1840–1916), a friend of Brahms (1833–1897), declared female cello-playing indecent.

In Europe, women appeared even more infrequently as *stage directors.* This function, as previously indicated, was often filled by former male singers who had lost their voices. The exception is Anna von Mildenburg (1872–1947), the former dramatic opera soprano, who became a stage director of the Salzburg Mozart festivals in Austria.

We will now move to the male role in musical performance, beginning with *male dancers.* Certain societies have limited some kinds of dancing to man. Some Melanesian tribes segregate their dances by sex. Extremely religious dances of certain American Indian tribes, Malays, Koreans, and Hindus are performed exclusively by men. More recently, Chasidism, a popular emotional movement among eighteenth century Jews in the former Polish provinces of Podolia and Walhynia, followed similar practices.

Just as women performed male operatic roles, male *singers* have performed female roles. Examples can be found in southern India and in modern Europe. In Europe, besides castrates, the so-called intermezzo opera in seventeenth century Vienna is a good example. Almost all roles were performed by men. Both Jesuit and Protestant schools sponsored performances where the younger boys took the female parts in school operas. As fundamentalist Protestantism frowns on opera, however, such performances were less frequent in Protestant schools than in Jesuit schools. Nevertheless, they were held occasionally at children's theaters in England; the Church of England, with its proximity to Roman Catholicism, tolerated these performances, while Calvinists, with their general dislike for the human body, protested them. Much of the Calvinists' opposition was motivated by the fear that such performances would tend to produce homosexuality.

In summary, we can say that where the dance and related musical performances are concerned, women have been predominant throughout musical history. There are, however, four occupations that have been almost exclusively handled by men: composer, librettist, conductor, and stage director.

AGE AND MUSICAL ACTIVITIES

Just as the participation of the sexes in music production has varied with geographic region and period, so has the role of various age groups. Although the majority of performers have always been adults, the role of children and adolescents has been significant. We must first differentiate between productions in which children participate but the leading parts are played by adults, and those in which children only are involved. Regarding the former, children participated in tribal singing in many preliterate societies (including those of the American Indians) by simply singing one octave higher than the adults. Needless to say, from the Christian Middle Ages to modern times, children have been involved in some form of congregational singing in the religious service. Sometimes we even find child soloists, as in German Lutheranism, which more than any other denomination emphasized the participation of all members in congregational singing. Children have participated in opera far less than in religious singing. As mentioned in the previous section, the parts of boys in eighteenth and nineteenth century operas were frequently sung by girls. However, in Mozart's *Magic Flute,* small boys may have been used for characters too young to be portrayed by a trained female singer.

When children do appear in operas they are more frequently used in choirs than as soloists. One example is the choir of children in the first act of Bizet's *Carmen.* Voice teachers and high-school choir conductors often take pride in training pupils for participation in large productions, especially oratorios. For many years, the "cantus firmus" in the opening double chorus of the *St. Matthew Passion* by Bach has been performed by school boys.

Normally, girls make the transition from childhood to adult singing without difficulty. The breaking of a boy's voice, however, can present a problem. In England during the Middle Ages, and today among modern Episcopalians, when the choir boys' voices begin to break, they are either sent to school or incorporated into a transitional age group. In both cases, they are trained until their voices have definitely become either tenor, baritone, or bass. Boys singing in the chapel of the French king were only reemployed as singers if, after breaking, their voices again became useful. If they did not, the boys were dismissed. Franz Schubert (1768–1824) and other musicians have remarked about the difficulties of passing through this stage. Their parents, teachers, and they themselves were often afraid that after breaking, their voices would not longer be of use in singing, consequently affecting their whole future.

In the situations just discussed, children play a relatively insignificant part within a performance. However, there are situations where children, possibly assisted by adults, may produce entire musical performances. Poor children have sometimes supported themselves by singing in the streets, as during the English Middle Ages. Children have performed operas in English castles and Jesuit schools. Orphans performed oratorios in eighteenth century Italy or sang in the court opera choruses of nineteenth century princes.

While orphan performance groups are relatively rare in music, the choruses and orchestras of high schools and similar institutions have been encountered more frequently. In the past, specifically in Europe, the school choir functioned primarily at school festivities and at celebrations corresponding to commencement day in American schools. While every institution of higher education had such a choir, student bands or symphony orchestras were infrequent. The humanistic gymnasium in Western and Central Europe, as well as the corresponding institutions where modern languages and natural sciences were primarily taught, considered everything not connected with scientific learning as unimportant and even distracting. More recently, in schools based on newer educational reform movements, performance in school orchestras has become part of the educational picture.

The situation has been somewhat different in the United States. In America, scholarship plays only one of many roles within the educational system. The school is supposed also to prepare boys and girls to become good citizens and to fully participate in community affairs. In many American communities the school becomes somewhat of a center of community life. Development of and participation in the school band or orchestra is a manifestation of this multiple interrelationship of educational and civic functions.

School theaters were also a rarity in European higher education during earlier times. Those few high schools that did develop theaters were usually sharply criticized by representatives of more traditional forms of education. Two iconoclastic innovators may be mentioned in particular: the school in Wiener-Neustadt (near Vienna) under the directorship of Ludwig Erik Tesar (1879–   ), which was renowned during the Austrian Republic for its orchestra; and the Odenwaldschule in Southern Germany under the direction of Paul Geheeb (1870–1961). In this boarding school, comedies of Molière, tragedies of Schiller, and even such classic Greek tragedies as the *Eumenides,* with choirs and rhythmic musical accompaniment, were performed. This exceptional phenomenon can be explained by the fact that the Odenwaldschule was closely connected with and derived from the German Youth Movement.

As in the case of orchestras, school theaters in the United States have not faced the academic criticism that those in Europe have. Moreover, North American cities are usually proud of a distinguished school orchestra or theater group. However, rarely has a European humanistic gymnasium or similar institution provided the members of the school orchestra with special uniforms. Musical performances were regarded as too insignificant to be distinguished by such distinctive attire. In the United States, the uniform of the school band has become a characteristic feature of urban life and sports events. Another factor is that for a number of reasons coeducation developed much earlier in the United States than in Europe, where education was traditionally for men. Accordingly, the American school band normally contained both boys and girls. The trend to eliminate differences between the sexes in almost every sphere of life was increasingly successful. Accordingly, many schools used the same uniforms for both sexes. This would not have been possible in the majority of traditionally-minded European schools.

At the age of fourteen, most European boys and girls leave school. They then may receive further education given in special institutions. Increasingly, every religious or political group tried to attract as many youths as possible into such institutions. The intention was to prevent boys and girls from becoming radicals, during the very sensitive puberty years, and instead to indoctrinate them with adult values. (Here we use the word "radical" in a purely formal sense of "not willing to make concessions.") Some of the groups did this on a very large scale, specifically Catholic and Socialist organizations. Among the various kinds of activities developed by such privileged institutions, music performed by the students played an important role. The aim was to attach the sentimental youth to the sponsoring adult group and value system of a religious or political nature.

Tutelage has been recorded throughout history. It existed in a more or less similar form in almost every Central and Western European country at the end of the nineteenth century. Quite different from other forms of tutelage, the German Youth Movement was exceptionally important to the development of music. Almost exclusively of German origin, it later influenced surrounding countries, such as Switzerland, to some extent. To elaborate on all the sociological, economic, and religious factors brought about by the German Youth Movement is impossible. We can only indicate the following.

In certain large cities, especially Berlin, around 1890, many upper-middle-class students in the humanistic gymnasiums were disgusted with the older generation. Life in the big cities, rationalization, and bureaucracy were considered proofs of an artificial existence as contrasted to the sincere, natural life these young people desired to lead. Food and beverage reforms were introduced, the consumption of alcohol and tobacco prohibited. New kinds of clothing appeared. Men started wearing short pants and open shirt collars. Whenever possible they avoided living in cities. Weekends and vacations were used for long trips on foot into mountains and woodlands. An outdoor life style, forgotten in Germany, was rediscovered. Unlike the sort of relationships found in big business, factories, and administrative offices, they wanted to experience more primary contacts, more direct face-to-face relationships.

That generation wished to be unique, neither stressing rationalistically-minded factory techniques and centralized organization, nor relying on postcapitalistic socialism. Therefore, they were almost obliged, independent of their original intention, to revert to a precapitalistic philosophy. They glorified life styles supposed to have existed before the industrial age and money economy. Just as a century before German Romanticism had rediscovered the various forms of folk life and local and regional customs of the Middle Ages, so these neoromantic youths rediscovered the old folk dances and forgotten songs of peasants, soldiers, and similar groups.

The German Youth Movement became one of the strongest impulses toward changing the entire structure of musical life. Young people no longer practiced the piano or violin, but played the old lute, the fiddle, and recorders on their hikes and trips. No longer did they attend operas, but instead danced to old rounds, while singing to the accompaniment of a few plucked instruments. The youth movement changed music in at least four ways: it renewed the neglected combination of voice, body rhythm, and instrumental accompaniment; it shifted from the modern separation of performer and audience, making them identical; it largely eliminated the professional musician and reinforced the importance of the amateur; and it eliminated the predominance of the individual star and emphasized the importance of the group, which was considered to be manifesting collective feeling.

Since many of the most characteristic representatives of the youth movement, retaining their ideology, later entered educational institutions of many kinds, their concepts and practices of music largely influenced both German education and other Germans. Moreover, the Hitler movement brought nationalism to the romantic concept of simple country life. The Hitler movement used many of the life styles that had been realized by the German Youth Movement, and changed them for its own nationalistic purposes. Thus, some of the music life of the German Youth Movement was infused into the life scheme of Hitler's Germany.

This short description of the essence of the German Youth Movement, and the enumeration of the spheres of musical life into which it spread, was considered important for inclusion here. Further details will be found in the section on musical education and on the relationships between political and musical changes.

ASSOCIATIONS FOR MUSIC MAKING

Professional Associations

So far we have dealt primarily with musicians as individuals. Obviously, most are also involved in group production. Therefore, we must now consider organizations for music production. We will temporarily exclude all organizations whose main aim is the maintenance or amelioration of the social and economic position of musicians. For this reason, guilds and unions will be discussed later under the economic aspects of music. First we will examine organizations whose members are brought together by the fact that they (at least occasionally) produce music. In this section, we will concentrate on stable professional associations. Itinerant associations, groups of foreigners, and amateur organizations will be taken up in three subsequent sections.

In tribal music, the oldest form of association we will consider, the distincton between professional and amateur group is inapplicable. For in the tribe, music is an essential manifestation of the life of the entire group. This belief is sometimes so exaggerated that no one is exempt from musical participation. The public and performers are identical.

In considering the family as a musical association, we will only examine those situations where many or all members of a family play together as a musical unit for an audience. We find this in many stratified societies, especially where performing music is regarded as somewhat hereditary. Koreans, ancient Hebrews, and various Celtic peoples are examples. In modern occidental culture this way of producing music is decreasing, but it was prevalent through the first half of the nineteenth century. In Europe, the Westphalian Romberg family is an example. This family contributed two composers, two bassoon virtuosos, and many clarinet, violin, and violincello virtuosos. From the United States, the Hutchinson family may be cited as a characteristic example. But these two families were actually rather itinerant groups.

Among groups of adults performing together as their main profession, the orchestra must be considered first. Many oriental and even primitive cultures had forerunners of the modern orchestra. These differed from the modern orchestra in that usually they did not appear alone but performed with singers and dancers. Giant orchestras in the Orient are only isolated examples of the power and wealth of an oriental despot.

In the occidental world the development of larger orchestral units occurred slowly. In many cases a division between chamber music ensembles and orchestras is nearly impossible to make. That was true for many of the earlier symphonies of Franz Joseph Haydn (1732–1809), who originally expected they would be performed by a double string quartet plus one double bass and a few winds (one of each kind, used soloistically). The best distinction may be made in the following way: Chamber music is performed with various instruments that are not duplicated. As soon as there is doubling of parts we perhaps have a small orchestra, but not a chamber ensemble.

The maintenance of small orchestras was long facilitated by the ability of many members to play more than one instrument, an ability that diminished with increasing specialization. With the rise of specialization, only instruments of very similar timbre and technique (such as oboe and English horn, or clarinet and bass clarinet) were played by the same performer. Growing specialization reduced even these combinations. In the very large orchestras, mainly in the United States, specialists play only the bass trombone or the double bassoon. Previously, relatively small orchestras were also maintained because the seventeenth and eighteenth century composers were primarily interested in melody and counterpoint, but not so much in timbre (as nineteenth century composers were). Thus, they left the decision as to which instruments should perform special parts to the discretion of the group. Even Handel permitted the musicians to decide whether some parts should be performed by flutes, oboes, or violins.

The occidental orchestra developed into string, wood, brass, and percussion sections. Besides the symphony orchestra, the less complete harmony orchestra (band), consisting of wood and brass instruments with percussion, and the even more incomplete group composed exclusively of brass winds with percussion, emerged. These two types were mainly used as military bands. Entirely new problems concerning the structure of orchestras arose through the appearance and development of recording techniques and the radio. These problems will be discussed elsewhere.

Most chamber music is written for the string quartet of two violins, one viola, and one violincello. This combination was established definitively by Hadyn, possibly preceded by Pietro Nardini (1722–1793) and a few others. In the majority of communities in Germany, Austria, and Switzerland that had court or city supported orchestras, some of the leading players formed such an ensemble and gave more or less regular concerts in smaller concert rooms. In America, the string quartet appeared later and less frequently than in the Old World, possibly due to the comparatively small number of American orchestras.

Chamber music is also written for various larger combinations of instruments than the string quartet. We will give both the combinations and the reasons for their origin, because their existence has modified the structure of chamber music ensembles. The most frequent types are compositions for the following instrument combinations: string ensembles for quintets, sextets, and even octets [such as those by Felix Mendelssohn (1809–1847) and Louis Spohr (1784–1859)], which are built by adding violins, a viola, a cello, and sometimes a double bass; combinations of piano with two to four strings with occasionally a double bass, as in Schubert's "Trout Quintet"; wind instruments, such as flute, oboe, clarinet, bassoon, horn, and possibly others, with or without piano; and finally, one wind, generally one of those just mentioned, with strings, again with or without piano. The use of more than one wind with various strings is found in sextets for two horns and strings by Mozart and Ludwig van Beethoven (1770–1827), the "Octet" by Schubert and the "Octet" and "Nonet" by Spohr.

Due to the difficulty of assembling the required virtuosi, music of this kind was seldom composed. However, seven factors favor such compositions:

1. A composer could, for purely acoustical reasons, desire the new combination. Mozart shifted from the string quartet to the quintet for this reason. He was interested in strengthening the middle voices and employed a second viola for his end. Beethoven, Brahms, and Anton Bruckner (1824–1896) imitated this combination.

2. A composer intended to write a traditional piano concerto (as developed under the influence of the sons of Bach, notably Philipp Eman-

uel). He lived at a rather small court, or anyplace where he had just a few instrumentalists for accompaniment, rather than a large orchestra. In Mozart's time, this situation produced some works for piano with one or two violins. Planned as piano concertos by necessity, they became chamber music compositions.

3. A monarch or powerful patron played an instrument and wished to play it in combination with others. He then ordered a composition of that kind. An example would be Mozart's unique composition for bassoon and cello.

4. An orchestral soloist had the same desire and was backed by his sponsor.

5. A musician was called to a court and expected to create new compositions. He wanted to participate in the performance. Since a complete string quartet was already there, he had to compose for a larger group. This is the origin of a kind of string quintet (different from the Mozartian) with two violincellos, invented by Luigi Boccherini (1743–1805), a composer and cellist. This new combination was imitated (for example, by Schubert), but less frequently than the two viola quintet.

6. A composer became acquainted with a virtuoso. The latter seemed to him especially able to express musical intentions. He then wrote compositions that allowed the virtuoso to show off his capabilities. Brahms, after having become acquainted with the clarinetist Richard Muhlfeld (1856–1907), composed two clarinet sonatas (later also arranged for viola), and combinations for clarinet and other instruments. However, Brahms was not an innovator in this sense. Instead, he used prior combinations, such as the clarinet quintet used by Johann Stamitz (1717–1757) in Mannheim, by Mozart, and by Karl Maria von Weber (1786–1826); or trios for clarinet, violincello, and piano, a combination employed by Beethoven. Spohr's case in the midnineteenth century was similar. He married a harp virtuoso who wanted to appear with him (he was a violinist) on the concert stage. That is the origin of his compositions for harp and strings, a combination seldom used.

7. A composer was a court conductor. He had at his disposal many chamber music virtuosos. Under such circumstances, compositions for many instruments could be written, rehearsed, and performed. The octet and nonet for strings and winds composed by Spohr, the conductor of the court orchestra in Cassel, are characteristic examples.

The newest group of instrumentalists, the jazz band, is primarily itinerant, and will accordingly be covered with other itinerant groups.

Next to instrumentalists, the opera ensemble is one of the most important musical organizations of modern times. The ancient Greek mystery play and certain oriental forms anticipated the modern opera. But what we have primarily in mind when using the term *opera* is a dramatic performance in which at least some of the characters do not exclusively talk but also sing. Such performances have really only existed since the Counter Reformation. Later, when dealing with the sociological background of special kinds of music, this situation will be explained.

Since their inception, opera ensembles have been primarily stable groups at the courts or in large cities, although the latter type is not as stable as it may appear. Such an opera theater may function for many years, even decades, but its members will change often, apparently more so than those of other orchestras. Very often, especially in the nineteenth century, singers were there for only one season. Since the end of the nineteenth century, opera has come more and more under state control, especially in Europe. Singers have often become state or city officials with accompanying privileges, such as pension rights.

Itinerant Associations

The possibility of developing itinerant groups of musicians depends on various factors: the size of the group, the distance to be traveled, the means of communication, and the capability and willingness of a public to pay relatively high prices, which possibly are necessitated by the first three factors. As to the size of the groups, the following can be stated: The larger an orchestra becomes, the less opportunity will it have to make a living as an itinerant group, traveling expenses being too high. The trend in the United States is an exception. The American attitude toward music differs from that of Europe in two ways. First, state and community support of orchestras is generally less than in Europe. Second, the percentage of persons who want to attend concerts regularly is relatively smaller. Both facts contribute to the traveling of large orchestras such as the Boston, Chicago, or Cincinnati Symphony to many cities lacking regular orchestras.

Similarly, the jazz band is largely an itinerant group since nightclub audiences often desire frequent changes of jazz groups. Chamber music ensembles, being smaller, have lower traveling expenses; but they also play to smaller audiences. (This is particularly true of string quartets). Chamber music ensembles have only recently become itinerant. Almost the first known examples are the two nineteenth century "Müllerquartets," composed of four brothers each, who performed in Rostock and Braunschweig, Germany. In both these and later cases, the members have had a permanent musical position, but are entitled to some leave of absence to play elsewhere, since both monarchs and city administrations wish their musicians to be known and honored elsewhere. Due to expenses, the larger ensembles can rarely travel. Accordingly, larger chamber compositions are usually performed by local musicians in their own city. In the relatively few cases in which they are performed by an itinerant string quartet, the latter has added a local pianist or double-bass player, for example, to perform the additional parts; or, conversely, a local pianist occasionally hires an outside string quartet to perform with him.

In the United States, chamber ensembles appeared relatively late. In the 1860s the repertoire of itinerant groups was increased by the ability of the membership to play flute and clarinet, as well as string instruments. The group could therefore be smaller and did not need to hire wind virtuosos for particular compositions. Traveling and other costs were consequently reduced. In more recent years, the traveling string quartet has become the predominant type.

The role of the itinerant orchestra or chamber ensemble in Latin America is even more restricted. The ruralness of the majority of these countries; the limited number of cities, which tend to be far apart; and undeveloped means of communication make itinerant groups impractical.

Before discussing traveling opera companies, a few words may be said about itinerant theater. Road shows that were at least partially religious in intent were performed by minstrels, jongleurs, and *Fahrende* in the Middle Ages, Italian Renaissance, and Counter Reformation respectively. Many oriental cultures have had similar shows. There are innumerable varieties of traveling shows in every culture, including many dialect and marionette theaters directed primarily toward the lower classes. All these types feature small ensembles and portable stage properties, unlike modern theater, which generally requires many actors, costumes, props, decorations, furniture, and other stage materials. This makes itinerant theater increasingly expensive and almost impossible.

An entire opera company is an even more difficult case. The problems of moving soloists, choir, and orchestra can be insurmountable. Italian opera companies traveled, but in an era of greater simplicity. The companies were small and their members tended to be versatile in their skills. Many could play several roles, often taking more than one part or even playing in the orchestra during a performance. Finally, Italian opera did not require as large an orchestra as the Wagnerian and post-Wagnerian. This is one reason why traveling opera troups performed in Italy until recently. The other reason is the tremendous popularity of Italian heroic opera among the rural lower classes. The individual singer is stressed over all other aspects and personnel of the opera. In non-Italian coun-tries, traveling opera vanished with the growing complication of scenery and orchestration and the shift (in the post-Wagnerian era) of audience interest from melody, aria, and voice to the totality of the musicodra-matic performance.

In America this shift occurred later and more gradually. Therefore, the older practice of traveling operatic groups continued, due in part to the reluctance of state and city governments to support local opera com-panies. Opera lovers had to attend performances by itinerant groups. Travel expenses were reduced by cutting the number of orchestra and ballet members. For example, when performing Charles François Gou-nod's (1818–1893) *Faust,* one such troupe changed the student dance scene into a female solo. Another group altered Guiseppe Verdi's (1813–1901) *Aida.* In the opera, a group of brass players precede the entrance of the King of Egypt, his daughter, Amneris, the high priest, and various court members. The march, to be played on a unique high trumpet known as the "Aida trumpet," required a number of trained brass players on stage. However, lacking personnel, this particular group used only its trumpet soloist for the scene.

As mentioned, independent ballet is usually itinerant; but having gen-erally been of foreign origin it will be covered with the itinerant foreign group.

Foreign Associations of Music Producers

We now turn to an examination of associations of foreign performers. Italian orchestras, just as individual Italian soloists, appear relatively early outside of Italy. Considering the undeveloped means of traveling, one can understand that only affluent persons or organizations could take the economic risk of inviting such groups. Examples range from the Czaress Anna in the eleventh century to the United States with its grow-ing wealth. Since the 1840s, Italian and later German orchestras have been highly esteemed in the United States. Conversely, during the two world wars, American military and jazz bands and symphony orchestras frequently toured Europe.

Foreign theater groups appear mainly under two circumstances: first, as a means of indoctrinating a subjected people; and second, when a spe-cial theater company or at least one of its leading actors has been ac-claimed by a foreign public. France epitomizes the first circumstance. In the seventeenth century, French invaders established the French theater when they took over the area now known as Belgium. Later, the Napole-

onic army also used French theater as an indoctrination tool, as did the
French occupying the German Rhine province after World War I. The
French, more than other Europeans, feel that their culture is the best; as
a result, they attempt to inculcate others with their customs. Comparatively speaking, the attempts of other countries at indoctrination by way
of theater are relatively unimportant. For instance, the Americans and
the British have made much less use of the stage in their respective zones
of military occupation.

Concerning the second circumstance, a theater or actor may be invited, or go of their own initiative, to foreign countries where they are
popular. Since they generally perform in their native tongue, performances attract a highly educated minority or the affluent (who see the program as a social event). Translations or comments in the program notes
increase the audience, but the performance will still not have a general
appeal. Sarah Bernhardt was a noted example of a touring popular actress. At the turn of the nineteenth century, she performed with her
theater troupe in many European countries, including Germany, even
though Franco-German relations were none too good at the time. But
Sarah Bernhardt and most of her audience were interested in Sarah,
rather than in a presentation of a French play. Most of the other performers were more or less unknown. The "divine Sarah" wanted to stand
in bold relief against lesser talents. A somewhat better example would be
the appearance of the "Düsseldorfer Schauspielhaus" in Paris. Although
its leader Louise Dumont [pseudonym for L. Heynen (1862–1929)] was
considered a remarkable actress, her fellow actors were chosen for their
compatibility with her.

This general survey of foreign theater reveals reasons for its limited
impact. Similar observations apply to foreign opera troupes—traveling
expenses are high, and so forth. There is however one factor that facili-
tates productions by foreign opera companies. The majority of an opera
audience is mainly interested in music, rather than in the dramatic text.
Comprehension of a foreign text is not a prerequisite for enjoyment.
Consequently, soon after its origin, and prior to extensive stage decora-
tion, orchestra, and chorus, Italian opera appeared in many places. Companies were invited by the Czar, for example. French opera companies
also toured, but more for political reasons. The United States, which has
spent so much money on outstanding foreign singers and conductors, has
seldom hosted foreign, especially European, opera companies. Expenses
are too high. The Metropolitan Opera in New York is less handicapped
than others by financial considerations. Nevertheless it prefers its own
orchestra and chorus, despite the fact that it obtains outstanding singers
from as far away as Bulgaria. Recently, prosperous Latin American coun-

tries such as Argentina have invited complete Italian or German opera ensembles.

Concerning foreign ballet companies, Italian dance groups sometimes appeared at the czarist court. Recently, Russian ballet has been widely acclaimed and considered unique.

Amateur Organizations

All musical groups discussed so far were professional. Amateur associations can be classified into four main types: amateur orchestras, singing associations, combinations of these two, and theater groups.

1. *Orchestras.* Orchestras were numerous in Austria during the eighteenth century; they performed the works of Haydn and his contemporaries. As involvment in music was essential for status, members of the upper middle class formed their own orchestras. Originally, they met in private homes, but the development of modern instruments complicated and enlarged orchestral performances, making it necessary for these amateur orchestras to move to more spacious quarters, such as assembly halls or city halls or restaurants. This shift entrained various consequences. Many orchestras insisted on not paying for rooms belonging to the city; sometimes they even requested financial assistance. Occasionally the members split into two groups. The majority continued to play their instruments, while well-to-do members withdrew from such participation and functioned as financial supporters. Other changes followed. Hiring a professional conductor became important and economically possible; occasionally it was even possible to hire professional musicians. The latter were often essential when none of the dilettantes could play recently developed instruments such as bass clarinet, English horn, or double bassoon.

Amateur orchestrast also played an important role with virtuosos. Traveling soloists frequently had difficulty advertising, selling tickets, and even securing a performance hall. The following pattern emerged: After coming to the city, a foreign virtuoso would first play, accompanied by an amateur orchestra, in a program sponsored by the orchestra. The amateur associations would then allow him to perform his own concert rent-free in their hall. The more orchestras depended on city or state support, rather than on amateur organizations, the less this reciprocity operated. Later it disappeared completely. The United States had a similar shift from amateur orchestras in the colonial period to professional organizations later.

In our days, there are more amateur wind ensembles than symphony orchestras. In France, local or regional groups known as *Fanfares* are largely composed of retired members of military bands—their members had previously had music as their main occupation. The fact that such brass instrumental associations in France are often composed of members of various social classes (including well-to-do rural landowners and factory workers) will be of interest to us later.

There are also many amateur associations for specialized instruments. One of the two characteristic types are the associations found especially in remote districts that employ obsolete national instruments, such as the harp and bagpipe societies of nineteenth-century Ireland, Scotland, and Wales. The *Zither* associations of southern Germany are similar. A flat-backed, plucked instrument that is played on a table, the *Zither* was used for centuries by relatively poor farmers and cattle breeders in the mountains of southern Bavaria and in neighboring Austrian districts. In the nineteenth century, largely due to the sponsorship of princes and the nobility, the *Zither* became more widely known. Many associations, especially in Bavaria, promoted it as a national instrument. The mandolin of Italian origin, and the guitar of Spanish and perhaps Arabic origin, as well as the accordion, while not as widely promoted, have also been cultivated by special associations, usually composed of members of the lower middle class. The essential fact is that these and many other instruments have never been part of the symphony orchestra. Their cultivation in amateur associations symbolizes, to some extent, a protest against state-protected musicians.

2. *Singing associations*. There are three main types of amateur *singing associations:* those exclusively for women, those for men only, and mixed choruses. The first type appeared in primitive cultures, the ancient Orient, early Christianity, and among medieval (mainly Celtic) peoples. In the Christian world, choirs of Catholic nuns are common, singing being part of their religious duties. Other female choirs are uncommon in the Western world, except for the glee clubs in women's schools and colleges. Some Protestant groups associate women with sin and temptation, and therefore restrict their role in religious worship.

Associations of nonprofessional singing men appeared in Western culture, such as soldier units and those connected with philosophical and political movements. One of the relatively few places where males exclusively gathered for social and cultural purposes were Masonic lodges. Special compositions for male voices have been written and performed there. In the late eighteenth and early nineteenth centuries, when Masonic ideas were popularized in the climate of religious liberalism, this custom spread to larger groups of anticlerical city burghers. In the Swiss democracy huge male choruses already sang before large audiences.

From there the custom spread to southern and then northern Germany in the early nineteenth century. It was then taken by emigrants to the United States.

An even greater role has been played by mixed choirs, primarily in churches, in music history. The attitude of a denomination toward music influenced its use of mixed choirs. Oratorio associations were one of the most characteristic types of mixed amateur choirs. In the time of Bach and his predecessors, those who sang chorales in Lutheran oratorios were members of the church choir and presumably true believers. They sang primarily from religious impulse. As religious interest decreased, oratorios shifted from the church to the concert hall; they became primarily secular affairs during the nineteenth century.

The singers in the choir usually were, and are still, members of the upper middle class, whose participation was motivated more by musical interest or social prestige than by basic religious feeling. As this kind of oratorio singing became more and more a social event, social differentiation among the choir members increased, especially in the larger cities. With the middle class rapidly increasing in wealth, particularly in many Central and Western European countries and in the United States, the middle-class wife could, almost universally, afford and was expected to have at least one domestic employee. At the same time, a growing appliance technology was simplifying housework. However, woman's emancipation was just getting under way. The upper-middle-class woman was not yet expected to work outside the home. Furthermore, except for volunteer work through church-sponsored welfare organizations, she was not yet permitted to participate in public life. What could she do, then, outside the home? Participation in more or less city-supported oratorio societies was one of the few opportunities available.

However, oratorio associations have diminished in the twentieth century, due to the breakdown of their social exclusiveness. Near the beginning of the twentieth century, lower- and lower-middle-class women began working (for example in factories) to earn a living. Finally, upper-middle-class women insisted on participating in public life, either by having jobs or by becoming involved in politics and public service. Through these activities, upper-class women came in contact with women of other social strata, and oratorio associations, dependent upon social exclusivity, were arrested in their development. Moreover, there were now other socially acceptable activities besides music. With the growth of industrialization and urbanization, interest in religion decreased, especially among the upper middle class in France, Switzerland, and Germany. Because of these factors, interest in oratorios diminished throughout Central and Western Europe, and later in the United States.

Vocal quartets and double quartets, which are considered too small to be politically dangerous, only flourish when larger associations (especially men's glee clubs) are forbidden for political reasons.

3. *Combined orchestral and vocal associations.* Many groups combined both singers and instrumentalists. Some organizations were founded to combine the enjoyment of good food, music making, and conviviality. Such a "convivium musicum" existed in Florence in 1470. In Germany, funeral fraternities played music at their friends' burial services. A separation comparable to that in singing societies then occurred; the well-to-do members paid higher fees, but did not participate in musical performances.

The "mastersingers" should be mentioned again. Originally, they were handicraft masters. Usually they met in a member's house, say in Frankfurt. Performers were not distinguished from audience. Detailed rituals admitted a person as an apprentice and later elevated him to master. Gradually these rituals were abandoned. The mastersingers simply became an association of craftsmen who, in their leisure time, came together for social purposes and to enjoy their own music. Although this occurred especially in Germany, similar developments took place in other countries. In Lyon, in the south of France, well-to-do members of the middle class regularly met to enjoy a very rich traditional dinner, featuring distinctive wines with every different dish. At these gatherings, they sang local songs, while some of their number played on the piano or other instruments. These gatherings helped maintain traditional local music.

4. *Theatrical organizations.* The amateur theater, which is often connected with music, exists in three types. The first is found in many folk cultures and in the more remote modern districts, such as the Celtic-speaking French province of Brittany. It performs mystery plays, whose content and ethics is closely linked to the total life of the people. The second type also persists in many countries. Unlike the first type, it is not particularly based on any special local or regional tradition, but imitates the theater of professional actors. Past examples include the powerful stage director August Wilhelm Iffland (1759–1814) who, around 1800 in Berlin, selected his professional actors from amateurs. In England and in the United States, amateur actors were still in high esteem around 1880. In some regions of the United States, attempts were made to systematically organize amateur productions. Central offices provided local amateur groups with material support, such as costumes.

The specific differences of the third type are seen in the light of the first and second types. Since the turn of the century, and especially since the end of World War I, a new concept of amateur theater emerged in

Europe, particularly in Germany. Actors no longer aspired to become professionals in the traditional sense. It was asserted that a young person with dramatic talent did not need extensive training in a dramatic academy or conservatory, and that such training would actually harm natural capacities. This claim was made in connection with simultaneous demands for a new expressionistic style, which was expected to express through characteristic movements what is essential, eliminating superfluous detail. This ideology was occasionally associated with the claim that proletarians should stress self-awareness and not imitate the bourgeoisie.

ON THE AUTONOMOUS INDIVIDUAL IN MUSIC

Having surveyed various types of individuals and groups involved in the production of music, we will now discuss the various degrees of individual autonomy associated with their roles in music.

When using the term *individual autonomy,* we refer to the following: Under what conditions does the individual arrive at independent conclusions about forms of musical style and technique and realize them through his own musical expression? How can he avoid being restricted by institutions that enforce their own concept of music? What kind of society not only toleraes, but appreciates and stresses individual expression, especially that of unique individuals?

In preliterate, folk, and even more complex cultures, a musical composition is considered a group manifestation, even when it was developed by one individual. The same is also true of the other arts in the Christian medieval world. Buildings, statues, pictures and miniatures, as well as musical compositions were created for the glorification of God, not the artist. Only Greek (especially Athenian) antiquity recognized poets and sculptors as individuals, although composers were not recognized. *The composer* as an individual creator has been given special recognition only since the beginning of modern individualism, anticipated by the Italian Renaissance. The earlier southern French troubadours, the northern French trouvères, and their German counterparts, the minnesinger, wrote both melody and lyrics for their songs. They are frequently considered among the first examples of individual composition in occidental history; they often glorified an individual woman. But even more than the Middle Ages, the Italian Renaissance represents the triumph of the individual over the group composer. Although restrictions and traditional rules remained, even such representatives of traditional music as church organists were often expected to compose or independently improvise in Protestant,

Catholic, or even Lutheran churches. But as organists are primarily instrumentalists rather than composers, their role will be more fully discussed later.

More than any other period, the nineteenth century, especially in its
impressionism and atonalism, saw the elimination of many restrictions.
The nineteenth-century composer represented unrestricted individualism.
The modern jazz musician also is expected to incorporate free improvisa-
tions into his performance. Primarily an instrumentalist, he will also be
discussed later.

Compared to the *composer*, the *librettist* is normally less able to assert
his individuality. His work is mainly a vehicle for the composer, and
gives the singers opportunities for showing their capabilities. Exceptions
may exist. For instance, a young unknown composer has few connections.
It may be advantageous for him to use a text written by a known librettist, who may then recommend the new work. The eighteenth-century
Italian, Metastasio, and the nineteenth-century Frenchman, Eugène
Scribe (1791–1861), are examples. Ironically, these two illustrate the limitations of the librettist. They wrote according to a scheme, with the same
numbers regularly appearing in sequence in each of their operas (such as
entrance choir, restaurant choir, and preger-ana'eto).

Another situation is when a composer, in collaboration with a writer,
adapts a popular work such as a dramatic play, a novel, or an epic song
as the text for a new opera. Sometimes he uses the work as written, with
only a few revisions. The German epic song *Der Trompeter von Säck-
ingen* by Victor von Scheffel (1826–1886) was made into an opera of the
same name by composer Victor Nessler (1841–1890). The symbolic drama
Die Versunkene Glocke by the highly admired German dramatist, Ger-
hart Hauptmann (1862–1946), was adapted by Heinrich Zöllner (1854–
1941) under the same title. Two examples of works used in their entirety
as opera texts are *Salomé* and *Elektra*, the plays by Oscar Wilde (1856–
1900) and the Austrian poet Hugo von Hofmannsthal (1874–1929), from
which Richard Strauss created his operas. In these instances, author and
composer both made autonomous artistic contributions. Such cases are
rare.

The development of individual autonomy for the *conductor* parallels
the case of the composer. We have already mentioned several forerunners
of the conductor: the Greek musician who beat the rhythm with his sandals, the Roman who used oyster shells for this purpose, the Arab employing castanettes, and the first violinist (or concertmaster) and harpsichordist who indicated when to begin playing a movement. However,
none of these were innovators, since all performed according to a musical
tradition. Tradition was still followed when conductors were no longer

instrumentalists and began watching to see that music was performed exactly as written. The conductor was not expected to provide his own individual interpretation. The "great" conductor emerged only after the rise of impressionism and subjectivism. This conductor does not feel that he is simply a link between the composer and listener, but that by his personality and corresponding individual interpretation he adds a new element to the composition. The public comes to hear not only the composition but also his interpretation.

Similar historical developments characterize the role of instrument *soloists*. However, percussion soloists were already distinguished from other instrumentalists in primitive and oriental cultures. This recognition was based on the belief that the welfare of the group depended on the accuracy of his magicorhythmic drumming. He was thus singled out for his collective function, not for his subjective interpretations.

In the Italian Renaissance the soloist was second in importance only to the composer; he could emphasize his own technical genius beyond the composer's intentions. During this period of increasing subjectivism, the personal feelings of the interpreter as well as those of the creator interested the audience. This development is closely connected with other changes in the social structure. Through the Reformation and the Counter Reformation, churches again came into power. The modern absolute state was emerging at the same time. Although in conflict, both powers restricted individual freedom. The individual was primarily tolerated when he threatened neither church nor state.

During the Italian Renaissance, musicians were admired for their technical virtuosity. Now the individual appeared as the performer of solo concerti, which were technically difficult, independent of exclusively musical considerations. The most difficult and consequently most important part of these compositions is the cadenza, a solo part without orchestra accompaniment, usually at the end of the various movements. Frequently it is a recapitulation or variation of the main themes of the concerto. The cadenza gives the soloist an opportunity to realize the potentials of his instrument—using double stops on the violin, for example. He may further display his technique by including complications such as pizzicatos. The latter, ordinarily, are not employed for primarily musical reasons.

The culmination of this development was the virtuoso who requested the composition of a concerto that would allow him to display his technical capabilities. For example, Niccolò Paganini (1782–1840) asked Berlioz to write a viola concerto for him. The same was true when a virtuoso of a special instrument composed extremely difficult concerti for himself. Again, the composition was not created for primarily musical reasons, but rather for the display of virtuosity. Apt examples of such compositions are the harp concerti and double-bass concerti composed by Domenico Dragonetti (1763–1846) and Giovanni Bottesini (1821–1889).

The individual is far less conspicuous among the orchestra members. However, there was a trend similar to that of soloists for some time. The concertmaster, solo cellist, and violist were supposed to be virtuosos. Up to Mozart's time, the orchestra normally contained only one of each woodwind instrument; their parts were thus largely considered solo parts. Modern orchestras are both larger and more collective than those of the past. As orchestras grew in size, instrumentalists became union members, which also shifted the emphasis from the individual to the collective.

Among instrumentalists, the organist deserves particular consideration. In regards to his playing, he is of course strictly bound by the rules and the ritual of his church. But his instrument, the individual pipe organ, is unique; each has its own structure, number of manuals, pedals, and registers. The organist, then, must adapt his style and technique to his instrument. Moreover, he is supposed to be able to improvise. Under certain circumstances he is expected to perform church concerts. This is especially true in Lutheran churches. The content of the program is partially in the hands of the organist, who may even be expected to perform his own compositions. Consequently, as performer as well as composer, the organist has some opportunity to introduce his own individuality.

More than the member of a symphony orchestra, the jazz musician has the opportunity to demonstrate his special talents through improvisation.

This survey of individual autonomy in music clearly shows at least one thing: Modern occidental individualism extends beyond the composer. At least as far as the formal and technical aspects are concerned, it has included the interpretive conductor and the solo instrumentalist.

Individualism is also found in theater acting and opera singing. In almost every preliterate, oriental, and medieval culture, the drama expressed communal and mystical cultic feelings of the group. Changes began during Hellenistic and Roman antiquity, and specifically with the Italian Renaissance, when the drama was expected to portray the poet's philosophical, ethical, political, or psychological concepts. This change also affected the actor. Rather than representing a group feeling, he was expected to reveal his individual traits, to distinguish himself from other actors portraying the same character in, say, a Shakespearian drama.

A similar development is perceived in the role of the *solo singer*. In certain preliterate societies, such as those of the American Indian, the tribe's shaman sang alone as part of his function. The same is true of various folk, Greek, and oriental cultures, as well as of occidental Christian medieval culture. Notwithstanding the fact that music was largely performed by the whole congregation during the Protestant Reformation, individual soloists were given a role. After having shifted from Counter Reformation Catholicism to Lutheranism, the oratorio gained greater importance for the soloist. Nevertheless, traditional rules were observed; solos were incorporated into the larger unit, which was considered more important than the subjective religious and musical feeling or technical capacities of the individual singer.

The greater potential for individuality allowed by the oratorio was anticipated by the role of the trouvères, troubadours, and minnesingers. The first impetus came during the Italian Renaissance, mostly in Italian opera where the dramatic unit was neglected. The main purpose of the performance was to give singers of both sexes the possibility of demonstrating their unique technical capabilities. (These singers included the two antithetical types, the castrate singing female parts and the woman playing male heroes.) This practice largely continued during the nineteenth century throughout Europe.

Wagner's musical drama was intended as a strong protest against these customs. Similarly, the German Youth Movement returned to simple forms of group singing. The Soviet doctrine of collective art rejected even further the utilization of musical performances as vehicles for exhibitions of virtuosity. Yet, despite these injunctions, soloists are of major importance in the contemporary artistic scene abroad.

The United States never ceased to emphasize the individual singer; individualistic philosophy remains dominant in the United States, and new art forms for many years tended to appear later in America than in Europe. Accordingly, the older forms remained viable in the United States after they had begun to be questioned in the Old World.

The development of *individual dance* parallels that of individual singing. Individual dance was found in the religious ceremonies of preliterate societies (such as those of the American Indians). Certain already complex Asiatic societies, such as in Korea and Japan, evidenced individual dancing. However, as in the case of the other arts, the solo ballet dancer really only exists in modern times. In Italy, the prima ballerina became as important as the coloratura soprano or the lyric tenor. This high esteem also continued after the shift from the original Italian ballet to the modern ballet, with its development of tragic and comic character. Individual characterization by each dancer became increasingly important. This trend has been evident also in the collectivist art of the Soviet era, carried over from the Czarist ballet.

Until recently, the stage director was simply an old actor who did his job in a routine fashion. The innovating stage director who gives unique interpretation to drama and opera appeared in the nineteenth and even more in the twentieth century. He might invent a scenario or change the historical setting of an opera by dressing the performers in costumes different from those normally called for by the script. The official Soviet theater claims that it expresses collective feeling, and not the subjective impression of the individual; but even there the stage director makes an individual contribution.

The *musicologist* appears, as already mentioned, only in very complex cultures, in which music and music theory are often still connected with institutionalized religion. The musicologist is bound by precepts, and even more by social beliefs. In this situation, he is a scholastic rather than a scientist. Thus, he is not expected to profess his own ideas and value judgments. An excellent example is the Chinese intellectual who deals with music. Only when a distinction is made between science and scholasticism does individualism occur. Due to their ideologies, Nazism and Soviet Communism minimally tolerate independent science, cultivating instead a more or less pure form of scholasticism. Consequently, only an official theory of music is tolerated.

The music *critic* also has only emerged recently and in relatively complex cultures. He is hindered in individual expression even more than the musicologist. Police states do not permit independent judgment. However, even where the press is free of state censorship, other powers, such as churches, political parties, and economically powerful groups, restrict freedom of the press, impeding the development of independent music criticism. Music critics normally are members of an editorial staff that must adapt its policies to the desires and values of dominant powers. The situation may be different only in complex societies. In big cities newspapers may be more independent because of the support of readers interested in the judgment of a particular critic. Hanslick, the music critic of the *Wiener Freie Presse* and a vigorous adversary of Wagner, was an example of such a powerful critic.

Every *teacher* is limited in his individual expression, being always supported by some organization. To a greater or lesser degree, he is expected to function as its representative. Because he contributes something new to the traditional knowledge of his students, he can in a sense function individualistically. The less the group (tribe, state, or church) he represents dominates spiritual life, the more he can function as an individual. Hence, the individualistic teacher emerges mainly after the Italian Renaissance, and especially with the onset of the nineteenth century. However, the current rise of modern industrialization has again produced antiindividualistic effects.

What applies to the music teacher also applies to the dance teacher and the music student. Only under those conditions conducive to individualism will they develop artistic personalities of their own. Conversely, when the group considers itself entitled to determine the "right" music and when it has the power to enforce its evaluations, student individualists will be hindered. They take the risks of not passing required examinations, being expelled from school, or enduring financial hardship.

The *instrument maker* has, for a long time, been a guild member and must adapt himself to its rules. These covered such areas as style of life, number of working hours, number of journeymen and apprentices, and prices for new material and finished products. But guild control of unrestricted competition also allowed him to devote all his time, energy, pride, and love to his product. He could work according to the individual wishes of the customer, whom he knew personally. This mixture of traditional rules and individual art remained after the Italian Renaissance. Amati, Guarneri, and Stradivarius were bound by some traditions; nevertheless, they built instruments in their own style. A similar situation occurred regarding the violin bow. The Frenchman François Tourte (1747–1835) has been called the "Stradivarius of the bow."

The shift from individual to industrial production a change associated with a change in values, occurred slowly. The traditional admiration for craftsmanship was replaced by admiration for financial success. To realize this end, one has to adapt himself to large-scale marketing conditions, which limit the opportunities for independent craftsmanship. The further development of larger economic units, such as trusts, restricted independent production even more. By necessity, many masters and apprentices were transformed into workers; it was no longer possible for them to do independent work as instrument makers. And, as a member of a labor union, a master is only one of many equal workers.

These findings can be summarized as follows: Under some circumstances, a human being stresses his own individuality. Under even fewer circumstances, this claim of the individual is recognized, and society gives him the opportunity to make value judgments, to realize them, and to manifest his own uniqueness. Society usually grants only the possibility to demonstrate technical superiority over others, and even this latitude is often restricted. Some persons ignore the limitations imposed on them by rules. They risk failure, but hope that perhaps under changed circumstances they will be rediscovered and appreciated after their death. This is especially true when basic changes concerning the essence and use of music are challenged.

Powerful institutions, such as the state, church, and university, struggle for their own independent power. In this process they first consider and declare themselves different from, or superior to, the sum of their individual members; and second, they persecute dissidents. The individual, however, will often not admit the institution's superiority. He may deny the right of the institution to impose its law, at least regarding his particular sphere of life. Consequently, he will be hindered, perhaps persecuted. In the long run, the individual may succeed, but new dogmatization, institutionalization, and group glorification occurs. Technology and industrialization do not presuppose a simultaneous individualization—new powers, such as mass production plants, trusts, and labor unions, spring up. The struggle continues between the individual, who desires to exercise his own judgment, and the large-scale institution, with its claim for dominance.

THE ANONYMITY OF MUSICIANS

The question of under which circumstances the musician remains anonymous is connected with the question of the individualist's role in musical life. The answers to both are not necessarily identical. Not everyone who is not anonymous is an individualist. For example, in many primitive cultures the solo singer or dancer is known personally by the audience, but he is not an individualist in the sense in which we have used this term. At the same time, remaining anonymous does not mean that one is not an individualist. Of course, in many cultures that understand and admire the activities of particular individuals, anonymity may be unimportant. However, an individual often has to remain anonymous just because he is considered important, such as when a powerful group considers him a threat to their existence. He is considered a revolutionary by the group, which represents tradition and has the power to enforce its will.

It is now obvious that the term *anonymity* denotes at least four sociologically different situations. These can be summarized as follows:

1. A group considers itself a value and entity different from and superior to the sum of its members. The member works as a representative of the organization. The honor of achievement belongs not to him, but to the group. Anyone desiring recognition for his work is regarded as a revolutionary. Individual members are inculcated by the group with the belief that anonymity is proper and desirable. The *object* of production forms the subject of our inquiry.

2. A society tolerates, even admires, the creative individual. This type of society recognizes the right of the individual to be known by name. In this case anonymity means that the individual or his function is considered so unimportant that he may as well remain anonymous. What should be examined are the *circumstances* of production, which are considered by a particular society to be unimportant.

3. In certain tradition-oriented societies, individuals have the right to criticize traditional forms, to reject them, and to work toward replacing them with others. However, because to do so involves risk, the individual will only try it anonymously or pseudonymously. The significant question is, What does the power group consider so important that it must be done anonymously to avoid risk?

4. A society needs large quantities of material or nonmaterial items, which it mass-produces. Nearly all those involved in production are anonymous; there are countless workers, clerks, and so forth. The sociologist is concerned with what the society believes to be so *necessary* that it must be produced by anonymous masses.

We may now illustrate these four conditions of anonymity with data on the process of music production, following our sequence of types of persons involved in the production of music.

1. The first type, in which anonymity is connected with the importance attributed to the work itself, as well as the group, is exemplified by the following: the composer of dances, folk songs, and heroic epics, transferred orally from generation to generation in preliterary cultures and early state societies; the poet of the text of such songs and epics; the solo singer and instrumentalist in the religious music performed by monks or similar groups; and the monk who copies musical scores.

2. The second category, in which anonymity is connected with the unimportance assigned to some kind of work, includes the following types: the librettist of earlier opera, whose name was often unprinted on score and program; the conductor (mainly his forerunners in antiquity and Mohammedanism, and the harpsichordist or first violinist) who indicated the beginning of the performance; the orchestral instrumentalist and the stage director, who have only recently been mentioned in the program notes; the actor and solo singer in itinerant troupes; and choir members in religious and secular singing.

3. The third type, individuals who find anonymity expedient due to their opposition to the group in power, consists mainly of musicologists and critics championing new ideas opposed to the value system of the dominant political, religious, or artistic group.

4. The fourth category includes those living in a period when there is a polarity between individualism and industrial mass production. Most are anonymous functionaries: workers, technicians, and clerks involved in the process of producting, distributing, and selling printed scores, instruments, records, and radio and television implements. There are also instrument teachers provided by factories and stores that have sold instruments to schools. Usually they simply return to anonymity after giving a few routine lessons.

There is also a trend toward nonanonymity, which has its origins in antiquity, but which has been especially pervasive since the Renaissance. It applies primarily to the composer, instrumental soloist, actor, singer (including the castrate), female dancer, musicologist, and the preindustrial instrument maker. In recent times, the conductor, orchestra member, stage director, and critic have gained increasing personal recognition.

The Practice of Using Pseudonyms

The use of pseudonyms occurs when musicians begin to be known by name after an era of anonymity. One may conceal his real name for various reasons, including:

1. The desire to avoid conflict or persecution may prompt the adoption of a pseudonym.

2. The musician comes from a relatively well-to-do family. If his family belongs to a religious demonination that disapproves of the public performance of music, for example, and considers it dishonorable to have an actor or singer in the family, the musician may wish to be known by a name other than his family name.

3. If his name is a very common one (such as Dupont in France, Smith in England, or Mueller in Germany), the musician may change to a more distinctive one. However, a common surname may be offset by an uncommon first name, eliminating any need to change. The famous late nineteenth-century violin virtuoso, Waldemar Meyer (1854–?), of Berlin, is a case in point.

4. A musician who comes from a nation little known in the musical world may find that his name is often mispronounced. If he wishes to become known in nations that play a greater role in musical life, he may change his name to suit the pronounciation of the area he desires to live in. The Czech violinist, Karl Halir (1859–1909), a friend of Brahms and collaborator with Joseph Joachim (1831–1907), is an example. In Czech his name was pronounced "Halirsch." Because no one in Germany knew what the accent on the "r" meant, or how the name should be pronounced, he dropped the accent and called himself Halir.

5. Because of the possibility of running into anti-Semitism an artist or his agent changes his name. For example, Bruno Walter's original name, Schlesinger, was changed by the theater director who hired him.

ON TYPICAL CONFLICTS AND INTERDEPENDENCY OF MUSICIANS

It would be a miracle if no conflicts existed between the various types of musical performers. Conflict does not refer to personal hostility, but to recurring antagonisms connected with interdependencies between various kinds of musicians. Economic conflicts will be considered later under the economic aspects of music.

More than anyone else, the composer is involved in conflict and is dependent upon other musicians. Generally, musicians' interpretation of a musical score will differ from the composer's. The conductor, instrumentalist, singer, dancer, or stage director may even see a new composition primarily as an opportunity to exhibit their special talents. As previously mentioned, eighteenth- and nineteenth-century composers of violin and wind concerti struggled with virtuosos who demanded technical difficulties. They expected compositions that would allow them to display their brilliance, disregarding musical necessity, logic, and the composer's intentions. Moreover, the composer was often dependent upon the structure of the orchestra he had at his disposal. Mozart became belatedly acquainted with the clarinet, more than a generation after it was invented. He immediately considered it to be of greater versatility than the previously favored double-reeded oboe. But he could not use the new instrument in many orchestral compositions, since not every orchestra for which he wrote had a clarinet player. Thus, he had to restrict himself to chamber music compositions, such as the clarinet quintet with four strings and the clarinet trio with viola and piano, for which he had sufficient players at his disposal. But even chamber music composers such as Boccherini were restricted by the limited number of performers available for certain instruments.

The vocal virtuoso may also alter, and even complement, the composer's original intentions. For example, Ludwig Fisher's (1745–1825) bass influenced Mozart's operatic writing. Utilizing the singer's extremely low voice, Mozart introduced an appropriately low D into an aria by Osmin in *The Abduction from the Seraglio*. As another example, Heinrich August Marschner (1795–1861), regarded as a forerunner of Wagner, has been most admired for his opera *Hans Heiling*. As an unknown, he had to add love arias to have this composition performed. Such arias suited the interests of the singers who wanted to demonstrate their versatility, but were detrimental to the structure of the opera.

The stage director may also cause the composer difficulty. Long regarded as unimportant, he gained power in the nineteenth and twentieth centuries, especially in court-supported opera houses, such as in Vienna. The Austrian composer, Wilhelm Kienzl (1857–1941), was made aware of this power. Kienzl is best known for his opera *Evangelimann,* which combines popular elements (melodies and characters of Viennese suburbs) with Wagnerian orchestral technique. At the drama's conclusion, the villain dies after having repented and obtained forgiveness from his brother, whose life he had ruined. A stage director wanted to include a choir of monks and nuns in this final scene. Kienzl thought this detracted from the central point of interest and successfully kept the monks out of the opera. Other composers have had similar problems with stage directors.

The conductor has his conflicts, too. Recently, young European conductors, schooled primarily in theory, are often resented by older, well-trained orchestra members. Lack of practical knowledge of instruments make the former a subject for jokes; the orchestra members tend to follow his directions minimally. Similarly, the stage director often has been trained almost exclusively in theory, and may never have performed in a stage play or opera. Sometimes, the trained actors and singers nickname him the "Latin Stage Manager," debasing his authority. Conflict between the stage director and the conductor and singers is even more typical, and perhaps inevitable, for their interests are often antithetical. The conductor and vocalists are mainly interested in the musico-acoustic aspects of performance. Consequently, both will place the singer at the location on stage where his voice sounds best. The stage director, who looks at the performance from the dramatic-optical point of view and who may be interested in a historically accurate setting, will place the singer in the most dramatically effective position.

VARIATIONS OF SOCIAL ESTEEM FOR MUSICIANS

As we have seen, conflicts between musicians are not rooted in economics alone. The social prestige that some musicians enjoy and that others would like to share is an equally likely cause. We propose to analyze the social status of musicians in six respects: (1) conditions under which the musician is considered to be socially inferior, dishonorable, or even an outlaw; (2) instances where high esteem and honor are accorded to musicians; (3) differences in esteem attributed to the players of various instruments; (4) the position enjoyed by the musicologist; (5) the esteem of the music teacher; and (6) the degree of esteem given foreign musicians.

1. In many societies, there are musicians who perform only for people of lower social strata. This is highly evident in the traditional Hindu caste society, and true of minstrels, jongleurs, and *Fahrende* as well as of all their successors, including the Gypsies. Such performers are disdained, even by the "decent" guild musicians, who may not always have high status themselves. Musicians are humiliated in many ways. For instance, a family (generally middle class) may object if their son or daughter wishes to become a professional musician, as we saw in examining reasons for the adoption of a pseudonym. Occasionally, members of the

nobility have had similar experiences; the family conflict of Hans von Bülow (1830–1894), the late Wagner conductor, is one of the best known examples. Similar problems arise when a nonmusician wishes to marry a musician. Typical is the desire of a son from the European nobility or upper middle class to marry an operatic singer.

Even if the lower status musician succeeds in becoming a member of a court ensemble (supported by a monarch or a noble), he has to overcome many humiliations. In the seventeenth century, monarchs made their musicians eat with the serfs. In the eighteenth century, they were often obliged to wear the same attire as the valets. The best known example is the contract Haydn had to sign. He agreed to always appear before his duke properly shaved, and with his hands washed. This situation later improved somewhat, particularly because during the nineteenth century musicians in many European countries became state or city officials and enjoyed the same social esteem as other officials of the same rank and salary group.

2. The status given to musicians frequently reflects reasons other than their musicianship. In the past, clergy in oriental and Christian cultures primarily enjoyed high esteem because they belonged to the estate of the clergy. When music is upheld as an intrinsic value, then the musician is honored for his talent. Accordingly, since the eighteenth century we find members of the nobility and even royalty in intimate relationships with musicians. The culmination of this development may be found in the relationship between Franz Liszt (1811–1886) and certain rulers of the Romantic Age, and especially in the friendship between Richard Wagner and King Ludwig of Bavaria (1845–1886).

The high social status of many musicians is evidenced by the fact that since the eighteenth century, many monarchs have performed with professionals before their court and guests of high rank. Numerous chamber compositions have been expressly written for such occasions. Sometimes the monarch went even further, forming a small ensemble (incorporating his own servants), in which he himself played just one of the various parts. Another form of honoring musicians consists in giving them an honorary salary for life, but this gesture can be regarded as a form of almsgiving.

To be the recipient of an honorary Ph.D. from an European university was far more significant. This was a rarely granted honor, especially in countries such as Germany. Here, someone not descended from the nobility who wanted admission into higher society needed an esteemed title. In the Old World, the highest honor a musician could attain was to receive the rank of nobility. Sometimes outstanding scholars (especially university professors and poets) living at a monarch's court were made members of the nobility. Well-known examples are Johann Wolfgang von Goethe (1749–1832), Friedrich von Schiller (1759–1805), and Johann Gottfried von Herder (1744–1808) in the epoch of German classical literature. The significance of conferring nobility on a musician, poet, or scientist is easily understood. He was now able to have social relations with the members of court nobility, to eat at the monarch's table, and to be with him on various occasions. But musicians rarely received titles. It would be a mistake to believe that the musician has enjoyed great esteem among the ruling classes, even in occidental modern times. Nobility, army personnel, and the industrial class, which dominate many countries, consider musicians, even more than intellectuals, as "good-for-nothings." However, admiring success, they may distinguish between world-renowned stars and the unknown artist.

3. Almost every society has some instrument that "decent musicians" do not use, an instrument whose use denotes that the musician belongs to a lower, almost dishonorable, class of performers. Hindu districts designate a type of flute as being exclusively for the use of lower castes. In certain small states of ancient Greece, the flute, harp, and lute were for many generations only instruments for slaves and foreigners. Even in modern times, honorable city musicians were not supposed to use instruments such as the bagpipe, triangle, or drum. Yet, changing circumstances produced different attitudes. For instance, after the Persian wars in Greece the flute began to be appreciated, and its player considered a decent musician. The modern violin succeeded in being recognized as more than just one of many orchestral instruments only after a long struggle against the older, flat-backed violas.

Conversely, an instrument originally regarded as traditional, even aristocratic, may lose its esteem. Such changes occurred even in traditional cultures in relatively remote districts. Up to approximately A.D. 1100, the Welsh almost exclusively used horse manes for strings of their harps. As the more complicated Irish harp spread through Wales, their own instrument, formerly played even at the feudal courts, became regarded as out of fashion. It became the instrument of the lower classes, even of beggars.

There are corresponding examples in the centers of modern occidental music. The "marine trumpet" is a string instrument with a single string to be bowed. It is not a trumpet and has nothing to do with "marine," the French word for navy. This instrument was highly esteemed, especially in Catholic countries, where it formed an indispensable part of the music performed by nuns. This may also explain the origin of its name. It was probably the "trumpet of Mary," used during the veneration of the Madonna. Whatever the case, high ranking ladies did not consider it beneath their dignity to play this relatively simple instrument. However, toward the end of the eighteenth century, it completely lost its prestige and became an instrument used by itinerants and beggars. The same thing happened to the French *vieille,* flat-backed but bowed, one of the many forerunners of modern string instruments. Just one of many more possible examples might be mentioned. A kind of small harp held by the left arm against the shoulder was a generally accepted instrument in Austria from the time of the minnesingers until the eighteenth century, where it was overshadowed by the development of the big concert harp, played with the help of pedals. In Austria, the former became a well-known instrument of itinerant musicians, who performed in lower-middle- and upper-lower-class restaurants and inns.

In contrast, in some groups certain instruments were regarded as the province of socially superior individuals. The master drummer has a higher status than other musicians among certain American Indian and central African tribes. In various Hindu groups, the same was true of the small flute, an instrument played by blowing through the nose.

Such phenomena are not exclusively characteristic of primitive or Oriental societies, but can also be found in occidental cultures. In ancient Greece, the *lyra* and *kithara* were played by the upper classes. The same is true of the lute and the *portative* (the forerunner of the organ) in the Middle Ages. In modern times, the viola, harp, guitar, and kettle drum were prestigious instruments in some areas. In parts of seventeenth century Germany, only persons of especially high rank were allowed to own these instruments and to have them played at their residences. Through the present, the bagpiper in the Scottish army, and the kettle drummer in the British army, enjoy privileges other army personnel do not share.

The general trend in modern orchestras is to require of every musician that he be completely trained at his instrument. Accordingly, the differences between various instrumentalists are eliminated to some extent. Nevertheless, certain differences have been maintained. For instance, too many boys become double-bass players, some because of the fellowships offered. Sergey Kussevitsky (1874–1951), a poor boy who wished to become a professional musician, could only obtain a double-bass fellowship. After becoming one of the few double-bass virtuosos, he shifted to conducting.

Even more students shifted to the double bass or viola, especially in France, because they failed as cellists. Those who participated in the final contest at the state-supported Paris Conservatory had often failed the final contest a year or two earlier. In many countries elderly violinists often maintain their orchestra position only by shifting to viola. This phenomenon is related to the viola's relatively insignificant symphonic role in the works of Johann Sebastian Bach to middle Beethoven. Renowned musicians such as Mendelssohn, Joseph von Wasielewski (1822–1896), and Joseph Joachim protested against the low rating of the viola, but in vain. More recently, some expressionist and atonalist composers, specifically Paul Hindemith (1895–1963), a violist himself, felt the viola suited their musical intentions. Their compositions required better trained violists, and thus helped raise the instrument's status.

4. The prestige of the musicologist also has undergone changes. Formerly he was demeaned from two sides: The musician regarded him as a theoretician, and consequently as inferior, while the typical university professor in Central Europe considered him half a practicioner and therefore not a true scholar. For a long time, he could not attain the rank of full professor in German universities. Within Catholicism, however, musicology had always been held in high esteem. The Benedictine monks were considered illustrious musicological forerunners, so that the study of Gregorian music was cultivated in Catholic universities, such as Freiburg in Switzerland. The same was true of the Schola Cantorum in Paris, which identified with Catholicism.

Whether Catholic or not, musicology was revered, if at all, among musically conservative groups. An example is the Berlin Royal Academy of Music in the late nineteenth century. Such men as Heinrich De Ahna (1835–1892), Halir, Robert Hausmann (1852–1909), H. von Herzogenberg (1843–1900), Joachim, Rudorff, and Emanuel Wirth (1842–1923) taught there. Admirers of Brahms, they helped make him known by performing his chamber works, in collaboration with the Joachim quartet. They opposed Wagnerianism, considering it a radical musical upheaval. Hence, they insisted on the systematic cultivation of musicology, particularly the history of the music they considered essential for the practical musician. This emphasis was rejected by the more revolutionary elements. Some even felt that music historians impeded the independent development of gifted young musicians and protested the emphasis given to musicology in musical education.

5. The female private music teacher has generally not been highly esteemed. She has frequently been an old spinster, perhaps originally from a relatively well-to-do middle-class family, and trained in music as a young girl in order to be able to support herself by teaching privately in the event that she did not marry. Until recently, and particularly in Europe, teaching music was one of the few career possibilities for a middle-class woman, due to social stratification.

The male private teacher is generally in a more advantageous position, being better able to combine teaching with another job. In some of the more bureaucratically organized European countries, status was obtained through appointment to a stable position as a state or city official. However, even with such appointments, music teachers often had to struggle to enjoy the same social recognition as other teachers in the same institution. The voice teacher in a French or German high school was considered inferior to the Latin, Greek, mathematics, and natural science instructors. In Germany, only the collapse of the monarchy (1918) brought the change that provided the high school music teacher with the same salary and social rank as other teachers.

The music teacher in the United States is in a different situation, his functions being broader than those of music teachers in European high schools. He is supposed to be able to lead at least a band, even a symphony orchestra, and should be familiar with many different instruments.

Music teachers in institutions that train future professionals enjoy higher status than high school music teachers. As previously indicated, the teacher of musicology in continental European universities had a long struggle for recognition. Furthermore, in many European countries, professional musicians received their training in conservatories of music rather than in universities. Like instructors in, say, schools of forestry, agriculture, or engineering, instructors in musical academies were considered second rate, academically, by university professors.

In North American colleges and universities the difference between theoreticians and practicioners, and between the teachers of older and newer branches of knowledge, is much less pronounced than in Europe. Consequently, music teachers in the United States, theoreticians as well as singers and instrumentalists, enjoy similar perquisites and esteem as teachers of science or economics who hold identical academic rank. However, in the United States businessmen enjoy greater prestige than in countries with a bureaucratic tradition such as Austria, Germany, the Netherlands, and Switzerland. Conversely, American intellectuals with state positions share a much lower prestige than the corresponding European, who actually approached divinity in pre-Hitler Germany. This comparatively lower regard for university and college instructors of course applies also to music teachers in America.

6. When dealing with various types of music producers, we mentioned the important role played by the foreigner. Accordingly, we should now look at the circumstances under which the foreigner enjoys greater prestige than the native musician. First, there are situations where it is advantageous to be of foreign origin. Certain nations were and are so revered in the musical world that their musicians had an aura of superiority cast about them. From the Renaissance on, in Latin American musical life a musician almost had to be Italian, to the point that non-Italians often italianized their names. Germans have held a similar status in other countries since the classical period (especially since Wagner became inter-

nationally admired). Musicians of other nations have rarely been revered simply for their particular national heritage. England, the United States, and Latin America have tended to be the greatest admirers of foreign musicians, especially composers. German conductors have enjoyed the greatest universal admiration, especially since the eighteenth century. Instrumentalists enjoyed similar prestige. Orchestras in the United States list many Germans and Italians in their program notes. French graduates of the Paris conservatory are frequently employed as woodwind instrumentalists.

The United States has also greatly admired visiting Italian and German orchestras, theater companies, and opera ensembles, an admiration comparable only to that given the Russian ballet. In the opposite direction, American jazz and military bands, and more recently symphony orchestras perform abroad frequently under official auspices. The rejection of foreigners often also has its genesis in politics, a topic that will be examined in greater detail elsewhere.

ON CLASS AND RELIGIOUS
FACTORS IN MUSIC

To this day, musical performance in certain tribal groups is largely connected with magicoreligious events. Musical performance is frequently regarded as an expression of the entire tribe; nonparticipation by even a single individual is thought to greatly damage the group. In such settings, a separate audience does not exist; performers and listeners form a total unit. Examples have been found among various totemistic cultures, as well as among such social groups as the Dajaks in Southeast Asia, and certain Hindu groups.

This kind of musical performance disappears with increasing specialization and general differentiation of labor. Differentiation between performers and listeners becomes more distinct in two ways. Performers and audience become separate units, and eventually special musical performances are given for selected audiences, thus creating new and various kinds of social differentiation. If the music is largely religious and ritualistic, and if the entire society is stratified according to ritualistic principles, special kinds of music and performance are accessible only to privileged groups. Among Hindus, for example, music sometimes reflects social standing.

The growing cultural stress on rational processes produces changes in the structure of audiences. This is seen especially in the increasing importance of political groups, which follows the decline of religious feeling and ritualistic segregation. Subconsciously, feelings of status superiority may still exist among the social elite, but even in Hindu society traditions of social caste are no longer as dominant in structuring musical life. The history of occidental music offers many examples of such social differentiation. The music performed by the troubadours in southern France, by the *trouvères* in northern France, and by the *Minnesängers* in medieval Germany was exclusively court music. Occasionally an exceptionally gifted musician not of noble origin, such as Biterolf at the 13th century court of Herrmann of Thüringen, was admitted to a singing contest. However, the audience consisted entirely of nobles, who were invited by the monarch. Gradually, changes occurred as the bourgeoisie grew in wealth and power, and imitated many customs, including the musical customs, of the previous elite groups.

MUSIC AND SOCIAL RANK OF AUDIENCES

This process of musical acculturation evolved in various stages. It can be illustrated particularly well by the history of seating arrangements at musical events. Originally the citizens were satisfied to simply be admitted to a performance. But in some cases the monarch granted certain persons special seating (for instance, in a balcony) for performances given primarily for him and his court. The construcion of special boxes allowed the lower classes to attend the same musical events as the upper classes. Those who wished to be considered socially superior could be physically isolated from the lower classes, although they shared the same room. The development of segregated seating in concert and theater halls obviously had an additional advantage in Latin countries, where tradition requires the husband and father to protect his wife and daughters from contact with other men. Although this cultural requirement has disappeared in many places, its impact is still felt in the many countries where boxes are sold only as a whole, making it often impossible to buy tickets for single box seats.

In certain musical theaters, there were two kinds of boxes. The traditional boxes were open, so that the ladies seated there could see the performance and be seen themselves by the rest of the audience, a factor they often considered of major importance. The other type of theater box concealed its occupants by wooden fences from the rest of the audience. These boxes were bought for the evening, perhaps by a gentleman escorting a married woman who did not want to be seen with a handsome young bachelor, perhaps by a gentleman accompanied by a woman whose profession or relation to him would compromise him.

In the nineteenth century it became increasingly customary to open theaters and concert halls to everyone who bought a ticket. At the same time, there was a rather strong social differentiation of the types of musical productions, prices, and theaters, which made the outstanding concerts inaccessible to the masses.

MUSIC AND THE MASSES

Certain kinds of music are associated with the lower classes. First, there is traditional folk music, which originates in and largely corresponds to the wishes and sentiments of the uneducated classes; it is performed almost exclusively for them. Even the performers are sometimes socially differentiated from those playing for the higher strata. Examples are the low caste Hindu musicians, the minstrels and *jongleurs* in France, and the *Fahrende* in medieval Germany. Some forms of comic plays that employ dialect songs and marionette theaters are survivals of this kind of lower-class art. With increasing rationalization of life and growing rationalization of art, these socially limited forms disappear. A new situation tends to arise, consisting of highly specialized art for the upper and middle classes, unrelated to the life of the masses.

It was under such circumstances that benevolent monarchs and especially democratically minded members of the middle class explored ways to bring the masses into direct contact with the culture and art of the middle class and the intellectuals. Popular theater groups, or concerts for the performance of musical compositions that originated in and were expressive of the higher classes, were organized and offered to the lower classes at very low prices. In this way, these compositions were made accessible to a wide audience, or were even made available to everyone by waiving admission fees. One example was found in Paris on the French national holiday, when the major state-supported theaters performed classical operas and dramas, and offered free tickets to all. Anyone who had the time and the patience to stand on the ticket line the evening before could see the performance. Similar attempts have been made in other countries, mainly since the end of the nineteenth century.

The culmination of mass art is represented by three recent inventions—movies, radio, and television. One reason these innovations spread so rapidly is that, despite their geographic locations and unlike other epochs, so many people presently share a variety of interests. It thus becomes economically advantageous to produce motion pictures, radio sketches, and television programs for the masses, despite tremendously high expenses.

However, differing religious and political convictions have produced opposing attitudes within and concerning the mass media. It is either argued that one cannot suddenly introduce cultural works to a group that lacks the background for their appreciation; or that even if the intentions of the sponsoring organizations are good, the entire style of presenting cultural works constitutes a condescending form of almsgiving; or the structure of the audience is debated. Persons familiar with the history of theater and music increasingly point out that the traditional unity of performers and audiences, based on common destiny, beliefs, and values, disappeared once the theater was opened to everyone. With this development, the only things listeners had in common were the ability to pay the same prices for tickets or a receiving apparatus, or sufficient time to wait for tickets to free performances.

ORGANIZATION AND MAKEUP OF AUDIENCES

This opposition did not stop with theoretical protests, but led to new kinds of theater. Mostly in Germany, but later also in neighboring countries, *Weltanschauung* (ideological) theaters appeared. For example, a Catholic theater consumer organization brought together members of the faith. The plays produced were often written and performed by Catholics, and were expressive of their religion. An example of similar structure, but based on a different philosophy, is the *Freie Volksbühne* (Free People's Theater). Originating in Berlin with the development of naturalistic drama, it leaned more and more toward socialism, and after World War I became increasingly a socialist theater consumer organization. Similar attempts, based on somewhat nationalistic concepts, prepared the way for the Nazi theater, which will be described later. The Communist attempt to propagate proletarian collectivity and culture in the German Republic is merely an extension of the direction of Soviet theater.

Whatever philosophic differences exist between various religions and political ideologies, their theater groups have one thing in common that distinguishes them from nineteenth and early twentieth century occidental theater and concert practice. They expect their audiences to be more than simply a number of persons who happen to be there that evening; they gather an audience united by a common philosophy of life, as in the Orient, in Greek antiquity, and during the Christian Middle Ages.

Some other forms of specialized audiences may be briefly mentioned. Wherever males enjoy special privileges, forms of music production for their exclusive enjoyment regularly exist. In the less complex cultures, magical elements are supposed to be involved in certain musical productions; special taboos that prevent women from participation in public affairs are also applied in this area. But where wives and unmarried daughters are supposed to be protected by their husbands and fathers against outside influences a double standard is practiced. Many practices strictly forbidden for women are permitted for men. For example, men of the upper and middle classes may visit variety and vaudeville theaters but their women may not. The composition of the audience clearly is of importance because it modifies the program. Jokes are male oriented. The program of the comic singer, especially the *diseuse* or the *chansonette* often reflects such a double standard.

Some musical forms, such as those employed in convents, are performed exclusively for women. The female branch of the Carmelites, especially the order established by Saint Theresa of Avila, represented the peak of this kind of music. A few other examples may be mentioned. In Turkey before World War I, Moslem women were not permitted to be present at entertainments performed for their husbands. However, postwar modernization produced certain concessions. Occasionally concerts of occidental music were first performed in Constantinople only for men, but were then repeated for an exclusively female audience.

Wherever formal education has existed, some kind of music has been performed either exclusively or primarily for children. Some of the choral and orchestral music performed by children and adolescents was performed mainly for the glorification of their school, as well as for the entertainment of other children. Similarly, the use of local dialects in puppet and marionette theaters appeals to children. Frequently, the plays used in these contexts are centuries old, as are the French *guignol* and the *Kölner Hanneschen* (the Cologne Little Johnny) theater. For centuries the latter traveled in the cities of the Catholic Rhine province, from one local fair to another.

The Southern German *Kasperle* traveled primarily in various Protestant districts of Germany, and indirectly influenced world literature and music. A poor itinerant puppeteer once performed in Frankfurt during the first half of the eighteenth century. A ten-year-old boy asked his father for pennies in order to see this play. He was so impressed that he never forgot the plot. He thought about it for seventy years. When he was eighty, he finished his own version. The little boy was none other than Goethe, and the drama written under the impulse of his youthful impression was *Faust*. Goethe's *Faust* became in turn the basis of all the operas, oratorios, and symphonies that made the Faustian destiny their essential theme. Among the better known are the opera by Gounod, an oratorio *The Damnation of Faust* by Hector Berlioz, and a *Faust* symphony by Franz Liszt.

To round out our discussion of the organization of audiences, a few words should be added concerning audience attitude and behavior during performances. Through this perspective, one can gain some insight concerning the relationship between performer and public, and consequently, the relative esteem enjoyed by the performer. During the classic period of Italian opera, and especially in the eighteenth century, it was customary to use one's opera box as a dining room during the opera performance. The eating may only have been interrupted when a popular singer performed a difficult aria. As the solo ended, and as soon as the dialogue resumed on stage, the spectators resumed their meals or conversations with relatives or friends. Visiting of other boxes also took place during the performance. This custom persisted even in the Grand Opera House in Paris during the nineteenth century. These and similar habits demonstrate the high interest in the performance of difficult solo arias, and the lack of importance attributed to dialogue, which actually contained the dramatic plot of the opera.

RELIGIOUS FACTORS

In many preliterate cultures, every kind of worship is connected with music, which is regarded as one of the essential conjurational means. An analysis of musical practices among the more complex religions and their surrounding literary cultures may best proceed by distinguishing between the essential kinds of music that are either permitted or forbidden. Normally, singing is not strongly opposed. Among the ancient Hebrews, an antiphony existed between the priest and the responding congregation. In this and similar cases, the essential variable becomes the role the congregation is expected to play within the antiphonal singing.

Changes in this role can be noticed in Christian practices. While the early Christians responded to the priests' recitations, singing increasingly became the function of the priest or of a choir during the Middle Ages. In the later Middle Ages, the reform movements that protested against the wealth of the church hierarchy insisted on the participation of the whole congregation in church singing. These demands were voiced by the Bohemian Hussites and to an even larger extent by other Protestant groups. Martin Luther (1483–1546) was musically inclined. He played the lute, sang every morning with his family, and considered congregational singing essential. Nor did Calvinism prohibit congregational singing; rather, it restricted the number of songs permitted during a service. One of the more extreme examples of such musical restriction may be found in the Christian Reform Church of the Dutch in the United States, which allows the singing of psalms only. This restriction is not based on opposition to congregational participation, but on a belief that hymns are too secular in character. Some textual restrictions exist among other Protestant denominations, but not against congregational singing itself.

Modern Catholicism was placed in an ambivalent position concerning the use of hymns in its liturgy. Through the Protestant movement, congregational singing had become very popular, so that Catholic worshippers also requested it. However, there was a tradition of small trained choirs singing the Ordinary in Latin during the High Mass. At the end of the eighteenth century, some leading Catholic bishops, influenced by ideas originating in Protestantism or the Enlightenment, introduced congregational singing into every kind of worship, including High Mass. This practice was gradually eliminated, and at present, the High Mass in Latin is sung almost everywhere by a trained choir. Congregational singing during Low Mass, however, continues in many countries, and is also found in some Sunday afternoon and evening liturgies.

In addition to congregational singing, special church choirs composed of members with some musical training exist almost everywhere in Christianity. We find them among the early Christians, in the cathedral of the medieval bishop, and even more so in the monasteries and convents of all orders, including the Benedictines and the mendicant orders of the Dominicans and Franciscans. The reform of church music during the Counterreformation (dating from Pope Marcellus) and the masses of composers such as Palestrina (1525?–1594) make such choirs indispensable. Accordingly, they have continued within Catholicism up to the present time.

Of all Protestant denominations, the Church of England retained the greatest part of the Catholic liturgy in its services. Accordingly, Episcopalians have cultivated church choirs, as have Lutherans. Calvinists experienced some conflicts on this issue. Choir singing presupposes the acceptance and cultivation of more complex forms of music, yet the true Calvinist considered these too secular. Accordingly, different attitudes exist to this day among the various Calvinistic sects. The same is true of several of the other Anglo-American Protestant denominations.

VARIATIONS IN THE USE OF INSTRUMENTS

Within religious services, the use of the organ must be distinguished from that of other instruments. We generally ascribe an especially religious character to the pipe organ, associating it mainly with church music. The organ has, however, played different roles in the history of music. Apparently it already existed in pre-Christian Rome. In the Byzantine Empire, at the Constantinople court of the emperor, it was used as a secular instrument to provide dinner music. Yet in Europe, especially under the protection of Charlemagne (742–814) and Benedictine monasteries, it became the principal religious instrument, and has remained so up to the present. Since the Reformation, Lutherans particularly have regarded it as the instrument characteristic of their faith. Wherever there are Lutheran groups, they will establish organizations to promote pipe organs. In the United States, organ music appeared largely through the influence of German and, to a lesser extent, Scandinavian and Finnish Lutherans. Other Protestant groups followed slowly. Some extremely zealous Calvinists and Anabaptists still exclude organ music from their religious services.

The history of other instruments within the church is far more complex. There is evidence that the western Asiatic Semitic peoples, among them the Phoenicians, neighbors of the ancient Hebrews, used percussion instruments in religious worship. Apparently, this is one of the reasons why the Hebrews increasingly eliminated the use of such instruments from their worship. Percussion instruments were identified with the religion of polytheists. Accordingly, later orthodox Judaism only used the shofar in temple worship. This primitive wind instrument is played on special holidays in memory of life in Palestine.

The situation is even more complicated in the Islamic religion, partly because of the greater cultural complexity of Moslem countries. Moslem religion originated in animal husbandry and nomadic life. Soon, and to a larger extent than occidental Christianity, it had to face the problem of invasion of cultural elements from ancient Greece. Consequently the attitude toward music in general, and the use of instruments in particular, was a changing and antagonistic one. Mohammed, as well as the older caliphs up to Ali, had forbidden the use of instruments in religious worship. Later the Arabs became familiar with the Greek author Aristoxenus of Tarentum and his musicotheoretical writings. These writings provided an impulse for further developments in musical theory. Moslems also became interested in physics, geometry, and acoustics through various sources. From a combination of all these elements, new and more complex instruments were developed, and originally used for secular purposes. But it became increasingly difficult to prevent their employment in the religious sphere, and although the theologians protested, the Abbassides permitted and even encouraged the use of such instruments in religious services within the mosque.

Analogous to developments among Moslems, strongly antagonistic concepts regarding the use of instruments in church developed in the Christian world. Some of the church fathers, such as Clement of Alexandria and Ambrosius, voiced strong opposition. Division among the Christian churches was connected with struggles concerning the definitions of the divinity and personality of Jesus. But this difference of opinion was not restricted to the followers of the pope. The Eastern church also debated the question; the Syrian Jacobites and Nestorians were especially strong adversaries of the use of instruments in church services. Other Eastern churches, although not as extreme, never tolerated more than very simple rhythmical accompaniments. The attitude of the Greek branch within the earlier Byzantine Empire was not entirely homogeneous. Many monasteries were rigorously opposed, while the emperor and many bishops and priests connected with his court did favor the use of instruments in church. The use of instruments was more favored by the Western theologians than by Eastern. Various popes, especially Benedictine popes, always produced and fostered music.

Musical instruments were probably much used for Western religious services during the Middle Ages. Again and again bishops elaborated synods and regulations forbidding the abuse of music, which suggests that music was customarily used in church services—if such customs did not exist, it would hardly have been necessary to protest so often against too great a use of them. In modern times the antagonism appearing within Catholicism was even greater. It should be remembered that the strict reformers of the Couner Reformation tried to eliminate everything the Catholic Church had borrowed from the Italian Renaissance and incorporated into the church. The attack against the use of instruments during the Mass was rigorous. Nevertheless, change occurred. During the seventeenth and eighteenth centuries, Catholicism lost much of the severity that had resulted from the Counter Reformation. Bishops from highly placed families often lived very secular lives. They were often major patrons of music, and used their great cathedral orchestras to embellish the celebration of Mass. They commissioned many great Masses written for large choirs with soloists and even with complete symphony orchestra accompaniment. Best known among these compositions are the Masses of Mozart, Haydn, and Beethoven.

The Ordinary, with prayers such as the Kyrie, Sanctus, and Agnus Dei, offers the composer an opportunity to demonstrate his ability to write for a large orchestra or to compose complicated coloratura arias. Because these prayers then became complex and repetitive and required much time to perform, it became necessary to provide a seat for the celebrating priest during the performance. This resulted in interruptions of the celebration of the Mass, the essential aspect of worship. For this reason, elaborate church music was opposed during the entire nineteenth and early twentieth centuries within various dioceses in Austria and Bavaria. Among the most successful of the opposition groups were various associations dedicated to St. Cecilia, which insisted on a return to simplicity and on the subordination of music to the religious aim. Finally, they were successful. Pope Pius X (1835–1914), representing an increasing rigor, insisted that the Mass be celebrated in such a way that neither the music nor other aesthetic elements would be predominant. Consequently, the use of instruments in Catholic churches was reduced.

This account of internal differences would be incomplete if we neglected the so-called "Liturgy Movement" in German Catholicism, which is connected both with Benedictine tradition and with a branch of the German Youth Movement. The German Youth Movement, which emphasized primary, personal relationships, regarded the Catholic liturgy as conducive to the promotion of such relationships and of feelings of Christian collectivity among the parishioners. They asserted that the altar should be placed in closer proximity to the congregation, and that the priest should celebrate Mass facing the congregation, so that the people could participate more directly in the celebration of the Mass and in the appropriate prayers. They also felt that the congregation, instead of saying their rosaries or other prayers, should be introduced to prayers more relevant to the celebration of the Mass. The idea of simplifying the liturgical music of the Mass again reappeared in connection with these discussions, sometimes it was claimed that the few instruments employed by the German Youth Movement (plucked instruments) should be used within the church. Although this movement found much support and sympathy among non-Catholics interested in these new forms of music, it was not in general very successful within the Church.

There were corresponding conflicts within Protestantism. Martin Luther, himself a musician, was not opposed to the use of instruments in religious worship, and therefore they are used in Lutheran churches. The best known examples are the oratorios and passions composed and performed by Johann Sebastian Bach, where a few instruments or even a complete orchestra joined the organ. Bach's Passions, as well as most cantatas, were originally composed for the worship service. Later, the Lutherans organized separate religious concerts in addition to the regular morning worship, in which the sermon was the essential aspect. These religious concerts, performed in the church at other hours, will be discussed more fully later. This development actually diminished the use of instruments within the main form of worship. Calvinism, as already mentioned, was almost always radically opposed to any use of instruments.

The use of instruments in Protestant revivalism needs special attention. We cannot, of course, give here a complete account of different developments of revivalism, but only discuss a few characteristic traits. In every institutionalized religion, there is a tendency to protest emotionally from time to time against increasing rationalization. Within Protestantism, the movement of Pietism is exemplary. Pietism started within Calvinism, shifted to Lutheranism, and was antithetical for a long time to dominant

Protestant orthodoxism. Later, however, Pietism formed an alliance with the orthodox group against the common enemy, Enlightenment. Although it apparently disappeared at the end of the eighteenth century, it resurfaced in the form of a powerful popular movement during and after the Napoleonic war. The more the intellectuals in non-Catholic countries shift to liberal theology or agnosticism, the more revivalist movements try to win over the masses, especially in the big cities and when the masses themselves move toward agnosticism or socialism.

Dominant groups and persons within Protestantism do not always protect or support such revivalistic movements, which is one of the reasons for splits and the formation of sectarian groups with pronounced emotional characteristics. The most successful of these is the Salvation Army, which exhibits certain Methodist influences. Musically speaking, these emotional movements place great emphasis on both congregational singing and the use of brass instruments. Trombone choirs or complete brass orchestras are used in the big revival meetings held in tents, large barracks, or even on the streets of large cities. Institutionized churches sometimes feel endangered by the appeal of these competitors, and counter with their own trombone choirs and brass orchestras.

Instruments were also employed in the religious mystery play, a form that existed widely in the Orient. Hinduism and some late forms of Buddhism employed it during festivals and pilgrimages. Music was a regular feature of these plays. The origin of Greek tragedy should also be noted. The cult of Mother Earth, of her son Dionysus, and of related phenomena, was built around religious plays with rhythmical musical accompaniment as a part of the whole worship. There is little evidence of such performances in Greek Orthodoxism, but much in Western Christianity. During the Middle Ages mystery plays were performed in the open air with rhythmical accompaniments. These performances formed part of the festivals for the glorification of a saint to whom a cathedral was dedicated, or whose shrine attracted pilgrims. Increasing interest in mysticism, fostered by Francis of Assisi (1182–1226) and his Franciscan order, also furthered the development of mystery plays. There is evidence that they could be found in remote districts in France in the seventeenth century. In Brittany they were performed in the native Celtic language up to recent times.

Organization of Religious Concerts

The early forerunner of the church concert may date back to the late Middle Ages, but it appears clearly as a consciously practiced form in the Catholic Counter Reformation in Italy. Philip Neri (1515–1595), whom we will meet again in connection with oratorios, together with members of his congregation, the Oratorians, built a music hall separate from their church and monastery. This hall was used to perform religious music outside of and different from the celebration of Mass, but these performances were nevertheless considered essentially religious. The extent to which the oratorio, with its various solo singers, originated from this practice has been explained elsewhere. Beginning in the seventeenth century, oratorios became a primarily Lutheran form of religious music, along with the church concert. The Lutheran church organist Dietrich Buxtehude (1637–1707) was one of the earliest to organize evening music services. His were held in the major Lutheran church building in the northern German city of Lübeck. His example was increasingly imitated by other Lutheran congregations. Many of the compositions of Bach and some of his sons were written for these occasions.

Gradually, as religious interest decreased, these performances became primarily aesthetic in nature. As a consequence, persons uninvolved with the religious content and intention of the music increasingly enjoyed such church concerts. By the later nineteenth century it often became difficult to classify such musical performances as religious; they were intended for a public that was supposed to buy tickets. Next to Lutheran churches, this kind of concert found favor in Episcopal churches. The religious mentality of the New England colonies was largely informed by the Calvinist and the Anabaptist traditions. This is, of course, one of the principal reasons why this form of church sponsored musical production developed so slowly in the United States.

Unlike oriental religions excepting early Buddhism and Jainism, the dance has been the least used of all kinds of musical performances in Christian worship. We have evidence that the ancient Hebrews performed religious dances in connection with some prophetic, emotional movements, as did the Chasidic Jews in the former Polish providences of Podolia and Walhynia. Within the Christian world only two similar examples can be cited: the dance of the priests during Mass in the ancient Ethiopian Coptic church, and the rhythmical dance performed by boys within the church in a few districts of Spain.

Language Differences of Religious Groups

The language used in religious singing is not a problem of major significance in non-Christian religions. Some later forms of Buddhism maintained Sanskrit as their sacred language long after it had been out of everyday use. The Parsees in southwest India and the remnants of the old Zoroastrian religion of Persia preserved their old Persian sacred language, which could only be understood by the learned priests.

Within Christianity, however, question of language is complicated. The Eastern churches celebrated the Mass and other liturgies in their native langues, such as Armenian, Syrian, and Ethiopian. But here too, the language used in everyday life changed, while the Church language remained stable, becoming a dead language understood only by the clergy. Where members of the clergy were isolated and became largely illiterate, even they could no longer comprehend the words used in ritual singing. Such situations gave rise to a peculiar problem. Since the days of the Crusades, Roman Catholicism had sometimes succeeded in bringing into contact with Rome at least parts of these national churches, where they were sometimes willing to reject their theory about the essence of Jesus and recognize the supremacy of the Pope. The latter would then grant them some concessions, among them the continuance of married priests and their traditional national liturgy. This liturgy usually was very popular, and its elimination would have threatened unification. Since the Crusades, therefore, individuals known as Uniates, who represent more than twenty different groups, although officially Roman Catholic, celebrate the Mass and other services in their traditional languages, some of which are old forms of Semitic or Indo-European language. They also retain their traditional music, which in part may be even older than the Gregorian chant of Roman Catholicism.

Concerning Greek Orthodox church music, complete uniformity of language doesn't exist. The Greek people to this day widely speak medieval Greek, which is quite different from ancient classic Greek. The majority of Slavic-speaking Eastern Europeans use Old Slavonic Church language. There are varying opinions concerning its origin. Old Slavonic is the language used by Cyril and Methodius when they translated parts of the Bible. They used these translations in missionary work north of the Byzantine Empire, among the people now known as Bulgarians. Slovanians. and Slovaks. In addition to the groups discussed earlier, some Greek Orthodox groups also joined Rome, and are also Uniates. The Church of Rome extended the same concessions to them regarding married priests, and continuance of their own traditional liturgy and music. Otherwise, with the exception of the words of the Kyrie eleison, Latin was used exclusively in the Roman Mass and all other celebrations until quite recently (to the mid-1960s).

The Protestant Reformation, in its opposition to Roman Catholicism, insisted on the use of the vernacular. For some time it looked as if the Roman church would make concessions toward singing in the native language, a practice that had rapidly become popular under the influence of Luther, John Calvin (1509–1564), and other reformers. However, as with other expressions of religious life, Rome insisted on maintaining Latin as an expression of the universality of the Church.

Organized opposition to the use of Latin arose again, especially at the turn of the eighteenth century. This protest came during a time when the papacy was relatively weak, and during which there was an increasing tendency to subject Catholicism to the control of absolute monarchs and more or less enlightened political governments. An attempt was also made to establish national branches of the Catholic church. This movement was especially hostile to the Jesuits, whose loyalty to the Pope and concepts concerning the use of sacraments were strongly disliked by the nationalistic Church disciples of the Enlightenment philosophers.

There were many adherents to the proposition that religious ceremonies, including the singing of High Mass, should use the vernacular. The Holy Roman Emperor, Joseph II and certain monarchs in Baden, Württemberg, and other German territories especially favored such a change. Among the bishops and theologians who insisted on the use of German in the celebration of High Mass, and who edited corresponding song books, Karl van Dalberg (1744–1817), Ignaz von Wessenberg (1744–1860), and Andreas Workmeister (1645–1706) became especially well known. However, by the convergence of various political and religious factors, the power of the Pope again increased rapidly a short time after the collapse of the Napoleonic Empire. The Society of Jesus, which had been abolished in the latter part of the eighteenth century, was reestablished. Movements in favor of a national and anti-Pope Catholicism declined rapidly, and attempts to have Mass sung in the vernacular were unsuccessful.

After 1870, the year in which the Vatican Council approved the doctrine of papal infallibility, there was a small-scale resurgence of singing in popular, national languages. Although the majority of Catholics accepted the new doctrine, small minorities influenced by certain priests and other intellectuals rejected it. They organized national Catholic bodies and called themselves Old Catholics or Christian Catholics. Such groups were created and remain in existence mainly in Germany, Switzerland, and Austria; more recently, they can be found in Czechoslovakia and even in the United States. All of them reintroduced national languages into their religious life.

Almost the entire spectrum of Protestantism eliminated Latin from its religious singing. The Episcopal ritual maintained some Catholic forms, and to a lesser extent there are Catholic survivals in some Lutheran districts. Some Lutheran groups retained the celebration of the Mass without Transubstantiation, which Catholicism regards as the most essential part. Thus altered, the Latin text for singing the Mass continued in use in some Lutheran congregations, at least up to the beginning of the eighteenth century. J. S. Bach's *Mass in B Minor* is an example of a composition not widely used in Catholic liturgy for this reason.

Parareligious Groups

Our survey of music and religious groups would be incomplete if we did not consider briefly some groups that fulfill functions generally met by religious organizations. Beginning in the eighteenth century, Masonic lodges became increasingly powerful in many countries. Often, as in the United States, they reflected conservative or upper-middle-class interests. In France and in other Latin countries of strong Catholic background, they represented the core of the anti-Catholic body politic. By being socially identified, they frequently influenced politics, public opinion, and culture, as well as musical life. Moreover, in some countries where Enlightenment and Catholicism combined, some Catholic believers, including priests, joined a Masonic lodge in the latter part of the eighteenth century. A notable example was Austria, where the combination strongly affected classical music. Mozart's opera, *The Magic Flute,* is perhaps the best known example of a blend of Masonic and Catholic ideas, as seen in the bass arias of Sarastro. Supposedly an Egyptian priest, Sarastro actually represents the Masonic order.

This blending of Catholic and Masonic ideas did not flourish for long. After the collapse of the Napoleonic Empire, Catholicism increased in power again and strongly opposed any connection with Masonic lodges. Nevertheless, the influence of the Masons on musical life did not cease. Like many institutions that have a basic philosophy, the Masons express themselves through collective singing. The majority of lodges are almost exclusively associations of men. While a number of compositions exclusively for male voices did exist, these were primarily religious, composed to be sung by monks in their monastery. Other vocal compositions were military or other patriotic songs. Accordingly, it was necessary to compose new works for the use in Masonic conventions and festivals, and the Masons thus represented an essential impetus toward composition for male choirs. Even in North America, and as early as the colonial period, Masonic choirs sometimes appeared before larger public audiences.

For similar reasons, other social movements and groups following some secular ethic sometimes felt obligated to write music or to order the composition of choral works for their own special use. Like the Masons, these groups are closely related to the deistic philosophy of the late seventeenth and eighteenth centuries, which was based in the theories of Locke (1632–1704), Voltaire (1694–1778), and similar optimistic believers in man's capacity to obtain truth without the help of revelations, sacred books, or church authorities. Deism had been the basic conviction of leading intellectuals during the French Revolution, who also wanted musical manifestation of this basic belief. Hymns composed to celebrate the memory of Bastille Day (July 14) clearly denote this attitude.

Similar developments can be observed in socialist music of the early nineteenth century. The followers of Saint-Simon (1760–1825), the Saint-Simonists, who shifted far away from the original concept of their master and considered themselves a new mystical religious group, wanted to celebrate their concept of a new humanity. Some of their members wrote choral works or commissioned works to be performed at their meetings. Saint-Simonism did not last long, however; the police dissolved the movement in France. Socialists, especially the workers, moved away from the theories of Saint-Simon and his adherents and embraced Marxism to a large extent. Communities that followed either the systems of the early French or English socialists such as Charles Fourier (1772–1837), Victor Considérant (1808–1893), and Robert Owen (1771–1858), or the ideas of some emotional Protestant movements that advocated the shift from private property to collective ownership, were founded. Some of these groups composed and performed their own music, which disappeared with these communities.

The positivistic philosophy of Auguste Comte (1798–1857) is closely related to the ideas of the French socialists. In his later work he proposed a religious cult to humanity-as-such, or to what he called "the Great Being." This positivism produced musical associations in France and elsewhere known as "positivistic associations" or "Auguste Comte associations."

These examples all represent a metaphysical shift from Christian fundamentalism, a shift that is apparent even when such groups included an element of new mysticism in their beliefs. Examples representing an even stronger shift to mysticism can be cited, along with examples of an increasing emphasis on rationalism and intellectualism within religion. The former are seen in those associations or lodges that contain old oriental elements, as the Mazdasnan group, which claims to represent an uninterrupted, continuing rejuvenation of Persian Zoroastrianism. Since the end of World War I it has found more and more adherents in the Old World as well as in Los Angeles and other American cities. Other groups of this type are the Theosophical Association and its splinter group, the Anthroposophical Society. The latter, founded by Rudolpf Steiner (1861–1925), tried increasingly to synthesize old Hindu belief with Christian elements. A former Protestant minister, Friedrich Rittelmeyer (1872–1938), joined this group, and insisted on the elaboration of a new ritualistic music adapted to the basic Hindu and Christian beliefs of this group.

Liberal Protestantism, in the European sense of the word, represents the increasing emphasis on rationalism in religion. Although the entire history of its development cannot be sketched here, we might mention its basic conviction, which originated during the Enlightenment. The Bible must be treated from the same philological and historical critical perspective scholars use to examine the sources of other religions. It is held, moreover, that such criticisms will not harm religion, but to the contrary will purify it from many elements that damage true religious feeling. Gradually, such a critical approach concerning the Bible did develop and enter the universities, including divinity schools in Germany, Switzerland, and, to a lesser extent, the Calvinistic Netherlands. As the phenomenon of liberal Protestantism is often of an intellectual and even rationalistic nature, it usually did not become the religious belief of the masses. Nevertheless, in some parts of Germany it did spread to larger groups within the established state church, including the ministry. Sometimes the wish for corresponding musical manifestations arose. The best known composer of such music is the German August Bungert (1845–1915).

In the United States more so than elsewhere, Protestant churches had taken on characteristics of social clubs, and the interest and antagonism surrounding various concepts of the Bible and of theology did not come to the fore as in Germany, Switzerland, and the Netherlands. Thus, while many denominations had conservative and liberal branches, the need for special musical expression of either viewpoint did not arise. The Pilgrims' Hymnal is one of the few known examples of musical compositions expressing a nonfundamentalist Protestant concept. This hymnal, composed for and adopted by the more liberal branch of the Congregationalists, is partially explained by the nonfundamentalist stress of certain Congregationalist groups. These groups had to struggle against the more conservative elements within their own denomination, however.

POLITICAL USES OF MUSIC

The use of music by antireligious associations should also be mentioned. During the French Revolution, increasing antireligious feeling manifested itself in the production of various operas, among them *Tarare* by Antonio Salieri (1750–1825), in which a member of the lower class struggles successfully against the priests. Another work of the same genre is *Les Rigueurs du Cloître* by François Berton (1784–1832). The title itself suggests disdain for the monastery, monks, and nuns. Some skits combined with music were sponsored and produced by the Soviets under Lenin with the intention of ridiculing the Greek Orthodox Church.

The state is second only to religious organizations in the sponsorship of music. Sponsorship can occur in two forms: The state financially aids an orchestra or theater that is not itself a state institution, or the music-performing body and its members are under direct state control and form a part of the state administration. The first way is often characteristic of periods of transition. Something originally of a private nature is unable to maintain its independence, so that some government body has to interfere. This situation has existed not only in Europe but very often in the United States, Latin America, and Australia. The second form goes back to ancient oriental societies, as in China and Korea. The performance of classical Greek tragedy was also sometimes accomplished as a function of the state. However, state sponsorship is now most frequent in modern Western and Central Europe and is a reflection of the general trend that characterizes these areas. Both conservatives and liberals encourage the elimination of private enterprise in various spheres of cultural life. Thus, large-scale music production increasingly came under state control, beginning in the 1880s. This trend, of course, coincided with the fact that modern symphony orchestras and opera ensembles have become so expensive that it is often necessary to free them from purely commercial viewpoints if compositions are to be performed according to the desires of their composers. The increasing possibility of unemployment among instrumentalists and singers who, afraid to be out of work, prefer to become civil service employees, supports this development. Their salaries may be lower than those privately employed, but they are guaranteed economic security. This applies particularly to pension privileges, which are especially important for a singer, who can easily lose his voice.

The two Paris opera companies, the Grand Opéra and the Opéra-Comique, are both state institutions. State control of opera is even more evident in Germany. With the exception of Hitler's period of power, Germany has been divided into many semisovereign states, originally monarchies, later republics, then *Länder*. The shift of the theater from a semiprivate affair of the monarch to the state-supported opera house had already occurred in the Bismarckian and Wilhelmian Empire. During the years of the Weimar Republic, this trend continued; consequently, even relatively small cities that formerly had been capitals of some of these small monarchies had relatively large state-supported theaters, including opera ensembles. In general, these state theaters were not dominated by a commercial attitude and enjoyed great artistic independence. In this respect, they differ from the theaters that formed a part of the state administration in the totalitarian systems of the Nazis or the Soviets, which employed theater as one of the many means of indoctrination.

Besides the state government, the community as a political subunit must be considered. This development largely parallels, and for similar reasons, the development of the state-supported and state-controlled theater. Groups of amateur instrumentalists often were at first partly supported by city money. Frequently an orchestra of instrumentalists who had other work as the main source of their income also received a small salary from the city. Finally, the city orchestra arose; nearly all its performers were city officials on a full-time, permanent basis. Some might receive a somewhat higher salary and formally teach instrumental music in a city-supported music academy.

The development of the city theater is somewhat more complex and gradual. It originated in Italian cities, in the form of an itinerant or stable group receiving permission to perform their opera or play in the town hall. Later, in Germany, cities owned theater buildings and appointed city theater directors. To some extent, such a director was an entrepreneur, but he was limited by a contract with the city which prevented him from determining the program or hiring special artists. The city theater originated directly from this semidependent situation. The director, as well as artists and workers of almost all kinds, were city officials who received their salary with precisely fixed rates as to paid vacations, insurance, and pensions. Theoretically, they were under the control of the city administration of the lord mayor, who acted in agreement with the city council. In actuality, they were under control of a committee, composed in proportion to the strength of the political parties represented in the town council. This committee would serve under the chairmanship of a representative of the lord mayor. Such a chairman often had other special institutions under his administration.

ON MUSIC, MUSICIANS
AND SPONSORSHIP

There are undoubtedly significant relationships between the social positions of practicing musicians and their audiences, on the one hand, and the musical characteristics of a given social milieu on the other. The rather complex relationship between sponsors and creative musicians needs detailed examination, as it tends to be quite influential in shaping the music of a given people and period. The musical attitudes and expectations of sponsors are largely shaped by popular concepts. It is often difficult to ascertain whether an individual is following his own taste or the views promulgated by an institutionalized sector of cultural life, such as a group organized to sponsor musical performances. In spite of this difficulty, the perspectives and musical ideas of individuals and those of organized groups must be analytically separated.

INFLUENCE OF RELIGIOUS LEADERS

Individuals who influence musical life must be of a social position that allows them not only to have musical preferences of their own, but to see them realized as well. Throughout history, such individuals have been often connected with religious institutions. Certainly this applies to the pope. Many popes during the Italian Renaissance liked and sponsored particular types of instrumental and vocal music. As theological changes occurred, and with the increasing power of the Catholic Counter Reformation, these compositions were considered too secular by later popes. An important example is Pope Marcellus, the first representative of the rigorous reform movement within the Catholic church. He made no concessions to Protestantism regarding its demands for changes in the hierarchy; instead, he published the various reform measures of his precursor and eliminated secularism from the church. The reorganization of the music of the Mass and the composition of nonsecular Mass music such as that by Palestrina was largely a product of this shift. Such changes were not however exclusively the result of one individual's influence; just as often they were instigated by a powerful group. Whatever the case, individual taste remained an important factor, and during the seventeenth and eighteenth centuries many cardinals and bishops commissioned compositions and performances that corresponded to their own personal taste. After the Counter Reformation the power of the pope had again decreased, even within the Catholic world, and bishops of noble origin tended to go their own way, usually under the protection of their monarch.

INFLUENCE OF ROYALTY

Monarchs in ancient China, Korea, Japan, Assyria, and in certain medieval Mohammedan states often interfered in the sphere of music. The occidental medieval Christian monarch, whose power was far more restricted by clergy and nobility, found his individual taste of less consequence. Even the so-called absolute monarch of relatively recent times was not completely independent, but rather limited by the power of his own trained and specialized bureaucrats. They usually allowed the monarch his musical preferences, however, since music was regarded as unrelated to politics. Consequently, the monarch's taste often dictated musical style. Such was the case at the imperial Viennese court, the French courts in Paris and Versailles, and in many small German courts.

Royalty used various means to affect musical practice. One must, of course, remember that the very presence of a monarch at certain performances was significant; his preferences determined what instruments were featured, which soloists performed, and what compositions were played. Furthermore, royal taste was imitated by the other members of the court and, when economically feasible, elsewhere. Royalty also influenced music by determining which talented individuals were chosen for higher training. Under the aegis of their monarch, many musicians were given the opportunity to perform in other countries. This partially explains why so many Italian musicians, composers and performers alike, appeared at German and Russian courts, and why, later, more than one German appeared at the czarist court.

Similarly, royalty granted members of the court ensemble time to play elsewhere; Duke Victor Amadeo of Turin, and his composer and virtuoso, Gaetano Pugnani (1731–1798), are an example. Another important illustration is the case of Mühlfeld, the clarinetist for whom Brahms composed chamber music. When the opportunity arose to perform one of these compositions outside the city of Meiningen, the Duke, also an admirer of Brahms, granted Mühlfeld a leave of absence. Such royal generosity was an important factor in popularizing Brahm's chamber music throughout Germany and England. Another example is the Prince of Lippe, whose personal fortune was so great, despite his small kingdom, that he could support a large court orchestra. He invited Brahms to give piano lessons to the princesses of his court. This stay in Detmold, the capital of Lippe, gave Brahms an ideal opportunity to complete work on a number of compositions. When the prince died childless, a distant relative from a far less wealthy side of the family succeeded him. This successor had no interest in music, and hence neither Brahms nor any other important musician was invited to court during his reign; the court orchestra was discharged immediately. The importance of the ruler's taste is therefore evident. It is, however, only one of the many sources of change in the political world that may modify the musical scene.

At this point in our discussion, it is sufficient to mention that certain rulers have preferred certain types of music. Charlemagne sponsored church music, for example, while many rulers during the period between the Italian Renaissance and the French Revolution were primarily devotees of the opera. Seldom does one hear of a monarch cultivating the oratorio or ballet. The Duke of Orléans (1674–1723), who served as regent for Louis XV until he reached his majority, was an exception; he had a strong interest in ballet. Another, though rare, example of royal interest in a specific kind of music be that of King Alfonso X of Castile (1221–1284), whose insistence on the systematic collection of old songs is one of the essential reasons why more old Spanish songs have been preserved than those of other countries. Rarely did a monarch assume personal responsibility for organizing music for the common people. One exception was Louis XIV (1638–1715), who developed a series of popular concerts performed by his own musicians in the Tuileries Gardens in Paris.

As already mentioned, monarchs not only sponsored certain performers and composers, but also dictated which instruments were to be used in solo performance. Various instruments were popularized through royal influence. Charles VI of France (1368–1422) stressed the use of harp, and made its fame. Certainly one of the most important changes in instrumental history was the increasing preference of the vaulted-back violin over the flat-backed instrument. Louis XIV, Elizabeth I (1533–1603), and certain rulers of small German territories were largely responsible for the shift. Another instrument that gained popularity under Elizabeth's sponsorship was the virginal. This forerunner of the harpsichord was especially suitable for this queen and her relatively small group of ladies-in-waiting because of its somewhat diminished volume.

Finally, we might mention royal interest, both musical and personal, in specific composers. We have already noted Brahms's invitation to Detmold. The encouragement of Orlando di Lasso (1530–1594) by King Albert of Bavaria is another example, and King Louis of Bavaria's patronage of Wagner is universally known.

INFLUENCE OF NOBILITY

The sponsorship of music by the nobility is second only to that of the royalty. Many composers have listed members of the nobility among their closest personal friends. Count Waldstein is remembered because Beethoven gratefully dedicated a sonata to him. Robert Franz (1815–1892) became, and has remained, one of Germany's most popular composers of lieder through the continual help of Baron Senfft von Pilsach. Another form of influence by the nobility was, as in the case of royalty, through preference for certain instruments and the commissioning of compositions, either solo or ensemble. The quartets and quintets for guitar and strings composed by Boccherini and Paganini were directly written on such orders. Mozart's "Duet for Cello and Bassoon" also belongs to this category.

Sometimes the protection offered by the nobility to itinerant musicians was not completely altruistic. During the classical period in Vienna, for example, the traveling virtuosos only received permission to organize their own concerts after playing gratis in the city palaces of noble courts. Although exceptional, similar situations existed in Czarist Russia. However, in many countries, the opportunity to play for a nobleman prepared the way to success, as at the medieval courts of the Mohammedan Umayyad dynasty, in medieval England and France, in the modern Scottish highland and surrounding island areas, in Czarist Russia, and last, but far from least, in the classical period in Austria. In almost all these countries, the city palaces were generally the sites of patronized performances. The nobility's sponsorship of theaters was less striking. Utilizing both professionals and their own servants, noblemen may have organized theaters on their estates, but seldom did they live in the city and own public theaters.

It is of course often difficult to distinquish between the music privately backed by members of the nobility, and the art they frequently and officially patronized as statesmen. Officially sanctioned music was often patriotic in character, as when Otto von Bismarck (1815–1898), after the founding of the German Empire in 1871, encouraged the composition of victory songs and other music glorifying this event.

SUPPORT FROM PRIVATE INDIVIDUALS

With increasing industrialization in the nineteenth century, general wealth in Europe and the United States was augmented, and members of the middle class patronized music. Opera houses not directly supported by the courts, the state, or the city, could often survive only through the financial benevolence of wealthy industrialists or businessmen. This was especially true in those cities where businessmen had become increasingly powerful, such as Hamburg, one of Germany's wealthiest seaports. The piano virtuoso Ignaz Moscheles (1794–1870), very much admired during the first half of the nineteenth century, could often only organize concerts for himself, alone or with an orchestra, if some wealthy individuals took the financial risk of purchasing a large number of tickets in advance. The same was true of many associations that organized oratorios or other vocal performances. Such cases were less frequent after the turn of the century in Europe, when such performances became increasingly state or city supported. In the United States, the custom remained until very recently, since its government sponsorship of music is infrequent.

The private enterpreneur did not appear until after the Italian Renaissance; until then, there had been little individual opportunity. His role probably began as the director of an itinerant theater group who hired individual performers on a contractual basis, and whose contracts clearly spelled out their relationship to the director. Such troupes, of Italian origin, also arose in France, where similar organizations were formed and later converted to permanent private theaters. Some privately owned theaters originated in amateur groups founded in England around 1800.

The concert as a private enterprise did not appear until much later. During the eighteenth century, however, the director of a private opera house would occasionally organize private concerts. During the latter part of the nineteenth century, the editor of compositions would set up an advance concert for an especially promising work. But such instances were exceptions.

ROLES OF IMPRESSARIO AND AGENTS

Another new role was that of the impressario, a position created from the part played by private secretaries to itinerant vocal or instrumental soloists. The formerly subordinate secretary gradually became the dominant figure to such an extent that an impressario might not only handle individual artists, but also found a large enterprise organizing the appearance of various soloists in many places. Commercially oriented, these enterprises forced gifted artists to adapt to their values. Programming must be geared to audience taste, while including numbers that will allow the performer to display his virtuosity. Publicity, of course, is among the principal duties of any theatrical agency. Performers not familiar with advertising technique often feel obliged to accept the rules of the agency. Only world-renowned artists confident of unqualified success can remain relatively free of commercialized agencies.

Nowithstanding the fact that individuals who sponsored music were often representatives of specific groups, there were differences between the situations in which individuals as such supported certain types of individual performers, and those in which an institution sponsored music. In the first instance, personal interests and tastes determined the choice of music; more general principles were applied in the case of institutional art. An analysis of the music of religious groups throughout the world illustrates this.

INFLUENCE OF ORGANIZED RELIGION

In considering relationships between organized religion and music, at least two essential problems have to be separately considered: the attitudes of religious institutions toward musical expression within the framework of worship, and the attitudes toward musical expression outside the framework of worship.

Most religious traditions have not been opposed to popular and traditional forms of dance. Only extremely unworldly, ascetic philosophies such as traditional Jainism and Buddhism have demonstrated such disapproval consistently. The Catholic Church even encouraged its missionaries to permit native pagan dances. However, some of the more ascetic forms of Christianity consider any type of sensual pleasure derived from physical activity sinful; prohibitions have existed, and still exist. Such attitudes have been found in the early writings of certain Eastern Church fathers and in Calvinism. Dancing, when not prohibited, is severely restricted in those countries where the Dutch Reform Church (or one of its branches) is the dominant religion, as in the Netherlands, Scotland, Hungary, western Switzerland, and parts of the United States (during the Puritan colonial period).

Although not as extreme as those regarding dancing, religious attitudes toward the playing of instruments are often similar. For some time Greek Orthodoxy, for example, frowned on even the use of traditional folk instruments. Roman Catholicism usually permitted the use of instruments, although there were a few exceptions at the beginning of the Counter Reformation. The majority of Protestant denominations have been tolerant. Calvinism, however, has consistently forbidden this type of musical expression.

Opera produced the strongest antagonism. Forerunners of the opera appeared during the Italian Renaissance, although its major development did not take place until the late sixteenth century, continuing through the seventeenth and eighteenth centuries. Opera developed primarily in Italy; very slowly, through imitation of Catholic operas, it found its way into Lutheran countries. Opera was more successful in the international trade city of Hamburg than in the more typical rural and feudal Lutheran districts. But even in Hamburg strong resistance from Lutheran ministers and *Kantors* had to be overcome. Calvinists were, and are, strictly prohibited from even attending opera. The impact of pietistic Calvinism on musical traditions is exemplified by the following situation. The Dukes of Mecklenburg in northern German had traditionally sponsored music and supported a court opera company. When Protestant Pietism, emotional and rigorous, entered Mecklenburg, the city's young duke converted to the religion and immediately discharged and exiled all court musicians, singers, and instrumentalists.

The oratorio, based on the traditions of the medieval passion play, found its greatest development in Italy during the Catholic Counter Reformation. The Congregation of the Oratorio, founded by Saint Philip Neri, performed sacred music frequently. Oratorio, a semidramatic performance, differed from opera in the absence of costumes. Beginning with the time of Buxtehude and Heinrich Schütz (1585–1672), and particularly with Johann Sebastian Bach and his sons, it became a characteristic expression of Lutheran religious feeling.

With the exception of Calvinist, Mennonist, and certain revivalist movements, the performance of dances and vocal and instrumental music outside of churches was not interfered with. However, new problems arose with the inception of radio broadcasting. The attitudes of various religious denominations toward this new technical invention varied. Even within the same religious body conflicts arose, and original position were often altered. The essential problem was usually whether, and in what form, religious services should be broadcast. We will explore this more fully in our discussion of the attitudes of various religious bodies toward the use of different kinds of music within their worship.

PRIVATE ASSOCIATIONS AS SPONSORS

Private associations of friends of the arts also played a role in sponsoring music. We have already discussed such arrangements in connection with the development of modern symphony orchestras. Frequently, association members were not even musicians, but only wished to support certain kinds of music. Therefore, they joined such organizations, and in exchange for high membership fees, received free concert tickets, often for an entire season. Although primarily consumer organizations, they sometimes acquired such large memberships that they became producer organizations, managing concert series and even their own recital halls.

In conjunction with church, state, and community, such private associations contributed far more significantly as sponsors of music than other institutions. Some Italian and English academies of science and music in the seventeenth and eighteenth centuries organized their own concerts, but these were unusual. More recently, industrial sponsorship has developed in the large cities of the United States. In the Soviet Republics, trade unions play a relatively important role in the education and entertainment of the factory workers; hence trade unions often organize concert and theater performances within the factory for their members.

MUSICAL INSTRUCTION AND SPONSORSHIP

The teaching of music is also of interest in considering the various aspects of musical sponsorship. A few possible answers to the question of who sponsors musical instruction can be suggested. First, let us examine those cases in which persons receiving a musical education are not expected to become professional musicians. In early oriental history, music was frequently taught in the royal court. Such cases were even more common in the European tradition, especially during the periods of centralized absolutism.

Next in importance to the royal court in musical training were the courts and households of the nobility. Feudal lords commonly trained their sons musically, even in the remote regions of czarist Russia. Many younger serfs also received such training, as the size of orchestras increased in modern times. Sometimes foreign musicians were hired to give lessons to both the landlord's family and the serfs.

Among the institutions offering musical instruction to those not planning to become professionals, the church or other religious organizations may be most important. As far back as the early Christian church, young people were taught psalm singing. In oriental and occidental monasteries, friars taught the younger brothers how to sing and play musical instruments. Similar instruction was given in cathedral schools. The Jesuits taught music in their humanistic gymnasiums and similar schools to those boys not intending to join the order. Among traditional Lutherans, the *Kantor* not only led the church choir, but also taught singing at the church-supported high school. Understandably, Calvinist and Anabaptist groups were more skeptical and reluctant regarding the teaching of music. Nevertheless, although very slowly and to a much lesser degree than other groups, they finally began to allow some musical instruction in their schools.

With the eighteenth century, control of education, and consequently musical instruction, moved from the church to the political community. In general, musical instruction was considered secondary to other branches of education in the institutions of higher learning in Central Europe. Musical training was given importance earlier in the United States than in Europe.

We will conclude with a few remarks concerning the sponsorship of institutions where future professional musicians received their training. In Europe these go back to the interest of certain monarchs of the absolutist period, when London's Royal Academy of Music was founded. As with so many institutions founded by royalty, the academies of music later came under state control. Because there was never a monarchy in America, and because the old European distinction between universities and vocational schools was not as sharply drawn, developments in the United States differed somewhat. Consequently, musical training has been offered at nearly all colleges and universities in the United States. Latin American countries generally followed European patterns of education. During the colonial period, the Spanish government supported musical instruction, but after the revolution led by Simón Bolívar (1783–1830), musical academies were established in the European pattern and were supported by the state. In today's totalitarian states such as Soviet Russia, and, earlier, Hitler's Germany, the entire field of music education has been brought under centralized state control, along with the control of other cultural institutions.

ON ECONOMIC ASPECTS OF MUSIC

Throughout history, much of musical activity has been connected with various economic aspects of social life. Among the more obvious considerations are the direct costs of musical productions, as related to the demand of the audience of musical "consumers." But there are hidden costs as well, which are customarily borne by the performers. To consider the extent and significance of the various economic links to music as directly as possible, we should first examine the employment status of musicians—who employs musicians and for how long, how and under what circumstances they can be dismissed—for without musicians there would be no making of music.

EMPLOYMENT STATUS OF MUSICIANS

The hiring of musicians was often the personal choice of a noble sponsor. When a king trusted the judgment of his outstanding court composer or conductor, he might delegate these decisions to him. Dittersdorf, contemporary court conductor of the classical Austrian composers, was given complete independence in selecting musical personnel. When routine musical productions were shifted from the court to the state theater, this function was delegated formally to a high government official. In Germany, under the monarchy, this official was often called the *Intendant*;

elsewhere he enjoyed similar titles and corresponding powers. Sometimes he was not a musician himself, but a man of high origin for whom some kind of official position was needed and who could not be employed in any other capacity. Occasionally aristocrats who had failed in the diplomatic service were assigned as general managers of the state theater. When the orchestra was city supported, the lord mayor was theoretically the employer of the musicians. Frequently a special official was entrusted with these functions, and under some circumstances the conductor of the city orchestra was allowed to decide on the hiring of orchestra members. These court, state, and city theaters and orchestras represent only a fraction of the entire range of musical institutions that provide opportunities for the employment of musicians.

To provide private enterpreneurs with musicians and bring the latter into contact with employers, musical employment agencies were founded. This kind of organization had its greatest development in Europe and the United States during the nineteenth and twentieth centuries. The person organizing this service made his living by asking for some commission for every job placement, in turn decreasing the earnings of performing musicians. Consequently, performers themselves built such agencies with the intention of eliminating the middle man between employer and employee. The greater the number of employers, and especially of employees, the less it became possible to use this arrangement. In general, this attempt by musicians to eliminate the fees of commercial agencies can be said to have largely vanished. In the United States, however, union-hiring halls play a prominent role.

Variations in Employment Terms

Musicians are often hired for a short time only—in many cases for only one or a very few performances. While this generalization holds for the majority of musicians, some courts tried as early as the late Middle Ages to secure a more permanent staff of regular musicians. The court of Burgundy was one of the first places where the regular musicians enjoyed life tenure in their position at court. Between the Italian Renaissance and the French Revolution, this example was gradually imitated elsewhere. As late as the nineteenth century, a probationary period often preceded the awarding of such a position. It may be mentioned, for instance, that in the era of later romanticism Heinrich Marschner, although he was already well known for some of his operas including *Hans Heiling,* only obtained his permanent life position after twenty years as court conductor. Nevertheless, such appointments increasingly became the rule not only in Germany but also in England in the later part of the nineteenth century.

In addition to the difficulty of obtaining a permanent position, the possibility of being fired on short notice remained relatively great. Of course, there are notable exceptions. Dittersdorf tells us of a bishop of high noble origin in the city of Grosswardein, Rumania, who decided to disband his orchestra, yet arranged that every one of his court musicians be paid in full for many months to come. Court orchestras were often dissolved soon after the death of their sponsors. Even after the shift of musicians from aristocratic court institutions to those supported by the state, similar situations occurred; for example, the fiscal relationship between the director of a theater and the city government that had chosen him and had placed the theater building at his disposal remained unclear. When a director resigned suddenly, no one knew who should pay the artists of his company. Even in such an institution as the Prussian Academy of Music in Berlin, directed by the world-famous player of Brahms, Joachim, Rudorff, the well-known teacher of piano (known to be conservatively minded) was fired by the government without Joachim's knowledge. In the United States musicians have also constantly faced the possibility of sudden unemployment. One major wave of dismissals occurred in the late 1920s when the new talking movies appeared, bringing almost immediate obsolescence to the relatively large movie house orchestras. Throughout history political events such as the French Revolution or the collapse of Czarism have caused general unemployment, affecting even those musicians who believed their positions to be secure.

LIFE STYLE OF MUSICIANS

To understand the attempts of musicians, political parties, and similar groups to improve the economic security of musicians, it may help to first look at their style of life. Many musicians succeed in enjoying extremely high incomes, and consequently live the life of a *grand seigneur*. These are usually successful conductors and traveling virtuosos, rather than the composers of works that later become known worldwide. The majority of musicians, however, have either had to live like the petty bourgeoisie or even in abject misery; there are countless examples of debt-ridden musicians. Mozart, who was buried with twenty proletarians in the same grave, is one of the world's best known examples of the inverse relationship between musical and economic success.

The economic situation becomes complicated partly because very often there are no clear understandings as to who bears what kind of direct expense. Who, for instance, is responsible for the purchase, upkeep, and payment of performance instruments? During the classical period of Lutheran church music, and continuing through the times of Johann Sebastian Bach, the cities as well as the church were usually so poor that they could not provide the instruments, making it necessary for the musicians themselves to purchase them. More recently the state or city came to own instruments of various kinds and could supply them to the musicians in their employ.

An even more complex problem was how to assign the costs of providing the costumes for theater and opera performers. Especially when of historical character, such costumes were and still are often expensive. Since costumes must somehow fit the actors, either the singers must own their own costumes or the theater must own a great quantity of costumes of all kinds and sizes, so that the actors can always find something suitable. Actresses, especially in Latin America, had costumes paid for by a friend, protector, or sponsor in return for sexual favors.

Artists without such personal sponsorship had to face financial hardships. A solo performer had to hire a concert hall and publicize his concert appearance widely if he wished to obtain monetary returns. In order to attract an audience of any size performers often found it to their advantage to first perform without payment in the palace of a member of the nobility or in a concert organized by an orchestra of amateurs. Only after such performances could an artist count on a larger public, because then the nobleman for whom he had played might buy a block of tickets or the association of amateurs would create publicity and allow him to use their concert hall rent-free. These arrangements have gradually disappeared since the middle of the nineteenth century where states- or city-supported orchestras became more common.

Difficulties for the solo performer persisted, however, due to the tremendous increase in competition among virtuosos. To be engaged to appear as a soloist in a concert organized by the city administration or by an association was only possible if the singer or instrumentalist had already gained an independent reputation through critical reviews in newspapers. How could young artists obtain such reviews in print? Almost the only possibility was to organize concerts on their own, in major cities with newspapers and critics of high reputation. Ordinarily the necessary organizational arrangements were handled through special concert booking agencies, which charged the solo performer for expenses, such as rental of the concert hall and publicity. One consequence of this practice, still to be observed in New York and other musical centers, is that a recitalist would perform highly difficult compositions to demonstrate his virtuosity to the critics, some of whom might leave after a third of the program in order to listen to part of another recital elsewhere, writing only a few lines on this recital within a general report on the musical events of the previous week. Often close friends, relatives, and fellow students of the performer comprised most of the audience. In Paris whoever could be found on the streets was often asked to listen to the recital. Legend has it that sometimes the unknown young performer even had to pay unemployed persons to come to his performance, so that the room might not be absolutely empty.

Many European countries were impoverished by the end of World War I. Maintaining musical life in the forms customary before 1914 became so difficult that these legendary solo recitals ceased almost completely. Other means of introducing solo performers were arranged by some music sponsoring societies. These societies organized concerts in which they offered performance opportunities to unknown young virtuosos. At such occasions as many as four or five artists might appear on the same program.

SOURCES OF EARNINGS OF MUSICIANS

These limited examples suggest that musicians frequently face expenses higher than those customary in other professions. To balance these observations we must consider how much musicians earn. Here it will also be necessary to distinguish between irregular and regular income.

Composing

Regardless of the nature of income, composers' earnings tend to be the most irregular for most of history. Until the beginning of the nineteenth century, there existed nothing that would compare with what is now called copyright protection. This meant that even if the composer was successful and found a publisher who would print his composition, anyone could copy the work by hand, perform it, or have it reprinted. Neither the original publishing house nor the composer could recover any financial compensation for their initial contribution. During the nineteenth century this situation began to change; several countries propagated laws forbidding the reproduction without consent, from the author or publisher, of any composition by hand, print, or performance. Several countries also extended this protection to a number of years beyond a composer's death, and a number of governments signed the

Geneva Convention by which this protection was extended to the signatory states. To this day, however, the protection remains incomplete, since some Latin American states and Russia are not part of the Convention.

In addition to governmental efforts, certain musicians and their admirers worked to extend this protection, as seen in the struggle over Wagner's *Parsifal*. According to Wagner's will, *Parsifal* was to be performed only in the festival theater of Bayreuth as a climax to the annual festivals. Yet according to the terms of the Geneva Copyright Convention, the exclusive right to print and perform ends thirty years after the death of the composer. Consequently, when that time came the New York Metropolitan Opera as well as some other theaters prepared performances of *Parsifal*. Wagner's family, who had made Bayreuth the center of a Wagnerian cult, protested, but were unsuccessful in the long run.

The twentieth century has seen copyright protection extended to jazz and to more recent musical movements. This development in copyright protection is especially marked in the United States, where even the sequence of a few notes is protected and the inclusion of such a sequence into another composition is ground for legal action. Economic agreements, especially with regard to the dissemination of music on the radio, have also been made between the United States and certain Latin American countries.

Publishing

In the past, finding a publisher willing to cover the costs of printing a musical composition was difficult. One of the ways to bypass this difficulty was to guarantee publication costs through using subscription lists. During the times of Haydn, when a composer played some of his works he would circulate such a list among the audience. People might then place orders for copies of the performed works. Sometimes a composer would go even further and send the list to a friend or protector in another city, as Haydn did for one of his string quartets. Another source of limited income was accepting commissions from a sponsor or an institution such as a theater; countless compositions were commissioned between the Italian Renaissance and French Revolution. The commissioning of compositions could also take another form. Persons well known as composers of special music have sometimes signed contracts with a publishing house, agreeing to regularly produce a certain number of compositions. Such arrangements were used in the United States as early as 1850 and are frequent in the popular music field.

Performance Royalties

Another form of providing income to composers is to grant them a certain percentage of the profits from the performance of these works. This arrangement has sometimes caused personal conflicts and has even led to legal proceedings, since it is extremely difficult to arrive at an exact breakdown of the costs of a given performance.

Performers

Throughout history, the economic situation of musicians has changed with the general economic conditions. It must be remembered that in precapitalistic times the income of those who did not engage in physical labor was largely derived from land rent. He who owned land enjoyed income. The landowner might loan or rent the land to tenants, or he might have slaves or serfs who worked the fields and were paid by him either in money or produce. When music was performed by members of the nobility it was not performed to secure an income. Similarly, the monk who performed music was not paid for his performance, if he was a member of a Hindu, Buddhist, or Christian monastic order that held collectively owned land, such as the Benedictines, Cistercians, Carthusians, and Premonstratensians. If there was pay in precapitalistic society it was generally in kind rather than in money. Like ministers, teachers, and other intellectuals, performing musicians were paid in fixed amounts of wine, beer, bread, fresh meat, or sausage. Another practice was to give them free meals in the houses of noblemen or burghers. In certain Lutheran communities, musicians, particularly church organists, would go in daily rotation from one house to another to be fed at the tables of the middle-class members of their congregations. Although examples are infrequent, occasionally members of the nobility seem to have also made a practice of providing a musician with a free room.

The irregularity of income and general economic insecurity of musicians is also seen in their dependence on gifts. The medieval minstrel, jongleur, or *Fahrende* often received gifts at court, which had the character of alms. In later days it is reported that Mozart and Muzio Clementi (1752–1832), the piano virtuoso and composer, received a piece of jewelry after having performed for persons of high rank. Many musicians were in such dire financial situations that they had to accept money from admirers or more fortunate friends in the form of gifts. Hector Berlioz, who long had to struggle for his existence, accepted money given to him by Paganini, who at the time was considered the world's leading violin virtuoso and enjoyed high income from the performance of his own concertos.

ON OLD AGE SECURITY OF MUSICIANS

As in other occupations, the problem of providing some form of economic support for aged musicians had to be faced. Frequently some form of ad hoc arrangement was worked out between financially more able friends and admirers. Occasionally special pension arrangements were provided, perhaps with the help of the monarch, municipal administrators, or associations of amateurs. Such was the case for Friedrich Chrysander (1826–1901), who was supposed to be the world's greatest authority on Handel at the end of the nineteenth century. He edited definitive editions of formerly unknown or unpublished compositions of Handel and was considered his outstanding biographer as well as one of the best performers of his music. At the occasion of the Handel Anniversary, the feeling grew among the organizers of the festival that Handel could not be honored better than by providing Chrysander with an honorary pension for the rest of his life.

MONETARY REWARDS

With the general trend toward specialization of labor in modern times, the payment of musicians in money more and more replaced the practice of payment in kind, which disappeared almost entirely. The practice of paying musicians by the performance instead of on a regular basis, however, remained in force till after the beginning of the modern symphony orchestra. In the United States this practice was still employed even when a more stable kind of payment had been instituted in European orchestras. Not all musicians, however, were concerned with earning a regular income from a stable source. Indeed there are musicians who refuse to accept a stable position, preferring to live a freer, though unstable, kind of life. The highly admired vocal and instrumental soloists especially would prefer gambling on earning very high incomes during their musical prime to settling for a rather pedestrian, though relatively secure, regular salary, in spite of the risk of being considered obsolete and not obtaining guaranteed engagements. More recently, arrangements have been made by some institutions to permit a known virtuoso to take paid leaves of absence so that he may continue to pursue his solo career. Frequently these solo appearances provide the artist with more income than their regular positions with the ensemble, which they maintain for the economic security they provide.

EARNINGS FOR TEXT WRITERS

For most of history, the income of the lyricist or librettist tended to be even more precarious than that of composers or performers. One of the few ways for the poet to obtain some income was to print the text at his own expense and have it sold before or during performances. Sometimes the booklet containing the text was dedicated, with permission, to a person of high rank, thus increasing the chances of selling it to a public accustomed to admiring everything somehow endorsed by a member of high nobility. Occasionally the nobleman might also condescend to pay the poet a sum in appreciation for having the text dedicated to him.

In a few cases, special arrangements were made when the librettist was aleady well known for his work. For example, during the seventeenth and eighteenth centuries, if the same opera was performed three times in the same place, the net proceeds of a performance would be paid to the librettist. After the Romantic era arrangements were made through agencies, prior to performance, as to the percentage of income to be received by the librettist.

EARNINGS FROM COMBINED MUSICAL SPECIALIZATIONS

To remedy the frequently unstable economic situation, musicians sometimes attempted to improve their finances by working at a second occupation, as mentioned earlier. Here our emphasis will be on the income provided by such combinations. In spite of their great variety, these individual arrangements can be classified in two basic ways. First, there are those individuals who considered themselves primarily as musicians and work at a second occupation so as to supplement their income from music, and second, there are those who are as proficient as professional musicians but do not consider themselves primarily as artists. They try to improve their basic income from other work by occasionally performing as musicians. Typically they are of lower-middle- or upper-lower-class occupational position. Examples are peasants and shepherds in the folk cultures in remote districts of southeastern Europe, individuals engaged in handicrafts, and middle or lower ranking office clerks. In some countries, after some years of service former members of a military band were entitled to a clerical position in the city administration. They then enjoyed the opportunity to supplement their basic income by playing in orchestras. These opportunities most frequently arose when the regular orchestra needed vacation substitutes or augmentation for the performance of modern symphonies. Such combinations of nonprofessionals playing occasionally in orchestras can be observed in different guises throughout the world. An example from the United States is the beginning of jazz, when part-time taxi drivers and others in similar positions added to their income by performing with a band. Schoolteachers also tend to supplement their income by working band jobs on weekends.

The majority of musicians would like to enjoy a fixed salary, if possible on a permanent basis. However, only since the turn of the twentieth century, in state- or city-supported theaters of Central and Western Europe, has the orchestra conductor become a salaried official on a permanent salary basis. Some instrumentalists, such as members of the papal orchestra in the Sistine Chapel or the opera house in Hamburg during the eighteenth century, received a regular salary at an earlier time than conductors. But even in these cases not every instrumentalist enjoyed financial security; his degree of security depended on the instrument he played. Horn players were among the favorites. During the eighteenth century the horn was improved, and shifted from a hunting to a symphonic instrument. Few knew how to play the improved instrument. As a result, horn players were so much in demand that they could demand guaranteed salaries. Kettle drummers enjoyed similar privileges when there was a great popularity of drums among the monarchs of the eighteenth century. A few instrumentalists, therefore, obtained much more favorable employment contracts than those enjoyed by players of instruments in greater supply. However, even those on regular salaries did not always enjoy the benefits of financial security. There are complaints on record that musicians, even of imperial orchestras, were not paid during periods of political insecurity.

THE SPECIAL SITUATION OF VOCALISTS

Professional singers have traditionally experienced anxiety about being able to sing well on command and being exposed to the risk of failing to earn income because of losing their voices. As in the case of instrumentalists, however, where there is great demand for a certain type of voice and few are in supply, singers with the desired voice have been in a strong position to negotiate for favorable terms of remuneration and for employment contracts running for several years. In the seventeenth and eighteenth centuries the castrates, who sang leading soprano roles such as the coloraturas, were among the favored singers. Once again, these long-term contracts did not absolutely guarantee the financial security of musicians. After the collapse of czarism, for instance, many financial contracts were invalidated by the Soviets, a move made easier by the fact that many young Soviet actors were ecstatically devoted to the new philosophy of their country and were willing to work for almost nothing.

Although long-term contracts, once they were gained, represented far greater security than that enjoyed by itinerant musicians, movements toward solidifying economic security remained one of the greatest concerns in all professions, and particularly the musical field, during the late nineteenth and early twentieth centuries. In Central and Western European countries this concern, of course, arose from the long tradition of financial insecurity. Many a young musician had difficulties in obtaining the hand of a sweetheart because of her parents' refusal to allow her to marry a young man whose financial future was so insecure. Peter Cornelius (1824–1874), who was later to compose *Der Cid* and *Der Barbier von Bagdad,* was rejected for that very reason by prospective parents-in-law. Robert Schumann, who wanted to marry Clara Wieck, encountered the same difficulty. Her father, himself a musician and well-known piano teacher, refused his daughter to Schumann; the possibility that Clara, although a trained pianist, might be obliged to live a life of insecurity as a musician's wife was unendurable to him.

Musicians also expressed concern about the lack of pensions for their widows at a time when government officials with far more limited training were enjoying such security. Band musicians in the United States were in especially precarious positions, since changing tastes of the public in popular music could render them suddenly unemployed.

ORGANIZATIONS FOR PROTECTING ECONOMIC SECURITY

Did musicians do anything to face these problems? As early as the eighteenth century Viennese musicians organized an association for mutual financial assistance. They performed benefit concerts, the proceeds of which were used exclusively for assistance to fellow musicians who happened to be in need. Such associations were created elsewhere during the nineteenth century, and both Franz and Richard Wagner tell us of similar associations in which they participated. To carry this idea of raising money one step further, Spohr, when court orchestra conductor in Kassel, organized an association for the specific purpose of aiding the widows of deceased musicians.

Musicians devoted much energy to organizing to obtain the right of pension, a movement that naturally encountered great difficulties. Even when the idea began to be accepted by employers it was not universally implemented. At the small German courts of the eighteenth century, whether or not a certain artist should receive a pension often depended on the whim of the monarch. During the nineteenth century the custom began to find wider acceptance, even in Czarist Russia. The arrangement of pensions began much later in the United States, and even then was practiced to a lesser degree than in Europe. This delay and corresponding limitation was largely due to the individualistic philosophy characteristic of the economic life in this country. For this reason, musicians along with the learned professions, have waited longer and received less in the way of pensions in the United States than anywhere else.

The amount of retirement pensions rarely reaches the level of earning of working professionals. Yet some exceptional practices must be mentioned. During the seventeenth and eighteenth centuries, outstanding members of the imperial orchestra in Vienna received full pay after retirement. Similar situations have been reported in regard to some other Central European orchestras; higher pensions have traditionally been paid in Europe than in the United States. Until very recently, full professors in German and other European universities received their full working salary after retirement. Pension rights in Europe customarily include widows' rights to pension, a practice also extended to musicians.

In spite of the overall improvement in the economic lot of musicians, few of them ever became wealthy. The main exceptions were among the already mentioned castrates in the eighteenth century or highly admired singers of the nineteenth and twentieth centuries. Then, too, the itinerant life often encouraged spending a great deal of money, and many well-known singers who had earned tremendous incomes ended their lives in poverty. One such individual was the operatic bass Karl Johann Formes (1810–1883), for whom Friedrich von Flotow (1812–1883) created the character of Plumket in his opera *Martha* and Carl Otto Nicolai (1810–1849) created the character of Falstaff in his *Merry Wives of Windsor*. Although Formes was admired in Europe as well as in America, he finally died in misery in San Francisco, a forgotten man. Among those who succeeded in retiring in wealth were two brothers of Polish origin: Edouard De Reszké (1855–1917) sang bass and Jean De Reszké (1850–1925) sang tenor. After having sung all over the world, including Paris and the New York Metropolitan Opera, they retired to their large estate in Poland.

As mentioned earlier, most composers whose work remained, or became, famous after their death usually were not able to build up a fortune from their income from composing. That, of course, is not true only of composers. Creative thinkers and artists who bring about innovations are usually considered revolutionaries in their fields, and are often accused of violating vested interests. Exceptions exist, of course. We are told of the great wealth that Matheson collected in eighteenth century Hamburg. However, he did not amass his fortune solely from composing music, but rather as the director of an opera house in which he himself performed as a conductor and singer. Or there was Giacomo Meyerbeer (1791–1864), whose work in Paris was the climax of the style of the heroic grand opera, most enjoyed by the Paris bourgeoisie. Richard Wagner was impoverished and debt-ridden for most of his life. Yet two factors enabled him to accumulate a large fortune in his later years: the friendship of the young King Louis of Bavaria, who gave him every opportunity to have his works performed, first in Munich and then in Bayreuth; and Wagner's second wife, Cosima, the daughter of Liszt, who was in a particularly good position to make of Bayreuth a musical center of international fame.

These composers and a few others who were economically successful changed their life styles to one of luxury. Only a few of them, such as Verdi, bequeathed their money directly to others less fortunate so that they might enjoy some security during their declining years. Verdi bequeathed a part of his fortune as well as a high percentage of the income from the sale of scores and piano arrangements of his operas and from performances to a house for retired elderly musicians. One who did not leave his money to some of his less fortunate colleagues was Matheson. He did bequeath some of his fortune to the Lutheran church, but with the idea that he should be buried there with a splendid funeral and with the accompaniment of a large orchestra.

Guild and Union Organizations

Another method of improving the economic circumstances of musicians was the organization of special associations for the purpose of reenforcing their strength and solidarity as members of a profession. Professional associations with the purpose of improving the economic lot of their members exist in two types: the guild and the union. The principal difference between them is that the guild membership is comprised of both employers and employees, who are united in their common social struggle against other professional, social, and occupational groups. The union normally contains only employees, who are united by a common struggle against their employers. The guild type of organization usually exists when the number of employees is relatively small in comparison to that of the employers. Under such conditions employees stand a relatively good chance of becoming employers in time. When employees outnumber employers by a large margin, an employee's chances of becoming an employer diminish almost to the vanishing point. At this point, the sense of common interest between workers and masters virtually disappears, giving rise to the founding of labor unions rather than guilds.

For many generations the majority of musicians' organizations were of the guild variety. In the medieval city there existed several musicians' guilds, rather than just one. Each of them enjoyed some rights, even privileges, and tried to hinder members of other guilds from becoming entitled to perform their particular kind of music. For instance, members of the guilds of trumpet, trombone, and kettle drum players would not be permitted to play string or woodwind instruments.

Performers excluded as inferior musicians by regular guild members also tried to organize themselves to protect their rights and improve their economic position. The wind instrument players who performed the relatively simple music at hunting parties given by members of the nobility were often simple peasants wearing special uniforms. At some German courts of the seventeenth century, there existed in addition to the official court orchestra a group called *Schalmeipfeifer* or hautbois players. They performed, on occasions of minor importance, on reed instruments that were forerunners of the modern oboe. These performers were not recognized as equals by members of the regular court orchestra. Therefore, they organized themselves in special guilds. Instrument makers, too, were oganized in special and ranked guilds. Although craftsmen, the makers of wind instruments were not considered the equals of those who made string instruments. Similarly, when the new instrument family of vaulted-back violins was introduced, a sharp separation occurred between the makers of lutes and similar plucked string instruments and the highly esteemed makers of the new violins.

Sometimes it may be difficult to ascertain whether an organization is a guild or a union. The unionization of musicians occurred especially in Germany, the country in which unions as defined above had their origin. Perhaps Germans more than other people were accustomed to living under discipline, at least as far as nonspiritual or material life is concerned. Consequently, a German, accustomed to obeying bureaucratic representatives of the state, could more readily extend that custom to union officials. Strong organizations of workers of all kinds originated in Germany earlier than in other countries. At the same time, there was always a strong feeling in Germany that sharp status differences exist between simple manual laborers and intellectuals. While the former were organized soon after the rise of industrialization in at least three ideologically different labor union movements (socialist, Catholic, and moderately liberal), some time elapsed before members of the intelligentsia, including musicians, organized corresponding groups. The Romantic composer Karl Maria von Weber (1786–1826) had initiated suggestions, but the essential impetus toward union organization derived from the competition between regular and military band musicians.

In Germany military bands were usually made up of sergeants who were on a twelve-year tour of service. Members of the infantry bands were expected to play string instruments as well as both woodwind and brass. With their versatility they were easy to use in symphony orchestras. Moreover, these military musicians were entitled to be employed in middle level positions in state, provincial, and city governments after their twelve years of service. Such positions permitted musicians with enough free time to continue their instrument playing and to participate as paid musicians in various kinds of performances. In larger communities, there was frequently such a large number of retired military band musicians that they formed complete orchestras of their own. To protect themselves against competition from retired and active military band musicians, regular musicians formed union organizations. In Germany the most important musicians' union was the *Allgemeiner Deutscher Musiker Verband*. It became increasingly powerful, and other attempted organizations, such as those supported by the Socialist Party, were far less successful by comparison.

When the trade union movement spread to throughout Europe toward the end of the nineteenth century, the organization of musicians was also attempted in the majority of European countries. Even Czarist Russia could not prevent the foundation and development of musician unions.

In the United States the idea of labor unions developed more slowly than in Europe. Individualism made the idea of unionization unpopular and caused unions to be considered by public opinion as un-American. The race problem also hindered the development of unions for some time, since Negroes and in the West Orientals were kept out of labor organizations. However, the rapid population growth in the cities along with the growing feeling of economic insecurity (especially since the Depression of the thirties) spread the belief that it was becoming less possible to ameliorate one's economic situation by one's own efforts. Accordingly, more and more workers in America shifted from their traditional belief in free enterprise and economic opportunity and joined organizations with the aim of protecting their social and economic interests against employers. Along with other unions, the American Federation of Musicians became strong. It succeeded in establishing minimum wages for all kinds of musical performances, and insisted that only union members were entitled to perform for public, including remote broadcast performances. The American example was followed in other countries as far away as Australia.

ON THE ECONOMIC ROLE OF THE AUDIENCE

Until now we have looked at the economic aspect of music making primarily by focusing on the musician and by examining such costs as the various expenses of performers and how they were met. This emphasis must be supplemented by asking what the costs are for the listener before music becomes available to the public. Today we are accustomed to purchasing tickets as a normal prelude to the enjoyment of musical performances. We should not forget, however, that this practice is relatively recent. Almost the entire range of music performed in connection with religion as well as music sponsored by monarchs or other persons of high rank was not accessible to the general public, even had they been able to purchase a ticket. The enjoyment of music was either the privilege of invited guests of high position or it was accessible without payment to members of the congregation as in the Roman Catholic High Mass or the Lutheran church concert. Even in our times there are some occasions at which admission is free to the public. A good example is offered by the bands in restaurants, cafés, and nightclubs. Yet the high prices charged for food and beverages in such establishments are actually a form of indirectly paying for the music.

Since the rise of opera and concert performances, attendance has generally been available only to buyers of tickets. As in most cases there are, however, a number of exceptions to consider. For example, since the eighteenth century it has been customary that those singers of the company who did not participate in the evening performance were entitled to free tickets. In some opera houses certain boxes, not perhaps the best ones, were reserved for them. The more important the role of critic became for musical life the more it was also necessary to provide complimentary tickets for the staff of various newspapers and critical reviews.

In some Latin countries and especially in Paris, a special type of listener who had the good fortune of attending performances without paying mainly were the *claquers*. They were hired by the *chef de claque*, who was responsible for providing the noisy applause desired by singers after special parts of their performances, such as the singing of the bravura aria. When such applause was strong, the singer could be expected to repeat his aria *da capo*, which increased his reputation. When a singer was uncertain about getting such applause, he would arrange for it with the *chef de claque*. The *claqueurs* were not paid for applauding, but they were supposed to start the applause whenever their master gave them the sign. When there was rivalry between various singers appearing on the same bill, the singers would buy a large number of tickets to build up such *claques,* thus incurring a major expense.

Another group received *billets de faveur* or tickets at reduced prices. The great theaters in Paris regularly sent these tickets to various state or city offices, where they were distributed among the staff. Holders of these tickets entered the theater by a special entrance, showing their tickets and paying extremely low admission fees. This arrangement apparently eliminated the accusation of bribery and may have existed elsewhere. Today, in general, attendance at musical performances tends to require some economic ability to absorb the costs of tickets and proper attire, and of course free time.

VARIATIONS IN THE DISTRIBUTION OF MUSIC

Once a musical composition has been performed it must also be reproduced so that it can be played in other places and be preserved for posterity. The necessity for reproducing music has always been somewhat problematic, regardless of the particular technology involved. In the majority of cultures, text and melody were not written down but transferred orally from one generation to the other. Lengthy epics, their simple instrumental accompaniment, and other vocal music were taught by the musicians of the older generation to the younger generation. This form of instruction entrained unconscious musical changes in the oral tradition. Neither were changes altogether avoided with the shift from the oral tradition to written copy, when special symbols, letters, or signs were introduced to indicate pitch and tempo. Using the medieval neumes of Christian culture, music was copied and recopied, especially by the Benedictines. Even after the invention of printing, the practice of hand copying continued among poorer people and in remote districts, as during the colonial and pioneer periods of United States history.

The invention of printing brought many changes. Composers began to become dependent on the owners of printing facilities. Without effective copyright protection, both the composer and the publisher faced the risk that the work would be copied by hand or reprinted elsewhere, making their investment in publication a complete economic failure. Numerous complaints were made by composers about the difficulty of finding a printer and about copies being made without their consent. The publication might be reprinted note for note elsewhere without giving the composer credit, or it might be changed without consulting him. Quintets for winds and piano were arranged for string and piano; a clarient quintet might be changed to strings because of the difficulty of finding a competent clarinettist for the part. Beethoven protested such modification, as did Weber and Johann Nepomuk Hummel (1778–1837) after him.

Even after some legal regulations were finally obtained, there were still other difficulties to be faced. An experience of Johannes Brahms may serve as an illustration. Although the major publisher of Brahms's music agreed to publish all his works, he nevertheless at first refused to publish certain ones because he believed that the piano part was too difficult for amateur musicians, thus limiting the market to only a few professional musicians. Similar objections were raised when Brahms shifted away from composing string quartets, since this type of chamber music had been increasingly popular since the days of Haydn. There was almost no demand for string sextet music, partly because travel for six would be far more expensive than travel for four, and partly because sextet music diminished the opportunities for participation in any one program on the parts of the second violist and second cellist. Consequently, Brahms had to overcome great difficulties before he saw his new kind of chamber music published.

Death presented another kind of difficulty, since a composer would often leave behind a number of more or less finished compositions, which his widow and other heirs, especially if they were in need of funds, would try to place on the market. The posthumous works of Alessandro Stradella for example, were sold for almost nothing. Mozart's poor widow also had a desperate struggle for the same reasons.

Such difficulties also occurred in the United States. Music publishing had already begun in the colonial era, mainly in Pennsylvania. There William Penn (1644–1718), as well as his successors, invited, or at least tolerated, heterogeneous religious groups. As their congregations increased, they needed more hymnals and began printing them. Since the printing of musical notation was extremely expensive, it would not have been possible to have special publishing houses for every single one of the many denominations. Thus, a peculiar situation arose. Notwithstanding that an enterpreneur had close personal connections with a certain church, he also printed the hymn books and similar publications of other religious groups. The song books for the Wesleyan Methodist Church were printed by a Quaker publisher. Even more important in the early history of music in America was Christopher Sower (1695–1758), who was a member of the Dunkers. He established a printing house with facilities for printing musical notation, and published religious music books for other denominations.

The role of textbooks in every field of education takes on a special significance in the United States. As already mentioned, education in music in the States shifted to institutions of higher education. Accordingly, in the United States textbooks for musical education and books of musical selections for choirs or other performances were printed by college or university presses to a greater extent than in other countries. Mention of this trend is worthwhile here because it is contrary to the more general support of private enterprise in the United States, where private enterprise, more than in the Old World, remained dominant and had the support of public opinion.

Once a composer had found a way of having his works printed, he still had to find ways of distributing them to prospective users. Various methods have been employed. One, the subscription list, has already been discussed. It worked much like the subscription lists used by virtuoso performers. Sometimes a composer, such as George Philipp Telemann (1681–1767), would circulate the list with the help of friends or individuals of high position in various cities before printing the work. Then, when he had the composition printed, the list of the people who had subscribed was included. Among those subscribing were many members of high nobility as well as eminent state officials. Mentioning their names served as a kind of advertising by endorsement. Telemann calculated that more people would be inclined to buy his compositions when it was known that persons of high social prestige had done so.

Specialty shops selling musical books or compositions as a rule did not exist in the eighteenth century. Therefore the printed music sometimes also announced that the composition could be purchased at the composer's private address. During the nineteenth century, censorship and similar limitations had diminished, so that privately owned bookstores were gradually established. Often they also sold printed music. The development, especially in larger cities, of a larger public of individuals interested in music created the need for specialty music shops. In addition to selling sheet music, these shops carried wind and string instruments, even pianos. Later, sound recordings, electronic playback, and recording equipment were also added.

Not much is known about the beginning of music shops in the United States. There are some occasional references to music shops in Boston even before 1800. With the growing interest in band music, the sale of trumpets, trombones, saxophones, and percussion instruments (and guitars) became the main object of American music stores.

Even in our age, with its highly developed printing and music reproduction equipment, the renting of music still plays an important role. Sometimes it is economically too risky to mechanically reproduce a modern composition with full orchestration; consequently it is made known that a certain composition exists and that a limited number of scores and instrumental or vocal parts may be borrowed from a rental or publishing house. This practice applies especially to the introduction of new operas. The mounting of a performance and the printing of the music are so expensive, in view of the great risk that the opera will be forgotten after a few performances, that often the renting of the music is the only economically feasible mode of initial distribution.

ON POLITICAL AND NATIONALISTIC DIMENSIONS OF MUSIC

In contemporary usage the term *politics* refers to the interplay of power groups, their leaders, and those aspiring to power within the context of the national state. Politics thus defined is a characteristic of our times. In earlier periods and cultures, long before the rise of the nation state, political relations were often defined by supranational antagonisms and conflicts, such as those between Christians and Mohammedans. With the rise of national and nationalistic concepts in society, governments usually became organized along national lines.

NATIONALISM AND MUSICIANS

Our survey of interrelationships between music and politics begins with an examination of certain aspects of the relationship between music and nationalism. First, we look at the political attitudes of musicians toward their own countries and toward concepts of nationality. Patriotism, of course, is widely found among musicians, many of whom are pleased when their own nation is victorious in war. But this attitude is not peculiar to musicians; rather, it is common among artists and intellectuals of any given period. What is of greater interest to this survey are those situations in which musicians insist that works by foreign composers be performed, even during times of war against the native states of the selected compositions. The French composers and patriots, Georges Bizet and Claude Debussy (1862–1918), although they disliked Germany, insisted that compositions by Wagner be performed in Paris during the Franco-Prussian war.

Since musicians tend to travel widely, they sometimes find themselves in situations where they must decide whether their loyalties should belong to their native land or to their country of residence. Franz Liszt, for instance, was born in Hungary, and although of German descent, was of the Hungarian nobility. While he resided mostly in Germany, he nevertheless retained sympathetic feelings for the land of his birth. Karl Goldmark (1830–1915), who was also born in Hungary, lived mostly in Vienna. During the 1870s Goldmark, in his opera *Queen of Sheba,* was one of the first to adopt Wagner's technique of orchestration without accepting his entire philosophy. He, too, maintained his sympathetic feelings for Hungary throughout his life.

The violin virtuosos Wasielewski and Joachim offer a different illustration. The former, of Polish ancestry, was greatly admired after 1870. Joachim, Hungarian and an intimate friend of Brahms, enjoyed a great reputation for being one of the world's most perfect performers of Beethoven and Brahms concerti and chamber music. Both settled relatively early in Germany and expressed strong pro-German sentiments, particularly during the Franco-Prussian war. Such patriotic enthusiasm in some cases developed into outright chauvinism; the most famous example is Richard Wagner.

What of the popular conviction which holds that there are certain types of music that best express the national feeling of a people? This conviction tends to develop more easily when people feel threatened by the predominance of the culture of a strong neighboring country. The Celts, for example, entertain such resentments toward the English. Hence, the Scottish highlanders insist that their music is basically different from that of the English and should be maintained as a symbol of their unique national character. That is one of the reasons why the Scottish army continues the use of bagpipe bands, which sound completely different from an English army band, or any other band in the Western world. The Welsh display a similar feeling, manifesting it in their musical contests called *Eisteddfodau,* which used to be held in Cardiff.

Although Germany had not been nationally united for centuries, a patriotic feeling began to develop during the nineteenth century. During this period many patriotic songs were written and performed, particularly in glee clubs and singing societies.

Up to the nineteenth century, Russia had been somewhat out of contact with occidental music, except for the occasional visits of traveling German and Italian virtuosos. Western patterns of orchestration and symphony and opera structure began to spread eastward to Czarist Russia. Among the Russian composers who adopted some of the Western techniques was Alexander Borodin (1833–1887). His compositions nevertheless remained essentially Russian in character. The practice of retaining certain elements of a musical tradition is also seen in the United States, where many national groups, such as the Finns and the Irish, settled in ethnic communities. Although avowedly loyal to America, they cherished their native music. American musicians and teachers insist that there is value in preserving the typical sounds of various national origins. Opposed to this pluralistic perspective one can also encounter the position that decries anything not typically American, typically German, or typical of whatever country one happens to be discussing. In Hitler's Germany, Wagnerians and anti-Wagnerians both criticized Jewish music as being "un-German." There were even some Americans who derided jazz as having too great a Negro element, which made it supposedly "un-American."

In some instances musicians have criticized the musical standards of their native country. Some Spaniards, for example, expressed a general feeling that Spain was backward as a country. These intellectual Spaniards felt that backwardness had been clearly demonstrated by their defeat in the Spanish-American War. Consequently, they insisted that their obsolete ways of life should be abandoned, including their folk music and dances.

National Music

We should also consider music that is not only supposedly national in character, but was in fact composed specifically for patriotic occasions. Naturally, all national anthems belong to this category. These are usually composed for the formation of a new state or the newly gained independence of a state. While these historic moments call for special music, they are not the only occasions for the writing of patriotic music. Whenever the patriotic sentiments of a nation are polarized, as in time of war, new songs are written reflecting sentiments of the people honoring their country or its armed forces.

Louis Spohr and Ignaz Moscheles in Germany, and Alexander Kastalsky (1856–1926) in Czarist Russia are all noted for their compositions in honor of home and country. Since Bolívar's revolution of independence,

Latin American countries have celebrated events of national importance time and again by special musical productions. Such music, other than national anthems, has included rhapsodies and symphonies whose titles include some national or ethnic identification. Niels Gade (1817–1890) and Edvard Grieg (1843–1907) of the Scandinavian countries and Modest Moussorgsky (1839–1881) of Russia have all composed important music evoking their countries. Secular oratorios, too, frequently espouse patriotic themes. A social situation that typically engenders patriotic music is that of a minority group caught in the pressures of discrimination. The Irish *Feis Ceoil,* founded in 1897 and celebrated annually in Dublin, includes the performance of oratorios that celebrate heroic Irish deeds. The Flemish, during the nineteenth century, when they felt endangered by the predominance of the French language in the industrial south, created a number of oratorios in the Flemish language by way of protest.

Operas, along with oratorios, frequently are used to express nationalistic feelings. Examples would include a number of Scandinavian composers. In Germany, in addition to Richard Wagner, his son Siegfried (1869–1930) composed many operas on national themes. Both father and son considered their works as direct expressions of the true German soul, and employed special musical techniques to this end.

A basic means for letting people know that a certain work is intended to express the national characteristics of a particular people is the use of rhythms typical of the people for whom the work is designed. One early example is the Czech composer Zach. Although the Czechs were not considered important in occidental culture toward the end of the eighteenth century, he included special Czech dance rhythms in his compositions. Zach left his native country and went to Vienna, and later to the court of the Bishop of Mainz in Germany, so that the Czech rhythms he had incorporated in his compositions became known in the musical world of his day. Beethoven, who was born and grew up in the western part of the Rhine province, can also be included within this frame of reference. In his youth he became familiar with certain rhythms used in the folk dances of the *Bergische Land,* the hilly district near Bonn. These rhythms became widely known through their inclusion in some of his minor compositions.

The incorporation of melodies from the folk music of a country have also added national color to certain compositions. Examples can again be found in Scandinavian music. Slavic composers, such as the Czech Bedřich Smetana (1824–1884), and Hungarian composers also included folk melodies in symphonic compositions. Such music has even been produced in the United States; various orchestral suites such as the *Indian Suite* by Edward MacDowell (1861–1908), and other compositions were supposedly based on American Indian melodies. Another composition of particularly American color is the *Appalachian Spring Suite* by Aaron Copland (1900–). The use of folk melody is far less common in chamber music. Eduard Hanslick, the outspoken opponent of Wagner, incorporated some personally collected folk melodies from the Austrian province of Kärnten into a piano fantasy.

Folk rhythms and melodies can be found in the nationalistic operas already mentioned. To even begin to enumerate all the operas composed in this vein during the German Romantic era would be impossible. Karl Maria von Weber and Peter von Lindpaintner (1791–1856) are two of the best known composers of these works in German. Weber's *Der Freischütz* became extremely popular. Folk melodies were also employed during the renaissance of the fairy tale opera at the beginning of the twentieth century. Engelbert Humperdinck's (1854–1921) *Hänsel und Gretel,* with libretto by Adelheid Wette (1858–1952), was a tremendous success for quite some time. This opera's great popularity was attributed to its extensive use of original Westphalian peasant and children's songs; although contemporary critics even accused Humperdinck of plagiarism, the trend of using folk melodies continued for twenty years. Approximately sixty German operas written during this period were based on fairy tales that had been collected by the Grimm brothers, and all of them incorporated melodic elements from folk songs. Although none was as successful as *Hänsel und Gretel,* one opera that did achieve a fair degree of popularity was *Dornröschen* by August Weweler (1968–1952).

Popular melodies were also used in Russia as indications of national character in music. There, romanticism culminated in the Slavophile Movement, whose outstanding writer Ivan Kireevski (1806–1856) expressed his conviction in the 1830s that the simple and illiterate Russian peasants represented the truest form of Christian life. Convinced of the religious and ethical superiority of the Russian people, Slavophiles refused to accept elements of Western culture. This religious and chauvinistic movement gave rise to literature depicting and glorifying Russian peasant life, to an intensive study of Russian folk music, and to the composing of relatively simple operas incorporating Russian folk tunes. These operas were produced on the remote estates of members of the Russin nobility, with serfs performing the principal roles.

Baron Haxthausen was noted for his interest in encouraging the development of this sort of music. A romantic, conservative German feudal lord who traveled through various remote Russian provinces under the protection of the Russian Czar Nicolai I (1796–1855) during the middle of the nineteenth century, he recorded his observations and thereby spread them among Central and Western European intellectuals.

Musical Localisms

Our survey of the adaptation of folk melodies in modern compositions points toward the use of cultural traditions of strictly local significance, since frequently folk rhythms and melodies are not representative of the whole of a nation but rather of some small local districts. They are also often expressed in some local dialect. During the Romantic period, scholars systematically collected old songs and encouraged the continued practice of local customs, mores, and arts. It is largely due to these efforts that musical elements of purely regional character have entered cultivated music.

Minority groups in countries also preserve the musical idioms of their own traditions. Portugal, because of its small size, and Switzerland, where the four language communities enjoy identical rights, do not have a minority/majority problem. All other contemporary European states contain larger or smaller population groups that define themselves as essentially different from the dominant majority. These minority groups frequently express the need of more or less developed cultural and administrative autonomy. Such minorities always represent an element of unrest, since these problems cannot be solved satisfactorily by the majority. Even if the boundaries between two states were changed to correct one minority problem, new minority groups would emerge on the other side of the boundary that had been changed to protect the original minority group.

In Europe, minority groups, especially when primarily rural, tend to maintain local customs, not the least important of which is their music. In the United States, however, the political situation has been somewhat different. Finns, Germans, Italians, and other minorities are not dissatisfied; they are loyal Americans whose native cultures, music, and so on are encouraged rather than hindered by the federal government. Soviet Russia also allows the different minorities it encompasses a certain amount of cultural autonomy, but the corresponding problems are somewhat more complex than in the United States.

INTERNATIONALISM AND MUSICIANS

Musicians' attitudes toward their native lands found expressions in national music, as seen in the foregoing examples. To round out the picture, we must also deal with musicians' attitudes toward foreign nations and the music of foreign nations. The more obvious political positions of musicians, such as Beethoven's admiration of the Danish struggle against English domination and Liszt's open sympathy for the Poles in their attempt to free themselves from Russia, may be disregarded in this connection. As these and similar situations are primarily political in nature and have little to do with national characteristics of music, fuller analysis belongs elsewhere.

At times, musicians from one country instruct musicians from a less musically advanced country in building musical forms. A relevant illustration is the development of Scandinavian opera. During the latter part of the eighteenth century the German musician Johann Gottlieb Naumann (1741–1801) was called to Denmark and Sweden. Naumann not only organized operatic performances, but even stimulated the composition of typically Scandinavian operas. A more recent development is the conscious use of foreign rhythmic and melodic elements in modern composition.

The history of musical borrowing and exportation is quite complex. One instance took place during the sixteenth century, when some of many wars in Europe extended to countries such as Turkey and Russia. The armies used in these wars were usually made up of unemployed persons recruited from overpopulated regions, many of whom came as strangers to European cities, bringing with them their native songs and dances. Others had also picked up Turkish and Slavic melodies and rhythms during their service in those nations, and through them these Eastern musical traditions became known in European cities.

"Foreign" themes were frequently introduced in Western operas. Although there were certain traditions a composer of classical opera was to follow, he could enhance the beauty of his works by incorporating new ideas, especially within less stringently regulated parts such as marches and military choruses. These parts were accompanied by music emphasizing brass and percussion instruments, and were therefore the most appropriate places for the introduction of new rhythms and melodies of exotic origin. During that classic period many operatic works were written in which Turks, Russians, Chinese, and other little-known people were given a major part. This trend can be observed in Neapolitan opera as well as in the works of Mozart, particularly *The Abduction from the Seraglio*. Less "exotic" musical themes can be found in a number of operas in which Scottish people were characterized wearing native costumes. One of these, in the repertoire up to our own day, was *Lucia di Lammermoor* by Gaetano Donizetti (1797–1848). A small number of operas depict American Indians.

In addition to the exotic dress and strange names, some of these operas incorporated rhythms of foreign origin, although the structure of musical harmony continued along more traditional lines. Of course, Western instruments do not easily lend themselves to the rendering of completely foreign tonal structure, especially since Chinese, Indian, and Turkish music often use scale tones unfamiliar to Westerners.

Romanticism, particularly the German variety, further contributed to musical innovation. Through the confluence of several factors, a great interest in the life and arts of primitive and exotic peoples arose. Besides the contributions this movement made toward the development of the social sciences, such as anthropology, history and philosophy, it also strongly influenced the evolution of music. No longer was the audience to be jarred by wild Islamic rhythms and shrill oriental sounds. Instead these themes were now fully incorporated into larger, more melodic works, giving them an oriental flavor. Many of the mazurkas written by Frédéric Chopin (1810–1849) can be said to be typically Polish, and Liszt and Brahms used Hungarian Gypsy melodies to enliven their works. Louis Spohr, another composer of the Romantic period, collected English and Irish melodies on his travels through the British Isles, and later incorporated them into much of his music, just as Daniel François Auber (1782–1871), Georges Bizet, and Léo Delibes (1836–1891) wove Spanish boleros into their operas.

As these characteristic examples of the Romantic era indicate, musicians borrowed musical elements from many foreign musical traditions. Their compositions were limited, however, by the temperament of the piano and the harmony of modern Western music, which restrict the ability to render oriental music. Impressionistic composers endeavored to remedy this problem by atonal music. Since they did not feel bound by the traditional rules of Western harmonic progression, they disposed of unlimited possibilities for creating a harmony atypical of the Western world.

Jazz

Musical elements of foreign national origin were also incorporated into the Western music form known as jazz. Even though contradictory theories abound regarding its origin and subsequent development, some generalizations can be made with a high degree of probability. For reasons not yet definitely established, African music tends to place strong emphasis on rhythm. As Negro slaves lived separately from their white slave owners, it was only natural that they continued to practice and cherish the musical forms they had known at home in Africa, and to hand them down to succeeding generations of slaves. These forms became the basis of the now famous Negro spirituals and blues. Other elements of African derivation that influenced the creation of the blues were a characteristic method of phrasing, and the melodic shifting to a flat third at the end of a phrase, even when the melody is composed in a major key. One should remember, however, that these African traits are not the only musical elements that characterize jazz. There are also at least three elements of Anglo-Christian origin, going back to the traditions of Scottish hymn singing, the custom of rhythmic body swinging in certain revival meetings, and the use of trumpets and trombones in the propaganda efforts of some missionary groups.

Religious Internationalism

Overemphasizing the national character of certain kinds of music can tend to obstruct the appreciation of such music between different nationalities. But music has also been said to have facilitated international contacts. A typical case is the use of the music of the Catholic Church, which has played an important international role. With relatively few exceptions, church music approved by Catholic authorities was used in almost every country espousing that faith, including Latin America. To a lesser degree this has also happened in Protestant religion, mainly in the Lutheran church. Lutheran church music was developed in northern and central Germany, and spread north to Scandinavia and Finland and south to the Baltic provinces of Czarist Russia, where a German Lutheran minority enjoyed political power for many centuries. During the colonial era of the United States, Lutheranism and its music spread further, especially through those who migrated to Pennsylvania.

Although the Calvinists were not noted for their interest in musical expression, they did help spread a certain amount of music. A French Calvinist hymnal edited by Ambrosius Lobvasser (1515–1585), thought to be of Alsatian extraction, was highly thought of and used in Calvinist missionary efforts elsewhere. It was even considered to be the most adequate expression of Calvinist religiosity in German, and during the seventeenth century was used for many decades in the comparatively few districts of Germany that adhered to the reform church. These areas included sections of the Rhine province around Elberfeld and Barmen, some cities in Westphalia, and some parts of the German section of Friesland, near the Dutch border.

More than other denominations, the tiny church of the Moravian Brethren was important in spreading a particular style of music to new countries. Being primarily of Czech origin and connected with John Huss (1369–1415), at first they used Czech in their singing. Persecution in Bohemia forced them to move to some districts of Lutheran Germany, where they continued singing in their native Czech. Eventually, however, they did translate their songs into German. Here, again, they suffered persecution and eventually migrated to Pennsylvania during colonial days, bringing their hymnals to their new home.

In discussing the technical difficulties of printing sheet music, we mentioned how this group provided songbooks for other denominations during the colonial period of the United States. In this manner, hymns of Hussite origin translated from the Czech found their way into the musical life of many of the English-speaking denominations of America. This interchange of musical expression between various American Protestant denominations has continued up to fairly recent times. For example, an interdenominational hymn society whose principal objective was the publication of hymnals to be used by all Protestant denominations was founded in New York in 1922. The society has also organized interdenominational hymn festival.

Recently, many outstanding Greek Orthodox priests and bishops have escaped from Soviet Russia and found refuge in the United States. Some Presbyterian groups in the United States have begun using music derived from the Greek or Russian Orthodox church. This phenomenon illustrates how closely music, religion, and political changes are intertwined.

Another way of introducing music across national boundaries is through the sponsoring of international competitions of the performing arts, some of which are directly connected with church life. An appropriate example of this kind are the international contests for Catholic Mass compositions. This type of cultural exposure is limited, of course, to composers, professional musicians, and priests who are especially concerned with church music.

A much larger public is attracted by various international competitions for amateur orchestras and *Fanfares*. These competitions are a feature of musical life in many Latin countries, and involve the use of brass instruments exclusively. They sometimes occur in connection with international fairs and offer opportunities for the display of musical bravado of the organizers of the exhibition; they also provide an opportunity to establish friendly personal contacts. International singing contests are naturally somewhat more restricted due to language barriers.

PROBLEMS OF TRANSLATION

Although difficulties of international contact, musical and otherwise, are increased by language barriers, they can be partially overcome by language translation. Almost at the very inception of Italian opera, translations of Italian librettos appeared, German was the language most often used. However, translation poses certain musical difficulties. Due to differences in speech pronunciation, the sound is altered. Even more important, there is the danger of altering the meaning of idiomatic expressions. Both German and English, for example, have vowel sounds and consonants that tend to be extremely guttural in contrast to the open vowels and frontally focused consonants of Italian, which are far easier to sing, particularly in the higher ranges. These pronunciation problems tend to affect the sound of Italian opera sung in these languages. Differences based in the idiomatic rendering of opera texts can be illustrated by German opera. Because of Wagner's penchant for alliteration, the texts of his operas are extremely difficult to translate. Alliteration, the practice of beginning each major word of a given sentence with the same consonant, involves a highly idiomatic sentence structure, which is always difficult to transfer to another language. In addition, it is next to impossible to use the same alliteration in the second language.

In the United States during both world wars, there was an aversion to hearing anything performed in German. The excuse was offered that performances should not be given in a language few understood. Eventually, however, these problems were resolved, and German opera was again performed in its language of composition.

METHODS OF SPREADING MUSIC BEYOND NATIONAL BOUNDARIES

Works noted for their profound musicological significance have occasionally been reproduced by international agreements among interested scholarly associations. State governments have also sponsored editions of the works of composers who many centuries ago had worked in their countries. One of the most important publications of this type is the series of *Deutsch-Oesterreichische Denkmäler*.

Another way in which music becomes known beyond its country of origin is through reviews published in news media and serious periodicals. Some of these cover new compositions and performances all over the world. The musical reviews by Johann Rochlitz (1769–1842) around the turn of the nineteenth century in the *Allgemeine Musik Zeitung* count among the first of such publications.

Last in historical development but not least in importance are various technical means of sound reproduction. Among these now widely available means must be considered long-playing tapes and records, film scores, and live and remote radio and television broadcasts.

MUSIC AND ORGANIZED POLITICS

So far we have considered the interrelationship of music and national membership and national feeling. The examination of various relationships between music and certain more closely defined forms of political expression, such as constitutions and specific forms of government, is our next focus of attention. The significance of such specific relationships is indicated by the sympathy or dislike exhibited by musicians (along with other intellectuals) toward certain political personalities. Beethoven, for instance, admired Napoleon (1796–1821), considering him an outstanding consul of the French Republic. During that period, Beethoven planned to dedicate to Napoleon the composition later called the Third or *Eroica* Symphony. But when Napoleon became a monarch and thus was no longer a republican, Beethoven, an admirer of the French Revolution, changed his mind. He did not wish to dedicate his new symphony to a monarch.

Political attitudes toward Napoleon III (1808–1873) varied among musicians. Liszt, Wagner, and Hans von Bülow admired him greatly, a feeling apparently connected with their general partiality for domineering men and their opposition to democracy. Other outstanding musicians of the same period strongly disliked Napoleon III. Joachim considered the new French Emperor the greatest enemy of German unification. Dislike for Napoleon III was not restricted exclusively to German musicians. Georges Bizet, whose fame as the representative of French operatic music was growing, harbored a violent aversion against the Emperor, as did other French artists and intellectuals. They considered Napoleon III an enemy of individualism and personal freedom.

Musicians as Supporters of Monarchies

Not all musicians espouse democratic aspirations. Bismarck was greatly admired in Germany for having unified the German Empire after democratic attempts to do so had failed. Many artists and intellectuals who might normally have been inclined toward republican ideals became his admirers. Among Bismarck's supporters were Brahms, as well as his friends Joachim, the violinist, and Heinrich von Herzogenberg, the pianist. Wagner, because of his particular concept of Teutonism, was not a wholehearted follower of Bismarck. Along with most German artists, Joachim rejoiced greatly over the victory of Germany over Napoleon III and the foundation of the second German empire in 1871. Countless

Germans, especially those with liberal or democratic leanings, had worked and prayed for German unification since the collapse of the first Napoleonic empire in 1815. Although unification was not realized by the constitutionalists in 1848, Bismarck succeeded where they had failed, earning the admiration of many Germans, including those who had not originally been friends of Prussia. This also applied to the majority of musicians. We know of no one who joined opposition groups. However, some Roman Catholics did oppose him during the 1870s, due to the struggle between Bismarck and their church (*Kulturkampf*).

Another interesting question is whether musicians entertain special attitudes toward political events. Only limited data are available on this subject. For example, little is known about the sympathies of musicians during the American Revolution, probably because music did not play a major role in colonial life. Data are also scarce in regard to the French Revolution. However, there seems to be little evidence of any robust opposition on the part of musicians in general. The revolution of 1830 also seems to have been sympathetically received by intellectuals, including musicians, as was the Belgian movement for independence. This movement, which also took place in 1830, resulted in Belgium becoming a constitutional monarchy and independent state. The revolutionary movements of 1848 were similarly favored by many German musicians, among whom were Cornelius, Moscheles, and Spohr. An outstanding supporter of this movement was Wagner, who actively participated in the rebellion.

German musicians were placed in a more difficult situation in 1866, the year of the Austro-Prussian war. Many German intellectuals embraced the Prussian cause in the belief that it could further the goal of national unity. Then as now, Vienna, the Austrian capital, was one of the leading musical centers, and many composers from a number of German states who had settled there were under the direct protection of the Austrian court and government. Thus, musicians of various national origins found themselves in competing camps. For example, Peter Cornelius, born in Frankfurt near the boundary between north and south Germany, evinced strong anti-Prussian emotions. Moscheles disapproved of the war in principle, considering it a war between brothers. Joachim was in an even more difficult position. Of Hungarian birth, he was completely assimilated into German culture as one of the most esteemed performers of Beethoven and Brahms in the world. He was also the leading musician at the court of the blind King of Hanover, who had embraced the Austrian cause and was at war with Prussia. Consequently, Joachim had to support his patron's stand, although along with many others in Hanover he gradually became aware that the Austrian cause was completely lost.

Consequently, he insisted that it would be of no interest to continue the war between the two German states, and that the interests of a unified Germany should be considered above those of the glory of Hanover. He therefore left Hanover and accepted a call, as professor, to the Royal Academy of Music at Berlin.

Musicians at Court

Musicians, like other individuals, entertain varying attitudes about the political events and personalities of their times and places. This much has already become clear through the examples already given. Now we need to examine more systematically the relationships between the attitudes of musicians and various political institutions. One should not be surprised to note that certain musicians have displayed great loyalty to their political superiors. Niels Gade and Edvard Grieg staunchly supported their monarchs. We must keep in mind that monarchies provided more opportunities for musicians to compose than any other form of government. Only monarchies commission coronation marches; they have also provided many opportunities to compose cantatas. The fact that some German musicians remained loyal to the imperial house of Hohenzollern after the collapse of the German monarchy indicates a loyalty to their means of livelihood. Many of these musicians had performed concerti and sonatas at court time after time and were treated like members of the royal family; their loyalty may have been affectionate as well as economic. Indeed, there may even have been a sense of indebtedness, which moved many artists to feel that they could not abandon the monarch, regardless of who was in power.

The fact that many prominent musicians were treated like members of the royal family they served indicates the high social esteem in which they were held. Actually, not only musicians but all artists and intellectuals were considered eligible for invitation to the royal court. When Germany became a republic, neither this high social position nor the opportunity for contributing their talents existed to the same degree for artists. In this light, the continued loyalty to former rulers and resistance to the republican form of government exhibited by many German musicians is easily understood. This does not imply that they sympathized with ultraconservative or reactionary movements, however. In fact, the only musician we know of who allied himself explicitly with monarchical causes to the extent of active participation was Franz Liszt. Liszt had been an admirer of Prince von Metternich (1773–1859) since before 1848. In addition to being the prime minister of Austro-Hungary, Metternich was the leading statesman of Europe during the period of the Holy Alliance (after the fall of Napoleon I). Above all Metternich was one of the most powerful enemies and persecutors of every democratic, republican, or even modern constitutional movement in Europe. This approach well suited Liszt's aristocratic and mystical concepts of the world.

That few noted musicians have openly professed admiration for democratic or republican forms of government can be easily understood in the light of their frequent appointment as court musicians and invitations to perform for the nobility, particularly in those European countries where Western art music developed. The only avowed republican we know of from the ranks of musicians was Cornelius, but even he may come to this position through his desire for national unity, which for a short period in 1848 showed some promising signs under the Frankfurt Parliament. Spohr and Moscheles professed sympathy for the constitutional limitation of monarchy, but only in a moderate way.

Musicians and Anticlericalism

Anticlericalism has occasionally been a tenet of political ideologies. During the period of the French Revolution, many intellectuals and artists became markedly anti-Catholic. In Germany, a corresponding development occurred during the era of the *Kulturkampf*, the previously mentioned struggle between Bismarck and the Catholic Church. At that time many intellectuals and artists supported the power position of Bismarck, among them many of the musicians who surrounded Richard Wagner, such as Hans von Bülow and Hermann Levi (1839–1900).

Musicians and Socialism

The attitude of musicians toward socialism has changed in time. We must, of course, keep in mind that prior to the emergence of Karl Marx (1818–1883) the socialist movement embodied most heterogeneous elements. During the pre-Marx period, many writers who were opposed to the ideas of the Enlightenment, to the laissez-faire system, and especially to the abolishment of the guilds, were called or called themselves socialists or communists. Among them were many conservative Catholics, particularly in France, who worked toward the reestablishment of feudal society. Moreover, some of these pre-Marxian socialists, whom Marx disdainfully referred to as "Utopians," had more or less romantic, mystical, or even religious inclinations. These factors should be remembered when trying to understand how the aristocrat Liszt could, at least for a period, display great sympathy for Saint-Simonism. This political and social movement had been elaborated by Prosper Enfantin (1796–1864) and Armand Bazard (1791–1832). It was clearly the mystical aspect of the idea of social collectivity that impressed Liszt. This becomes apparent when we realize that he was at the same time strongly opposed to Pierre-Joseph Proudhon (1809–1865), who then represented the most anarchistic wing of pre-Marxian socialism. Proudhon had however impressed a number of contemporaries favorably. For a while he even held the admiration of Hans von Bülow, who later reversed his position completely. During the same period, Wagner was greatly interested in Bakunin (1814–1876), the anarchist, and his work.

For all these men socialism and anarchism represented a means of stemming the tide of the rising middle classes and capitalism. Later forms of socialism became highly organized through labor unions and cooperatives, and were consequently more and more bureaucratically structured. Understandably, then, socialism soon became the butt of many jokes on the part of romantically minded musicians, who admired individualism and were full of contempt for the masses. Hugo Wolf (1860–1903), who was one of the first composers to use Wagnerian orchestration as accompaniment for popular music, was one such musician. Despite Wagner's early political views, he had many followers who almost idolized the heroes in the class wars of history, and who protested against Bismarck's application of violence in his battle with the rising socialist movement. One of the most notable of these political critics was Hermann Levi, the conductor of *Parsifal* in Bayreuth.

Regarding the contemporary Soviet state, an artist has but two alternatives—he can either become a supporter of the system or leave. Accordingly, many musicians left Russia. Those who stayed, together with new recruits who moved to Russia, became outstanding representatives of Soviet music.

MUSICIANS AND ANTI-SEMITISM

Anti-Semitism has influenced musical life in the Western world more immediately than any other political or social ideology. To present here the full historical background of the development of this cancerous point of view would, of course, be impossible; only those few aspects directly affecting musical life can be touched upon.

Throughout Europe many of the restrictive laws against Jews were gradually abolished after the French Revolution, but only in theory. In practice many professions and positions, particularly those government positions enjoying high social status, remained inaccessible to those of Jewish birth. Consequently, Jewish people were forced into many less popular professions in Europe. In addition to the fields of business, medicine, dentistry, and law, however, there were other professions Jews were allowed to enter, and did enter in large numbers.

Among the various artistic pursuits, becoming a musician was the most popular calling among Jews, probably because music was more international and fewer expressions of anti-Semitism were found among musicians. But when the movement to provide permanent employment security succeeded and orchestra members and music teachers became public officials with rights to old age pensions, regular employment opportunities within music became scarce for Jewish people. Since it was quite difficult for Jews to obtain official positions in the community, even in the realms of music or art, a relatively high percentage of free-lance actors, singers, and other performers were Jews. This fact was later incorporated as a tool in anti-Semitic propaganda.

Excursus on Anti-Semitism

The term *anti-Semitism* covers a variety of heterogeneous movements which, however, share certain characteristics, so that they can be discussed under three main headings. The oldest of these is the religious antagonism between Christians and Jews, the dominant source of conflict during the Middle Ages and various periods in modern times. When interest in religion diminished during the nineteenth century, religious persecution gradually waned. In the large Western and Central European cities Jews did not identify as strongly with their religion, and many rabbis moved away from orthodoxy to embrace more liberal Judaic concepts that did not greatly differ from certain religious ideas of liberal Protestant ministers.

The second sphere of anti-Semitic expression is primarily economic. In many Central European countries Jews were not only involved in big business; many lived in small cities where they were store owners and were involved in the livestock trade. Because of this they were almost the only personal representatives of the capitalist order with whom the middle and lower class peasants and the lower middle class of the small cities, especially the handicraft men, came into contact. All these more or less rural groups asserted that they suffered economically from the development of large capitalistic enterprises. But being of a petty bourgeoisie mentality, they wanted to keep their very small properties. Accordingly, they were opposed to any kind of socialism that had developed since the Industrial Revolution. Dissatisfied with capitalism and opposed to any kind of socialistic future, they became the admirers of a precapitalistic past, and by so doing, advocates of the feudal system. Feudal landholders also knew that their own power was decreasing with increasing industrialization. Thus they believed that they could not stand alone any longer; they needed allies and found them in this dying class of small property owners, innkeepers, and master craftsmen. This alliance was formed under the banner of struggle against the common enemy, modern capitalism. Capitalism, in turn, was supposed to be represented to the highest degree by Jews. Anti-Semitism became the slogan of this alliance of feudals and lower class precapitalists. This economic form of anti-Semitism became a direct political power, most directly in Germany and Austro-Hungary, and also sometimes in France. In general this movement received little support from members of the intelligentsia, except from a few Lutheran ministers and some high-school teachers who hoped for the reestablishment of feudalism and the guild system.

In order for the movement to attract intellectuals and artists, anti-Semitism needed, in addition to the romantic, precapitalistic ideology, a theory with scientific pretensions. This led to the third phase in the development of anti-Semitism—racism. Racism appeared as one of the many applications of Darwinism. The claim was that one human group might be superior to others and thereby might be entitled to any useful means of survival. Just as some industrialists have used Darwin's theory to argue against state-supported social welfare policies, many people have used it to justify the oppression of minorities. Germans in particular have used this theory to justify the persecution of Jews. Under its aegis, frequent alliances against Jews were formed between conservatively-minded orthodox Lutherans and atheistic Darwinists.

One should remember, however, that anti-Semitic developments took place not only in Germany and Austria-Hungary. Somewhat similar forms of anti-Semitism originated and developed in Czarist Russia, affecting the life of Jewish musicians even more than in Central Europe. For example, musically gifted Jewish children were not, for a long time, eligible for admission to the state musical academies. If a Jewish child did eventually succeed in gaining entrance to such an academy, severe restrictions were imposed. The situation for Jewish musicians did not improve until during the last decades of Czarist rule. However, even then Jewish musicians and artists, along with other Jewish intellectuals, continued to harbor strong feelings against the Czar.

Anti-Semitic Musicians

This general background should be kept in mind as we consider the role of anti-Semitism in music, the position of Richard Wagner, and the role of music during the Hitler and Soviet eras. Naturally, a musician's attitude toward anti-Semitism depends somewhat on whether the musician himself is Jewish. Jewish people, we must remember, were among the few in artistic circles who vigorously opposed anti-Semitism.

But there was also a certain trend toward the end of the nineteenth century to repress one's Jewish origin as much as possible. If one's name made assimilation impossible, the practice was to change it. In fact, this common practice in Europe has occurred even in the United States, as recently as the first half of the twentieth century. Other Jews, such as Joachim, who were already largely assimilated into Western culture, converted to Christianity and had their children baptized. Joachim continued to protect Jewish musicians, however; to cite one example, he sharply protested an attempt to fire the violinist Jacob Grün (1837–1916) because he was Jewish. Joachim also opposed Richard Wagner's anti-Semitic attitude. Joachim's custom of protecting Jewish musicians caused him a great deal of trouble. Rudorff, a pianist whose political views were ultraconservative, told Joachim that he should publicly refuse further association with Jews. No one else in the Brahms front was so blatantly verbal, although remarks similar to those made by Beethoven and Cornelius were made regarding the so-called Jewish commercial mentality. Brahms's intimate friend Herzogenberg however protested against not hiring musicians for being Jewish.

The Case of Richard Wagner

A vast literature deals with speculation as to whether Richard Wagner was of Jewish origin. Some have pointed out that his mother was an intimate friend of the actor, Ludwig Geyer (1780–1821), and have even gone so far as to suggest that Geyer was Wagner's father; others have spent much energy and many words refuting the same assumptions. Some have tried to prove that Geyer was a Jew, while others have maintained that he came from an old Lutheran family. Of course, the answer to this question does not interest us here; the example is mentioned merely to convey something about the atmosphere in which anti-Semitism within music operated in Europe.

Wagner's anti-Jewish sentiments were part of his universal sociopolitical philosophy. The full exposition of his philosophy required several decades. It had not yet appeared during his Romantic period when he wrote *Lohengrin, The Flying Dutchman* and *Tannhäuser,* but began to emerge in the *Ring* and *Tristan and Isolde* as well as in some of the theoretical works of the later period. Many writers have pointed to differences between the young revolutionary Wagner of 1848, who was noted for his identification with and support for the anarchist Bakunin, and the later Wagner, who, as an intimate friend and protégé of the King of Bavaria, made a direct commitment to Christianity in his last work, *Parsifal.* Although these obvious differences in his views exist, Wagner espoused certain primary concepts throughout his life. Basic to these was his deeply-rooted protest against such dominant attitudes of the nineteenth century as bourgeoisie, capitalism, rationalism, and the tendency to measure anything qualitative in a quantitative manner.

He was also deeply pessimistic throughout his life, a tendency that increased in later years. This pessimism is expressed in the operas of *Der Ring* in which the heroic characters—Wotan, Siegmund, and Brünhilde—are defeated, while the elements of darkness, especially represented by Alberich, king of the dwarfs, are victorious. Wagner was not versed in the works of Arthur Schopenhauer (1788–1860), the pessimistic philosopher, at the time he composed the Ring. It has been established that he had, up to then, not even heard of Schopenhauer, nor did the two meet. Schopenhauer, however, became familiar with the work of Wagner and rejected it completely. This would be consistent with what is known about Schopenhauer, who downgraded everyone except himself and those few thinkers he considered his imperfect predecessors. In his later years, however, Wagner was greatly influenced by Schopenhauer's thinking, as is obvious in the plot of *Tristan,* whose hero not only had to die but wanted to.

As has already been mentioned, *Parsifal,* his last work, expresses themes consistent with Christian thinking—although Amfortas dies (in this opera), he is "saved"—and also contains elements of Buddhism. The dominant theme of the opera is the hope of finding a better world, free of this world's evil, to live in. This theme is elaborated in the plot's various human relationships. Rather than attempting to help each other by improving the conditions of this world, the various characters pity themselves and others for being obliged to live in this worst of all possible worlds. This Buddhist attitude is directly related to views of Schopenhauer. This philosopher had first brought together elements of German transcendentalism with romantic ideas introduced into Western thought by the von Schlegel brothers, August Wilhelm (1767–1845) and Friedrich (1772–1829). Wagner proceeded to combine ideas of Schopenhauer with ideas that had no connection with the philosophy of the Frankfurt pessimist. The philosophical struggles between the kingdoms of light and darkness were combined by Wagner with real struggles between "superior" and "inferior" peoples in the plots of his operas.

The basic story of *Der Ring* is derived from an Icelandic legend that dates to the time shorty after A.D. 1000. This legend expresses the pre-Christian religion of Scandinavia and contains highly pessimistic elements. In the Scandinavian religion of pre-Christian times, the gods are defeated and must die. However, Wagner's rendition is far more pessimistic than the Nordic mythology, which includes indications of hope that a better world will come after the catastrophe of the gods. That Wagner found his version of Nordic legends congenial to his concept of the world is not surprising. He considered Nordic philosophy, along with his own, to be basically different from Christianity and other Western European, Western-Asiatic religions. He also construed a similarity between the Hindu philosophy, his own and that of the Norsemen, an amalgamation that was consistent with the findings of Franz Bopp (1791–1867), who recognized similarities between Scandinavian languages and those of India. It was Bopp who classified these languages as one family of Indo-European languages. The theory of similarity of race was based on these linguistic relationships. Eventually, the concept of an Aryan race developed.

In the next phase of development, the Aryan race concept was fused with Darwinian theory. Darwin's notion of the "survival of the fittest" was applied in such a way that the conclusion was reached that this Aryan race was superior to any other race, and especially superior to the Semites. The concept of Aryan superiority then crystallized further in the idea that the Nordic peoples were the elite of the Aryan race, and that superiority was manifested in their pessimistic religion. Not only were the Semites considered inferior, but the Hebrews, who were largely responsible for the origin and philosophical context of Christianity, were by far the most inferior of all Semitic peoples. Even though the superiority of the Aryan race was proved erroneous, this metaphysical and pseudoracial antagonism later fueled interpersonal animosity based on more general social and economic hostilities.

In Wagner's operas, Norsemen represent a feudal and regimented society in which craftsmen are organized in guilds and enjoy great professional honor. *Die Meistersinger,* the least pessimistic of all Wagnerian operas, depicts the glories of the craftsmen of Germany. In stark contrast, the Semitic peoples, especially the Jews, represented an antiheroic, commercial view of the world. In *Der Ring,* Alberich, king of the dwarfs and ruler of the dark kingdom, gained his power from stealing previously undiscovered gold from the bottom of the Rhine. For Wagner, Alberich

represented capitalism and the Semitic mentality. Thus the battle between the kingdoms of light and of darkness was reduced to the struggle
between Teutonic Norsemen and Jews.

Richard Wagner's denigration of modern commercialism should not be
confused with socialism's criticism of the capitalistic order. If because of
his anticapitalistic views Wagner is to be considered a socialist, as some
biographers have insisted, then it must be insofar as he preferred a feudal,
guild-organized society. Wagner's ideas were held by many anti-Semitic
groups of his own time, and also by Hitler's followers. One may say without exaggeration that Wagner was one of those German intellectuals and
musicians who helped prepare the way for Nazism. Indeed, few musicians
have influenced political developments as extensively.

The Wagner Cult

The King of Bavaria helped Wagner build his own theater in Bayreuth,
giving every kind of official protection besides. An essential fact is that
this theater, the *Bayreuth Festspielhaus,* was never intended primarily for
musical events; rather, it was to be the center of a new cult, a new world
concept, even a new religion. The unlimited supply of money devoted to
this end came largely from the sale of Wagner scores and arrangements
and from performance royalties. At the festivals the most famous conductors, stage directors, singers, and instrumentalists were engaged. These
artists believed that it advanced their careers to be called to Bayreuth. A
special journal, the *Bayreuth Blätter,* was founded with contributions
from world-famous writers who adhered to Wagnerian concepts. Many of
them settled in Bayreuth for long periods of time. Perhaps the most
famous of these was the French Count Gobineau (1816–1882), a major
expounder of German superiority. In addition to his immediate family,
Wagner also involved other relatives in the project at Bayreuth, including his two famous sons-in-law Houston Stewart Chamberlain (1855–
1927) and Henry Thode (1857–1920). Thode is well known as a musicologist and historian, while Chamberlain, although of English origin,
became one of the most articulate advocates of German superiority over
other nations, including his native England. All these activities joined
together in promoting Wagnerianism not only as a musical movement
but also as a complete world concept. During the latter part of the
nineteenth century and the beginning of the twentieth century, few
musicians protested against the Wagnerian philosophy.

Gosima Wagner, Wagner's second wife, was an admirer of and in steady
contact with such men as Ludwig Scheman, who propagated Gobineau's

ideas of German superiority, and Heinrich von Treitschke (1834–1896), historian and German advocate of neo-Machiavellianism. Treitschke insisted that state and statesmen should be completely free of all religious and ethical considerations and that the sole consideration of politics should be the pursuit of power, disregarding justice. Cosima Wagner also became an open admirer and protector of Wilhelm Ahlwardt (1827–1900), a former primary school teacher who was elected to the Reichstag on an anti-Semitic program. Ahlwardt made such wild assertions about well-known Jewish members of the business community that leaders of other successful anti-Semitic parties, such as the conservative Liebermann von Sonnenberg (1848–1911) and the democratic Otto Böckel (1853–1923), announced publicly that they had no connection with him. Adding Cosima's activities to those of her husband, one can understand why their philosophy and its manifestations are said to having helped prepare the way for the anti-Semitic persecutions in Hitler's Germany.

MUSIC AND POLITICAL CHANGE

When a country is ruled by a monarch the simple fact of his death can be a significant event for musicians, especially when music performances at court are a private matter to the monarch and have no connection with the state government per se. A musician may then find himself out of work for a variety of reasons. For example, the successor to the throne may have no interest in spending money in the support of orchestras or operatic productions. He may also be an outright antagonist of music for reasons of personal or religious taste. This happened several times when new rulers of small German courts espoused a pietistic version of Protestantism and considered opera and anything related to it as too secular, if not downright sinful. Another type of situation occurred when a monarch had a favorite court musician, who might have been regarded as something of a musical dictator while under the protection of the royal throne. Once the ruler was dead or dethroned, voluntarily or otherwise, such a musician had to rely on his own resources with no one caring what happened to him. Such a case was that of Gaspare Spontini (1774–1851), an Italian composer of traditional grand opera in the early part of the nineteenth century who was the protégé of the Prussian King Frederick William IV (1765–1837). When the king resigned in favor of his younger brother, Spontini lost his position at court almost immediately and was soon forgotten.

A monarch's death may have an even stronger impact on music when it marks the end of an epoch, as when Louis XIV of France died in 1715 after reigning for more than seventy years. A time of uninterrupted war, his reign had brought the state near bankruptcy more than once. With his death, the determination of the French people to bring about a change found expressions that also had their effect on music. Louis XIV had favored operas dealing with war, and whose heroes were generals and other military men; with his demise, heroic opera lost favor in France.

Changes in governmental forms also affect the development of music. Changes such as political revolutions have sometimes been adumbrated in musical productions. One of the more famous examples is *The Marriage of Figaro* by Mozart. The libretto represents condensation of two comedies by Beaumarchais (1732–1799), *The Barber of Seville* and *The Marriage of Figaro*. On the surface they appear as tales of intrigue with happy endings yet they clearly contain satirical elements. The Count Almaviva wishes to enjoy the feudal custom of "ius primae noctis," the right of a feudal landlord when two of his serfs marry to enjoy himself with the bride on the wedding night. But Mozart turns the tables on Count Almaviva; the valet Figaro becomes the victorious hero, and Almaviva emerges as the villain. Since Mozart's works were usually performed in the presence of nobility, this particular point, although the opera's main point, was somewhat modified and shaded over in order not to offend his patrons. Nevertheless, the bourgeois audiences understood satire very well, which helped to promote the popularity of this opera.

When the repressive political situation became intolerable for members of the upper middle class and for intellectuals in France, the general feeling found frequent expression in operatic works. The opera *Tarare* by Antonio Salieri may serve as an example. It is the story of a man of humble origin who wins out over priests and nobility. Such pieces were also written in the New World. Musical comedies satirizing those who remained loyal to the British crown were common during the colonial period of American history.

However, the outbreak of a revolution has far greater influence for musical change than do the events which lead up to it. Musical practices which had been protected by the ousted government as expressions of its rule are almost immediately cast aside with a completed revolution. For example, the Italian opera buffo, a favorite of the French king and his court, disappeared after the French uprising. When the revolutionary movement spread to the area now known as Belgium, which was under Austrian control at the time and was referred to as the Austrian Netherlands, the use of the German and Italian language in opera performances stopped as well.

Music and Revolutions

The impact of a successful revolution upon the musical life of any country does not consist only of the elimination of certain forms of music. Even more important, new types of music intended to reflect the attitudes of the victorious revolutionaries are created. Usually a new national anthem will be written. The "Marseillaise" originated in this way, as did "La Brabanconne," which glorified the successful Belgian revolution in 1830. Moreover, the new heads of government are usually not content with the creation of only a new anthem, but wish to introduce other forms of music to celebrate the victory of their philosophy of life. With the French Revolution, popular songs were written to express a deistic type of world concept. New operas glorified the revolution. New ballets were composed and performed on the new national holidays. In these performances the male dancers wore the long pants introduced by the insurgents, instead of the *culottes* of the vanished regime.

Occasionally an aborted revolution provides inspiration for a later rebellion, and the anthem of the previous uprising is adopted as expression of the movement. For instance, although the "Marseillaise" was outlawed after the collapse of the Napoleonic empire in 1830 and again in 1848, it was immediately revived by each respective group of rebels and proclaimed as their own song of revolution. This was true of other countries as well, since the Greeks and Hungarians adopted the "Marseillaise" as their own after changes of government.

Wars of independence influence the musical expression of a country even more than revolutions. After achieving independence, almost every Latin American country did away with the songs of Spain or Portugal. They produced their own songs and choral music to express and symbolize new concepts of state and society and their sense of patriotism for the new state.

Of course, a successful counterrevolution may also have powerful effects on music. As mentioned, the Marseillaise was forbidden regularly after each successful reestablishment of monarchy in France. Rouget de Lisle (1760–1836), its composer, died penniless.

Music and War

Not only revolution, but all kinds of war and national upheaval affect the musical expression of a people. The most telling effect of national crises upon the musical scene is the shortage of funds for the financing of new musical ventures, since the whole economy is usually geared to achieving victory. There is evidence that as early as the end of the

Middle Ages, musicians were complaining that Maximilian I (1459–1519), Emperor of the Holy Roman Empire, had stopped paying them in order to use his money exclusively for military purposes. Similar things have taken place in more recent periods. Frequently, musicians who did not have lifetime or permanent contracts were discharged when during wartime it appeared necessary to withdraw funds from artistic projects.

Throughout history, the performance of music written by enemy nationals is reduced, if not outlawed altogether in war time. The heat of national feeling was so increased by the rise of chauvinism in the nineteenth and twentieth centuries that performers and composers of a foreign origin even remotely resembling that of the enemy found it nearly impossible to obtain employment. This was particularly true during World War I and II. Although musicians felt this problem more intensely in Europe, it also existed in the United States.

~ One must not assume, however, that war has only negative consequences for music. Wars may spur the production of new music and the performance of certain older forms as well. Much music is introduced anonymously under highly emotional conditions, such as songs written by soldiers on the field of battle. Songs, choral music, and musical stage productions are composed, published, and performed to celebrate victory. Legend has it that as a young boy Euripides, one of the three great Greek writers of tragedy, was the member of a choir that performed in celebration of the decisive Greek victory over Persia. Through the ages renowned composers have been commissioned to write music in celebration of a victory. Others have written such music from their own inspiration and patriotic fervor. Brahms and Wagner wrote music so nationalistic that it won the hearts of a people inspired by their victory in the Franco-Prussian war of 1870.

The end of armed conflict does not necessarily imply the end of the war's influence on musical life. Often a war is followed by the military occupation of enemy territory, which may result in the prohibition of the performance of that country's patriotic music. France employed this practice immediately following 1680, the French Revolution, and the Napoleonic wars in its occupation of the Rhine province of Germany. More recently, of course, the French army also occupied Germany after the World Wars, when Germany was also occupied by American, Russian, and British troops. In the French occupied zone the German people were forbidden, after World War I, to sing their local songs in praise of the Rhineland; the British and American troops placed no such restrictions on the Germans. One of the results of French occupation in any period was a rash of new French compositions designed to demonstrate the superiority of French over German culture.

What we have said about the effects of military occupation on the music of the occupied and conquering countries applies equally when the victors amalgamate the conquered lands with their own territory and thereby create a new country. Even if the old style of music of the newly attached people is not officially repressed, it will generally disappear in the course of time. The centuries-old harp playing of the Irish people disappeared when Ireland came under English control. Many other examples exist. Certainly, there are positive influences as well as negative. The conquering country may have developed a more sophisticated musical culture, which is passed on to the people of newly occupied countries. While outlawing the native music of a country, the French have added new works to enrich the culture of the land they have taken over. The reverse may also be true, as when the Spanish conquered some Arabian territories. It was Spanish music that was enriched by the culture of the conquered Arab peoples. Spanish music was also enriched by the conquest of Holland and Belgium. These generally far more advanced countries also enriched the pictorial arts of the conquering Spaniards.

MUSIC IN TOTALITARIAN STATES

In spite of the rich palette of social forces that colored musical life, none influenced its fate more profoundly in a short span of time than the great political changes that occurred in Europe after the end of World War I. Among totalitarian states, the Hitler and Stalin governments deserve special analysis for our sociological view of music. The political roles of the totalitarian governments of Mussolini (1883–1945), Marshall Pétain (1856–1951), and General Franco (1892–1975) will first be mentioned, even though their influence on music was not nearly as extensive as that of Hitler and Stalin. In Italy and Spain the spark of music was so completely identified with national feelings that neither Mussolini nor Franco considered it necessary to impose any essential changes. Pétain's government was primarily a short-lived puppet state under Hitler's specific control. Pétain's only obligation was to follow the orders of the Third Reich, which cared little about whether French music would be changed.

Excursus on Totalitarianism

Hitlerism or Nazism did not fill an ideological void. It built on a long tradition of conservative and antiindividualistic thought in various sectors of cultural life. Consumer associations had already aimed at unifying artists and audiences under a common philosophical opposition to the individualistic Renaissance ideals of *ars pro arte*. Collectivist protest against occidental individualism manifested itself in a variety of romantic and youth movements at the turn of the current century, among other things. Hitler's superstate can be viewed as an attempt to give political expression to this antiindividualistic perspective, as the official German definition of music, under Hitler, testifies. Music was not supposed to have anything to do with aesthetics or enjoyment, much less the social life of the upper classes. It was rather to express a national enthusiasm for the Nietzschian theory of the superrace adopted by the Nazis. Musical practice was to promote audience awareness of and pride in belonging to the Aryan Race. Germans were expected to surround themselves with Aryan music, and were encouraged to learn to play instruments in order to further glorify the Fatherland and the Führer. In other words, appropriate amateur as well as professional performances were considered an essential manifestation of national feeling. During the Nazi period, when a 14-year-old boy joined the Hitler Youth, he was invited to join one of the many fife and drum corps or marching bands of the movement and was taught to play, if necessary, an instrument. In physical education, emphasis was shifted from gymnastics to eurhythmics in order to further involve music in daily life. One may find it noteworthy that the various forms of youth music were not practiced primarily for audience enjoyment, but rather as part of a political education that glorified the Führer and the Fatherland.

In a totalitarian state, the term *political party* has a rather specific connotation. Instead of uniting the citizens' struggle for power, membership in the party identifies the elite within the elite. In the case of Nazi Germany, party membership afforded the opportunity of showing that one was a true believer in and adherent of Nazi dogma, willing and able to behave accordingly. Thus, everything connected with the party was surrounded with a nationalistic and emotional aura. For example, the Nazi Party reacted to the discussion of controversial issues such as popular elections as decadent manifestations of a democratic, and therefore non-Aryan, mentality. Hence, democratic decision-making was eliminated from party caucuses, which resembled ecstatically conducted religious revival meetings. Martial music played an essential role at party caucuses, where fife and drum corps and marching bands were used to create an atmosphere of patriotism.

Although this type of music as performed by amateurs was considered essential to life in the Nazi state, professional musicians had not been eliminated from the scene but continued to work within a change of function. Outstanding among the requirements, of course, was service to the Führer. In fact, without such service they were not tolerated. In this way all musicians, amateur and professional, were organized into the overarching institution of *Die Reichsmusikkammer*.

Governmental Control of Music in Hitler Germany

The top institutional layer of governmental control of musicians was the Reichsmusikkammer, which included in its jurisdiction everyone from the youngest Hitler Youth drummer to the serious composer of symphonies and operas. This institution also included all of the economic aspects of music, from publishing houses to retail outlets, bringing them under unified control. Governmental control also included all of the amateur associations specializing in popular music.

The frequency of political occasions on which to perform music was, as we have seen, very high and was expressed by the term *Gebrauchsmusik*. This word cannot be translated literally, but a meaningful rendering goes as follows: Music was not to be viewed as an art confined to concerts, which would stand out in bold relief against daily living. Rather, it should be an integral part of daily living and permeate every waking moment. Music was to start in the home and family, where it was not only to be appreciated but performed as well, beginning as soon as the youngest child was capable of holding an instrument in his hands. Simple types of flute music, comparable to modernized forms of the old *Blockflöte,* were performed by very young children, who were also taught old folksongs that might otherwise have been forgotten. Composers of regional music were encouraged to compose new folk tunes based on old rhythms and melodies. Modern symphonic compositions also contained, in the last decades, melodic elements of popular and regional origin. Folk singing and the playing of simple instruments came to fill much of leisure time. University students were admonished to abandon the traditional drinking songs, which had been collected in the *Commersbuch* for over a hundred years and had been sung at thousands of student conventions and academic holidays. Drinking songs were to be replaced by reviving the old form of collegium musicum, which had nationalistic as well as academic characteristics.

The Nazi leaders also displayed their own peculiar preferences in instruments. Strings were considered effeminate, as opposed to the more masculine brass and woodwinds. Brass instruments were especially favored for their volume. Choirs of trumpets and trombones, which had been common in Lutheran churches for centuries, were adopted for general use. They were stationed on the towers of churches and town halls so that everyone throughout the surrounding countryside could hear them. Many older compositions by Bach and his predecessors and their admirers were transposed and reproduced for use by these trumpet and trombone choirs.

Of course, military music was heavily sponsored by the Hitler state. While every government with a standing army has a military band, in most countries they are lucky to enjoy secondary rank. Most professional musicians, particularly those involved with classical music of any kind, are usually disdainful of military bands, with their emphasis on wind and percussion instruments. In fact, the army itself tends to accord but little honor to those who play in its own band; few commissioned officers, if any, participate. They are usually staffed with privates and noncommissioned officers only, including the band leader. Within Nazi Germany, however, bandmasters in the military were given officer rank and the opportunity to advance within the officer corps.

Another indication of these changes in musical practice was the emphasis given to instruments that had either been eliminated from symphonic orchestras or had never been so used, such as mandolins of all classes (including mandolas and mandacellos which had lower ranges) and the bandoneon in all of its ranges. These instruments had always been popular with the German people, and with Hitler's rise to power were included in various public bands.

The Nazi takeover of institutions also had consequences for the German theater. Although municipalities retained some control as in the old German tradition, the state now held the power to interfere with program selection and the frequency of performances. Opera, too, was restricted and made subject to the Hitler concept of the political and social functions of music. Much emphasis was placed on Wagner. Because of the philosophy expressed in the *Ring* and *Die Meistersinger,* Hitler and his entire entourage considered Wagner their forerunner. Other manifestations of the Germanic spirit were fostered in a variety of regional musico-dramatic productions. Prior to the rise of Hitler, many of these amateur forms had been considered, like military music, inferior. Now local and regional productions by itinerant artists (even those who used marionettes) who spoke largely in dialects were considered as characteristic expressions of German life. In order to appreciate the renewed sympathy for local and regional folk art during the Hitler era, one must remember that provincialism has always been considered a particularly German trait. Under Hitler, *Kasperle* theaters in Southern Germany, *Hanneschen* in the Rhine provinces, and similar dialect theaters in other districts were raised from obscurity to the level of officially sponsored institutions.

Hitler's Germany also gave renewed emphasis to dance and body rhythm. These phenomena, already known before Hitler's rise to power, were now incorporated into Nazi culture and used as symbols for the new philosophy of life. Speech choirs (*Sprechchor*) had been introduced earlier, during the Weimar Republic. Their recitations were accompanied by orchestral music and interpretive dancing, and were combined with the traditionally accompanied eurhythmic speech choir and reintroduced by the Hitler movement as an expression of group feeling.

Movies in Hitler Germany

Totalitarian movements tend to promulgate ideological views according to which collective life is more important than that of individuals. The cinema involves group activities more completely than any other artistic medium, both in the production and reception or appreciation phases. In order to gain a fuller understanding of the role of collective experience and the use of the cinema during the Hitler era, a brief excursion into the history of the moving pictures is called for. Technical innovations in art have always initially been used to express and even to imitate established forms. The technological advances of the film had first been perfected at a time when other art forms, such as painting, offered opportunities for highly developed individualistic interpretations. The rising preference for individualistic rather than stereotypic expression can be seen in the great admiration showered upon stars of the dramatic and operatic stage. The new medium, in keeping with this historical trend, at first elaborated traditional themes of the theater of the times, namely the individual love affair. Many early films were adaptations of previously successful stage plays, which were expected to repeat their commercial success in the new medium. The background music for these movies employed the musical styles then current. Originally played to cover up the noisy projection equipment, this background music later developed into a musical form particularly suited to underline the action in the film. In the early days, however, the background music often bore little if any relation to the story content of the films. With the change over from silent to sound movies in the late 1920s, unrelated background music disappeared. Although the music of the movies changed, romantic love themes, by popular demand and the business sense of movie producers, retained a dominant position in the plots of motion pictures.

When the Nazis came upon the scene in Germany, they insisted that the movies be used as a propaganda device in the consolidation of their regime. Their image of the new Germany permitted no place for the cultivation of the subjective feelings of a beautiful girl or a handsome young man, either in the arts or in life. Therefore, it was argued, movie plots should expose the public to the collective customs and the way of life of a great number of people. Moreover, changes in personal life spheres should be linked to significant political changes of the times, and ought to find expression in the movies. In this way, the new national German film was to change not only the romanticized theme of the cinema, but its entire artistic concept. For example, the actors would be the German people, the Hitler Youth or the Brown Shirts, rather than featured film stars. This transformation is exemplified in *"Hitlerjunge Quex"* (September 1933; camera: Konstantin Tschet). The main character, Quex, was to represent the youth of the new Hitler Germany. The plot is set off against the traditional society, in which liberal and democratic themes are portrayed as decadent.

The change to the propaganda films was easily accommodated and even supported by the development of the new style of film music, with musical accompaniment related to the plot. The interpretative musical accompaniment in films of this period frequently incorporated patriotic music in the form of marches, trombone choirs, and the use of fife and drum corps and similar forms sponsored by the party.

Radio Broadcasting in Hitler Germany

Many of the observations regarding the Nazi attitude toward the use of films may also be extended to radio. Radio broadcasting had been under limited state control under the Weimer Republic. This had been facilitated by the introduction of a mixed ownership system, half private enterprise and half state. The Weimar coalition government had been relatively tolerant of a broad range of political views. In fact, with the exception of some extremist views, spokesmen for almost every political position could use the radio. A great variety of viewpoints came to be represented on the air, whether political, economic, religious, or philosophical in basis. Although the Republic had made little use of radio for presenting government attitudes and positions on various issues, this medium became the official voice of the government beginning with the very day of Hitler's assumption of power.

In the 1920s, a great deal of time had been assigned to music programs. Even these programs were now to be used to further the objectives of the regime. A telling example concerns the scheduling of programs that emphasized local musical materials. The Hitler regime, as will be recalled, directed various party offices and associated scholarly resources toward documenting the cultural heritage of the various Germanic tribes. In keeping with this orientation, performances of local and regional theater were encouraged to employ the traditional vernacular. Radio, too, despite its wider audience and primarily because of its broader coverage, was also directed to feature local dialects, folk songs, and instrumental music. Germans were to be shown that they should be proud of their diversified heritage, which distinguished them from migrant peoples who had no sense of their own cultural traditions.

Although radio broadcasting was used extensively as a political propaganda instrument, Hitler was quite ambivalent about the accomplishments of modern technology and abstract science. Machine technology, especially, was considered an outgrowth of urban intellectualism, which in turn was regarded as less German than the more simple national emotions. This attitude may have been responsible for the preference of live over recorded music during the Third Reich. It was said, for example, that mechanically reproduced sound was not able to render immediate emotions. At any rate, radio programming took on a decidedly more regional character under the influence of the new government, and it may well be that the same currents influenced the field of musicology.

In German universities there had been a highly developed tradition of scholarship in musicology, which was carried on by a number of internationally known music historians and theoreticians. In fact, a large percentage of all musicological work and studies had been done in Germany. Historical work was also of interest to the new regime, which recognized that German scholars had gained international reputations in this field and that continued support would enhance the Third Reich. At the same time, preoccupation with purely intellectual forms of inquiry and the pursuit of abstract art were officially discouraged.

Since musicological scholarship was to help in the creation of a music supposed to be a true emanation of the German national character, appropriate musicology was encouraged and most music publications continued to appear. Music historians were persuaded to investigate previous instrumental forms in order to assess their possible revival in a more contemporary cast. Once it had been decided that the *blockflöte* had a Germanic derivation, it was heavily promoted and incorporated in different performance settings. Music scholars were also expected to collect traditional and folk songs. Systematic collections of texts and melodies were commenced in the various regions of Germany. After appropriate analysis they were to be published, expurgated of any alien elements that might have contaminated them.

Musical criticism in major newspapers had also been widely read abroad. It was permitted to continue during the Nazi years, although not without official guidelines. Prior to the rise of Hitler, many Jewish scholars had been active also in this field. Their work was now repressed as

being "negative" in character. "Positive" criticism was to offer suggestions by the critic on how the performance of a work would better help
in building a new German music full of national feeling. Positive music
criticism was to turn into a branch of political propaganda, a part of the
overall indoctrination program aimed at imposing the Nazi vision on
the total life experience of all Germans.

These selected observations on certain aspects of musical life in Germany during the Hitler period illustrate how changes in political structure can bring about major changes in performance practice, musical involvement, and even scholarship. Another series of examples can be
offered from the case of the Soviet Union which, though similar in some
respects, will be quite different in others. These differences are notably
related to variations both in political and musical traditions.

Music in Czarist Russia

Since we are not able to exhaustively treat the full history of musical
development of Czarist Russia, any conclusions based on the changes in
musical practices of the Soviet state will have to remain tentative. However, in order to get some comprehension of the changes the Soviet attitude brought, selected traits will be examined on which information
from the Czarist period has been available to this writer. On the basis of
this selection an attempt will be made to assist the reader in comparing
the similarities and essential differences between the Nazi attitude toward
music and that of the Soviet state.

Russian history had been outside the realm of Western cultural development until approximately 1700 and the reign of Peter the Great
(1672–1725). The vast areas of Russia had been Christianized by Greek
Orthodox missionaries from Constantinople rather than Rome. Differences between Eastern and Western Christianity are quite remarkable,
since there were intellectual movements that influenced the West but
that never touched the East. A few of these elements may be mentioned.
First, there was Roman law with its extreme concept of individual ownership of property; also, Aristotelian logic and its goal of providing rational
proof for religious belief. Further, natural philosophy and certain applications in the form of chemistry, engineering, and industrial technology
had formative influences on Western critical thinking. In Russia, however, there were districts that had been completely separated culturally
from the West. Some areas had been under Mongolian control for more
than 250 years. Because of this heritage, the Greek Orthodox Church was
accommodating in its doctrine and submissive to political rulers to an ex-

tent not experienced in other Christian groups. This religious teaching helped to strengthen the trend toward collectivism among the subjected Russian masses.

Russian music had also remained virtually untouched by Western developments for many centuries. Church music in Russia consisted mainly of simple vocal music used for congregational singing, which was copied over and over by the Basilian monks in their monasteries. Rural populations also amused themselves with old folk dances and songs, accompanied by a few relatively simple plucked instruments. To the Western ear, this folk music had a melancholy, even mystic, quality. It was characterized by minor thirds and the use of modal scales, even on such happy occasions as festivals and dances, and on sacramental occasions such as weddings and christenings.

Musical instruments and forms such as the organ as developed by Benedictine monks, polyphonic singing and instrument playing, and the use of stringed instruments to be played with the bow, which had become customary in Western society failed to reach Russia. Such musical forms as opera, oratorio, suite, symphony, and various kinds of chamber music were not indigenous to Russia. Some of these became known in Russia just before, and to an even greater extent, during and after the reign of Peter the Great. Because of the Czar's sponsorship of Western music, this more complex music was cultivated almost exclusively at court. There it was encountered by the landowning nobility and by a relatively small number of upper-middle-class business and industrial leaders. In spite of self-conscious attempts by a few Russian composers, especially Peter Ilich Tchaikovsky (1840–1893), Alexander Borodin, and César Cui (1835–1918), to combine traditional Russian melodies and rhythms with techniques of Western orchestration, they still did not succeed in reaching the broad masses and found only limited public appreciation of their music. The people were mainly of rural extraction and without viable connections to the social elite. The music they produced was the music of the simple folk continuing their old folk dances and songs.

Government Control of Music in the Soviet Union

With this brief sketch of musical practices in Russia in mind, one will realize that the Soviet government faced a cultural situation quite different from that which Hitler could manipulate on becoming the dictator of Germany. In contrast to the variety of intellectual movements foreshadowing the rise and acceptance of Nazi ideologies, the Bolsheviks found not a single native movement that could be considered as a predecessor to their own. Far more so than in Germany, Russian communists began to establish a new world of art for the people. By the same token, this meant that few concessions had to be made to an existing establishment.

To understand more fully the practice of musical life under Russian communism, one may find it helpful to review some of its basic ideas and views on social development. The Soviet leaders were faced with the task of building up a system of modern economic production in a very short time. This they had to accomplish in a country where hardly any tradition of technological know-how existed, compared with Central and Western European agriculture and industry. Convinced that Russia would have to fight major wars in the course of the revolution, the leaders saw the necessity of feeding their own population numbering in the millions, and of simultaneously building an army, a navy, and an air force. Because of the inadequate transportation network that had been built by the czars, these tasks were even more complicated than they would have been in the West. To accomplish this monumental social and technological transformation all obtainable manpower was needed; tremendous emphasis was placed on work that contributed to developing the proletarian state. Hence, the state accorded special honors to all those connected with this work. To this day the Soviet worker enjoys great prestige. For a long time, citizens of the Soviet state even celebrated weddings at the factory or other place of employment to emphasize the social importance of work.

The Soviet attitude toward the value of physical labor influenced the official position toward art in general and music in particular. Just as the technical education offered to a young worker was largely given within the factory or in close connection with the work involved, so theatrical and musical education were closely connected with economic life. This relationship between practical work and music can be analyzed with regard to both organization and content. In regard to organization of economic activities, one must realize that there were varying degrees of direct state control over different types of work. A high degree of control was found in the industrial sector of life, including the related activities of mining and communications. Farming on the other hand was more decentralized, so that local and regional chapters of labor unions had a certain degree of autonomy.

One essential feature of combining artistic performances with activities of the work place concerns the homogeneity of the audience. For example, the performance of music could be arranged for an audience consisting exclusively of members of the labor union of one factory. At such occasions the performers would be made up both of professionals and amateurs. As in Germany, the Soviet system organized amateur performers through labor unions into orchestras, theater troupes, and even opera performance groups. During such amateur performances representatives of the professional cultural institutions would also sometimes be present. If one of the amateur performers seemed especially gifted for an artistic career, he would be selected, encouraged, and given an opportunity for specialized study in his particular art. Thus, in Soviet Russia the same system by which technically gifted young people were selected to be sent to special training schools was adapted for developing artistic talents.

The location and curricula of these schools for higher artistic training also reveal a characteristically Soviet trait. Such academies were almost always connected with institutions for artistic performances, such as repertory theaters. These are still to be found in almost every large city of Russia, particularly in the capitals of Soviet Union republics. There the resident artists—actors, singers, instrumentalists, and dancers—are all employees of the state. Many of them also work as instructors in the professional schools connected with their particular theater. Students in these schools not only receive theoretical training, but also gain practical experience as performers in the associated theater soon after beginning their instruction.

As has already been stated, unlike Hitler the Soviets found few ideological traditions that could be elaborated directly for their political purposes. In fact, the Soviets considered czarist history as an evil in itself. When for Joseph Goebbels (1897–1945) the performance of old German music or of the works of Richard Wagner presented no ideological problem, the Soviets had to decide whether or not they could accept and perform music that had originated in czarist times. In keeping with Soviet ideology, there was the commitment of leading the people to believe in true Marxian philosophy with its claims that changes in all spheres of life are determined by and manifestations of prior changes within the economic sphere. Thus, changes in all forms of art must be accounted for by economic factors. The Soviet regime claimed to be working toward the most complete of all economic and social changes in history. They therefore argued that the traditional music created during the epoch of the czars would naturally be affected by the social attitudes of that period, and would have to be abolished.

In certain areas the changes in Soviet society did not conform to Marxian ideology. Two important modifications were Lenin's (1870–1924) decision to keep agriculture under local or regional control, and the obvious turnabout from Marx's original intention to bring about world conquest by converting individual countries to the Soviet plan by peaceful means. Nor was music confined to the narrow interpretation of Marxian concepts. Since according to official policy music was to belong to the working people, but had not under the czars, rather than break altogether with musical tradition, older forms of music were to be adapted to the new class situation. Consequently, assimilationists and other less radical groups had their say with regard to music. They argued that there are types of art that are politically neutral by nature, these could be adapted to the needs of the new society. Among such works are stage plays by Shakespeare (1564–1616) and Gogol (1809–1852). Even though he had become quite religious near the end of his life by advocating the realization of the principles laid out in the Sermon on the Mount, Tolstoi (1828–1910) was included with these writers. Of course, the Soviets struck the Christian and ethical references from his work, making it appear that the author of *Resurrection* had only described realistic vignettes from the life of various social groups. The Soviets welcomed any artist who would vividly and "realistically" describe life as the Soviets pictured it. This was particularly so when an author also made a point of derrogating, in the most lurid terms, the living conditions as they had existed in the days of the czars and other nobility. Bizet's *Carmen* met with official approval for its portrayal of the living conditions of workers and the reprehensible conduct of Spanish officers.

During the early years of Soviet rule an expressionistic movement developed. A few lines or movements symbolized the essential aspects of life that all of the people had in common. In music, interest was displaced from melody to the creation of special sound effects that were supposed to express dramatically this kind of human experience. Besides these developments in individual art forms, emphasis was also given by dance troupes to the movement of the human body in simultaneous rhythmical movement. This form of Soviet art combined three expressionistic elements that had largely been used separately in the West: eurhythmic mass movement, mass choral speaking groups, and instrumental accompaniment of a purely rhythmical nature.

In order to teach these new art forms considered so valuable to the state, new educational institutions had to be founded. Sending gifted boys and girls to the conventional state-supported art schools was no longer adequate. The Soviet state built new schools for the teaching of body rhythms and also training institutions for the modern character ballet in many of the larger cities of Russia and in the capitals of various non-Russian Soviet Union republics. Here young people aged twelve to fourteen were accepted as pupils. They studied there for several years, receiving artistic instruction in addition to a complete academic high-school education.

The fate of artistic independence of the various minority groups in the Soviet Union is of some interest. Some of these minority peoples spoke Slavic; others, of Mongolian origin, spoke Ural-Altaic languages. These minority nations had seen several changes under czarist rule. For example, there had been increasing pressure to Russify these people and convert them to the Greek Orthodox religion, especially when the Pan-Slavic movement under Konstantin Pobyedonostzev, a former tutor of Czar Alexander III (1845–1894), had come into power. The situation of some of these groups had become so bad that many were inclined to join revolutionary movements against the czar. Many revolutionary leaders, foremost among them Joseph Stalin (1879–1953), had come from these minority groups. After the Soviet accession to power, some of these minorities began to enjoy somewhat greater freedoms. Under Lenin, however, members of the Christian religious community, particularly the Greek Orthodox, suffered persecution.

Moslems had far less to suffer than under the czars, who had considered them of inferior social status. Consequently, the Moslems along with other minorities were expected to support the new regime. Additionally, they became more united with each other and the rest of Russia through Stalin's policy of strengthening the Soviet Union by systematically bringing the various Slavic and Mongolian peoples under Moscow's control.

In order to successfully unify the Soviet states, the leaders felt it important to make friends with peoples such as the Serbs and Croatians before subjecting them. One procedure was to convince these groups, each in turn, that they would continue to enjoy cultural autonomy, even when under Soviet rule. As a result, religious persecution diminished and a kind of cultural decentralization began to take place within the Soviet Union. The decentralization was, however, restricted entirely to cultural spheres. Industrial production was not decentrailized. It was considered essential to bring mining, communications, and all other areas pertaining to industry under strict central supervision.

Among the means employed to propagate Stalin's programs was the policy of protecting the drama, music, and dance of minority people. Relatively old and forgotten national folk songs and dances were systematically cultivated, taught, and performed in modernized form in state-supported theaters. Even old Jewish theater plays were protected by the state, although Jewish theater, particularly the famous *Habima,* was basically religious in nature. The Soviets also granted equality of social position to the Gypsies.[1] More importantly for us, they founded and sponsored Gypsy theaters, where plays dealing with various aspects of Gypsy life were combined with the performance of Gypsy music. In these theaters the Gypsies would often glorify the Soviets, who had given them rights instead of the persecution they had suffered everywhere else, particularly in Hitler's Germany.

Movies and Radio Broadcasting in the Soviet Union

In propagandizing their ideology and socialist art, the Soviets made even more extensive use than Hitler of modern communication technology. This relative preference can easily be understood by recalling that the Nazi movement considered modern communication technology tainted by Jewish commercialism, urban intellectualism, and Anglo-Saxon pragmatism. In contrast, the Bolsheviks were not restricted by racist and romantic notions. Indeed, Karl Marx had sharply distinguished between the romantic utopian socialisms and his own materialistic system. Another essential difference was the positive recognition given to modern technology by Marx and post-Marxian socialism and communism. For Marxists not the machine but the methods of its use by the bourgeoisie were branded as the enemy of the proletariat. Once the political revolution was successfully accomplished, technical means of all varieties should be used to improve the economic situation of the masses. Through these means, opportunities for both urban and rural workers to participate in spiritual life were to be increased. Hence, the Soviet state employed sound recordings, broadcasts, film, and later television in its educational efforts. By means of these technical devices, the masses, including all minorities, could be indoctrinated using their native languages. Moreover, even the remotest village could be supplied with recordings of every musical art form considered worthwhile by leading Soviet educators.

Films especially were given a prominent role in popularizing Soviet teachings. These films were produced to convey the experiences, values, and history of the masses. Frequent subjects of historical films were the

---

[1] Gypsies are a nomadic group of mixed Hindu and Slavic origin. Their language is also a mixture of Hindu and Slavic, and they have a culture of their own with regard to literature and, especially, music. They stress rhythms and the use of strings, especially the violin. When performing in groups, their musicians play by following the leader, who is usually the only member of the group able to read music. The relationship between Hungarian music and that of the Gypsies is too involved to be dealt with here in any great detail.

demonstration of the heroism of rural serfs and poor urban people in the Russian past. Other subjects were various peasant revolts and urban revolutionary movements. In addition to these primarily political subjects were films on the new technical works, railways, mining facilities, and canals built since the establishment of the Soviet state. A typical story would deal with the construction of a railway line through an Asiatic desert under the supervision of Stalin himself, and how the life style of previously poor Mongolian tribes becomes improved through this project.

In the Soviet film the role of music became different from that customarily associated with movies. In the advanced films of Eisenstein, for example, the separation between spoken lines and musical accompaniment vanished. Some impressionistic music was also used as accompaniment. Although many of these developments were not entirely new, they had played a minor role in the West. A particularly characteristic feature of Soviet film music, however, is the replacement of instruments by the use of human voices. Frequently collective singing even replaces spoken dialogue. This may represent the culmination of nonindividualistic expressionism in film music.

Radio has been used in the Soviet state for the same purposes of politicalization as all the other technical means of communication. Although the listener cannot see the announcers or performers, he is nevertheless supposed to gain a realistic understanding of the entire situation. Therefore, expressionistic sounds are frequently incorporated into radio productions. In fact, the proper use of sound effects is more important in radio productions than in any other medium.

ON FORMS OF MUSIC
AND FORMS OF SOCIETY

In this essay we explore the linkages between various kinds of music and societal settings. For example, we will try to see to what extent special kinds of music such as mixed choirs, woodwind chamber music, comic opera, or other forms are connected with or even caused by certain societal structures. We will first explore what regularities can be established about some form of interrelationship between society and the special qualities of musical sounds.

QUALITIES OF SOUND

The literature does not say much about the relations between musical sounds and social structure. Although reports and analyses of the music of preliterate society exist, much study remains to be done in the field of primitive music. Similarly, our knowledge concerning the music of the more complex ancient Oriental and pre-Columbian cultures is also quite limited. Accordingly, only a few observations can be made here dealing with these materials.

One major problem discussed in this field concerns the use of pentatonic musical scales. This term denotes the partition of the octave into no more than five intervals. This type of tonal scale has been reported to have existed in many places, such as among aborigines of central and south Australia and some early California Indian tribes, as well as in the Inca Empire and its surrounding Indian tribes. Remnants can still be found in remote districts. There is also evidence of its use in ancient China and in pre-Christan Egypt. The pentatonic system has also continued in use among some Celtic-speaking people in remote districts such as the Hebrides Islands in the west of Scotland.

There is little more specific information that can be cited as to the processes of the distribution of pentatonic music. There is certainly not enough evidence to permit us to advance a broader generalization, since the cultures we have mentioned are extremely different from one another. On the basis of existing evidence, to assert that under similar social or economic conditions similar scale relationships have been established would be untenable. Cultural diffusion from the high Andes of the Inca Empire into the lowlands suggests, however, that music and culture can be distributed by diffusion. But even though that diffusion seems to have specifically incorporated the pentatonic scale, along with many other cultural elements, to assume that cultural goods were diffused between districts as far removed from each other as Australia, China, Egypt, the Celtic islands, and the Inca Empire must be considered, at the least, as highly improbable on the basis of our present knowledge. Traditional explanations for the appearance of identical phenomena in remote districts—independent parallel development, diffusion, or human migration —cannot be used to adequately explain the appearance of the pentatonic scale in these various geographic locations. Because these cultures developed in regions very distant from one another, the migration theory is extremely difficult to prove. Perhaps new evidence will become available through excavations or through the discovery and deciphering of older reports. Only further study may make it possible to reach more specific knowledge of the diffusion of musical scales.

Evidence is also incomplete in the related question regarding the cultural preference for or predominance of the minor mode over the major. That Slavic peoples, especially the eastern Slavs, use the minor mode almost exclusively is known. The varying distribution of the minor mode even within the Slavic people, however, emphasizes anew the difficulty of explaining this phenomenon. Yet there is a striking difference in thinking between the mystically inclined Eastern Slavs and the far more rationally minded Western Slavs. The difference may be related to some extent to the strong difference between the Greek Orthodox and Roman Catholic outlooks on life. But to consider the predeliction for the minor mode as something especially Greek Orthodox would again be impossible to maintain, since there is indeed a great variation in the use of the minor mode among the Russians (the largest) and other Greek Orthodox population groups. Among the regions of the Byzantine Empire, where Greek Orthodoxy originated, we do not find the minor mode used any more frequently than among other peoples. On this basis we cannot offer any general statement about the interrelationship between the use of the minor mode and certain societal or even religious characteristics.

Little is known regarding the use of special musical pitch. It has been observed that American Indians do not show a great preference in the use of fixed pitch. When asked to repeat a succession of notes performed by them just a few minutes before, American Indians were usually incapable of repeating the tonal sequence at the same pitch.

Nor can anything definite be said about the preferential use of vocal register. Here countless cultural as well as physiological factors can play a role. Moreover, geographical and climatic factors may possibly influence the structure of the voice. Extremely high altitude and the degree of humidity have been suggested as factors that influence a singer's capacity to produce very high or low sounds, but up to the present time these physiological discussions have been hypothetical. Some statement can be made, however, about the interest in and preference for high or low sounds in certain societies. As far as the development of vocal culture in occidental society is concerned, great interest in producing very high sounds with the voice did not exist before the Italian Renaissance. The middle and low registers were dominant in medieval church music, especially in the recitatives sung by monk choirs. Only later was the melody shifted to a higher vocal pitch. Usually a high voice now holds the melody. This practice is the linguistic and etymological origin of the term *tenor,* which denotes the kind of vocal range that holds the melody. With the Counter Reformation, emphasis was given to the capacities of some male voices to produce extremely high sounds, even up to high C. This development is paralleled by the training given to female singers to enable them to produce extremely high sounds. The castrates have to be largely explained as having been introduced to serve the same interest. Emphasis on high-pitched voices was also manifested in the fact that operatic roles for the lower vocal register become rather unimportant in Italy during the seventeenth and eighteenth centuries, at least for some time. The use of mezzo-sopranos or even contraltos was almost negligible. In Italian comic opera, the mother of a marriageable daughter or an elderly housekeeper, both more or less comic characters, traditionally sing in the lower register. Thus, the young sweetheart who sings the extremely high coloratura aria stands out in bold relief against characters of secondary importance.

This interest in high tones produced by young voices was paralleled by interest in high sounds produced by instruments. In the second half of the seventeenth century the new string instrument with the vaulted back, that is the violin, became increasingly preferred to the older, flat-backed lute-type string instruments. The new instrument was and is far more capable than its forerunner of pleasantly producing high sounds, because of the use of harmonic overtones. This characteristic is one of the essential causes of the increasing preference for the violin. High vocal and instrumental sounds were found to be more brilliant than the middle and lower ones. This is consistent with other developments of this particular culture, in which much interest was attached to brilliance. Some reasons for this will emerge when we examine the relationship between forms of music and kinds of society, and the relationship between the rise of opera and concert performances and the Counter Reformation.

Concerning the role of musical rhythm in culture, we can say without exaggeration that in the majority of cultures rhythm reigns dominant over every other musical element. The reason for this is obvious. To a great extent music is intertwined with religious elements. Even when religious belief and practices decrease in importance, customs and means of procedure developed in primarily religious epochs retain some cultural presence. For example, a great many religious practices were initially of magical character. As we know, the effect of magical procedures was largely, if not entirely, dependent on the correctness of the ritualistic performance of sung or spoken words and of correctly executed movements. Exact memorization of all the various words and movements was especially difficult in eras that had no written symbols to denote their sequence. Rhythm can be more easily impressed into man's memory than words, body movements, or musical melody. Thus rhythm can be viewed as the most fundamental musical expression. Traditionally, it has been given great emphasis. All reliable reports tell us about the dominant role of rhythm among the music of African Negroes and American Indians. Studies of the oldest written sources of the Hindus and other oriental people provide evidence of a similar role of rhythm. The music used in the theater of ancient Greece had its origin in forms of religious worship that employed rhythm. Even the classical dramas of Aeschylus and Sophocles assign an essential role to rhythm. Rhythm was also fundamental to the music performed among Moslems, especially under the rule and at the court of the Umayyads. Christianity also linked musical practices to religious worship, at least for most of its history. Of course, the extreme use of rhythmical emphases in dances performed within the celebration of the Mass by priests of the old Ethiopian sect is somewhat of an exception. In general, however, rhythmic expressions can be found almost everywhere in the Eastern as well as in the Western traditions.

Most "classical" (fine art) music of Europe is differentiated from the music of other cultures by a lessened emphasis on rhythm; greater importance is given to other aspects of music production, especially melody. Only quite recently and under special circumstances has rhythm been reemphasized in occidental musical life. At times this emphasis appears in connection with an emphasis on the human body—political movements such as the German Youth Movement of the 1920s emphasize physical culture, as has already been mentioned.

The limited materials available on the interrelationship between society and the special qualities of musical sounds permit tentative generalization only in regard to pitch (vocal register) and to rhythm.

FOLK MUSIC

Folk music should be considered as a separate form of music. Music that has not been composed by individuals or groups who are known as musical specialists and music that is usually performed without sharp distinctions between performers and audience and without overriding economic concerns is included here with traditional folk music. This kind of music can be performed almost everywhere and normally is not considered a value in itself. Instead it is performed in connection with events that represent high points in the life of the people involved. In Italy, for example, where the veneration of Mary plays an important role in the life of the people, holidays and places of worship connected with Mary are centers of folk music performances. In Scandinavia, covering icy terrain to meet socially may require endurance and other skills. Songs to be sung on these travels and to celebrate the surmounting of such difficulties form an important part of Scandinavian folk music. In Brazil, the raising of livestock forms the focus of life on many large ranches, and so folk music is centered around ranching events. Numerous examples of a similar nature could be mentioned from other parts of the world. We might add that certain music used in a great many theaters has similar characteristics, whether vocal or instrumental and whether performed by marionettes or live actors. In such cases it is often difficult to decide whether a performance belongs to traditional folk music or may better be classified as a kind of art music.

ART MUSIC

In contrast to folk music, the origin of art music is usually known. Even if the individual composer is not identified, the group from which the music originated is known. We may not know the specific composer of the rhythmical accompaniment for a Greek tragedy or the name òf the Benedictine father who composed the recitatives sung by the members of his order, but we can identify their special group and consider that group as sociologically different from others. Art music has normally been produced for a special and differentiated audience rather than for everyone in the tribe or community; it generally presupposes some knowledge of rules that are accepted as valid within the producing group. Finally, art music is more complex than folk music; there is usually more than one part, often with elaborate accompaniment. This description implies that there are marginal cases in which it is most difficult to draw the line between folk and art music.

Instrumental Art Music

The simplest instrumental music is based on only one instrument or part, in contrast to that with a more or less logical structuring of multiple parts. Another simple form is composed of only one movement, which may combine several instruments or parts; that is, of course, one of the older forms and appears in countless special types. The march may be singled out for mention because it appears in almost every complex society. When groups of people walk in step, they find the necessity of walking in rhythm; the march provides a basic rhythm to fill this need. Marches are used by militaristic societies and by athletic associations. Various professional groups adopt marches written for their use as a kind of trademark.

The more complex a culture, the greater is the inclination to create instrumental music that consists of sequential parts or movements that are intended to form a unit. These movements follow one another in a special order that is considered to follow some logical scheme or at least to be sensible. This form of music, with very few exceptions, is exclusively found in occidental culture, and is derived, apparently, from a sequence of different dances. Such music is connected with a society in which there was time to perform such dances, and where enjoyment in listening to music grew until a relation between dancing and music was no longer necessary and music was listened to for its own sake. The origin of the suite can be traced directly to some of these factors.

The upper classes, especially the nobility in courts and castles, had developed a highly complicated art of dancing during the baroque period. When certain movements of these dances became so complicated that they could no longer be executed by nonprofessionals, it became the custom to let dancers and even instrumentalists perform some of them. The terms used to denote the individual movements in a suite, through the nineteenth century, clearly reflect this origin—*gavotte, allemande,* and *passacaglia* stand for dance movements. During the seventeenth century, with the Age of Reason, bureaucracy and an increasing interest in mathematics and physics fostered the trend toward rationalization also in the field of music. Consequently, the suite began to be replaced by more logically structured forms of instrumental music. Since the second part of the eighteenth century only a few suites have been composed. The only successful nineteenth century composer of suites was the Bavarian Franz L. Lachner (1803–1890), who composed his suites in a conscious protest against the predominance of concerti and symphonies. Lachner considered the restriction to these forms deplorably narrow and thought that concert programs should be enriched by forms different from those customarily performed. Moreover, in keeping with the ideas of German Romanticism, Lachner protested against the systemization and rationalization of life as being too overpowering and exclusive in its appeal to intellectual responses.

With the exception of Lachner, the interests of composers, producers, and the public had shifted to musical forms with more rational structures. Three of these forms will be discussed here. The first and oldest is the concerto grosso. It is composed of various movements, each of which is divided into special parts. In the concerto grosso there are either two instrumental groups of approximately the same size that perform antiphonally, or a smaller group, consisting of only a few instruments, which interrupts the playing of a larger orchestra. This form of composition remained popular through the middle of the eighteenth century. Handel and Telemann are considered representative composers employing this form.

The trend toward systemization did not stop with the concerto grosso. Two other forms were introduced, the symphony and the solo concerto. The symphony is also made up of several movements, but differs from the suite, for example, in that it is not simply a sequence of dance movements somewhat connected with one another by the kind and number of instruments involved and by the similarity of the key signature used. The symphony, rather, presents at least two main themes in the first movement. These may reappear in any of the three or four movements. The symphony became the characteristic musical form of performance at orchestral concerts at the end of the eighteenth and the beginning of the nineteenth centuries. After some predecessors whose compositions are often difficult to classify, Haydn, Mozart, and Bethoven became masterful developers of the symphonic form. Orchestral compositions of this period are usually in the form of classic symphonic music.

Solo Instrumental Compositions

The solo concerto appeared at approximately the same time as the symphony through the convergence of various sociological factors. One factor is outstanding; the increasing interest in the unique capacities of the individual performer. The concerto grosso had already provided some opportunities for certain musicians to display their special abilities, but because even the smaller group within the larger orchestra was usually playing as a unit, the individual virtuoso could not yet stand out in bold relief against his fellow musicians. Some of the earlier symphonies, especially those by Haydn, used wind instruments in a soloistic sense. Although they gave the soloist some opportunity to show his ability, the opportunities were restricted to rather short passages. Many virtuosos, as well as the audience, found these passages insufficient. Increasingly, compositions were asked for in which the individual performer would have more possibilities to display his capacities as a soloist to conquer certain technical difficulties. Thus the solo concerto was originated for the exceptional few, usually for one solo instrument with orchestra accompaniment. Various compositions by Mozart for violin and orchestra, or those for flute and harp, or for oboe, clarinet, bassoon, and horn with orchestra accompaniment are examples. Several of Mozart's compositions were actually on a borderline between the solo concerto and the symphony. Mozart recognized this and called such compositions *symphonia concertanti*. The most frequent type of concerto remained, through the nineteenth century, the one for a single solo instrument.

Among solo instruments the violin must be considered the most important. The Stradivarius, named for its original maker, has been considered since its inception the most satisfactory instrument of its kind, especially for its ability to produce the extremely high and pure tones that had become so popular. For a long time more concerti were written for the violin than for any other instrument. After the violin, the piano ranks next in importance. With the increasing size of audiences, larger concert halls were needed, which in turn required instruments producing greater volume. After many trials, the instrument makers had succeeded in shifting away from manufacturing the older keyboard instruments, such as the virginal and the harpsichord, which produced sounds by plucking the strings. The new keyboard instrument vibrated the strings by striking them with hammers, one for each string, and became the piano as we know it today. Although often accompanied by a full symphony orchestra, it could clearly be heard in the back of even the largest hall. The new instrument was also capable of producing a far greater variety of tones than were its predecessors. Due to its versatility, the demand for piano concerti was soon second only to that for violin concerti. The compositions of the sons of Johann Sebastian Bach, especially those of Philipp Emanuel Bach, were forerunners of the piano concerto as we know it today.

In the era of rising individualism, musicians like other professionals wanted to be recognized and looked for opportunities to prove their uniqueness. This search provided a stimulus for composing solo concerti starting with the middle of the eighteenth century. These were written for most instruments with few exceptions. It was some time before the cello appeared as a solo instrument—since initial interest in the family of vaulted string instruments was in those producing high-pitched tones, there was less initial interest in shifting from the older viol family to the newer instruments with middle and lower registers. Therefore while the older instrument in the higher register gave way to the violin and gradually disappeared, the newly invented cello was used for a long time only to back the orchestra as a general bass. Only Boccherini, who played the cello, and Haydn succeeded in introducing the cello as a solo concerto instrument.

The viola was also far less popular than the violin for use in solo concerti. It, too, has a lower register than the violin and played a relatively minor role in orchestral compositions. When the violin was predominant, viola players were considered inferior in their tonal production and were not allowed in the regular violin section of the orchestra. These instrumentalists did not search as much as others for an opportunity to show off their musicianship and instrumental technique. Since concerti were very often composed on the request of virtuosos, the demand for viola concerti was limited. There are only a few concerti for the viola that were composed during this period. Later, the orchestral role of the viola changed. This came about gradually. First, the German Romantic inclination toward everything mystic and melancholy was well suited to the use of the somewhat nasal tone of the viola. Robert Schumann and Karl Maria von Weber gave important parts of this formerly neglected instrument—for example, solo arias in Weber's *Freischütz* are accompanied by the viola. A second impulse came from French Romanticism, which shifted from subjectivism to a form of musical impressionism, with Hector Berlioz as its most explicit representative. Berlioz's compositions no longer centered around the elaboration of melody, rhythm, or pitch but included experimentation with sound, color, and timbre. Time and again he tried to invent new combinations of timbre, which is why he was greatly interested in incorporating those wind instruments that were either invented or strongly modified in his day, namely the English horn, the bass clarinet, and the bass tuba. He also expressed his desire to shift from the classical timbre combinations by giving stronger emphasis to the viola. The climax of Berlioz's employment of the viola is in his symphony *Harold in Italy*. Here he used the technique of designating persons, landscapes, or situations by special themes and frequently reappearing melodies. Since the main theme, that of the hero, is regularly played by the viola, *Harold in Italy* approximates a kind of viola concerto.

The interest in concerti during that era even included the double string bass. In its usual construction, this instrument does not belong to the modern violin family; it is built, particularly in regard to the back, more like the older bass viol, which gives it a great volume of sound but little purity of tone. As in the case of the cello, there was not much interest in treating the double bass as a solo instrument. However, many double-bass players were considered better musicians than violists. These instrumentalists requested concerti for double bass, and some composers tried to satisfy them. Haydn's solo concerto for this instrument, as well as a few other compositions, were written for this purpose. Yet the number of solo concerti for this instrument remains rather small.

Some solo performers composed concerti for their own instruments and performances. Dragonetti and Bottesini were the two most successful virtuosos as composers, but their compositions have been played infrequently since their death. These concerti, which demand the correct execution of rapid passages on the fourth string, are so difficult that few individuals can perform them. Besides their composers, only August Miller, Lobercht Goedeke, and Sergey Kussevitsky prior to the time he began conducting have performed them.

Countless concerti for the entire range of wind instruments were composed during that same period. These instruments had already been used soloistically in the symphonies of Haydn, Dittersdorf, and their contemporaries. It had therefore been demonstrated that it was possible to expand the shorter solo passages within symphonies into complete solo concerti. A nonmusical influence on this development was the increasing preoccupation with rural life that had emerged in French Literature. Even royalty played at being farmers, without doing any manual labor; because they felt that there was something wonderful about the life of the peasants. This notion was not restricted to people of high social rank. Jean-Jacques Rousseau (1712–1778) popularized the idea that the true embodiment of man was only to be found far away from the city in the simplest rural surroundings.

The shepherd with his reedy shepherd's pipe was considered most characteristic of innocent country life. With the increased interest in rustic living, an interest developed in woodwinds, due to their resemblance to the instrument used by shepherds. The most popular woodwinds were the oboe and the flute. Since they had become so interested in learning to play these instruments in their leisure time, it was natural that society people were also anxious to hear these woodwinds played by professionals in concert. A form of chamber music thus arose combining the flute or oboe with a few strings. Mozart may also be mentioned in this connection as one of the most successful composers of chamber music and solo concerti for wind instruments.

The decline in the soloistic use of wool instruments coincided with the rise of the symphonic form during the nineteenth century. The most dominant instruments in the symphony became the strings, which explains why the interest in wind instruments appeared to decrease during this time and fewer concerti were composed for them. As wind instruments decreased in popularity for solo performance, composers began writing chamber music for them instead of long concerti. Brahms, for instance, composed his pieces combining clarinet, strings, and piano on the suggestion of the clarinet virtuoso Muhlfeld.

Concerti were also composed for certain nonsymphonic instruments. With the democratization of music in the nineteenth century, special organizations were founded to sponsor performances for guitar and mandolin. Performers who were considered or believed themselves to be outstanding asked for opportunities to display their soloistic skills. Concerti were composed for these instruments, and other uses were also found for them. They were occasionally combined with other symphonic instruments in chamber music ensembles for strings and winds.

JAZZ

The study of the origin of jazz and of the main steps in its development is of special interest to the student of sociological elements in the history of music, since a number of rather specialized sociomusical phenomena converge in this musical genre. When peoples from various African tribes and regions were brought to North America as slaves, some owners or slave masters permitted them to have some time off from work and to spend this time in each other's company. This time was often passed in singing and dancing to aboriginal rhythms and to music improvised in the new setting. For accompaniment, relatively simple instruments were often made by the performers.

After the abolition of slavery, Negroes continued some of the traditions of this musical idiom. Since these musicians usually considered a line of work other than music to be their main occupation, the next step consisted of shifting from a nonmusical occupation to music making as the main source of income. Performers joined together, increased the number of instruments, and included more recently invented Western instruments. Among these was the saxophone from France, usually the alto "sax." Relatively small groups generally formed traveling bands that went from one restaurant or nightclub to another, improvising on traditional or popular melodies according to the rules of a developing convention. Not only Negro musicians, but others as well turned to this new form of music. Among those who turned to jazz for their livelihood were some instrumentalists who had formerly belonged to symphony orchestras. The interest in jazz among musicians increased when this form of music created a demand for top-notch players of instruments that had not been highly valued or used soloistically within the symphony orchestra. Specialists in the trombone, double bass, and kettle drum became indispensable in jazz bands. Clarinetists who were used to the bass clarinet frequently changed over to playing the alto "sax," which is actually a modified bass clarinet. Although a brass instrument, the saxophone used the traditional clarinet mouthpiece, which is a combination of wood and reed. The increasingly popular acceptance of jazz made it a financially rewarding occupation. Many new careers were created, and some jazz musicians attained international stardom.

VOCAL MUSIC

The Oratorio

Keeping in mind our previous general references to vocal music, the oratorio and the opera will now be examined more directly. Among the direct forerunners of the oratorio were such religious practices in the Christian Middle Ages as mystery plays produced on certain religious holidays. Other antecedents were certain types of hymns sung by monks in their monasteries, and some of the secular vocal music of the Italian Renaissance, which was later suppressed during the Catholic Counter Reformation. Oratorio performances, although purely religious in char-

acter, were to be understood by the masses as well as by priests and intellectuals. The aim was to reach even illiterate members of the lower
classes.

This form of music was introduced by Philip Neri, who was later declared a saint, with the help of his order, the Congregation of the Ora-
tory. The term originally described an area in the monastery between
the main sanctuary and the dormitory, and was later applied to the kind
of music performed there. Neri's new musical form was intended neither
for a purely dramatic performance nor for simple narration. The lyrics
usually dealt with periods in the life of Jesus, the apostles, some saints,
and heroes of the Old Testament. As a rule a given singer would represent several characters. There was some dialogue between two characters,
generally in recitative. If the audience was unfamiliar with details in the
life of the characters, they would find following the action rather difficult.
For this reason a narrator was introduced; this role became the main feature distinguishing the oratorio from other forms of vocal music. Forerunners of the oratorio form are seen in the Middle Ages, but as they
have no narrators they cannot be considered modern oratorios.

The same region that gave birth to the oratorio also encouraged operatic developments more than any other part of the world. When interest
began to grow in this new type of musical drama, the oratorio lost some
of its popularity in Catholic Italy; later refinements in this form occurred
mainly within the Protestant realm. In this connection some aspects of
the religious teaching of Episcopalians and Lutherans, who aligned themselves neither with the Catholic Counter Reformation nor with Calvinism or Anabaptism, should be mentioned. Episcopalians are neither as
liberal as the Catholics under Jesuit influence concerning the controversy
of free will, nor as conservative as Calvinists and their related groups on
the subjects of original sin and predestination. Theological attitudes of
Episcopalians and Lutherans are not as receptive to the enjoyment of
the senses as Catholics nor as restrictive as, say, Presbyterians, Methodists,
Baptists, and the like. These theological positions are reflected in their
attitude to different forms of music. Unlike Catholics, some Lutherans,
for example, do not allow opera performed in costume. But neither do
they prohibit all forms of dramatic music, as do the Calvinists, whose
music is restricted to simple hymn singing. Since the oratorio is neither a
dramatic operatic performance nor a simple religious song, it conforms
closely to Lutheran belief, which also takes a middle ground. Consequently, oratorio music could develop in Lutheran regions, and mainly of
course in Germany, the home of the Lutheran movement.

The Episcopal church, as is generally known, retained a number of

Catholic forms and institutions, including some forms of music. In England, the Episcopal Church of England did not conflict with the commercial orientation of many of its people.

A telling example of a musician who worked within several religious frameworks is the story of George Frideric Handel, who was born in Halle, in central Germany, a short distance from Leipzig, the city of Bach. Handel was raised in a Lutheran environment, receiving the corresponding education. Considered especially gifted in music, he was sent to Italy, then the dominant country of music, to receive advanced musical training under the guidance of Catholic musicians. On his return, his oratorios, like some of Bach's music, were considered too secular by certain religious groups. Pietism had been introduced in Halle, and the substitution of Calvinistic severity for certain more liberal Lutheran practices was called for. Because Handel had been raised as a Lutheran and had received a Catholic musical education, his prospects for wide acceptance of his compositions and financial success were not great. Greater promise for success existed at an Episcopalian court. Accordingly, his greatest fame was acquired during the years he spent in England.

We have seen how the oratorio developed primarily within the Lutheran orbit. Toward the end of the eighteenth century the forces of the Enlightenment became so powerful that even religion and its institutions began to be rationally questioned, causing a decrease of interest in religious music and a concomitant decrease of popularity for oratorios. The nineteenth century saw a renewed interest in the oratorio, but under completely changed circumstances. It was then that the oratorio shifted from church to concert hall. Mendelssohn, a man without extended Lutheran connections, became the new protagonist of this art form. The structure of the performing body had also became completely different. In the days of Bach, and even more so of his predecessors, the choral parts in Lutheran oratories were sung by church choirs. Thus, true believers were singing with religious fervor. Yet with Mendelssohn, performance of an oratorio in a concert hall became a secular production. Members of the choir were usually people of the upper middle class who were interested in music or thought to gain social prestige by being associated with such a cultural cause.

While the singing in such a choir was no longer motivated by religious conviction, it became more and more socially homogeneous. As this kind of musical performance became recognized as a social event, status differences between choir members attained special significance. Soon several organizations of this kind would exist in the larger cities, often with the members divided according to their social standing in the community. During the last half of the nineteenth century, another social change

contributed to the growing participation in this type of choral production. With the rising standard of living of the middle class, many families acquired at least one domestic servant. At the same time, technological advances simplified housework. Accordingly, middle-class women
had less work to do at home than their ancestors. Yet, middle-class wives
and daughters were not allowed by the conventions of the times to work
outside the home nor to participate in public or political activities other
than church connected welfare services. Consequently, these women had
very little choice in what they could do on their own socially, except to
take part in choral groups. Choral groups were more or less supported by
the community, and membership presupposed moderately high social
status. With the beginning of the acceptance of the movement toward
woman's emancipation early in the twentieth century, these flourishing
musical organizations soon began to decline.

Woman's emancipation advanced rather rapidly. Through these activities upper-class women came into social contact with their sisters of lower
status, diminishing the claim to exclusiveness that had been so basic to
the social prestige of oratorio associations. In addition, religious involvement was tremendously challenged by industrialization and the growth
of large cities. The upper middle class lost interest in religion more
rapidly than did the nobility and lower middle class. When all of these
factors converged the appeal of oratorio choir participation and performances diminished rapidly.

The Theater

Before focusing extensively on opera, we will look at more general aspects of the theater. Throughout the major portion of human history,
the theater meant exactly the opposite of what it means today to the
average contemporary theater-goer. Contemporary theater attendance
usually involves something of a search for new experience. Even when the
content of the play is familiar, a new experience is still expected—for
example, the audience may want to see how a certain actor performs an
interesting part. In these respects, modern theater is completely different
from the theater of primitive and Oriental peoples and the theater of
antiquity and the Christian Middle Ages.

Throughout history, in the majority of cultures, theaters were connected with and sponsored by one of the dominant social institutions,
such as church or state. The content of the performance was usually
based on a shared basic belief common to all members of the audience
and taught by the sponsoring institution. Theater was used by these in-

stitutions as one of several means of self-glorification and indoctrination. Thus, when people attended a performance they knew what they were to expect; when they left they had once again been confirmed in the truth of their traditional belief and its ethics. The symbolism of the situation is revealed by the use of the concealing masks worn by the actors of many cultures. These stylized masks represented saints, divinities, and heroes of the sponsoring groups. The nature of modern theater is connected with the decomposition of traditional medieval institutions and the increasing emphasis on the individual in modern life. The modern individual does not conceive of himself primarily as representing a traditional group and its mores. He begins to compare various forms of life, to develop a critical mentality, and accordingly to have the desire for new experiences. Attending the theater is just one among the many possibilities available to satisfy this desire.

The Opera

The opera represents a special case within the development of theater. Consequently, it requires some detailed description. The Italian Renaissance was a new way of life which resulted from the convergence of various economic, social, political, and religious factors, and represented a revolution in all aspects of life. But the man of the Italian Renaissance was afraid to introduce anything too new or unexpected. Therefore, as with most revolutionaries, he wanted to justify his innovations by showing that they retained some traditions established from the past. This explains some of the emphasis given to Greek antiquity during the Italian Renaissance. Renaissance man did not simply imitate antiquity, but rather glorified it in the belief that the classical Greeks had already provided the model of what he wanted to become. With this objective in mind he rediscovered, collected, and edited old texts. He excavated ancient sites and tried to reconstruct the original appearance of these remains of antiquity. However, in doing so he tended to seek primarily those traits he could conveniently use to justify the kind of life he himself wished to live. Thus, these men rebuilt a kind of mythical past—they departed from the realities of ancient times to suit their own convenience, and then proceeded to imitate their own version of the past.

Among the forms of art practiced in ancient Greece they discovered tragedy. This dramatic form had been combined with music, although the actual music scores remained relatively unknown. Being ignorant of the exact music used in Greek theater but familiar with recitatives and other forms of church music combining words with music, Italian Renaissance scholars assumed that the Greek theater was musical rather than spoken drama. Italians of that period considered the ancient art forms as the most nearly perfect ever having existed. Thus they originated the idea that perfect drama should be sung rather than spoken. Here lies the origin of occidental opera, which at least in some countries and cultures became one of the most used and discussed kinds of dramatic art and music. In addition to the reasons discussed above, many social and religious factors also contributed to the development of this art form.

Many factors worked together to cause the decline of the Italian Renaissance after a mere two centuries. Detailed discussion is not possible here. We may only comment that the Protestant Reformation represented an ascetic protest against the secular spirit of the Renaissance and of the Roman Church. Another contributing factor was the origin and development of the modern centralized state. Naturally, a state holding absolute and concentrated power was a strong deterrant to any form of individualism. Last, but not least, religious feeling, threatened by Protestantism, moved to reorganize itself through the Catholic Counter Reformation. In this movement the Roman Church refused to make any concessions to Protestantism regarding dogma or the hierachical structure. The Church did however recognize that the world had changed, that completely new life styles had originated, that it was not possible to reestablish the society of the high Middle Ages, and that concessions to the changed environment had to be made. Such concessions were made in the fields of ethics, economics, and the arts. The Roman Church began to relinquish control over many areas of culture and tolerated a separation of powers. For example, secular art forms independent of the church art were allowed, as long as these works did not deal with religious topics.

Nevertheless, the Church continued its involvement in politics to the same or even greater degree. Since the political sphere remained closely connected with the Church, a prohibition against treating political subjects in art also existed. Therefore only the personal sphere of the individual remained as subject matter for the arts, and only in a restricted sense. The individual was not allowed to express his own ideas on religion or ethics. Therefore, personal love affairs were the main topic of artistic expression in that era.

It was during the Counter Reformation that opera got its start and was promoted. While the individual as such was only tolerated outside the religio-ethical sphere, he was granted recognition for activities outside of church life and especially where special talents were concerned. Opera became the principal kind of music outside the church, and it dealt almost exclusively with love affairs. Opera provided individual singers with many opportunities to develop and display their technical prowess by giving them highly complicated arias to perform. Due to the restrictions imposed by the Church, musical drama could not deal with any type of psychological or ethical problem. The amount of acting ability needed was thus limited. Complicated arias became the essential part of opera, relegating every other aspect to secondary importance. One of these secondary aspects of the opera was the overture.

In the beginning of Italian opera, the theater doors remained open during the performance of the overture, allowing the public to enter, find seats, and visit with their friends while it was being played. The same treatment applied to the performance of recitatives, although they were dramatically essential. Nevertheless, during those passages members of the upper class did not listen but visited with their friends in other boxes. A further indication of the lack of importance attributed to the recitatives was the frequent practice of not printing the whole text of the passage in the score, but only providing cues for entrances and cut offs. Furthermore, when translated from Italian into other languges the libretto did not include recitative passages.

Although the name of the librettist often remained unknown, to look at his work for a moment may prove interesting and provide us with additional insights into some of the values of the period. Our first observation might be that the heroes of Italian opera often belong to other, frequently exotic, nations. Countless operas deal with Turks, Hindus, Persians, and Chinese. Montezuma, the last Aztec king, is one of the heroes, as well as the heroine Inca girl, Cora. Even the American Indian is sometimes found in this role. Oddly enough, however, while these Asiatic and American heroes and heroines are costumed in the authentic dress of the place of origin, they are made to act and speak as typical Europeans of the seventeenth and eighteenth centuries.

This interest in exotic peoples can easily be understood; Europeans had been discovering new continents and becoming acquainted with their natives as far back as the end of the fifteenth century. Adventurers and tradesmen told about their peculiarities and religious missionaries wrote reports that were widely read and discussed. Frequently these reports did not jibe even in essential points. One can imagine the astonishment within the Catholic world when two such outstanding religious orders as the Jesuits and the Dominicans wrote completely different accounts of the Chinese and Hindus. On the other hand, if one created a story about Hindus or Persians rather than about Italians or Spaniards, the writer could avoid the danger of being accused by the censor of interference in contemporary political affairs or of insult to a friendly nation. Finally, and equal in importance, the interesting costumes of these foreign people served to satisfy, at least in part, the desires of the audience for new experiences.

Peasant life was another dominant theme in many operas. Around the middle of the eighteenth century rural life became an object of scientific investigation as well as of general interest. Agriculture was especially emphasized in France after the death of Louis XVI (1754–1793), who was accused of having brought France to the verge of bankruptcy with his emphasis on city life, money, and manufacturing. Since the life of the peasant was supposed to be close to nature, it was considered to be the truest form of life; the supposedly idyllic life of shepherds became a frequent opera theme.

Anticipating the French Revolution, protest against tradition was glorified in this period. By combining the emphasis on the simple life with admiration for those who oppose the establishment we have an explanation for the rise of a new type of operatic plots. These plots revolved around the Robin Hood type of character—an outlaw from the established community with a band of followers to assist him in robbing the rich in order to aid the poor, the weak, and the innocent. Of course, the plot also provided the happy ending: The outlaw is restored to his rightful place amid the accolades of the people as the curtain falls. During the French Revolution itself, rebellion was painted in a less romantic form. By that time the rebel was regularly involved in politics, struggling bitterly against monarchs and priests in an effort to restore simplicity to the life of his people.

Fantasy reappeared as a reaction against the rationalism of enlightenment, revolution, and the Napoleonic Empire. This movement, generally known as Romanticism, not only emphasized the unique characteristics of different national traditions by rediscovering folk tales and legends, but also assigned importance to the occult. More than any other national group, German Romantics stressed the ghostly realm. Among the composers dealing with spectres and phantoms were Lindpaintner and Marschner. Marschner's *Hans Heiling* was the direct predecessor of Wagner's *Flying Dutchman*. Added to the Wagnerian tradition of ectoplasmic apparitions we have fairy tale operas such as *Hänsel and Gretel*. In these operas, the good, the poor, and the persecuted always prevailed. Fairy tale opera diminished in popularity for a time, to rise again around the turn of the twentieth century in reaction against a naturalistic realism that had developed during the nineteenth century.

The trend toward realism began with Italian opera and was known as "*verismo*." Two outstanding examples of realistic Italian opera are *Cavalleria Rusticana* by Pietro Mascagni (1863–1945) and *Bajazzo* by

Ruggiero Leoncavallo (1858–1919), who is probably better known for *I Pagliacci,* another opera dealing with reality as he saw it. *Verismo* arose as a result of a feeling of monotony in traditional forms, and can be traced also to the English, French, and German novel as well as to the Scandinavian drama of Ibsen (1828–1906) and Björnson (1832–1910). Wagner's work also reflected the change from tradition at this time. However, his Nordic pessimism and deemphasis of melody had little appeal for Italian tastes. In fact, the operas mentioned above were a direct Italian response to the heaviness of Wagnerian music. As might be expected, both Wagner and the Italian composers had many imitators, most of whom achieved little in the way of recognition and whose works were regarded as nothing but worthless imitations.

With the fading of interest in fairy-tale opera a new type of realism arose, adapting the impressionistic orchestrations of Berlioz and Wagner to psychologically interesting texts. This development is reflected in the works of the English poet and playwright, Oscar Wilde, and of Austrian Hugo von Hofmannsthal, as set to music by Richard Strauss in his operas *Salome* and *Elektra.* In fact, Strauss departed from his more extreme impressionism in these works and went so far as to reintroduce, in these later operas, such an old-fashioned form as the coloratura aria.

Comic Opera

Although it has certain links to grand opera, comic opera had some development of its own. Various factors converged in its history that require some sociological explanation. Wherever there have been human beings there have been moments for laughter. Hence, there are representative examples of comic art in almost every culture, though music has not apparently been the most important of them. (Many kinds of so-called comic music actually do not deserve this name, but should rather be called entertaining music.) Certain instruments have sometimes been used to intentionally produce comical sounds. We know that the bagpipe and bassoon were so used by Austrian composers. Wenzel Müller (1767–1835) used them in this way in Vienna at the beginning of the nineteenth century. Later Lortzing a German composer of opera, did the same at the end of the Romantic period. Even Wagner used the bassoon in this way at the end of the second act of the *Die Meistersinger.* More recently, the trombone has often been used in jazz for comic effect.

There are other known attempts to produce humorous musical effects within other forms of music. Comic intermezzos have occasionally been incorporated into serious mystery plays and oratorios. Works by the

French composer Lully contained such passages, as did certain Italian operas, Yet all of these examples are unimportant when compared with comic opera itself. Comic opera is a combination of the Italian *opera seria* and forms of comic theater that developed within the sphere of the spoken theater. Above all, the Italian commedia dell'arte was significant in this development. The influence of this form on the origin and growth of comic opera was so great as to deserve more detailed description.

Commedia dell'arte arose in Italy, spreading from there primarily to Catholic countries. In Spain it appeared under approximately the same name—*Comedia del arte*. French comedy before Molière followed the same line, as did many German comedies of more or less local or regional character. To a lesser extent something similar could also be found among Protestant peoples. The name highlights the special kind of humor that is essential to this art form, which was largely based on the art of improvisation. The amusing details were often not fully elaborated, but rather left to the discretion of the actors, who made their jokes at special places in the script. They might do so by using local situations and events as the butt of some of their jokes. The performers thus had some independence of interpretation. The principal roles consisted of typical characters who appeared again and again in all the various plays belonging to this category.

Most important of these characteristic roles was the part of the merry valet. He was not devised independently by writers of the Italian Renaissance, but had already existed many centuries before Christ in the old Roman play in which he was a jolly slave who assisted his master in complicated situations. Brighella, as he was often called in Italian comedies, had been discovered by the pioneers of the Italian Renaissance as they delved into antiquity. A faithful servant, he was usually willing and able to use any means available to help his master. One of the best known successors of the Brighella part was the French Scapin whom Molière presented in his earlier comedies. Another manifestation of this character was Bernardo in the eighteenth century Viennese comedy. Hanswurst in Germanic countries and Johnny Pudding in England may have had the same beginning. The rationalism and enlightenment of the eighteenth century was not fertile ground for this kind of popular art. One of the most powerful leaders in the field of German theater, Johann Christopher Gottsched (1700–1766), partially succeeded in banishing Hanswurst from the official stage.

Another type of character was Kölner Hanneschen who has been discussed in another context. Although Hanswurst and Kölner Hanneschen were quite different from one another they had one thing in common. They were, ordinarily, both cast as spirited young boys of lower social origin who are able to scout out and master any situation. This reflects, to a great extent, on the self-glorification of lower-class people. One example may clarify this trend. There is an old Cologne dialect version of the Doctor Faust story. The great scholar enters into a contract with the devil who, in the end, is victorious. But Faust has a valet, Johnny Sausage from Cologne, who also makes a bet with the devil. While the great scholar is defeated by the devil, his merry servant wins the bet and the devil is obliged to pay Johnny twenty-five cents. This story clearly depicts the self glorification of the poorer classes who considered themselves able to handle any and every situation, even to outwit the devil himself.

Another typical role is that of the village idiot. He too has had many names, two of which became especially well known. First there was Dummer Anton ("stupid Anthony"), a role made famous by Emanuel Schikaneder (1751–1812). At one time in Vienna, Schikaneder was owner and director of a theater, as well as its stage manager, librettist, and actor. He is known also in music history for having written the text for Mozart's *Magic Flute*. Schikaneder performed the part of Papageno and is responsible for the fact that Mozart made the latter a harmless and stupid fellow. Schikaneder insisted on performing the role which, incidentally, goes back to the commedia dell'arte. Another character of this kind was Tuennes, who also spoke the Cologne dialect and usually appeared with bright red hair and a huge nose.

Among the more or less traditional comic characters was the Italian Pulcinella. The French version of this character, which spread to other countries and up to recent times, was called Polichinelle, and is hunchbacked and cross-eyed. Apparently Charchet, one of the principal comedy characterizations of the southern Belgium marionette theater, goes back to the same source as does Schael of Rhineland comedy. "Schael" means cross-eyed in Cologne dialect. In this version the deformed back is no longer a characteristic trait, but like his predecessors Schael thrived on intrigue.

Some characters in the plot indicate, by their name, that they are not conceived as individuals but as typical representatives of an occupational group. Among them are the doctor (*Il Dottore*) and the captain (*Il Capitano*). The latter, of course, represented an epoch in which all continents were explored and were unceasingly at war. In the typical captain plot, the captain told about all his great adventures in remote countries to which none of the listeners was supposed to have been. Unfortunately for him, someone present had also been to the place under discussion or participated in the war. This person told the audience that the captain had been anything but a hero. In other countries a similar character was called Bramarbas.

We now come to the role of Pantalone. He was usually a rather old man who was either the father or the guardian of a beautiful girl. Ordinarily he was a wealthy man with great plans for the young lady in question. When he was the girl's father he wanted her to marry some other wealthy man, and when he was merely her guardian, and a bachelor, he wanted to marry her himself. In the original story, Pantalone was a native of the city of Venice, one of whose favorite saints was St. Pantaleone. Since Venice is supposed to be a city of much cold weather, due to her many canals, the older men were entitled to wear trousers in contrast to the custom of shorter pants for the younger generation. During that era, Pantalone was one of the few men who wore the long trousers that were later named for him in French as *pantalon*. French revolutionaries wanted to show in their attire, as well as by their actions, how different they were from the hated ancient regime. Consequently they abandoned the *culotte* type of short trousers and began to wear long pants adapted from this comic Venetian character. In English, we can trace the words "pantaloon" and "pants" to this character.

What is the sociological significance of these humorous characters? They provide us with a key to the understanding of the mentality of the period, and of the commedia dell'arte. Although international navigation and trade were already a part of the world scene during the period under discussion, we cannot say that a truly capitalistic attitude existed as yet. Il Capitano and Pantalone, who were connected with navigation and trade within the script, were frequently made to appear ridiculous, and their ends were usually defeated before the play concluded. In a typical plot the handsome young lover, with the help of his valet, wins his beautiful sweetheart against the will of Pantalone, and despite all his money. At the end, youth and nature enjoy victory over the power of money and calculation.

Comic opera combines many aspects of both commedia dell'arte and Italian *opera seria*. Although at first it only spread to other Catholic countries, comic opera was finally taken up by Protestant countries and was even imitated in some degree in nineteenth century Czarist Russia. Some of the principal comic opera figures are identical to those already described for commedia dell'arte, although the names may have been changed. The only difference is that of singing (opera) as opposed to speaking (comedy theater). The merry valet is sung by the buffo tenor, while the elderly father or guardian is usually a buffo bass. The term *buffo* indicates the special vocal technique used for comedy, in contrast to the normal style of the lyric tenor or basso profundo. The doctor and captain also appear regularly, the wet nurse and the beggar and/or stutterer (often called Tartaglia) are seen less often. Mozart used this tradition in *The Marriage of Figaro,* in which Bartolo continues the tradition of Pantalone. His stammering judge Don Curzio is a modernized form of the older Tartaglia.

The fact that the rich bourgeois was depicted as a comic figure during this period, while the land-owning nobility, the clergy, and the royalty escaped being subjects of dramatic or musical wit is easily explained. Up to and including Mozart's *The Marriage of Figaro,* opera was largely performed at the courts of nobility, clergy, and royalty of Italy, France, Germany, and other Western European countries. It follows, naturally, in the course of human nature (and thus as a sociological rule) that any individual of high station in life does not wish to see his peers ridiculed in the plot of a play or opera. He would rather watch comedy centered about people of some social position lower than his own. This situation did not change until after the French Revolution, when Trinchera wrote the opera *La Tavernola Aventorosa* using a priest as his comic figure. Even then, however, he was imprisoned for having done so. The notable exception to this trend was the type of comic opera with humorous monarchal figures performed in Venice, which was a republic.

During the nineteenth century the situation changed, at least in some countries. France, for example, became less and less religiously oriented; one finds priests depicted in humorous roles, especially in vaudeville. But this is already much closer to the more recent form of the operetta than to the classical comic opera.

The Operetta

Some distinction may be useful at this point between the classic type of comic opera and the operetta of the nineteenth century, which is characterized by a greater use of dance rhythm than had been common previously. The rhythm is the famous Viennese waltz, which dates back to an Austrian peasant dance called the *Ländler* that was practically unknown up to the end of the eighteenth century outside of the native districts. Sociologically speaking, a characteristic trait of the operetta was that the main characters of the plot were members of the aristocracy.

The sociological background of the operetta follows. The Viennese opera audience was primarily made up of relatively conservative members of the middle class. These people were not at all inclined to revolution; on the contrary, they admired the nobility and would have considered it a great honor to be invited to participate in their social life. Psychological research has shown that many spectators in the theater tend to project themselves into the action on stage, sometimes to the extent that they feel personally involved. This tendency explains the high degree of enjoyment experienced by middle-class audiences as they watch a play or operetta about those whose lives were lived in luxury. Furthermore, these middle-class people enjoyed dancing as much as did the nobility. Being Viennese, it was natural that the waltzes introduced in these operettas should become their favorites. And since the heroes of these productions frequently were monarchs or military men of the Balkan States, they represented topics of current political interest. As can be seen, many factors worked together to create popularity for this type of performance. The Strauss family members Joseph, Johann, and Eduard wrote and conducted one operetta after another in this fashion.

This sociological background of the Viennese operetta explains not only its success but also its limitations. The sector of the middle class that sang Schubert's songs, danced to Viennese waltzes, and listened to Johann Strauss (1825–1899), Millöcker (1842–1899), and similar composers gradually decreased in numbers and slowly began to die out. Industrialization produced a generation involved in a more rapid tempo of life, and with other interests to contemplate than the amorous adventures of Balkan dukes. Moreover, the rapid rise of the lower-middle, or wage earning, class was taking place almost everywhere. This new lower-middle class, and even more so, the traditional wage-earners were involved in the capitalistic production process. Their effective contacts with other social classes were limited to dealings with industrial producers, bankers, engineers, and other occupations that were more or less dependent on industrialists. The affairs of the nobility, especially the nobility of Austria, Hungary, and the Balkan States, lay completely outside their field of interest. The aspiration of the working class for upward movement was directed toward the world of businessmen and engineers. In keeping with these changes in the social class structure, structural support for the nineteenth century operetta diminished rapidly.

Declining popular interest in operetta plots was also connected with diminishing marriage taboos. In the operetta the lovers had to overcome serious social obstacles concerning the suitability of the partners before they can marry. Frequently the plot provides an ending where the beautiful girl is not at all an unsuitable mate. She is not a poor Gypsy girl, but the lost daughter of a powerful nobleman. Yet the subject of social suitability decreased in topical interest with the abatement in family-arranged marriages. Finally, one should mention that the operetta originated in a period of ample leisure time for the theater-going public. Operettas normally took an entire evening. The new generation was living at a faster pace and wanted more diversity of entertainment in the limited leisure time left to them. As a result, the operetta was replaced by listening to short skits on the radio, in nightclubs, or cabarets, where many heterogeneous experiences could be enjoyed in a relatively short period of time.

The Melodrama

Before we consider the subjects of dance and the more recent forms of music, a few words about some other older forms of musical theater need to be added in order to complete the picture. The term *melodrama,* at present, is often used in a rather sarcastic sense to denote plots in which the girl is unbelievably innocent and the villain inconceivably wicked. Melodrama today represents a kind of dramatic performance that exaggerates and oversimplifies everything; all is black and white, and there is no gray. Yet the original meaning of the Greek word *melodrama* was quite different. It denoted a kind of musical performance in which the lines were spoken to the accompaniment of music. Although this combination of music and drama had been in existence for hundreds of years, it did not become popular nor even much recognized until the end of the eighteenth century. At that time, Rousseau, who had considered himself a composer for quite some years, began to emphasize this form of theater in his work. Rousseau's following included members of the dissatisfied upper-lower and lower-middle classes, but was primarily composed of members of the aristocracy. Consequently, Rousseau's emphasis on melodrama became widely known. Yet with the rapidly disappearing interest in Rousseau after the French Revolution, interest in melodrama also faded. The technique was later used mainly to create special effects within the whole of a larger opera. Among the better known examples are the beginning of the second act of Beethoven's *Fidelio* and the appearance of the devilish Samiel in Karl Maria von Weber's romantic opera *Freischütz.*

MUSIC AND DANCE

As far as we know there is not a single society without dances. This widespread diffusion of the dance may be related to the fact that dancing was connected with magic in many societies. Dance could either avoid the powerful effect of evil spirits or induce blessings from the spirits for the benefit of the participants or even for the entire group. There is conclusive evidence that dances are performed for this purpose among peoples in the Sudan, among Melanesians, and among American Indians. Similar phenomena are also found in more complex civilizations, as among the Malayans, Chinese, Koreans, and Japanese. We have remnants of such originally magic dances among the terpsichorean activities of ancient Greece. Within Christian ritual, religious dancing was limited to the Ethiopian Coptic church, Spain, and, until recently, Latin America.

In the analysis of particular examples it is often difficult to determine whether one is dealing with dancing for magic purposes or with a form that might better be called dance theater. This problem arises especially when the dancers wear masks in their performance. Many masks clearly denote their origin; animal masks indicate that the dance is a sort of animal imitation. In such cases the whole phenomenon can be traced back to totemism or similar forms of primitive religion in which animals were considered superior to human beings. In ancient times man feared the animals and considered it important to obtain the protection of such powerful creatures.

In the more complex cultures, however, we find occurrences that doubtlessly should be called dance theater. Since Greek times, some of these performances have also been in the form of pantomimes. This kind of dance actually exists among all known peoples. Modern ballet, when it is character ballet, as well as the czarist and the Soviet character ballet, are modern representatives of this tradition. All of these ballet forms share as an essential feature that nearly the entire body is used in the movements of the dance and that musical instruments are merely used as accompaniment for these movements. This consideration helps to explain the range of instruments used in connection with the dance. The most elementary, and apparently the oldest, form of accompaniment for dances is that of hand clapping, which is found in various folk dances even today. It was also used in connection with the religious dances of the Ethiopian church.

Next to the use of the body, including the hand clapping, natural objects have frequently been adapted to supply a rhythmic accompaniment. Many percussion instruments are made from gourds or from wood, as are certain kinds of rattles used in Central Africa and New Guinea and in other relatively primitive cultures. A further development was in the use of string instruments, which were played by plucking the string rather than by bowing. The religious dances of ancient Greece were accompanied in this way. The Greeks also used wind instruments made of reeds, as did the people of ancient Egypt and western Asia, where some are still in use. This distribution is connected with the presence of frequently flooded rivers; reeds grow easily in stagnant water. These early wind instruments were the forerunners of the modern oboe. Even the so-called portative, a more complex wind instrument and an early predecessor of the modern organ, was used to accompany certain dances. The organ has not always played the primarily religious role it has had in the churches of our Western culture. In many of its earlier forms and in the Byzantine Empire, it was considered a most secular instrument.

As instrumentation differed in various cultures, so did occasions for dance. In the ancient Greek and the Byzantine empires hiring dancers to perform during banquets, while the high-ranking guests ate and drank, was considered fashionable. One event at which dances are used in almost every civilization is the wedding. The only variation seems to involve who is doing the dancing. In ancient Greece, for example, weddings were celebrated by having boys perform dances with the accompaniment of the Greek *kithara* and *aulos*.

Sword dances played a prominent role in feudal cultures. During these periods the primary occupation of the nobility was war; their leisure time was used for training themselves and their sons in the military arts. Sword dancers symbolized heroic deeds performed in battle. These dances were widely cultivated in Spain, which saw 700 years of almost uninterrupted religious wars against the Mohammedans, which were fought under a feudal type of leadership.

Dances are used at funerals in some cultures. This may be an expression of religious belief or superstition to either conjure up or ward off evil spirits, since many societies expected to such spirits to wipe out the whole family or even tribe in the case of a death. Even in more complex cultures, we find dirges performed at the time of death in combination with conventional dance steps that are clearly the remnants of earlier dances. The use of dancing in connection with events of a more or less religious nature has been maintained in certain folk traditions, and even in some more sophisticated cultures, through our own times.

Western civilization, especially in modern times, has witnessed the rise of the dance for its own sake, or more accurately for the personal pleasure of viewers and participants. Consequently, dancing has lost much of its ability to express the values of an entire group and has taken on an existence sui generis as an element of entertainment and a value in itself. The custom, first encountered in feudal times, of entertaining guests by encouraging them to share in the dance at court has thus been imitated and adapted to our own times by the urban middle class.

In our discussion of opera during its early days we saw that various parts were interconnected by dialogues and musical recitatives, to which few of the audience would listen. In the same sense opera ballet frequently became just one number among others in the development of Italian opera, as well as in the French and German versions. Just as the coloratura role in the opera was composed for the primadonna so that she could display her technical excellence, the opera ballet offered female dancers a chance to display their technique. This characteristic of classical ballet is given emphasis in the convention of dressing the dancers in costumes that are thought to be very beautiful and to enhance the perfection of their bodies, even though they have little if anything to do with the period in which the opera is set. Often opera ballet functioned more as an interlude than as an integral part of the opera plot. That the ballet became a value in itself, almost disconnected from the dramatic performance, is illustrated in another example from the history of this art form.

During the seventeenth and eighteenth centuries, especially under the rule of Louis XIV, ballet was immensely popular. Even the king would sometimes participate in it. During this time ways were also explored to incorporate ballet performances into plays, whether tragic or comic. One such example was *Le Malade Imaginaire,* a comedy by Molière. It was staged in the court theater, in the king's presence. To please this royal audience, Molière contrived to add a ballet, with a somewhat artificial effect. Essentially, the plot is as follows: A very wealthy man is under the care of physicians who convince him that his life is in immediate danger if he does not follow their advice in every detail. The physicians surround him constantly and charge exorbitant fees. His relatives later convince him that his doctors are only out to fill their own pockets at his expense, and are not really doing him any good. The relatives suggest that if the hypochondriac really wants to remain in good health and never get sick again he should become a physician himself. In order to do this, he need not study medicine, but only to receive a medical degree. The final scene includes the ballet, in which the degree of Doctor of Medicine is conferred on the patient. The audience knew, of course, that besides ridiculing the medical profession this ending was designed to satisfy a high society audience that prefered ballet to almost any other muse.

The form of the classical ballet continued throughout the eighteenth century and well into the nineteenth. At this time a trend toward character ballet appeared. The czarist Russian ballet especially became known as a proponent of this form.

Some concluding comments need now to be made concerning social dimensions of folk and social dancing, insofar as this activity, too, has been exposed to the forces of change. Changes in social and popular dancing essentially came from two directions. Old folk dances were rediscovered by the German Youth Movement and similar Romantic and nationalistic or ethnic revivals. These dances had continued to be practiced in remote areas, but without any connection with the social dances of the affluent. The revival movement of folk dances, as it were, counteracted the separation between body movement and song of ballet dancing, and reintroduced the traditions of dance so predominant in the majority of cultures: the total involvement of dancers in the combination of song, dance, and instrumental rhythmic accompaniment.

Other dancers went even further by insisting that dancing was to include the entire body. That process rediscovered very old forms that were now referred to as *eurhythmics*. The full history of the eurhythmic movement cannot be given here, yet some outstanding names should be mentioned, such as Emile Jacques-Dalcroze (1865–1950), Mary Wigmann (1886–1973), Rudolf von Laban (1879–1958), and Rudolf Bode (1881–1970). The whole movement was closely connected with the general inclination to turn away from rationalism and intellectualism and give emphasis instead to nature and emotion, as it had found intellectual expression at the beginning of the nineteenth century. The adherents of this movement argued that body rhythm was closely related to the natural rhythm of the universe. Moreover, the assertion was made that man had become too intellectualized and had lost contact with nature. Many phenomena characterizing our own time are considered to be expressions of decadance and are explained by this loss of contact with nature.

BIBLIOGRAPHIES

SOCIOLOGY OF MUSIC:
TITLES SELECTED AND ANNOTATED
BY PAUL HONIGSHEIM

Abert, Hermann. *Die Lehre vom Ethos in der griechischen Musik*. Leipzig: Breitkopf & Härtel, 1899.

Abraham, Gerald (Ed.). *Grieg: A Symposium*. Norman: University of Oklahoma Press, 1950.

———. *Eight Soviet Composers*. London: Oxford University Press, 1944.

Abraham, Otto, and E. M. von Hornbostel. *Studien über das Tonsystem und die Musik der Japaner*. Leipzig: Breitkopf & Härtel, 1903. [On the puppet theater; morals of the people on the stage, etc.]

Abrahamsen, Erik. *Eléments Romans et Allemands dans le Chant Grégorien et la Chanson Populaire en Danemark*. Copenhagen: P. Haase et fils, 1923. [Based on much material. Main thesis is that in Germany Gregorianism was changed by German elements.]

Acevedo, Hernández. *Canciones Populares Chilenas*. Santiago: Ediciones Ercilla, 1939. [Popular, not scholarly.]

Ackerknecht, Erwin. "Das Lichtspiel in seinem organischen Zusammenwirken mit den anderen Einrichtungen der Bildungspflege." *Bildungspflege*, 1:3–7, 1919.

———. *Das Lichtspiel im Dienste der Bildungspflege*. Berlin: Weidmannsche Buchandlung, 1918.

XX   ———. "Lichtspielreform ohne Lichtspiel." *Volksbildungsarchiv*, 6(3), December 1918.

Adler, Cyrus. *The Shofar—Its Use and Origin*. Washington, D.C.: U.S. Government Printing office, 1893.

Adler, Guido. "Musik in Oesterreich," in Studien zur Musikwissenschaft. *Gesellschaft zur Herausgabe von Denkmälern der Tonkunst in Oesterreich*, vol. 16. Vienna, 1929.

XA ———. "Zur Vorgeschichte der Denkmäler der Tonkunst in Oesterreich," in *Studien zur Musikwissenschaft. Gesellschaft zur Herausgabe von Denkmälern der Tonkunst in Oesterreich*, vol. 5, Vienna, 1918.

Adorno, Theodor W. "Ideen zur Musiksoziologie." *Schweizer Monatshefte*, **38**:679–691, November 1958.

———. *Dissonanzen: Musik in der verwalteten Welt*. Göttingen: Vandenhoeck & Ruprecht, 1956.

———. "On popular music." *Studies in Philosophy and Social Science*, 9(1):17–49, April 1941.

XX ———. "Fragmente über Wagner." *Zeitschrift für Sozialforschung*, **8**, 1939.

———. "Über den Fetischcharakter und die Regression des Hörens." *Zeitschrift für Sozialforschung*, 7:321–356, 1939.

———. "Zur gesellschaftlichen Lage der Musik." *Zeitschrift für Sozialforschung*, 1:103–124, 356–378, 1932.

Adrio, Adam. *Die Anfänge des geistlichen Konzerts*. Berlin: Junker, 1935. [All concerts and editions indicated in detail. Also new editions are often cited. Some things of use to us.]

Akeret, Kurt. *Studien zum Klavierwerk von Maurice Ravel*. Zurich: Hug, 1941.

Albani, Emma. *Forty Years of Song*. London: Mills & Boon, 1911.

XX Albrecht, Hermann Alexander. *Das Englische Kindertheater*. Dissertation Halle-Wittenberg, Halle: Buchdruckerie des Waisenhauses, n.d. [Elze as *Referent*. Relevant also concerning choir boys.]

Aldrich, Putnam. *Ornamentation in J. S. Bach's Organ Works*. New York: Coleman-Ross, 1950.

Almeida, Renato. *Historia da Música Brasileira*. Rio de Janeiro: F. Briguiet, 1942. [With vast material, bibliography, alphabetic *Lexikon* of contemporaries.]

Alvarez, Juan. *Origenes de la Música Argentina*. N.p., 1908. [Popular, not scholarly.]

Amster, Isabella. *Das Virtuosenkonzert in der Ersten Hälfte des 19. Jahrhunderts*. Berlin: G. Kallmeyer, 1931. [Brilliant, truly sociological, with detailed table of all composers, concerts, editions, performances, etc.; also discusses all solo recitals of secondary significance.]

Anderson, Joannes Earl. *Maori Music with its Polynesian Background*. New Plymouth, New Zealand: Thomas Avery and Sons, 1934. [Polynesian music interrelationship; relevant because of the Peru-Polynesian.]

Anderson, John. *The American Theatre*. New York: Dial Press, 1938.

Anderson, William Robert. *Music as a Career*. London: Oxford University Press, 1939.

Andreesen, Alfred. *Das Landerziehungsheim*. Leipzig: Quelle & Meyer, 1926.

Anheisser, Siegfied. "Der Einklang von Ton und Wort," in *Jahrbuch des Westdeutschen Rundfunkes*. Cologne, 1929.

Anton, Karl. *Beiträge zur Biographie Carl Loewes*. Halle: A. S. M. Niemeyer, 1912. [Very critically based on knowledge of material, some things usable.]

Apel, Willi. *The Notation of Polyphonic Music, 900-1600*. Cambridge, Mass.: Mediaeval Academy of America, 1942.

Appel, Margarete. *"Terminologie in den mittelalterlichen Musiktraktaten."* Dissertation Berlin, 1935. [Constructed by herself from study of *Traktate*.]

Armitage, Merle (Ed.). *George Gershwin.* London: Longmans, 1938.

———. *Igor Strawinsky.* New York: Schirmer, 1936. [With many collaborators (coauthors?).]

Armstrong, Robert Bruce. *Musical Instruments,* vol. 2. Edinburgh: Constable, 1908. [Detailed description of variously arranged harp ensembles. Not as sociological as his work on Irish-Scottish harps.]

———. *Musical Instruments,* vol. 1. Edinburgh: D. Douglas, 1904. [Panegyrical, romantic, cites O'Curry.]

Arnold, Elliot. *Finlandia: The Story of Sibelius.* New York: Holt, 1941. [Largely narrative, much based on Ekman.]

XX Arnold, Hermann J. "Puppenspiel in Amerika." *Jugendvolksbühne,* 3(6), August 1932.

Aronson, Rudolph. *Theatrical and Musical Memoirs.* New York: McBride, Nast, 1913. [Prints many letters; otherwise everything based on personal recollections.]

Artaria, Franz, and Hugo Botstiber. *Joseph Haydn und das Verlagshaus Artaria.* Vienna: Artaria, 1909. [Panegyrical, but with some useful source references.]

Arvold, Alfred G. *The Little Country Theater.* New York: Macmillan, 1922.

Ashson, Joseph Nickerson. *Music in Worship.* Boston: The Pilgrim Press, 1943.

XA Asaf'ev, Boris W. Vladimirovic. "Chopin's Mazurken," in *Chopin Almanach,* Chopinkomitee in Deutschland. Potsdam: Akademische Verlagsgesellschaft Athenaion, 1949.

Aubry, Pierre. *Trouvères and Troubadours.* New York: Schirmer, 1914.

———. *La Musique et les Musiciens d'Eglise en Normandie au XIIIe Siècle.* Paris: H. Champion, 1906.

———. *Les Plus Anciens Monuments de la Musique Française.* Paris: H. Welter, 1905. [Entirely paleographic.]

———. *La Musicologie Médiévale, Histoire et Méthodes.* Paris: H. Welter, 1900. [Catholic, authorized by bishop; but protests against Rome's interference in questions of the history of the liturgy.]

———. *L'Inspiration Religieuse dans la poèsie musicale en France du Moyen Age à la Révolution.* Paris: Bureau de la Schola Cantorum, 1899.

Auer, Leopold. *My Long Life in Music.* London: Duckworth, 1924. [A lot on conditions of music in the Rhineland.]

Auerbach, Cornelia. *Die Deutsche Clavichordkunst des 18. Jahrhunderts.* Kassel: Bärenreiter-Verlag, 1930. [All without exact historical proof.]

Avery, Emmet Langdon. *Dancing and Pantomine on the English Stage, 1700–1737.* Chicago: University of Chicago Library, 1934. [A part of a dissertation.]

XX Bab, Julius. "Das eine Theaterproblem." *Junge Menschen,* 6(2), February 1925.

———. "Film und Kultur." *Bildungspflege,* 1(7):200, April 1920.

Bacharach, Alfred Louis (Ed.). *British Music of our Time.* Harmondsworth: Penguin Books, 1951.

Bacher, Joseph. *Die Viola da Gamba.* Kassel: Bärenreiter-Verlag, 1932. [Short bibliography on youth movement; critical, historical, with quotations.]

Badger, Alfred G. *An Illustrated History of the Flute.* New York: Firth, Pond, 1853. [Actually an advertisement; irrelevant, also as far as the Boehm-Gordon controversy is concerned.]

Balfour, Henry. *The Natural History of the Musical Bow.* Oxford: Clarendon Press, 1899. [Some quotations, but mostly based on museum studies. Apparently doesn't know Ratzel.]

Banning, Helmut. "Johann Friedrich Doles," in *Schriftenreihe des Staatlichen Instituts für deutsche Musikforschung,* no. 5. Leipzig: Kistner & Siegel, 193—. [Based on careful source studies.]

Baresel, Alfred. *Das Neue Jazzbuch.* Leipzig: W. Timmermann, 1929.

Barnes, Harry Elmer, Howard Becker, and Frances Bennet Becker. *Contemporary Social Theory.* New York: Appleton-Century, 1940. [Essential things of the *orientalische* culture. Economic ethics of the religious fostered by occidental religion has powerfully inhibited the economic attitude in the Orient, p. 635, and similarly, p. 843.]

Barnett, John Francis. *Musical Reminiscences and Impressions.* New York: B. W. Dodge, 1906.

Barry, Phillips, Fannie Hardy Eckstorm, and Mary Wnslow Smyth. *British Ballads from Maine.* New Haven: Yale University Press, 1929.

Bartenstein, Hans. *Hector Berlioz' Instrumentationskunst und ihre Geschichtliche Grundlagen.* Strasbourg: Heitz, 1939.

Bartók, Béla, and Albert B. Lord. *Serbo-Croatian-Folk Songs.* New York: Columbia University Press, 1951. [Very scholarly music theoretical treatment, but not much that concerns us; some things concerning distribution.]

Batalha Reis, Pedro. *Da Origem da Misica Trovadoresca em Portugal.* Lisbon: Tip de J. Ferdandes, 1931. [Wholly based on archive materials; proof that there were such. Partly popular music, represented by the *jogral* (p. 133). At the courts there also was *joasch.* Also Moorish musicians at the courts fasc. XII (239). Folk music. Repeats himself in discussing support; same in treating social position.]

Bauer-Lechner, Natalie. *Erinnerungen an Gustav Mahler.* Leipzig: Tal, 1923.

Baum, Richard Hellmuth. *Joseph Wölfe.* Kassel: Bärenreiter-Verlag, 1928. [On archbishop's court and music, also England.]

XX   Baumann, Paul. "Der Rhythmus in der Erziehung." *Soziale Zukunft* 5–7. Dornach: Der kommende Tag, n.d.

XX   Baumann-Dollfuss, Elisabeth. "Eurythmie." *Soziale Zukunft* 5–7. Dornach: Der kommende Tag, n.d.

Bäumler, Wilhelm. *Das katholische deutsche Kirchenlied in seinen Singweisen. Von den fühesten Zeiten bis gegen Ende des 17. Jahrhunderts.* Freiburg: Herder, 1886. [Started by Meisters, completed by Joseph Gotzen. Largely bibliography; bishop's regulations, etc. Quite useful.]

Bax, Sir Arnold Edward Trevor. *Farewell, My Youth.* London: Longmans, 1943. [Especially details as traveling pianist.]

Bayard, Samuel Preston (Ed.). Hill Country Tunes. Philadelphia: *American Folklore Society,* 1944. [Very critical, with exact indication on which day, played by whom, where he learned it, and from whom.]

Beaumont, Cyril William. *Puppets and the Puppet Stage.* London: The Studio Ltd., 1938. [A survey, also historical; not much that is new. Punch, Hanswurst, Karagheuz. No particular historical explanation.]

XX   Bech, Heinrich. *Das Judentum in der Musik.* Breslau: Deutsche Verlagsanstalt, 1926. [Dedicated to Paul Bekker, phenomenological, etc.]

Bechler, Leo, and Bernhardt Rahm. *Die Oboe und die ihr verwandten Instrumente.* Leipzig: C. Merseburger, 1914. [Refers to old books, e.g., Mersenne, Praetorius, etc. Manesse manuscript of songs *(Liederhandschrift)*.]

Beck, Earl Clifton. *Songs of the Michigan Lumberjacks.* Ann Arbor: University of Michigan Press, 1941. [Chiefly North Michigan.]

Beck, Jean Baptiste. *La Musique des Troubadours.* Paris: H. Laurens, 1928. [Historical.]

Becker, Carl Ferdinand. *Die Hausmusik in Deutschland in dem 16., 17. und 18. Jahrhunderte.* Leipzig: Fest, 1840. [Listing of chorales that developed from folk songs.]

Becker, Howard. *German Youth.* New York: Oxford University Press, 1946.

Becket, Wheeler. *Music in Warplants.* Washington, D.C.: War Production Board, War Production Drive Headquarters, August 1943.

XX   Beckler, H. "Ein Beitrag zur Kenntnis der Musik bei den Australischen Ureinwohnern." *Globus,* 1868, p. 82 ff. Cited by Hager, Karl. In Dissertation Jena. Hamburg: Schatke, 1822. [On the music of some primitive peoples.]

Beckmann, Gustav. *Das Violinspiel in Deutschland vor 1700.* Leipzig: Auslieferung bei N. Simrock, 1918. [Based on the study of manuscript materials, only in libraries abroad. Not for our purposes. Much history of technique.]

Bedbrook, Gerald Stares. *Keyboard Music from the Middle Ages to the Beginnings of the Baroque.* London: Macmillan, 1949. [Mostly history of instruments.]

Beecham, Sir Thomas. *A Mingled Chime.* New York: Putnam, 1943.

Beethoven, Ludwig van. *Konversationshefte.* Berlin: M. Hesse, 1941–1942.

———. *Unbekannte Skizzen und Entwürfe.* Bonn: Verlag des Beethovenhauses, K. Schroeder, 1922, 23 pp.

———. *Beethoven über eine Gesamtausgabe seiner Werke.* Veröffentlichungen des Beethovenhauses in Bonn, no. 1. Bonn: K. Schroeder in Komma, 1920.

———. *Beethoven's Letters: A Critical Edition with Explanatory Notes by Dr. A. C. Kalischer, Translated with Preface by J. S. Shedlock.* London: Dent, 1909.

Bekker, Paul. *Wagner, das Leben im Werke.* Stuttgart, etc.: Deutsche Verlagsanstalt, 1924.

———. *Das deutsche Musikleben.* Stuttgart: Deutsche Verlagsanstalt vereinigt mit Schuster und Löffler, 1922. [Originally written in 1916.]

———. *Franz Schrecker, Studie zur Kritik der modernen Oper.* Berlin: Schuster und Löffler, 1919.

XX   Beling, Else. "Der Ausschuss für Volksvorlesungen in Frankfurt." *Volksbildungsarchiv,* 1(4), December 1910.

Belvianes, Marcel. *Sociologie de la musique.* Paris: Payot, 1950.

Benet, Laura. *Enchanting Jenny Lind.* New York: Dodd, Mead, 1939. [Broadly narrating.]

Benjmain, Lewis Saul. *Stage Favourites of the Eighteenth Century.* London: Hutchinson, 1928. [Exclusively biographies, not very critical.]

Bennet, Joseph. *Forty Years of Music, 1865–1905.* London: Methuen, 1908. [The author is primarily a music critic.]

XA   Bennet, Tom. "Arranging music for radio," in *Music in Radio Broadcasting,* Chase. New York: McGraw-Hill, 1946.

XA   Benzer, Willi. "Musik in der Provinz," in *Musikerziehung,* Adler, Karl; Willi Benzer, and Hermann Keller. Kassel: Bärenreiter-Verlag, 1929, 132 pp.

Berendt, Joachim Ernst. *Dass Jazzbuch*. Frankfurt: Fisher-Bücherei, 1953.

Berger, Arthur Victor. *Aaron Copland*. New York: Oxford University Press, 1953.

Berger, Francesco. *Reminiscences, Impressions, and Anecdotes*. London: Low, Marston, 1913. [The author is primarily a conducting teacher.]

Bergmann, Leola N. *Music Masters of the Middle West*. Minneapolis: University of Minnesota Press, 1944.

XX Berlepsch-Valendàs, Hans von. "Der Wegwart." *Blätter für lebendiges Schauen und Gestalten*, Erich Nippold and Hans von Berlepsch-Valendàs, eds. 1(2), October 15, 1925. Wolffenbüttel: Kallmeyer, 1925.

Berlioz, Hector. *Memoirs of Hector Berlioz from 1803 to 1865*. New York: Knopf, 1932.

Bernar, Alfred. *Studien zur Arabischen Musik auf Grund der gegenwärtigen Theorie und Praxis in Ägypten*. Leipzig: Kistner & Siegel, 1937. [Theory of influences; daring, with much literature: Idelsohn, Romanet. Builds on his own recordings in Egypt.]

Bernhard, Edmond. *Apologie du Jazz*. Brussels: Les Presses de Belgique, 1945. [Only a few things of use.]

Bernstein, Nikolai Davidovitch. *Russlands Theater und Musik zur Zeit Peters des Grossen*. Riga: A Gizycki; Leipzig: P. Pabst, 1904. [Glorification of Peter the Great; nothing that is new; no sources.]

Berqquist, Nils William. *Swedish Folk Dances*. New York: Barnes, 1910. [Collected in the villages during the nineteenth century by students. Material in the Skausen Museum near Stockholm; here printed with annotations, performance edition. Pictures, with music.]

Berrien, William. *Report of the Committee of the Conference on Inter-American Relations in the Field of Music*. Washington, D.C.: U.S. Department of State, 1940. [Some things relevant.]

Berten, Franzi. *Franz Benda, sein Leben und seine Kompositionen*. Essen: Druck von C. W. Haarfeld, 1928.

Bessaraboff, Nicholas. *Ancient European Musical Instruments*. Boston: Harvard University Press, 1941. [Systematic, detailed description. Follows the scheme *Membranophon*, etc. Each again historical.]

XX Beyer, Georg. "Lorbeerkranz und Bettelstab," aus dem Schicksalsbuch der Kölner Theater in Monatsblättern der freien Volksbühne Köln. Jahrgang 1, no. 9, May 1932. Festausgabe 10 Jahre freie Volksbühne.

Bie, Oskar. *Der Tanz*. Berlin: J. Bard, 1919. [Aestheticizing, aristocratic.]

Bieber, Margarete. *The History of the Greek and Roman Theater*. Princeton: Princeton University Press, 1939. [Repeats much that has been known for long; a few things that are new.]

Biedenfeld, Ferdinand Leopold Carl, Freiherr von. *Die Komische Oper der Italiener*. Leipzig: T. O. Weigel, 1848. [Anecdotal. Not relevant.]

XX Bienath, Ernest. *Die Guitarre seit dem III. Jahrhundert vor Christi. Eine Musik-und Kulturgeschichtliche Darstellung mit genauer Quellenangabe*. Berlin: A. Haack Verlagsbuchhandlung, 1907. [Goes back very far: Egyptians, Hittites, etc. Very exact indication of secondary sources. Mentions guitars.]

Birge, Edward Bailey. *History of Public School Music in the United States*. Philadelphia: Oliver Ditson Co., 1937. [Details concerning Lowell Mason, etc.; based on sources.]

Bispham, David. *A Quaker Singer's Recollections*. New York: Macmillan, 1920. [The author is a Wagnerian of Philadelphia Quaker Singers.]

Bitter, Werner. *Die Deutsche Komische Oper der Gegenwart*. Leipzig: Kistner & Siegel, 1932. [Especially Part III. The text problem based on many sources and much material.]

Bittermann, Helen Robbins. *Harun al-Rashid's Gift of an Organ to Charlemagne*. Cambridge, Mass.: Medieval Academy of America, 1929.

———. *The Organ in the Early Middle Ages*. Cambridge, Mass.: Medieval Academy of America, 1929.

Bizet, Georges. *Lettres à Un Ami, 1865–1872*. Paris: Calmann Lévy, 1909. [His letters to Galabert himself. Primarily critique of his attempted composition, occasionally also describing conservatory affairs; relevant only for the latter and for the question of *Praemierung* of foreigners.]

———. *Lettres de Georges Bizet*. Paris: Calmann Lévy, 1907. [Relevant because of Commune, Napoleon III, and attitudes toward Wagner and Germany.]

XA   Black, Franck J. "Conducting for radio," in *Music in Radio Broadcasting*, Chase. New York: McGraw-Hill, 1946.

Blaukopf, Kurt. *Musiksoziologie*. Vienna: W. Verkauf, 1951.

XX   Blaux, E. Notes et documents inédits à l'Opéra Comique et quelques [antécédents?] pendant la Révolution. Extraits de L'Exdess musicale de Lyon. Paris: Fischbacher, 1909. [Very short book; prints documents.]

Blegen, Theodore Christian, and Martin B. Ruud. *Norwegian Emigrant Songs and Ballads*. Minneapolis: University of Minnesota Press, 1936. [Among other things, many poems by which departing emigrants are celebrated in Norway. (18-23) Songs of how bad things were in Norway. (Songs refer to emigrating Mormons. *Not by Mormons!*)]

Blesh, Rudi. *Shining Trumpets, A History of Jazz*. New York: Knopf, 1946. [Some things important.]

Bloch, Paul Jacques. *Der deutsche Volkstanz der Gegenwart*. Giessen: Kindt, 1927. [Elze as *Referent*. Naumann and Franz Schulz.]

Blom, Eric. *Music in England*. West Drayton: Penguin Books, 1947.

Blume, Friedrich. *Two Centuries of Bach*. Trans. Stanley Godman. London: Oxford University Press, 1950. [First published 1947 by Bärenreiter-Verlag.]

Blumner, Martin. *Geschichte der Sing-akademie zu Berlin*. Berlin: Horn & Raasch, 1891.

Bobillier, Marie. *La Musique Militaire*. Paris: H. Laurens, 1917. [Includes primary history of instruments; short bibliography; no indication of sources.]

———. *Musique et Musiciens de la Vieille France*. Paris: F. Alcan, 1911.

———. *Les Musiciens de la Sainte-Chapelle du Palais, Documents Inédits, Recueillis et Annotés*. Paris: A. Picard et fils, 1910. [Almost exclusively documents; in chronological order; some things useful.]

XX   ———. *La Musique Sacrée sous Louis XIV*. Paris: Editeur de la Schola Cantorum, 1899. [Short, without indication of sources.]

Bochet, Henri. *Le Conservatoire de Musique de Genève*. Geneva: 1935. [With several supplements.]

XX   Bode, Rudolf. *Gymnastik und Jugenderziehung*. Munich, n.d.

———. *Rhythmus und Körpererziehung*. Jena: E. Diederichs, 1925, 90 pp.

Böhme, Erdmann Werner. *Die Frühdeutsche Oper in Thüringen*. Stradtroda: E. & Dr. E. Richter, 1931. [Certain things, on place of orchestras, courts, etc., quite relevant.]

XX ———. "Soziale Schilderung Thüringer Musiker im Jahrhundert des Baroks," *Monatshefte Thüringens*, February 1931. [Cannot be located; quoted in Böhme's *Die Frühdeutsche Oper in Thüringen*.]

Böhme, Franz Magnus. *Geschichte des Tanzes in Deutschland*. Leipzig: Breitkopf & Härtel, 1886. [Based on sources, especially old German poems.]

XX Böhme, Fritz. "Der Tanz in der heutigen Kultur," *Die Freude*, 2(9), September 1925. Egesdorf: Robert Lauer Verlag, 1925.

Boehn, Max von. *Puppen und Puppenspiele*. Munich: F. Bruckmann, 1929. [Volume I on puppets only. Volume II a history of the puppet theater, *not* systematic, in which some things are useful.]

Boelza, Igor. *Handbook of Soviet Musicians*. London: The Pilot Press, 1943.

XX Bofinger, (no initial). *Lyrik in Dichtung und Rundfunk*. Berlin: Reichsrundfunkgesellschaft, 1929.

Bohe, Walter. *Richard Wagner im Spiegel der Wiener Presse*. Würzburg: K. Triltsch, 1933. [Goes back to L'Ester in Munich and Everth in Leipzig; not evident who was the *Referent*.]

XA Bohnstedt, Werner. "Erwägungen zum Thema Film und Radio als Gegenstände Soziologischer Erkenntnis," in *Reine und angewandte Soziologie, ein Festausgabe für Ferdinand Tönnies zu Seinem 80. Geburtstage*. Leipzig, 1936.

Bolte, Johannes. *Die Singspiele der Englischen Komödianten und ihrer Nachfolger in Deutschland, Holland und Skandinavien*. Hamburg und Leipzig: L. Voss, 1893. [Studies of theater history edited by Berthold Litzmann. Good, useful details.]

Bondy, Curt. *Die proletarische Jugenbewegung in Deutschland*. Lauenburg: Adolf Saal, 1922.

Bonnassies, Jules. *Les Spectacles Forains et la Comédie Française*. Paris: E. Dentu, 1875. [With some sources in the few notes.]

Bontoux, Germaine. *La Chanson en Angleterre an Temps d'Elisabeth*. Oxford: John Johnson at the University Press, 1936. [An imposing volume with facsimile reproduction of notes, reproductions of texts. with bibliography. Based also on study of manuscripts.]

Borcherdt, Hans Heinrich. *Das Europäische Theater im Mittelalter und in der Renaissance*. Leipzig: J. J. Weber, 1935. [With selected excerpts and sources in notes at the end of the book.]

Borgerhof, Joseph Leopold. *Le Théâtre Anglais à Paris sous la Restauration*. Paris: Hachette, 1912. [Addresses itself almost exclusively to dramatic plays.]

Borris, Siegfried. *Kirnbergers Leben und Werk und seine Bedeutung im Berliner Musikkreise um 1750*. Kassel: Bärenreiter-Verlag, 1933. [Of limited use.]

Botstiber, Hugo. "Geschichte der Ouvertüre und der freien Orchesterformen," in *Kleine Handbücher der Musikgeschichte nach Gattungen*, August Kretzschmar, no. 9, p. 274. Leipzig, 1904–1922. [Occasionally there are specific citations, also scores and information on location of manuscripts.]

Böttcher, Hans. "Musiksoziologie," *Melos*, 10:188–191, 1931.

Bourgault-Ducoudray, Louis Albert. *Etude sur la Musique Ecclésiastique Grecque.* Paris: Hachette, 1877. [Many details on scales; problems of susceptibility to reform and modernization for practical purposes.]

Bournot, Otto. *Ludwig Heinr. Chr. Geyer.* Leipzig: Siegel, 1913. [Intended as Germanic; based on much historical, archival material.]

Bouteron, Marcel. *Danse et Musique Romantiques.* Paris: Le Goupy, 1927. [Narrating, in anecdotal manner.]

Brahms, Johannes. *Johannes Brahms im Briefwechsel.* Berlin: Verlag der Deutschen Brahms-Gesellschaft, m.b.h., vols. 1–16, 1908–1920.

Brake, Franz Josef. *Moderne Spieloper.* Munich: Franz, 1886. [Without any relevance; deals with Conradin Creutzer, Millöcker, Johann Strauss, Suppé, etc.]

XX Brandenburg, Hans, and Rudolf von Laban. "Schwingende Gestalten." *Die Freude,* 2(9), September 1925. Egesdorf: R. Lauer Verlag, 1925.

Brandstetter, Renward. "Die Hymnen der Dajakischen Tiwah Feier," in *Festschrift. Publication d'hommage, offerte au Paul Wilhelm Schmidt,* pp. 189–192. Vienna, 1928. [Refers to A. Hardeland, *Dajakische Grammatik,* Amsterdam: T. Müller, 1858; where in the appendix the hymns are transcribed.]

XX Brauberger, Johann. *Musikgeschichtliches aus Böhmen.* Prague: J. Taussig, 1906. [Some things useful.]

Brauns, David. *Traditions Japonaises sur la Chanson, la Musique, et la Danse.* Paris: J. Maisonneuve, 1890. [Entirely popular, uncritical, without indication of sources.]

Bredow, Hans. *Vier Jahre deutscher Rundfunk.* Berlin: Reichsdruckerei, 1927.

Brewer, Francis Campbell. *The Drama and Music in New South Wales.* Sydney: C. Potter, 1892. [Published by the Authority of the New South Wales Commissioners for the World Columbia Exposition, Chicago, 1893.]

Brewster, Paul G. (Ed.). *Ballads and Songs of Indiana.* Bloomington: Indiana University Press, 1940. [Collected with help of students, doesn't include songs of foreign groups.]

Bricqueville, Eugène de. *Notice sur la Vielle.* Paris: Fischbacher, 1921. [Aristocrat, dilettante; founder of a society for old instruments; panegyrist of the vielle; apparently much traveled; no indication of sources.]

———. *Le Livret d'Opéra Français de Lully à Gluck.* Paris: Maison Schott, 1887. [No attempt at historical explanation; some sources; no bibliography.]

Bridge, Sir Frederic. *A Westmünster Pilgrim.* London: Novello, 1919. [Especially important, concerns music education of children.]

XX Brinkman, Karl. "Sieht der Jugendlihce lieber Schauspiel, Oper oder Film. . . ," *Jugendvolksbühne,* 2(10). Berlin. 1932.

Broadbent, R. J. *A History of Pantomime.* London: Simpkin, Marshall, Hamilton, Kent and Co., 1901. [Popular, goes back down to Hindus.]

Brodbeck, Albert. *Handbuch der deutschen Volksbühnenbewegung.* Berlin: Volksbühnen-Verlags-und Vertriebs, g.m.b.h., 1930, 439 pp.

Brodde, Otto. *Johann Gottfried Walther (1684–1748), Leben und Werk.* In Dissertation. Kassel: Bärenreiter-Verlag, 1937. [Elze as *Referent,* Korti.]

Brömse, Peter. *Flöten, Schalmeien und Sackpfeifen Südslawiens.* Brünn: R. M. Rohrer, 1937. [Based on the author's own travels; very painstaking; useful to us; much on social position, making of instruments, etc.]

Brown, Thomas Allstone. *History of the American Stage.* New York: Dick and Fitzgerald, 1870. [Alphabetic list of reachable actors, including singers, who performed in America, including those who returned to Europe; e.g., Felicitas von Vestvali.]

Brücker, Fritz. *Die Blasinstrumente in der altfranzösischen Literatur.* Giessen: Selbstverlag des Romanischen Seminars, 1926. [Based on study of sources, very useful.]

Bruckner, Anton. *Gesammelte Briefe, Gesammelt und hrsg. von Franz Gräflinger.* Regensburg: G. Bosse, 1925.

———. *Gesammelte Briefe, Neue Folge, Gesammelt und hrsg. von Max Auer.* Regensburg: G. Bosse, 1925.

Bruni, Antonio Bartolommeo. *Un Inventaire sous la Terreur.* Paris: G. Chamerot, 1890.

Brunner, Hans. *Das Klavierklangideal Mozarts und die Klaviere seiner Zeit.* Augsburg: Dr. B. Filser Verlag, g.m.b.h., 1933.

Brush, Gerome. *Boston Symphony Orchestra.* Boston: Printed for the Orchestra, 1936. [With descriptions and characteristics.]

Bruyr, José. *Maurice Ravel, ou le Lyrisme et les Sortilèges.* Paris: Plon, 1950. [Largely narrative.]

Buck, Sir Percy Carter. *The Oxford History of Music, Introductory Volume.* London: Oxford University Press, H. Milford, 1929.

Buddensieg, Hermann. "Vom Geist und Beruf der freideutschen Jugendbewegung." *Schriftenreihe des Rufers,* no. 2. Lauenburg: A. Saal, 1924.

XX   Bücken, Ernst. "Aufgaben der Musikwissenschaft für die Musikpädagogik in der Schule." *Die Musikpflege. Monatschrift für Musikerziehung, Musikorganisation und Chorgesangswesen,* 1(9), 1930. Leipzig: Quelle & Meyer.

Bücken, Ernst. *Musikalische Charakterköpfe.* Leipzig: Quelle & Meyer, 1925. [No annotations; article on Metastasio and on chief representatives of music aesthetics in the nineteenth century. Useful.]

———. *Der heroische Stil in der Oper.* Leipzig: Kistner & Siegel, 1924. [Almost exclusively analysis of style.]

———. *München als Musikstadt.* Leipzig: Siegel (R. Linnemann), 1923? [Popular, with general indication of literature at the end. Very historical.]

Bücker, Josefine. *Der Einfluss der Musik auf den englischen Wortschatz im 16. und 17. Jahrhundert.* Dissertation Cologne, 1926, 113 pp.

Buhtz, Ernest. *Die Mittelschule. Im Auftrage des Zentralinstituts für Erziehung und Unterricht.* Leipzig: Quelle & Meyer, 1926, 162 pp.

XX   Bulk, Fritz. *Die Gitarre und ihre Meister.* Berlin-Lichterfelde, Lankwitzer strasse 9: Schlesniger'sche Buch und Musikalienhandlung, n.d., (Preface, 1925). [Greatly detailed, apparently based on studies in the instrument collection of Dr. Rensch in Munich.]

Bulliet, Clarence Joseph. *How Grand Opera Came to Chicago.* Chicago: Printed and published privately, 194–.

Bülow, Hans Guido von. *Neue Briefe.* Munich: Drei Masken Verlag, 1927, 727 pp. [Especially to Klindworth; also to Cosima and daughters.]

———. *Briefe und Schriften.* Leipzig: Breitkopf & Härtel, 1895–1908.

Bumpus, John Skelton. *A History of English Cathedral Music 1549–1889.* New York: Pott, 1908.

Burchenal, Elizabeth. *Rinnce na Eirann, National Dances of Ireland.* New York: Barnes, 1924. [Systematically collected, set for piano, with pictures; description of the individual dances; pictures show boys in white breeches and white shirts, girls in Irish national costumes. Collection of dances now danced in Ireland; from viewpoint of continuation of national dances in contemporary America. First Round and Country Dances.]

———. *Folk-Dances and Singing Games.* New York: Schirmer, 1909. [From viewpoint of their continuation in America's university groups; so in foreword by Lather H. Gulick.]

Burge, William. *On the Choral Service of the Anglo-Catholic Church.* London: G. Bell, 1844. [Based on the reports of old sources.]

Burlin, Natalie. *The Indians' Book.* New York: Harper, 1923.

Burmester, Willy. *Fünfzig Jahre Künstlerleben.* Berlin: A. Scherl, g.m.b.h., 1926. [Youth and travel recollections, etc. Little sense for the exotic, e.g., Japanese art.]

Burney, Charles. *The Present State of Music in Germany, the Netherlands and United Provinces.* London: T. Becket, 1773.

Burton, Frederick Russell. *American Primitive Music.* New York: Moffat, Yard, 1909, 284 pp. [Useful concerning solo singing or for entertaining others, etc.]

Busch, Fritz. *Aus dem Leben eines Musikers.* Zurich: Rascher, 1949.

Busoni, Ferruccio. *Letters to His Wife.* Trans. Rosamond Ley. London: E. Arnold, 1938. [With travel reports.]

———. *Fünfundzwanzig Busoni-Briefe.* Vienna: H. Reichner, 1937. [Almost exclusively music philosophy; also critique of the compositions of the addressee and critique of her newspaper articles.]

Cain, Georges. *Anciens Théâtres de Paris.* Paris: Charpentier et Fasquelle, 1920. [Without indication of sources.]

Calcaño, José Antonio. *Contribución al Estudio de la Música en Venezuela.* Caracas: Editorial "Elite," 1939. [Aperçus, collected articles. Detail, Indian instruments, Negro instruments, especially drums.]

Calvé, Emma. *My Life.* Trans. Rosamond Gilder. New York: Appleton, 1922.

Calvocoressi, M. D. *Glinka.* Paris: H. Laurens, 1911?

Campardon, Emile. *L'Académie Royale de Musique au XVIIIe Siècle.* Paris: Berger-Levrault, 1884. [Prints lots of records, all from the Archives Nationales. Always the same.]

XX Campoi, Ruben M. *El Folklore Músical de la Ciudades.* Mexico City: Publicación de la Secretario de Educación Publica, Talleres linotipográphicos, "El Modelo" 1930. [A few facts that are relevant.]

Cardeza, María Elena. *Historia de la Música Americana.* Buenos Aires: Talleres gráficos "Buenos Aires," 1938. [Popular; enumerations of Indian music; details on modern composers, orchestras, etc., that are not relevant. Exists in another similar version.]

XA Cardinal, R. L. "Music in industry," in *Music and Medicine*, Dorothy M. Schullian and Max Schön. New York: Schumann, 1948.

Carniti, Antonio. *In Memoria di Giovanni Bottesini*. Crema: T. la Moderna, 1922. [With detailed bibliography of all publications.]

Carse, Adam von Ahn. *The Orchestra from Beethoven to Berlioz*. Cambridge: W. Heffer, 1948. [Continuation of the author's corresponding book on the eighteenth century.]

———. *The Orchestra in the Eighteenth Century*. Cambridge: W. Heffer, 1940. Reprinted 1950. [Here the 1950 edition used. Some things in it are relevant for us.]

———. *Musical Wind Instruments*. London: Macmillan, 1939.

Carter, Huntly. *The New Spirit in the Russian Theatre, 1917–1928*. London: Brentano, 1929.

Castillo, Jesús. *La Música Maya-Quiché*. Quezaltenango: Tip. E. Cifuentes, 1941. [Full of daring statements without the documentation one would desire; e.g., concerning the affinity of Maya language and Arabic.]

Castro, Joannes de. *Methodus Cantus Ecclesiastici Graeco-Slavici*. Rome, 1881. [Reprinted in modern notation with texts. With lengthy introduction.]

Cauer, Friedrich, and Agnes Molthan. *Lyzeum und Oberlyzeum*. Leipzig: Quelle & Meyer, 1926.

Cazalet, William Wahab. *The History of the Royal Academy of Music*. London: T. Bosworth, 1854. [Prints many documents, etc.]

Cernicchiaro, Vincenzo. *Storia della Musica Nel Brasile*. Milan: Fratelli Riccioni, 1926. [Very comprehensive, but the usual scheme.]

Chamberlain, Houston Stewart. *Mein Weg nach Bayreuth*. Munich: F. Bruckmann, 1937.

———. *Die ersten zwanzig Jahre der Bayreuther Bühnenfestspiele, 1876–1896*. Bayreuth: L. Ellwanger vorm. T. Burger, 1896. [Details, but at the same time Germanic.]

Chapman, John Kemble. *The Court Theatre and Royal Dramatic Record*. London: Chapman, 1849? [Not critical; has access to official materials.]

Chappell, Louis Watson. *Folksongs of Roanoke and the Albemarle*. Morgantown: The Ballad Press, 1939. [On North Carolina.]

Chase, Gilbert. *Music in Radio Broadcasting*. New York: McGraw Hill, 1946. [Almost every article of use to us. Also on law, television, instrumentation, etc. Some of the articles appear in this bibliography.]

———. *The Music of Spain*. New York: Norton, 1941.

Chauvet, Stéphen. *Musique Nègre*. Paris: Société d'Editions Géographiques, Maritimes et Coloniales, 1929.

Chavarri, Eduardo López. *Música Popular Española*. Barcelona and Buenos Aires: Editorial Labor, 1929. [Popular, does not give sources.]

Chávez, Carlos. *Toward a New Music*. New York: Norton, 1937.

Chevalier, Maurice Auguste. *The Man in the Straw Hat, My Story*. London: Odhams Press, 1950.

Chevalley, Heinrich. *Hundert Jahre Hamburger Stadt-Theater*. Hamburg: Broschek & Co., 1927.

———. *Arthur Nikisch, Leben und Wirken*. Berlin: E. Bote & G. Bock, 1922.

Chopin, Fryderyk Franciszek. *Chopin's Letters*. Collected by Henry Opieński; trans. from the original Polish and French, with a preface and notes by E. L. Voynich. New York: Knopf, 1931.

Chorley, Henry Fothergill. *The National Music of the World.* London: W. Reeves, 1882. [Unclear.]

Chrysander, Friedrich. "Geshcichte der Braunschweig-Wolfenbüttelschen Capelle und Oper vom 16. bis 18. Jahrhundert." *Jahrbücher für Musikalische Wissenschaft,* 1:147–286, 1863. [Based on archive materials, some details concern social position; important.]

Chybinski, Adolf. *Beiträge zur Geschichte des Taktschlagens.* Leipzig: Breitkopf & Härtel, 1912. [On 1500–1800. Based especially on works of theorists and what these demand for the conductor, and the position of conductors in their writings.]

XX *Le Cinéma des Origines à Nos Jours.* Préface par Henri Fescourt. Paris: Editions du Cygne, n.d. [Many collaborators, illustrated fat volume, not scholarly.]

Clark, Kenneth Sherman. *Baltimore, "Cradle of Municipal Music."* Anniversary edition. Republished by the City of Baltimore, 1941. [Offprint; details on financial crisis.]

XX Clearing, Carl. *Music and Jägerei.* Kassel: Bärenreiter-Verlag, 1937. [Many biographies, songs, partly with music, panegyric; nothing that is essential.]

Clokey, Joseph Waddell. *In Every Corner Sing.* New York: Morehouse-Gorham, 1945.

Cocks, William Alfred. *The Northumbrian Bagpipes.* Printed for the Northumberland Pipers Society. Newcastle upon Tyne: Northumberland Press, 1933. [Says that he collected all of this because of a few rhymes (p. 3).]

Coerper, F. "Tätigkeit der Gesellschaft von Volksbildung." *Volksbildungsarchiv,* 1:349–360, 1910.

Coeuroy, André, and André Schaeffner. *Le Jazz.* Paris: C. Aveline, 1926.

Coirault, Patrice. *Recherches sur Notre Ancienne Chanson Populaire Traditionelle.* Vannes: Imprimerie Lafolye Frères, 1927–   [Over 680 pages, all told, without any table of contents. Important, pp. 516–521. Points out very slow means of communication. Possibility of independent identical development under similar circumstances, if the reactions of the Indians in question are similar (p. 519). Based on sources and direct data.]

Collet, Henri. *L'Essor de la Musique Espagnole au XXᵉ Siècle.* Paris: M. Eschig, 1929. [Extols Spanish music and its renown abroad. Enumerates all orchestras, chamber music societies, virtuosos, etc. Prix de l'Institut d'Etudes Historiques.]

———. *Le Mysticism Musical Espagnol au XVIᵉ Siècle.* Paris: F. Alcan, 1913. [Based on *Chroniqum*; no exact indication of time, but apparently existing down to seventeenth century; but also based on archive sources.]

Combarieu, Jules. *Histoire de la Musique.* Paris: A. Colin, 1925–1930. [Several volumes. Reduces many things to the mystical. Very important for a great number of pianists. Vol. II, 1920 edition. Pp. 3–41 on Italian opera and role of love, etc. Pp. 369 and 370, briefly detailed on concert life and *concerto grossi.* Pp. 189–206 on Italian sonafa for violin and violin concerts.]

Conrad, Michael Georg. *Wagners Geist und Kunst in Bayreuth.* Munich: E. W. Bonsels, 1906. [Including the incriminated question of intellectual theft and the court decision concerning Conried, New York v. Conrad.]

Conran, Michael. *The National Music of Ireland.* London: J. Johnson, 1850. [Popular, not based on sources—although on O'Connor and Walker.]

XX *Constitutions and By-Laws of the Mendelssohn Memorial Society of Philadelphia.* Instituted October 15, 1866. Philadelphia: Inquirer Book and Job Print, 1867. [Short.]

Contamine de Latour, Emmanuel. *Chants Nationaux de l'Amérique Latine.* Montdidier: E. Carpentier, 1912. [Short introduction, otherwise a collection of the texts of the national anthems.]

Cooper, Martin. *French Music from the Death of Berlioz to the Death of Fauré.* London: Oxford University Press, 1951.

Coopersmith, Jacob Maurice. *Music and Musicians of the Dominican Republic.* Washington, D.C.: Division of Music and Visual Arts Department of Cultural Affairs, Pan American Union, 1949. [The text follows in Spanish in the same volume with detailed bibliography. Cites very old sources like De Las Casas and Oviedo.]

Corder, Frederick. *A History of the Royal Academy of Music.* London: F. Corder, 1922. [Details concerning founding.]

Corle, Edwin. *Igor Stravinsky.* New York: Duell, Sloan & Pearce, 1949.

Cornelius, Peter, *Literarische Werke.* Leipzig: Breitkopf & Härtel, 1904–1905.

Cortijo Alahija, L. *Musicologia Latino-Americana.* Barcelona: Maucci, 1919? [Introduction on pre-Columbian music. Popular. Then detailed enumeration of individual countries, virtuosos, orchestras, and schools in modern times. Not relevant.]

XX Courant, M. *"Chine & Corée." Encyclopédie de la Musique,* vol. 1. [Strictly scholarly.]

Courlander, Harold. *Haiti Singing.* Chapel Hill: University of North Carolina Press, 1939. [Based on travels, knows the Haitian French, often cites Herskovits.]

Cox, John Harrington. *Folk Songs of the South.* Cambridge: Harvard University Press, 1925.

Creuzburg, Eberhard. *Die Gewandhaus-Konzerte zu Leipzig.* Leipzig: Breitkopf & Härtel, 1931.

Crosten, William Loran. *French Grand Opera, An Art and a Business.* New York: King's Crown Press, 1948. [Popular, journalistic, but based on precise references to newspapers.]

Cucuel, Georges. *Les Créateurs de l'Opéra-Comique Français.* Paris: F. Alcan, 1914. [For beginners only, doesn't mention sources.]

Cui, César. *La Musique en Russie.* Paris: Fischbacher, 1880. [Author is half French, was Russian officer for a long time. Texts of Romantic operas (pp. 164ff.) Historical, objective.]

Czach, Karl Rudolf. *Friedrich Wilhelm Rust.* Dissertation Essen, 1927. [List of sources; some things relevant, concerning middle-class audience and house music.]

Daly, John Jay. *A Song in His Heart.* Philadelphia: Winston, 1951. [The story of a Negro songwriter and singer.]

Damrosch, Walter Johannes. *My Musical Life.* New York: Scribner, 1923. [Personal reminiscences.]

Danckert, Werner. *Claude Debussy.* Berlin: W. de Gruyter, 1950.

———. *Geschichte der Gigue.* Leipzig: Kistner & Siegel, 1924.

Daniel, Francisco Salvador. *The Music and Musical Instruments of the Arab.* Henry George Farmer, Ed. London: W. Reeves, 1915. [Factual critique and supplementation of his French book published in Algiers in 1879. Contains biographies. Daniel was the director of the Paris conservatory during the Commune.]

————. *La Musique Arabe; Ses Rapports avec la Musique Grecque et le Chant Grégorien*, Algiers: A. Jourdan, 1879. [Also exists in the corresponding English edition with additions by Henry George Farmer. The main thesis concerns Arab music and Greek origin.]

Dannemann, Erna. *Die spätgotische Musiktradition in Frankreich und Burgund.* Strasbourg: Heitz, 1936.

Daube, Otto. *Siegfried Wagner und die Märchenoper.* Leipzig: Deutscher Theaterverlag, M. Schleppegrell, 1936. [Panegyrical.]

Dauney, William. *Ancient Scotish Melodies.* Edinburgh: The Edinburgh Printing and Publishing Co., 1837. [Some details, based on old manuscripts, 1666.]

Davies, A. Harold. "Aboriginal Songs of Central and Southern Australia." *Oceania*, 2: 454–467. Melbourne: Macmillan, 1932. [Concerning voice level, etc. His own important experiences.]

Davis, Arthur Kyle. *Folk Songs of Virginia.* Durham, N.C.: Duke University Press, 1949. [Detailed collection which indicates origin (Irish, etc.); lengthly introduction on classification of railroad songs.]

Davis, Carol Berry. *Songs of the Totem.* Juneau: Empire Printing Co., 1939.

Davison, Archibald Thompson. *Protestant Church Music in America.* Boston: Schirmer, 1933, 182 pp.

Debussy, Claude. *Correspondance de Claude Debussy et Pierre Louÿs 1893–1904.* Paris: J. Corti, 1945.

————. *Lettres à Deux Amis.* Paris: J. Corti, 1942.

————. *L'Enfance de Pelléas.* Paris: Dorbon-Aîné, 1938. [New things on finances, concerns place of publication.]

————. *Correspondance de Claude Debussy et P. J. Toulet.* Paris: Le Divan, 1929. [Much of it irrelevant, but significant for time of First World War.]

————. *Lettres de Claude Debussy à Son Editeur.* Paris: A. Durand et fils, 1927.

Degen, Dietz. *Zur Geschichte der Blockflöte in den Germanischen Ländern.* Kassel: Bärenreiter-Verlag, 1939. [Critical; influenced by youth movement.]

Deiters, Heinrich. *Die Schule der Gemeinschaft.* Leipzig: Quelle & Meyer, 1925.

De Lafontaine, Henry Cart. *The King's Musick.* London: Novello, 1909.

Delius, Clare. *Frederick Delius, Memories of My Brother.* London: I. Nicholson and Watson, 1935.

De Lorenzo, Leonardo. *My Complete Story of the Flute.* New York: Citadel Press, 1951. [Very snotty and conceited.]

Demuth, Norman. *César Franck.* New York: Philosophical Library, 1949. [Much of it very subjective.]

————. *Ravel.* London: Dent, 1947.

Densmore, Frances. *The American Indians and Their Music.* New York: The Womans Press, 1936.

Dent, Edward Joseph. *Opera.* Harmondsworth: Penguin Books, 1949.

————. *Foundation of English Opera.* Cambridge: The University Press, 1928.

DeRensis, Raff. *Mussolini Musicista.* Mantova: Paladino, 1927. [Essentially on Mussolini's personal taste and his own playing.]

DeRobeck, Nesta. *Music of the Italian Renaissance.* London: The Medici Society, 1928. [Not much that is new, rather popular, with bibliography.]

Despois, Eugene André. *Le Théâtre Français sous Louis XIV*. Paris: Hachette, 1886. [Based on studies of the theater archive, especially the Comédie Française. No bibliography.]

XX *Deutsche Tonkünstlerzeitung. Officielles Blatt des "Reichsverbandes deutscher Tonkünstler und Musiklehrer Eingelragenen Verein."* Berlin. Mainz: Verlagsanstalt Deutscher Tonkünstler A. G.

Deutsch, Leonard. *A Treasury of Slovak Folk Songs*. New York: Crown Publishers, 1950, 127 pp. [Based on older collections, e.g., Ruppeldf's. Introduction by Adam P. Lesinsky.]

Deutsch, Otto Erich. *Schubert, A Documentary Biography*. London: Dent, 1947. [With an enormous philological apparatus, list of persons, etc., not very relevant for us.]

———. *Das Freihaustheater auf der Wieden*. Vienna: Deutscher Verlag für Jugend und Volk Gesellschaft, m.b.h., 1937.

Dickinson, Alan Edgar Frederic. *The Art of J. S. Bach*. London: Hinrichsen Edition, 1950. [Mostly analysis of works.]

Dickinson, Edward. *The Oberlin Conservatory of Music*. Oberlin: Oberlin College Library, 1923. Informational Bulletin, no. 1. [Short, some of it useful.]

Dieckmann, Jenny. *Die in Deutscher Lautentabulatur Überlieferten Tänze des 16. Jahrhunderts*. Kassel: Bärenretier-Verlag, 1931.

Diem, Nelly. *Beiträge zur Geschichte der Schottischen Musik im XVII. Jahrhundert nach bisher nicht veröffentlichten Manuscripten*. Leipzig: Hug, 1919. [Referent H. Riemann and H. Köster. Predominantly historical and philological.]

Diemer, Hermine. *Oberammergau und sein Passionsspiel*. Munich: C. A. Seyfried, 1910. [Popular, local, and sentimental. Some of it important.]

Dietz, Max. *Geschichte des Musikalischen Dramas in Frankreich*. Vienna: Groscher & Blaha, 1886. [Claims in introduction that it is based on handwritten materials in the Bibliothèque Nationale and libraries of the Conservatoire. Much of it important and useful for us.]

Ditters von Dittersdorf, Karl. *Lebensbeschreibung*. Regensburg: G. Bosse, 1940.

Djoudjeff, Stoyan. *Rythme et Mesure dans la Musique Populaire Bulgare*. Paris: Champion, 1931. [Primarily on musical topics—rhythmical problem. Important for combination, etc.]

Dokkum, Jan Dirk Christian van. *Honderd Jaar Musiekleven in Nederland*. Amsterdam: Uitgegeven door het Hoofdbestuur, 1929. [Panegyrical, sentimental, only a few things important.]

Dolge, Alfred. *Pianos and Their Makers*. Covina, Calif.: Covina Publishing Co., 1911–1913. [No notes or critical apparatus.]

XX Donastra, Rev. Père K. A. de. "Essai d'une Bibliographie Musicale Basque," in *Cahiers du Centre Basque et Gascon d'Etudes Regionales*. Bayonne: Editions de Musée Basque, 1932. [French and Spanish forms of baroque music in the Basque country.]

Doncieux, George. *Le Romancéro Populaire de la France*. Paris: E. Bouillon, 1904. [By comparing the various tunes, intends to get to the original tune that corresponds best to the original text. Details. Source criticism. Proof that often, when memory failed, lines from other poems were substituted, e.g., pp. 460–461, no. XLIV.]

XX Donike, M. L. "Wir vom Sprechchor." *Jugendvolksbühne*, 3(5), June 1932.

Dörffel, Alfred. *Geschichte der Gewandhaus Concerte zu Leipzig*. Leipzig: Breitkopf & Härtel, 1881–1884.

Döring, G. *Choralkunde in 3 Bänden*. Danzig: Bertling, 1865. [Protestant; connected with Winterfeld; based on precise sources.]

Douen, Orentin. *Clément Marot et le Psautier Huguenot*. Paris: Imprimerie Nationale, 1878–1879. [With many historical examples and printing of notes. Strongly anti-Catholic.]

Douglas, Charles Winfred. *Church Music in History and Practice; Studies in the Praise of God*. New York: Scribner, 1937. [Episcopalian, with exact bibliography; references to recorded hymns, etc. Prosaic, ultimate purpose is practical.]

Dräger, Hans Heinz. *Die Entwicklung des Streichbogens und seine Anwendung in Europa (bis zum Violinbogen des 16. Jahrhunderts)*. Kassel: Bärenreiter-Verlag, 1937. [Among other things, figurative art is used as a source.]

Dreetz, Albert. *Johann Christian Kittel*. Berlin: Druck P. W. Nacken Nachflg., 1932. [Based on accurately indicated source materials; useful observations on Dalbug.]

Drewes, Heinz. *Maria Antonia Walpurgis als Komponistin*. Borna: R. Noske, 1934. [*Referent* Kroyer. Important concerning studies.]

Droux, Georges. *La Chanson Lyonnaise*. Lyons: A. Rey, 1907. [Second part especially important. Survey of many various literary matters, also culinary societies in the nineteenth century that cultivated local songs. Some even gave public concerts where new Lyonese songs were presented, e.g., by women. Some very Bohemian and short-lived.]

Drüner, Otto. *Die Deutsche Volksballade in Lothringen*. Frankfurt: Verlag M. Diesterweg, 1939. [Much about Gemeinschaft. Personality as expression of the Gemeinschaft, pp. 8–9. Some things important; some daring assertions.]

Ducharte, Pierre Louis. *La Comédie Italienne*. Paris: Librairie de France, 1925.

Duey, Phillipp A. *Bel Canto in its Golden Age*. New York: King's Crown Press, 1951. [Important concerning castrates. Often cites Franz Haböck, *Die Kastraten und ihre Gesangskunst*, Stuttgart: 1921.]

Dufourcq, Norbert. *Documents Inédits Relatifs à l'Orgue Français*. Paris: E. Droz, 1934. [Ordered by periods, within them by schools in the various regions. Based on unpublished source studies.]

Duhamel, Maurice. *Les Premières Gammes Celtiques et la Musique Populaires des Hébrides*. Paris: Rouart, Lerolle, 1916. [Based on detailed knowledge of all Celtic music.]

Du Moulin-Eckart, Richard. *Cosima Wagner*. Munich: Drei Masken Verlag, 1929–1931.

Duncan, Edmondstone. *The Story of the Carol*. London: The Walter Scott Publishing Co.; New York: Scribner, 1911. [With facsimiles, pictures, quotations from historical sources.]

———. *The Story of Minstrelsy*. New York: Scribner, 1907.

Duncan, Isadora. *The Art of the Dance*. New York: Theater Arts Inc., 1928.

XA Dunham, Elvin L. "Production of musical programs," in *Music in Radio Broadcasting*, Gilbert Chase. New York: McGraw-Hill, 1946.

Durán, Gustavo. *14 Traditional Spanish Songs from Texas*. Washington, D.C.: Music Division, Pan American Union, 1942.

Durand, Jacques. *Le Cinéma et Son Public*. Paris: Sirey, 1958.

Ebert, Alfred Leopold. *Attilio Ariosti in Berlin*. Leipzig: Druck von Giesecke & Devrient, 1905. [Prints much abbreviated material from records.]

Eckardt, Andreas. *Koreanische Musik*. Leipzig: Verlag Asia Major im Komm, 1930, 63 pp. [Very important concerning solo and group dance, etc.]

Eckert, Heinrich. *Norbert Burgmüller*. Augsburg: Dr. B. Filser Verlag, g.m.b.h., 1932. [Based on source studies.]

XA Eckhardt, Otto. "Der Musikunterricht," in *Die Mittelschule. Im Auftrag des Zentralinstituts für Erziehung und Unterricht*, Ernst Buhtz. Leipzig: Quelle & Meyer, 1926.

Eddy, Mary O. *Ballads and Songs from Ohio*. New York: J. J. Augustin, 1939. [Among other things, materials from pages of old family albums or Bibles.]

Edgerly, Beatrice. *From the Hunter's Bow*. New York: Putnam, 1942.

Ehinger, Hans. *Friedrich Rochlitz als Musikschriftsteller*. Leipzig: Breitkopf & Härtel, 1929. [*Referent* Nef and Zinkernagel. Based on source studies; of use for musical newspaper history.]

Eichborn, Hermann. *Die Trompete in alter und neuer Zeit*. Leipzig: Breitkopf & Härtel, 1881, 118 pp. [Some things concerning *Zunft*, fees.]

Eichenauer, Richard. *Musik und Rasse*. Munich: J. F. Lehmann, 1937.

Einstein, Alfred. *Schubert, A Musical Portrait*. New York: Oxford University Press, 1951.

———. "Italienische Musik und Italienische Musiker am Kaiserhof und an den erzherzoglichen Höfen in Innsbruck und Graz." *Studien zur Musikwissenschaft*, 21:3–52, 1934. [Includes materials from the contemporary archive of the Austro-Hungarian Joint Ministry of Finance, Vienna, the co-called musicians' fascicle Austria.]

Ekman, Karl. *Jean Sibelius, His Life and Personality*. London: A. Wilmer, 1936. [Mostly narrative.]

Elkin, Robert. *Royal Philharmonic*. London: Rider, 1946. [Historical. Survey of compositions performed in England for the first time; survey of program of concerts. Based on archive studies.]

Ellis, William Ashton. *Life of Richard Wagner*. London: K. Paul, Trench, Trübner and Co., vol. 1, 1900; vol. 2, 1902; vol. 3, 1903; vol. 4, 1904; vol. 5, 1906; and vol. 6, 1908. [Greatly expanded from vol. 3 on, as compared with Glasenapp; entirely independent from vol. 4, with no allusion to Glasenapp left even in the title.]

XA Ellman, W. "Das Musikleben in den deutschen Universitäten," in *Musik im Volk*, Stumme. Berlin: C. F. Vieweg. 1939.

Elson, Louis Charles. *The National Music of America and Its Sources*. Boston: The Page Co., 1915.

Emmanuel, Maurice. *The Antique Greek Dance*. New York and London: J. Lane, 1916.

Emmanuel, Maurice. "Grèce," in *Encyclopédie de la Musique et Dictionnaire du Conservatoire*, Paris: n.d.

Engel, Egon. *Die Instrumentalformen in der Lautenmusik des 16. Jahrhunderts*. Dissertation Berlin, 1915. [Concerning lute music as predecessor of string music etc.]

Engel, Gabriel. *Gustav Mahler, Song-symphonist*. New York: The Bruckner Society of America, 1932.

Engländer, Richard. *Johann Gottlieb Naumann als Opernkomponist*. Leipzig: Breitkopf & Härtel, 1922. [Kretzschmer and Stumpf as *Referenten*. Based on sources.]

Eppstein, Hans. *Nicolas Gombert als Mottenkomponist.* Würzburg: Buchdruckerei, Mayr, 1935. [Chapter 1 is of use.]

XX Epstein, Wilhelm. "Kino und Volksbildung." *Volksbildungsarchiv,* 5(3), September–October, 1913.

XX Erdberg, Robert von. "Programgestaltung." *Volksbildungsarchiv,* 5(2), March 1947.

Erdmann, Hans, and Guiseppe Becce. *Allgemeines Handbuch der Filmmusik.* Berlin: Schlesinger, 1927.

Erlanger, Rudolphe von. *La Musique Arabe.* Paris: P. Guenther, 1930. [With French translations of the Arab philosophers al-Kindi, Avicenna, etc., with detailed commentary.]

Ernst, Georg, and Bernhard Marshall. *Film und Rundfunk. 2. Internationaler kath. Filmkongress. 1. Internationaler kath. Rundfunkkongress.* Munich: Verlag Leohaus, 1929, 432 pp.

Erskine, John. *My Life in Music.* New York: Morrow, 1950.

Erskine, John. *The Philharmonic-Symphony Society of New York.* New York: Macmillan, 1943. [With much material concerning works performed, etc.]

XX Esponos, Victor. *El "Quichote" en la Musica, con Prólogo de José Maria Peman.* Barcelona, 1947.

Esser, Ben. "Die Wiederbelebung der Volksmusik und die Lehrerbildung." *Mitteilungen der Pädagogischen Akademien in Preussen,* no. 1. Berlin: Weidtmann, 1926.

Euting, Ernst. *Zur Geschichte der Blasinstrumente im 16. und 17. Jahrhundert.* Berlin: Druck von A. Schulze, 1899. [Description of the instruments and discussion of their use in operas, etc., not relevant.]

Ewen, David. *The Story of George Gershwin.* New York: Holt, 1943.

———. *Music Comes to America.* New York: Crowell, 1942.

Ewens, Franz Josef. *Anton Eberl.* Dresden: A. W. Limpert, 1927. [Some things of use in section 1.]

Faber, Frédéric Jules. *Histoire du Théâtre Français en Belgique.* Brussels: F. J. Olivier, 1878–1880. [Based on vast material, which he prints much of.]

Fallet, Edouard Marius. *La Vie Musicale au Pays de Neuchâtel du XIIIe à la Fin du XVIIIe Siècle.* Strasbourg: Heitz, 1936. [Collection of musicological treatises—by Karl Nef, vol. 20.]

XX Farfan, Policarpo Cabalero. *Influencia de la Música Incaica en el Cancionero del Norte Argentino.* Buenos Aires, 1946. [Strictly scholarly, with knowledge of the instruments and scales of other peoples.]

Farmer, Henry George. *Concerts in Eighteenth Century Scotland.* Glasgow: Hinrichsen, 1945.

———. *Sa'adyah Gaon on the Influence of Music.* London: A. Probsthain, 1943.

———. *Turkish Instruments of Music in the Seventeenth Century.* Glasgow: The Civic Press, 1937. [Important concerning music guilds.]

———. *A Further Arabic-Latin Writing on Music, attributed to al-Farabi.* London, 1933. [Very philological; important for transformation of theories.]

———. *An Old Moorish Lute Tutor.* Glasgow: The Civic Press, 1933. [Four texts original litogr. Translation, comment, some items very important, re-migration of the notation systems.]

———. *Studies in Oriental Musical Instruments*. I. Series, London: H. Reeves, 1931. II. Series, Glasgow: The Civic Press, 1939. [Specialized history of origin and migration of instruments; based on precise source studies of the Arabic historical sources. Much in favor of Arabic origin. Chinese and occidental string and plucked instruments. Almost nothing on social position, etc.]

———. *Music in Mediaeval Scotland*. London: W. Reeves, 1930.

———. *A History of Arabian Music*. London: Luzac, 1929. [Includes Mohammed's own wedding; based on Arabian sources.]

———. *The Rise and Development of Military Music*. London: W. Reeves, 1912. [No bibliography; many biographical details; much concerning instruments.]

Farrar, Geraldine. *The Story of an American Singer*. Boston: Houghton Mifflin, 1916.

Federmann, Maria. *Musik und Musikpflege zur Zeit Herzog Albrechts*. Kassal: Bärenreiter-Verlag, 1932.

Felber, Erwin. *Die indische Musik der vedischen und der klassischen Zeit*. Vienna: Hölder, 1912.

XA   Felber, Erwin. "Die Musik in den Märchen und Mythen der verschiedenen Völker," in *Report of the Fourth Congress of the International Musical Society*. London: Novello, 1912.

Fellerer, Karl Gustav. *Deutsche Gregorianik in Frankenreich*. Regensburg: G. Bosse, 1941. [A bit folk-oriented, also in its terminology; much based on sources.]

———. *Orgel und Orgelmusik, ihre Geschichte*. Augsburg: Dr. B. Filser Verlag, g.m.b.h., 1929. [Almost exclusively history of instruments, not relevant for us.]

———. *Der Palestrinastil und seine Bedeutung in der vokalen Kirchenmusik des 18. Jahrhunderts*. Augsburg: Dr. B. Filser Verlag, g.m.b.h., 1929. [Catholic, dedicated to Adolph Sandberger. Based on sources.]

Fellman, Hans Georg. *Die Böhmsche Theatertruppe und ihre Zeit*. Leipzig: L. Voss, 1928. [Some things of use.]

Fellowes, Edmund Horace. *English Cathedral Music from Edward VI to Edward VII*. London: Methuen, 1941. [On sources; collection of music historical detailed description of all English composers.]

Fenby, Eric. *Delius as I Knew Him*. London: G. Bell and Sons, 1936.

Fenton, William Nelson. *Songs from the Iroquois Longhouse*. Washington, D.C.: The Smithsonian Institution, 1942.

Fenwick, J. W. *Instruction Book for the Northumbrian Small-pipes*. Newcastle upon Tyne: Northumberland Press Limited for the Northumbrian Pipers' Society, 1931. [Exclusively technical description.]

Finger, Charles Joseph. *Frontier Ballads*. Garden City, N.Y.: Doubleday, 1927. [Entirely unscholarly, but includes important Outflow songs.]

XX   Fischer, Hans W. "Feste." *Die Freude*, 2 (9), September 1925.

Fischer, Kurt von. *Griegs Harmonik und die Nordländische Folklore*. Bern: P. Haupt, 1938.

Fischl, Viktor (Ed.). *Antonin Dvořák, His Achievement*. London: L. Drummond, 1943.

Fisher, William Arms. *Notes on Music in Old Boston*. Boston: Oliver Ditson Co., 1918. [Not very original.]

Fitzgibbon, Henry Macaulay. *The Story of the Flute*. London: W. Reeves; New York: Scribner, 1929, 291 pp. [Very comprehensive, many interesting descriptions, no indication of sources.]

Flanders, Helen Hartness, Elizabeth Flanders Ballard, George Brown, and Phillips Barry. *The New Green Mountain Songster*. New Haven: Yale University Press, 1939. [Many changed versions of those collected in England by Child.]

Fleischer, Heinrich. *Christlieb Siegmund Binder*. Regensburg: G. Bosse, 1941. [On detailed source studies.]

Fleischer, Herbert. *Strawinsky*. Berlin: Russischer Musik Verlag, 1931.

Fleischer, Oskar Reinhold. *Die Germanischen Neumen*. Frankfurt: Frankfurter Verlags-Anstalt A.G., 1923. [Fundamentally based on deciphering.]

———. *Neumen-studien*, vols. 1–3. 1 & 2, Leipzig: F. Fleischer, 1895–1904. 3, Berlin: Verlag von Georg Reimer, 1904.

Flemming, Willi. *Die Oper*. Leipzig: P. Reclam, 1933.

Fletcher, Alice Cunningham. *Indian Games and Dances with Native Songs*. Boston: Birchard, 1915. [Not very scholarly.]

———. *Indian Story and Song*. Boston: Small, Maynard, 1900. [Important concerning Indians and groups; perhaps exaggerating.]

Flood, William Henry Gratton. *The Story of the Bagpipe*. New York: Scribner, 1911.

———. *The Story of the Harp*. London: The Walter Scott Publishing Co.; New York: Scribner, 1905. [Sentimental; discusses Celtic harp; many details; inexact citation of sources; bibliography, without indication of edition, in the appendix.]

Font, Auguste. *Favart: L'Opéra-Comique et la Comédie-Vandeville aux XVIIᵉ et XVIIIᵉ Siècles*. Paris: Fischbacher, 1894. [Historical, many details on roles, etc.; some things on content and rustic personages on separate sheet.]

Foote, Henry Wilder. *Three Centuries of American Hymnody*. Cambridge: Harvard University Press, 1940. [Not denominationally limited, going far back to colonial period. Based on old material.]

Foss, Hubert James. *Ralph Vaughan Williams*. London: Harrap, 1950. [Includes Williams's autobiography.]

Fouque, Octave. *Michael Ivanovitch Glinka*. Paris: Au Ménestrel, Heugel et fils, 1880.

Fox-Strangways, Arthur Henry. *The Music of Hindostan*. Oxford: Clarendon Press, 1914.

XX   *Frankfurter Bund für Volksbildung. Ausschuss für Volksvorlesungen. Bericht über die Jahre 1925–1926 bis 1928–1929*. Frankfurt: Union Druckerei, 1929. [Primarily enumerations.]

Fransen, Jan. *Les Comédiens Français en Hollande au XVIIᵉ et au XVIIIᵉ Siècles*. Paris: Champion, 1925. [Entirely historical, based on very much old material.]

Franz, Robert. *Robert Franz und Arnold Freiherr Senfft von Pilsach; Ein Briefwechsel 1861–1888*. Berlin: A. Duncker, 1907. [Very personal, often terribly irritated and sensitive, many conflicts; some of it important.]

XX   Fredenthal, Albert. *Musik, Tanz und Dichtung bei den Kreolen Amerikas*. Berlin: Hausbuch-Verlag Hans Schnippel, 1913. [Popular, especially songs, with much attention to their origin. Based on actual transcriptions; apparently not on recordings. Also from manuscripts found with native musicians by the author. Only a few works quoted, but does quote legation, friends, etc., who collected the things in question.]

Frehn, Paul. *Der Einfluss der Englischen Literatur auf Deutschlands Musiker und Musik im 19. Jahrhundert*. Düsseldorf: G. H. Nolte, 1938. [Some Hitlerism artificially blown up; otherwise some things not so useful.]

Frensdorf, Victor Egon. *Peter Winter als Opernkomponist.* Erlangen: K. B. Hof und Universitäts Buchdruckerei von Junge und Sohn, 1908. [With biographies and analysis of works.]

XA Freund, Ernst Ferdinand. "Rhythmische Gymnastik und Körpererziehung," in Körperschulung Künstlerische, Ludwig Pallat and Franz Hilker. Breslau: Ferdinand Hirt, 1925, 168 pp.

Friederici, Franz. *Geschichte des Vereins der Liederfreunde zu Königsberg.* Königsberg: R. Leupold, 1906. [Quite harmless, well founded.]

Friedländer, Arthur Meyer. *Facts and Theories Relating to Hebrew Music.* London: H. Reeves, 1924. [Very short, Jewish influence on art.]

Fry, George. *The Varnishes of the Italian Violin-Makers of the Sixteenth, Seventeenth and Eighteenth Centuries, and Their Influence on Tone.* London: Stevens and Sons, 1904.

Fülop-Miller, René. *The Motion Picture in America.* New York: Dial Press, 1938.

Fülop-Miller, René, and Joseph Gregor. *The Russian Theater: Its Character and History.* Philadelphia: Lippincott, 1929. [Not much that is new.]

XX *Fünfzig Jahre Hoftheater. Geschichte der beiden Wiener Hoftheater under der Regierungszeit des Kaisers Franz Joseph I.* Vol. 1, *Hof Burgtheater von Rudolph Loth.* Vol. 2, *Hof Operntheater von Julius Stein.* Vienna: Alexander Duschnitz, 1898. [Quite Byzantine, panegyrical, with many collaborators.]

XX *Funkalmanach 1930. Offizieller Ausstellungskatalog zur grossen deutschen Funkausstellung, 1930.* Berlin: Rothgisser und Diesing, 1930.

Gabrilovich, Osip. *An Open Letter to the Music Critic of the New York Tribune.* Munich: A. Schmid, 1911.

Gade, Niels Wilhelm. *Aufzeichnungen und Briefe.* Basel: A. Geering, 1894. [Many details of his youth at Leipzing.]

Gaer, Joseph (Ed.). *The Theatre of the Gold Rush Decade in San Francisco.* California: Library Research, 1935. (Mimeograph.) [Primarily a listing of pieces produced.]

Galpin, Francis William. *The Music of the Sumerians and Their Immediate Successors, the Babylonians and Assyrians.* Cambridge: The University Press, 1937.

———. *A Textbook of European Musical Instruments.* New York: Dutton, 1937.

Ganz, A. W. *Berlioz in London.* London: Quality Press, 1950, 222 pp. [Includes many hitherto unpublished letters.]

XX Garalda, Miguel Querol. *La Música en las Obras de Cervantes.* Barcelona: Ediciones Comtalia, 1948.

Garay, Narciso. *Tradiciones y Cantares de Panama.* Brussels: Presses de l'Expansion Belge, 1930. [Subdivided by provinces, very popular, usually as a travel journal.]

Garden, Mary, and Louis Biancolli. *Mary Garden's Story.* New York: Simon and Schuster, 1951. [Autobiography.]

Gardien, Jacques. *L'Orgue et les Organistes en Bourgogne et en Franche-Comté au Dixhuitième Siècle.* Paris: E. Droz, 1943. [Big volume, gigantic material, archival.]

Gardner, Emelyn Elizabeth, and Geraldine Jencks Chickering. *Ballads and Songs of Southern Michigan.* Ann Arbor: University of Michigan Press, 1939.

Garnault, Paul. *La Trompette Marine.* Nice: L'Auteur, 1926. [The author a former captain of the navy, dilettante. Much material, with indication of sources and pictures. Very much about navy bugler. Includes bibliography.]

Gastoué, Amédeé. *Les Primitifs de la Musique Française*. Paris: H. Laurens, 1922. [Without indication of sources, but with general bibliography.]

———. *L'Art Grégorien*. Paris: F. Alcan, 1920. [Short and popular, but based on knowledge of new editions of old sources.]

Gatard, Augustine Anselm. *Plain Chant*. London: The Faith Press, 1921.

Gautier, Théophile. *The Romantic Ballet as Seen by Théophile Gautier*. London: C. W. Beaumont, 1932. [His theater critique of the ballet of the Eisler, etc., in Paris, 1837–1848.]

XX Gebertus, Martinus. *De Cantu & Musica Sacra*, vols. 1 and 2. Typis San Blasianis, 1774. [A classic work; includes many musical examples in vol. 2; usually transscribed.]

Geiringer, Karl. "Isaac Posch," in *Studien zur Musikwissenschaft. Gesellschaft zur Herausgabe von Denkmälern der Tonkunst in Österreich*, vol. 17. Vienna, 1930.

———. "Paul Peuerl," in *Studien zur Musikwissenschaft. Gesellschaft zur Herausgabe von Denkmälern der Tonkunst in Österreich*, vol. 16. Vienna, 1929.

Gergely, Emro Joseph. *Hungarian Drama in New York*. Philadelphia: University of Pennsylvania Press, 1947.

Germa, Maurice. *L'Art Scandinave*. Paris: Didier, 1874. [Dedicated to Gobineau; but in the epilogue, p. 32, against "Sacomanie"; it seems also Scottish music derived from the Germanic; completely undocumented.]

Gérold, Théodore. *La Musique au Moyen Age*. Paris: H. Champion, 1932.

Gerson, Robert A. *Music in Philadelphia*. Philadelphia: Theodore Presser, 1940. [Based on much material. History of the Philadelphia Orchestra; old instrumental groupings; church music, operas, school music, etc.]

XX Gerst, Wilhelm. *Das Theater der Kulturgemeinschaft*. Innsbruck, n.d.

Gervais. André Charles. *Marionettes et Marionettistes de France*. Paris: Bordas, 1947. [Practical instructions, with autobiography. Nothing special on music.]

Gilbert, Douglas. *Lost Chords, the Diverting Story of American Popular Songs*. Garden City, N.Y.: Doubleday, 1942. [A history of the hit song.]

———. *American Vaudeville, Its Life and Time*. New York: McGraw-Hill, 1940.

Gillhoff, Gerd Aage. *The Royal Dutch Theater at the Hague, 1804–1876*. The Hague: M. Nijhoff, 1938.

Gilman, Samuel. *Memoirs of a New England Village Choir*. Boston: Crosby, Nichols, 193–. [Short, popular; typical for American description, of use.]

Glasenapp, Carl Friedrich. *Richard Wagner's Leben und Werken*. Kassel: C. Maurer, 1876–1877. [Not very important.]

Glasenapp, Carl Friedrich. *Siegfried Wagner*. Berlin: Schuster und Loeffler, 1906. [Hitler could have written this.]

Glen, John. *Early Scottish Melodies*. Edinburgh: J. & R. Glen, 1900.

Glenewinkel, Hans. *Spohrs Kammermusik für Streichinstrumente*. Dissertation Nienburg (Weser), 1912. [Dissertation for Sandberger. Place of publication not indicated.]

Glyn, Margaret Henrietta. *About Elizabethan Virginal Music and its Composers*. London: W. Reeves, 1934.

XX   Goarts, Hans. *Die Opern Heinrich Marschner's.* Leipzig: Breitkopf & Härtel, 1912. [Based on the studies of the previously lost Marschner documents. Inaugural Dissertation, Bonn, with comments by L. Wolf.]

Goffin, Robert. *Jazz from Congo to Swing.* London: Musicians Press, 1946.

———. *Aux Frontières du Jazz.* Paris: Editions du Sagittaire, 1932.

Goldberg, Isaac. *George Gershwin, A Study in American Music.* New York: Simon and Schuster, 1931.

———. *The Tin Pan Alley. A Chronicle of the American Popular Music Racket.* New York: The John Day Co., 1930. [Journalistic, shoddy.]

XX   Goldmark, Karl. *Notes from the Life of a Viennese Composer.* Trans. Alice Goldmark Brandeis. New York: Albert & Charles Brothers, 1927. [From memory as octogenarian; much concerning first performances; conflicts with conductors.]

Goldschmidt, Hugo. "Claudio Monteverdis Oper: Il Ritorno d'Ullisse in Patria." *Sammelbücher der Internationalen Musikgesellschaft,* 9:570–592, 1907–1908. [Important on comical person.]

———. *Studien zur Geschichte der Italienischen Oper im 17. Jahrhundert.* Leipzig: Breitkopf & Härtel, 1901–1904.

Gombosi, Otto. "Jacob Obrecht, Ein stilkritische Studie." *Sammlung Musikwissenschaftlicher Einzeldarstellungen, no. 4.* Leipzig: Breitkopf & Härtel, 1925, 87 pp. [With many musical examples and much material.]

XX   Gonzales-Sol, Rafael. *Historia del Arte de la Música en el Salvador.* San Salvador: Imprente Mercurio, 1940.

Goodman, Benny, and Irving Kolodin. *The Kingdom of Swing.* New York: Stackpole Sons, 1939. [Very anecdotal, some things useful.]

Goslich, Siegfried. *Beiträge zur Geschichte der deutschen romantischen Oper Zwischen Spohrs "Faust" und Wagners "Lohengrin."* Leipzig: Kistner & Siegel, 1937. [Very useful, especially concerning position of the court theater, municipal theater, conductor, court opera composer. Attempt of popular tunes in operas, tunes in Romanticism, etc.; some things important.]

Goss, Madeleine. *Bolero: The Life of Maurice Ravel.* New York: Holt, 1940.

Gounod, Charles François. *Autobiographical Reminiscences.* London: Heinemann, 1896.

Grandenwitz, Peter. *The Music of Israel.* New York: Norton, 1949. [Bibliography.]

———. *Johann Stamitz.* Brünn: R. M. Rohrer, 1936.

Graf, Max. *Composer and Critic.* New York: Norton, 1946.

XX   Grant, F. *The Choirmaster and the Clergyman.*

Grant, John. *Piobaireachd: Its Origin and Construction.* Edinburgh: John Grant, 1915. [No indication of sources, but evidently based on gigantic collected communications, and on old manuscripts and prints. Also based on book by Donald McDonald, 1822. With musical examples.]

Grant, Margaret, and Herman S. Hettinger. *America's Symphony Orchestras and How They Are Supported.* New York: Norton, 1940.

Graves, Alfred Perceval. *The Celtic Song Book.* London: E. Benn, 1928.

Gray, Cecil. *Sibelius.* London: Oxford University Press, H. Milford, 1931.

Gregor, Joseph. *Geschichte des Österreichischen Theaters.* Vienna: Donau-Verlag, 1948, 334 pp.

———. *Kulturgeschichte des Balletts.* Vienna: Gallus Verlag, 1946.

Greilsamer, Lucien. *L'Anatomie et al Physiologie du Violon, de l'Alto et du Violincelle.* Paris: Delagrave, 1924. [Primarily technical development with documents relating to history of technique; not relevant for us.]

Gressmann, Hugo. *Musik und Musikinstrumente im Alten Testament.* Giessen: J. Ricker, 1903. [In *Religionsgeschichtliche Versuche und Vorarbeiten,* Albert Dietrich and Richard Wünsch eds., vol. 1. With many references from Old Testament. Some use.]

Grieg, Edvard Hagerup. *Briefe an die Verleger der Edition Peters, 1866–1907.* Leipzig: C. F. Peters, 1932. [Some things useful.]

Griffith, Frederic. *Notable Welsh Musicians.* London: F. Goodwen, 1896. [Details on Welsh living in London. Not very specific.]

Griggs, John Cornelius. *Studien über die Musik in America.* Leipzig: Breitkopf & Härtel, 1894. [Largely based on reports of American newspapers. Not much that is new; generally on traveling operas; question of government support.]

Gronowicz, Antoni. *Sergei Rachmaninoff.* New York: Dutton, 1946.

Gross, Rolf. *Joseph Hartmann Stuntz als Opernkomponist.* Würzburg: Dissertations Druckerei & Verlag K. Triltsch, 1936.

Grössel, Heinrich. *Georgius Otto, ein Motettenkomponist des 16. Jahrhunderts.* Kassel: Bärenreiter-Verlag, 1933. [With detailed bibliography, based on very exact sources.]

XX Grosset, Joanny. "Inde. Histoire de la Musique depuis l'Origine jusqu'a Nos Jours," in *Encyclopédie de la Musique,* vol. 1. [Entirely scholarly.]

Grout, Donald Jay. "Seventeenth century parodies of French opera," *Musical Quarterly,* 27:211–219, April 1941. [Supported by much material, including Lully.]

Grunsky, Carl. *Richard Wagner und die Juden.* Munich: Deutsch Volksverlag, 1920, 96 pp.

Gulik, Robert Hans van. *The Lore of the Chinese Lute: An Essay in Ch'in Ideology.* Tokyo: Sophia University, 1940, 224 pp. [Based on Chinese sources, with detailed listing of literature.]

Gura, Eugen. *Erinnerungen aus meinem Leben.* Leipzig: Breitkopf & Härtel, 1905. [Very conceited, always describing his successes; only some things useful.]

XX Gutman, Hans. "Die Generalallüre der Zahmheit Melos." *Zeitschrift für Musik,* 10 (5,6), May-June, 1931.

Gwynn Williams, William Sydney. *Welsh National Music and Dance.* London: J. Curwen, 1933, 165 pp. [Based on study of Celtic sources.]

Haas, Robert Maria. "Die Musik in der Wiener Deutschen Stegreifkomödie," in *Studien zur Musikwissenschaft. Gesellschaft zur Herausgabe von Denkmälern der Tonkunst in Österreich,* vol. 12. Vienna, 1925.

———. "Die Wiener Ballet-Pantomime im 18. Jahrhundert und Glucks Don Juan," in *Studien zur Musikwissenschaft. Gesellschaft zur Herausgabe von Denkmälern der Tonkunst in Österreich,* vol. 10. Vienna: Universal Edition, 1923.

Haböck, Franz. *Die Kastraten und ihre Gesangskunst.* Stuttgart: Deutsche Verlags-Anstalt, 1927. [Quoted in *Bel Canto in its Golden Age,* Phillip Duey. Bibliography.]

Hackett, Karleton Spalding. *The Beginning of Grand Opera in Chicago, 1850–1859.* Chicago: The Laurentian Publishers, 1913. [Concerning individual singers, guest performances.]

XX   Hadley, Henry. *Azaro, an Opera Libretto by David Stevens, Historian.* Grand Opera Season. Chicago: Opera Association, Inc., 1917–1918.

Häfker, Herrmann. *Kino und Erdkunde.* Munich: Volksvereins-Verlag, 1914.

XX   Hagan, Karl. *Über die Musik einiger Naturvölker.* Hamburg: Schatke, 1882. Dissertation, Jena. [Cites others, e.g., *Ein Beitrag zur Kenntnis der Musik bei den Australischen Ureinwohnern,* H. Beckler, Globus, 1868.]

Hague, Eleanor. *Latin American Music.* Santa Ana, Calif.: The Fine Arts Press, 1934. [Based on travel reports; has rich bibliography.]

XX   Halevy, Daniel. *Nietzsche & Wagner 1869–1876.* Paris: La Revue, 1 December 1897. [Irrelevant for us.]

Hamel, Fred. *Johann Sebastian Bach.* Göttingen: Vandenhoeck & Ruprecht, 1959.

———. *Die Psalmkompositionen Johannes Rosenmüllers.* Strasbourg: Heitz, 1933. [Based on source material, very useful.]

XX   Han, Sophie. *Notes on Chinese Music.* Peabody Bulletin. Baltimore: Peabody Conservatory of Music, series 30, no. 1, December 1933. [Popular, without footnotes or indication of sources. Nothing useful.]

Handschin, Jacques. *Das Zeremoniewerk Kaiser Konstantins und die sangbare Dichtung.* Basel: Rektoratsprogramm der Universität Basel für die Jahre 1940 und 1941, 1942.

Handy, William Christopher. *Father of the Blues.* New York: Macmillan, 1941. [Author himself a Negro from the South. Important.]

Hannikainen, Ilmari. *Sibelius and the Development of Finnish Music.* London: Hinrichsen Edition, 1948.

Hanslick, Eduard. *Vienna's Golden Years of Music.* New York: Simon and Schuster, 1950. [Selection of his critiques, especially *Lohengrin, Tristan, Meistersinger, Parzival,* Bayreuth *Ring*; important introduction on house music.]

———. *Aus Meinem Leben.* Berlin: Allgemeiner Verein für Deutsche Litteratur, 1894.

———. *Geschichte des Concertwesens in Wien.* Vienna: W. Braunmüller, 1869–1870. [Very one-sided, his own standpoint.]

Haraszti, Emil. *La Musique Hongroise.* Paris: H. Laurens, 1933. [Useful details; cites historical books, refers to Hungarian games.]

Harcourt, Raoul d'. *La Musique des Incas et Ses Survivances.* Paris: P. Geuthner, 1926.

Harding, Rosamond Evelyn Mary. *The Piano-forte.* Cambridge: The University Press, 1933. [No bibliography, but many learned appendixes.]

XX   Hardt, Ernst. *Die Kunst im Rundfunk. Vortragsabend der Reichsrund-funkgesellschaft im ehemaligen.* Berlin, February 1928.

Harms, Rudolf. *Kulturbedeutung und Kulturgefahren des Films.* Karlsruhe: G. Braun, 1927, 70 pp.

Harris, Rex. *The Story of Jazz.* New York: Grosset & Dunlap, 1955.

XA   Hartmann, Paul. "Musikpflege," in *Das Gymnasium,* Otto Morgenstern. Leipzig: Quelle & Meyer, 1926.

Harwell, Richard Barksdale. *Confederate Music.* Chapel Hill: University of North Carolina Press, 1950. [Some things important, concerning publishing houses, music supply trade, theaters and movies.]

Hase, Herman. *Joseph Haydn und Breitkopf & Härtel.* Leipzig: Breitkopf & Härtel, 1909. [Panegyrical, but has some useful source materials.]

Haskell, Arnold Lionel. *Ballet.* Harmondsworth, Middlesex: Penguin Books, 1955.

———. *Ballet to Poland.* London: Adam & Charles Black, 1940.

———. *Ballet Panorama.* London: B. T. Batsford, 1938.

———. *Balletomania.* New York: Simon and Schuster, 1934. [Autobiographical.]

XX ———. *The Ballet in England.* London: The New English Weekly, n.d. [Short, some historical survey.]

XA Hasse, Karl. "Musikerziehung und Universität," in *Musikerziehung,* Karl Adler, Willie Benzer, and Hermann Keller. Kassel: Bärenreiter-Verlag, 1929.

Hatherly, Stephen Georgeson. *A Treatise on Byzantine Music.* London: A. Gardner, 1892. [Very scholarly discussion of Byzantine theory; based on analysis of examples of Byzantine music.]

Hauptmann, Moritz. *The Letters of a Leipzig Cantor.* New York: Novello, 1892.

Hausegger, Friedrich von. *Richard Wagner und Schopenhauer.* Leipzig: F. Reinboth, 1892, 52 pp. [Impotrant concerning connection.]

Haweis, Hugh Reginald. *Music and Morals.* New York: Harper, 1900.

XX Hawel, Walter. *Praxis des Lichtbildunterrichts für Schulen, Jugendpflege-Organisation, Vereine.* 2nd ed. Cologne: Gilde Verlag, 1929.

Haxthausen-Abbenburg, August F. L. M. *The Russian Empire: Its People, Institutions and Resources.* London: Chapman and Hall, 1856.

Heckel, William. *Der Fagott.* Leipzig: C. Merseburger, 1931. [At the Centennial; based on first edition, published 1899. Details concerning the history of the factory *Almenraeder.*]

Heer, Josef. *Der Graf von Waldstein und sein Verhältnis zu Beethoven.* Leipzig: Quelle & Meyer, 1933. [Based on archive sources.]

Hegar, Elisabeth. *Die Anfänge der neueren Music Geschichtsschreibung um 1770 bei Gerbert, Burney und Hawkins. Sammlung musikwissenschaftlicher Abhandlungen,* vol. 7. Leipzig: Heitz, 1937, 86 pp. [Important concerning eighteenth century.]

Hein, Hellmuth Gunther. *Das Plagiat in der Tonkunst.* Cologne: Druckerei W. May, 1937. [Many details.]

XX Heinrich, Hugo. *John Wilbye in seinen Madregalen. Veröffentlichungen des musikwissensch. Instituts der deutschen University Prag,* no. 2. Augsburg: Benno Filser, 1932. [Some things useful.]

Henry, Mellinger Edward. *Folk Songs from the Southern Highlands.* New York: J. J. Augustin, 1938.

Hensel, Olga. *Vom Erleben des Gesangs.* Augsburg: Bärenreiter-Verlag, 1925, 56 pp.

Hentoff, Nat, and Albert J. McCarthy (Ed.). *Jazz.* New York: Rinehart, 1959.

Hering, Hans. *Die Klavierwerke F. v. Hillers.* Dissertation. Düsseldorf, 1928.

XX Hermann, Albert von. *Antonio Saliere. Eine Studie zum Gedenken seines Künstlerischen Wirkens.* Dissertation. Wien. Vienna: Verlag von Adolf Rabitschek, 1887. [Concerns German operas, somewhat important, with indication also of the older literature.]

Herskovits, Melville Jean. *Life in a Haitian Village.* New York: Knopf, 1937. [Bibliography.]

Herzefeld, Friedrich. *Königsfreundschaft, Ludwig II und Richard Wagner.* Leipzig: W. Goldmann, 1941. [Based on correspondence; objective, also concerns König.]

———. *Minna Planer und ihre Ehe mit Richard Wagner.* Leipzig: W. Goldmann, 1938. [Pro A. Wagner, but, on the whole, objective, with much citation of correspondence.]

Herzog, George. "A Comparison of Pueblo and Pima Musical Styles." *Journal of American Folklore,* vol. 49, 1936.

———. *Research in Primitive and Folk Music in the United States.* Washington, D.C.: Executive Offices, American Council of Learned Societies, 1936. [Almost all methodology, bibliography, and record list.]

Heseltine, Philip. *Frederick Delius.* London: John Lane, 1923. [Not much that is new.]

Hess, Heinz. "Die Opern Alessandro Stradella's." Publikationen der international Musikgesellschaft 2(3). Leipzig: Breitkopf & Härtel, 1906, 93 pp. [Based on source material.]

Hickmann, Hans. *Das Portativ.* Kassel: Bärenreiter-Verlag, 1936. [With detailed historical discussion.]

Hill, Ralph (Ed.). *Music, 1950.* Harmondsworth, Middlesex: Penguin Books, 1950.

Hill, William Henry, Arthur F. Hill, and Alfred E. Hill. *The Violin-Makers of Guarneri Family.* London: W. E. Hil and Sons, 1931.

Hiller, Ferdinand. *Erinnerungsblätter.* Cologne: M. du Mont-Schauber, 1884. [In loose sequence, some things important concerning Russia, Spain, etc.]

———. *Künsterleben.* Cologne: M. du Mont-Schauberg, 1880. [In loose sequence, some things important, but much based on personal meetings.]

Hindenmith, Paul. "Forderungen an den Laien." *Freiburger Theaterblätter,* Intendanz des Stadttheaters, 1930–1931.

Hipkins, Alfred James. *A Description and History of the Piano Forte and of the Older Keyboard Stringed Instruments.* London: Novello, 1896, 130 pp. [Not relevant for us; history of construction.]

———. *Musical Instruments, Historic, Rare and Unique.* London: A. and C. Black, 1921.

Hislop, David Hall. *Our Heritage in Public Worship.* Edinburgh: T. and T. Clark, 1935.

Hobson, Wilder. *American Jazz Music.* New York: Norton, 1939. [Important.]

Höcker, Karla. *Begegnung mit Furtwängler.* Gütersloh: C. Bertelsmann, 1956.

XA Höckner, Hilmar. "Music," in *Das Landerziehungsheim,* Alfred Andreesen. Leipzig: Quelle & Meyer, 1926.

Hodermann, Richard. "Geschichte des Gothaischen Hoftheaters 1775–1779," in *Theatergeschichtliche Forschungen,* Berthold Litzmann, no. 9. Hamburg: L. Boss, 1894, 183 pp.

Hoffmann, Rudolf Stephan. *Erich Wolfgang Korngold.* Vienna: C. Stephenson, 1922.

Hoffmeister, Karel. *Antonin Dvořák.* London: John Lane, 1928.

Högg, Emilie Rosa Margarete. *Die Gesangskunst der Faustina Hasse und das Sängerinnenwesen ihrer Zeit in Deutschland.* Dissertation. Königsbrück i. Sa., 1931 [Very important; attitude toward women singers.]

Hol, Johannes Cornelis. *Horacio Vecchi's Weltliche Werke.* Strasbourg: Heitz, 1934. [Based on sources. Essential especially concerning influence of folk music.]

Holland, Arthur Keith. *Henry Purcell.* London: G. Bell & Sons, 1952.

Holland, Henry Scott, and W. S. Rockstro. *Memoir of Madame Jenny Lind-Goldschmidt.* London: J. Murray, 1891.

Holst, Imogene. *Gustav Holst.* London: Oxford University Press, 1938.

Honigsheim, Paul. "Soziologie der Kunst, Musik und Literatur," in *Die Lehre von der Gesellschaft: Ein Lehrbuch der Soziologie*, Gottfried Eisermann, ed. Stuttgart: Enke Verlag, 1958.

———. "Musikformen und Gesellschaftsformen," in Bernsdorf, *Die Einheit der Sozialwissenschaften*, W. Bernsdorff and G. Eisermann, eds. Stuttgart: Enke Verlag, 1955.

———. "Musik und Gesellschaft," in *Kunst Und Technik*, Leo Kestenberg. Berlin: Volksverband der Buecherfreunde, Wegweiser-Verlag, 1930.

———. "Bewegungs und Sprechchor, expressionistische Musik und die Kommende Theaterkultur." *Die Rampe* 7(4), December 1928–January 1929.

———. "Die Soziologischen und Soziopsychologischen Grundlagen des Kinos." *Der Bildwart*, 7(10-11), October–November 1929.

———. "Die Soziologischen und Soziopsychologischen Grundlagen des Rundfunks und der Radiomusik," in *Discours au Congrès de Musique Radiogénique*. Göttingen, May 1928; Berlin, 1929.

———. "Die Bohème." *Kölner Vierteljahres Hefte für Soziologie*, 3:60–71, 1923.

XX   ———. "Volkshochschule und Kino," in *Volkshochschule und allgemeines Bildungswesen*, Egbeing. Cologne, 1923.

XA   ———. "Übersicht über die bestehenden Volksbildungseinrichtungen und Strömungen," in *Soziologie des Volksbildungswesens. Schriften des Forschungsinstituts für Sozialwissenschaften in Köln*, vol. 1, L. v. Wiese. Munich, 1921.

XA   ———. "Umrisse einer Geschichtsphilosophie der Bildung," in *Soziologie des Volksbildungswesens. Schriften des Forschungsinstituts für Sozialwissenschaften in Köln*, vol. 1, L. v. Wiese. Munich, 1921.

Hood, George. *A History of Music in New England*. Boston: Wilkins, Carter, 1846. [Detailed history especially of internal conflicts concerning women's participation in song. Choirs and organ based on old sources, especially of old publications.]

Horch, Franz. *Die Spielpläne Max Reinhardts 1905–1930*. Munich: R. Piper, 1930. [Theater playbills as source for cultural history.]

Hornbostel, Erich Maria von. "Die Massnorm als Kulturgeschichtliches Forschungsmittel," in *Festschrift. Publication d'Hommage, Offerte à Paul Wilhelm Schmidt*. Vienna, 1928, pp. 303–323 [With much ethnological and historical detailed literature.]

Horne, Lena. *In Person, Lena Horne*. New York: Greenberg, 1950. [Negro singer.]

XX   Horsch, Rudolf. "Jugend spielt." *Der Turm. Blätter der Bundes-Erziehungsanstalt*, **6** (2), June 1931.

Horton, John. *Some Nineteeth Century Composers*. London: Oxford University Press, 1950. [Sketchy, always emphasizes the European as against the national.]

Houghton, Norris. *Moscow Rehearsals*. New York: Harcourt, Brace, 1936.

Howard, John Tasker. *The Music of George Washington's Time*. Washington, D.C.: U.S. George Washington Bicentennial Commission, 1931. [With very much material; also information on new editions of eighteenth century; music performed and composed in America.]

Howe, Mark Antony De Wolfe. *The Boston Symphony Orchestra: An Historical Sketch*. Boston: Houghton Mifflin, 1914, 279 pp. [Listing of members and duration of their membership. The second edition in the first few chapters is a verbatim reprint of the first, but in different format and with changed pagination.]

Hübner, Herbert. *Die Musik im Bismarckarchipel.* Berlin: B. Hahnefeld, 1938. [Differences between music and dances of men and women. Entirely based on the *Kulturkreis* theory. Useful.]

Hudson, Arthur Palmer. *Folksongs of Mississippi and Their Background.* Chapel Hill: The University of North Carolina Press, 1936. [With lengthy introduction, history, national life, and music in Mississippi.]

XX Hughes, H. V., O.S.B. *Latin Hymnody. An Enquiry into the Underlying Principles of Hymnodism.* Church Music Monography, no. 5. London: The Faith Press, 1922. [Catholic within a collection that is chiefly Episcopalian. Historical, popular, no indication of sources.]

Hughes, Russell Meriwether. *The Gesture Language of the Hindu Dance.* New York: Columbia University Press, 1941. [Short, with many pictures; based on travels. Knows Sanskrit. Introduction by Henry R. Zimmer.]

Huguenin, Elisabeth. *Die Odenwaldschule.* Weimar: H. Böhlaus Nachf., 1926, 83 pp.

Huigens, Caecilianus. "Blasius Amon," in *Studien zur Musikwissenschaft. Gesellschaft zur Herausgabe von Denkmälern der Tonkunst in Österreich,* vol. 18. Vienna: 1931.

Hurn, Philip Dutton, and Waverly Louis Root. *The Truth about Wagner.* New York: Frederick A. Stokes, 1930, 313 pp.

Hurok, Salomon. *Impressario.* London: Macdonald, 1947.

Hutchings, Arthur J. B. *Delius.* Toronto: Macmillan, 1948, 193 pp.

XX Hutchins, Charles Lewis. *Annotations of the Hymnal.* Hartford, Conn.: The Church Press, 1872. [Episcopalian; history of texts; includes proof of nonconformist church songs.]

XX Idelsohn, Abraham Zebi. *The Kol Nidre Tune.* Hebrew Union College Annual, vols. 8, 9. Cincinnati, 1931–32. [With much documentation. Very cautious in historical judgments.]

———. *Jewish Music in Its Historical Development.* New York: Holt, 1929. [Very useful.]

Ihlert, Heinz. *Die Reichsmusikkammer.* Berlin: Junker, 1935.

Indy, Vincent d'. *La Schola Cantorum: Son Histoire depuis Sa Fondation jusqu'en 1925.* Paris: Bloud & Gay, 1927. [Delightful stories, biography of the instructors; awards and award winners. A symposium, many authors.]

XX Institut für Theaterwissenschaft an der Universität Köln. Tätigkeitsbericht, 1927–1928. [Also on puppet plays and shadow plays.]

Iselin, Dora Julia. *Biagio Marini.* Hildburghausen: Druck von F. W. Gadow & Sohn, g.m.b.h., 1930. [Does not give sources, but includes musical examples.]

Isnardon, Jacques. *Le Théâtre de la Monnaie.* Brussels: Schott frères, 1890. [Had access to the whole archive material.]

Istel, Edgar. *Revolution und Oper.* Regensburg: G. Bosse, 1919. [Almost exclusively dealing with Wagner and his revolution of music; hardly relevant.]

———. *Die Entstehung des Deutschen Melodramas.* Berlin: Schuster & Loeffler, 1906. [With very much detail, based on source studies; very important book.]

Ivchenko, Valerïan Iakovlevich. *Thamar Karsavina.* London: C. W. Beaumont, 1922. [Panegyrical.]

Jackson, George Pullen. *The Story of the Sacred Harp, 1844–1944.* Nashville: Vanderbilt University Press, 1944. [Stories collected by farmers, then used interdenominationally; originally Baptist hymnal.]

————. *White Spirituals in the Southern Uplands.* Chapel Hill: University of North Carolina Press, 1933. [Based on studies of hymnal histories of several denominations.]

XX   Jackson, (no initial). *Album of the Passion Play at Oberammergau.* [No place, publisher, or date. Apparently written in the 1870s, popular, fat volume. [Details on individual scenes.]

Jäckel, Kurt. *Richard Wagner in der Französischen Literatur.* Breslau: Priebatsch, 1931–

XX   Jacobi, Heinrich. *Jenseits von Musikalisch und Unmusikalisch. Voraussetzungen und Grundlagen einer Musikkultur.* Mitgeteilt auf dem II. Kongress für Aesthetik und allgemeine Kulturwissenschaft. Berlin: October 1924. Zeitschrift Aesthetik und allgemeine Kunstwissenschaft. Jahrgang, 1925, vols. 1–4. Stuttgart: Enke, 1925.

Jacox, Francis. *Bible Music.* London: Hodder & Stoughton, 1871. [Fat volume, but entirely unscientific. Always digresses into other periods, in anecdotal form.]

Jahrbuch für Volksliedforschung. Berlin: Walter Gruyter, 1928–1938, vol. 7, 1941; vol. 8, 1951; beginning with vol. 15, 1970, published Berlin: Schmidt Verlag. [On the whole not nationalist; many details. Investigations; also concerning collection of songs by Annette von Droste-Hülshoff.]

Jaide, Walther. *Deutsche Schwerttänze.* Leipzig: B. G. Teubner, 1936, 44 pp. [Nothing detailed on origins. Detailed description of the individual dances.]

James, W. N. *A Word or Two on the Flute.* London: Paine & Hopkins, 1826. [Historical chapter on flutes of antiquity including Apuleius, only thing useful for us. On German and English flutes; on modern flute virtuosos; aperture, etc.]

Jameson, Raymond de Loy. *Trails of the Troubadours.* New York: The Century Company, 1926. [Anecdotal.]

Jammers, Ewald. "Der Gregoreanische Rhytmus," *Sammlung Musikwissenschaftlicher Abhandlungen*, vol. 25. Carl Nef. Strasbourg: Heitz, 1937, 188 pp [Strictly scholarly and philological.]

————. *Das Karloffizium "Regali Natus."* Strasbourg: Heitz, 1934. [Strictly philosophical and scholarly.]

Jankélévitch, Vladimir. *Maurice Ravel.* Paris: Rieder, 1939.

Jeanroy, Alfred, Louis Brandin, and Pierre Aubry. *Lais et Descorts Français du XIIIe Siècle.* Paris: Welter, 1901.

Jelagín, Juri. *Taming of the Arts.* New York: Dutton, 1951.

Joachim, Joseph. *Briefe von und an Joseph Joachim.* Berlin: J. Bard, 1911–1913.

XA   Jöde, Fritz. "Die Musik im Kindesalter," in *Music im Volk*, Wolfgang Stumme. Berlin: C. F. Vieweg, 1939.

————. *Musikschulen für Jugend und Volk.* Wolfenbüttel: G. Kallmeyer, 1924, 64 pp. [His chief theory.]

Johnson, Frances Hall. *Musical Memories of Hartford.* Hartford: Witkower's, 1931. [Development into orchestra and chamber music.]

Johnson, H. Earle. *Musical Interludes in Boston (1795–1830).* New York: Columbia University Press, 1943. [Fundamental, based on sources; with much reprinting of advertisements, etc. Announcements of recitals, musical supply and instrument dealers, private music teachers, and musicians, especially the von Hagen family, Mr. and Mrs. Grampen, and Dr. Jarken.]

Johnson, James. *The Scotish Musical Museum*. Edinburgh: W. Blackwood and Sons, 1839. [Collections of volumes with indication of origin to be found in old printings, musical notations, etc.]

Johnson, James C. *The Introduction of the Study of Music into the Public Schools of America*. Chicago: Kindergarten Literature Co., 1893. [Very short, harks back to Lowell Mason.]

Johnston, Alfred Wintle. *The Sword Dance, Papa Stour, Shetland, and Four Shetland Airs*. London: Viking Society for Northern Research, 1912. [Very short, with tunes; based on Walter Scott and other printed travel journals. Important on solo singing before a dance.]

Jourdan-Morhange, Hélène. *Ravel et Nous*. Geneva: Editions du Milieu du Monde, 1945. [Anecdotal.]

Journal of the English Folk Dance and Song Society. London: Sharp, 1932 ff. [Many specific examinations of individual dances, also of Indians.]

Jullien, Adolphe. *L'Eglise et l'Opéra en 1735*. Paris: A. Detaille, 1877. [Ecclesiastic conflicts are described in detail.]

———. *Les Spectateurs sur le Théâtre*. Paris: A. Detaille, 1875.

XX   Jürgens, Alfred. "Von Isadora Duncan bis Mary Wiegmann." *Die Freude*, 2(9), September 1925.

XA   Justi, Hans. "Hausmusik als Führungsgabe," in *Musik im Volk*. Wolfgang Stumme. Berlin: C. F. Viewig, 1939.

Kaestner, Rudolf. *Johann Heinrich Rolle*. Kassel: Bärenreiter-Verlag, 1932. [Eighteenth century, also Frederick the Great. Very important.]

XX   Kahlbeck, Max. *Das Bühnenfestspiel zu Bayreuth. Eine kritische Studie*. Breslau: Schletter, 1877. [Satirical; Wagner's grandchild.]

XX   Kaplan, Max. "A sociological approach to Music and Behavior." *The American Journal of Occupational Therapy*, January-February, 1950.

———. *Music in the City*. Pueblo: First mimeographed edition, 1944.

Kapp, Julius. *Geschichte der Staatsoper Berlin*. Berlin: M. Hesse, 1937.

———. *Franz Schreker, Der Mann und Sein Werk*. Munich: Drei Masken Verlag, 1921.

Karpath, Ludwig. *Siegfried Wagner als Mensch und Künstler*. Leipzig: H. Seemann, 1902, 42 pp. [Short, panegyrical; some things useful concerning folkloristic origin.]

Karsavina, Tamar. *Les Souvenirs de Ballets Russes*. Trans. Denyse Clairouin. Paris: Plon, 1931.

XX   Karthaus, Werner. *Musik. Aus Theorie und Praxis der rheinischen Volkshochschule Düsseldorf*. Düsseldorf: Verlag der Volkshochschulgemeinde, 1926.

Kasten, Otto. *Das Theater in Köln während der Franzosenzeit*. Bonn: F. Klopp Verlag, g.m.b.h., 1928.

Kaudern, Walter Alexander. *Musical Instruments in Celebes*. The Hague: M. Nijhoff, 1927. [Critical discussion of the origin of Hindus, Mohammedans, Christians, Chinese, on basis of races, with detailed examples.]

XA   Keefer, Lubov. "The Beethovens of America," in *Romanticism in America*, George Boas, ed. Baltimore: Johns Hopkins Press, 1940. [Important details on Heinrich, Wunderkinder, people who are composers, virtuosos, dealers, and publishers at the same time. Romanticism, literary, also on Indian operas.]

Keh, Chung Sik. *Die Koreanische Musik.* Strasbourg: Heitz, 1935. [Useful because of the various types of musicians.]

Keiner, Ferdinand. *Die Madrigale Gesualdos von Venosa.* Leipzig: Breitkopf & Härtel, 1914. [First part useful.]

XA Keller, Hermann. "Gedanken zu einer Reform des musiktheoretischen Unterrichts," in *Musikerziehung,* Karl Adler, Willie Benzer, and Hermann Keller. Kassel: Bärenreiter-Verlag, 1929, 132 pp.

Kempers, Karel Philippus Bernet. *Jacobus Clemens non Papa und seine Motetten.* Augsburg: Dr. B. Filser, 1928, 109 pp. [Based on sources with detailed bibliography of the sources. Useful.]

Kennedy, Hans. *Die Zither in der Vergangenheit, Gegenwart und Zukunft.* Tölz: F. Fiedler, Musik Verlag, 1896, 207 pp. [Hoping and grumbling in a snide fashion.]

Kinscella, Hazel Gertrude. *Music on the Air.* New York: Viking Press, 1934. [A hodgepodge on all kinds of musicians who were on the air.]

Kinsky, Georg. *A History of Music in Pictures.* London: J. M. Dent, 1937.

———. *Die Originalausgaben der Werke Johann Sebastian Bachs.* Vienna: H. Reichner, 1937.

XA ———."Das Musikhistorische Museum von Heyer," in *Köln als Stätte der Bildung,* Joseph Theele and Adam Wrede. Cologne: Gonski & Co., 1922.

XX Kinzl, Wilhelm. *Meine Lebenswanderung.* Stuttgart: Ergelhorn's Nachfolger, 1926.

Kirby, Percival Robson. *The Musical Instruments of the Native Races of South Africa.* London: Oxford University Press, H. Milford, 1934. [Everything verv accurately documented; also data concerning Hottentots.]

———. *The Kettle-Drums.* London: Oxford University Press, H. Milford, 1930.

Klages, Ludwig. *Vom Wesen des Rhythmus.* Kampen auf Sylt: N. Kampmann, 1934.

———. *Vom Kosmogonischen Eros.* Jena: E. Diederichs, 1930.

———. *Der Geist als Widersacher der Seele.* Leipzig: J. A. Barth, 1929.

———. *Zur Ausdruckslehre und Charakterkunde.* Heidelberg: N. Kampmann, 1927, 389 pp.

XX ———. "Zur Psychologie des Volksliedes." *Der Rhythmus. Zeitschrift für gymnastische Erziehung, Mitteilungen der Bodebunder,* 5(3), July–September 1927.

Klatt, Fritz. Die geistige Wendung des Maschinenzeitalters. Potsdam: A. Protte, 1930, 124 p.

XX ———. "Die Arbeit eines Jahres." Bericht über die Freizeit des Volkshochschulheimes auf dem Darss. 1928. Im Selbstverlag des Verfassers, 1929.

———. *Das Gegenspiel.* Jena: E. Diederichs, 1925.

Klefisch, Walter. *Arcaldelt als Madrigalist.* Cologne: Buchdruckerei Orthen, 1938. [Kroyer as *Referent.* Some things can be used.]

Klein, Hermann. *The Reign of Patti.* New York: The Century Co., 1920. [Evidently on basis of personal acquaintance; a number of documents in the appendix.]

Klob, Karl Maria. *Die Komische Oper nach Lortzing.* Berlin: "Harmonie," Verlagsgesellschaft für Literatur und Kunst, 1905. [Not important, especially sentimental criticism, indication of content.]

Klose, Friedrich. *Meine Lehrjahre bei Bruckner.* Regensburg: G. Bosse, 1927.

Kloss, Erich. *Zwanzig Jahre "Bayreuth," 1876–1896.* Berlin: Schuster & Loeffler, 1896. [Pro-nationalist.]

Kluckhohn, Clyde, and Leland C. Wyman. *An Introduction to Navaho Chant Practice.* Menasha, Wis.: American Anthropological Association, 1940.

Klusen, Ernst. *Das Volkslied im Niederrheinischen Dorf.* Potsdam: L. Voggenreiter, 1941. [With superimposed Hitlerism, otherwise some things useful.]

XA Knorr, Ernst Lother von. "Musik im Haus," in *Music im Volk.* Wolfgang Stumme. Berlin: C. F. Vieweg, 1939.

Kobald, Karl. *Beethoven, seine Beziehungen zu Wiens Kunst und Kultur.* Zurich: Amalthea-Verlag, 1927.

Kobbé, Gustav. *Opera Singers.* Boston: Oliver Ditson Co., 1904. [*Kitsch,* much advertising, no pagination.]

Koch, Edward Emil. *Geschichte des Kirchenlieds und Kirchengesangs der Christlichen, insbesondere der Deutschen Evangelischen Kirche.* Stuttgart: C. Belser, 1866–1877.

XX Koch, Ludwig. *Schallplatte, Sprechmaschine und ihre kulturelle Mission.* Funkalmanach, 1930.

XA Koczirz, Adolf. "Exzerpte aus den Hofmusikakten des Wiener Hofkammerarchivs," in *Studien zur Musikwissenschaft. Gesellschaft zur Herausgabe von Denkmälern der Tonkunst in Österreich.* Vienna, 1913–1934.

Kolodin, Irving. *The Metropolitan Opera, 1883–1935.* New York: Oxford University Press, 1936. [With a lot of material.]

Komma, Karl Michael. *Johann Zach und die Tschechischen Musiker im deutschen Umbruch des 18. Jahrhunderts.* Kassel: Bärenreiter-Verlag, 1938. [Somewhat nationalistic.]

Kommissarzhevskii, Fedor Fedorovich. *Myself and the Theater.* New York: Dutton, 1930.

Kommissarzhevskii, Fedor Fedorovich, and Lee Simonson. *Settings and Costumes of the Modern Stage.* London: The Studio Ltd., 1933. [Mostly pictures.]

Komorzynski, Egon von. *Der Vater der Zauberflöte.* Vienna: P. Neff, 1948.

Kool, Japp. *Das Saxophon.* Leipzig: J. J. Weber, 1931. [Very professional; history of invention; history of struggles over the saxophone.]

Korson, George Gershon. *Pennsylvania Songs and Legends.* Philadelphia: University of Pennsylvania Press, 1949.

Korte, Werner. *Studie zur Geschichte der Musik in Italien im Ersten Viertel des 15. Jahrhunderts.* Kassel: Bärenreiter-Verlag, 1933. [On the whole only for tradition and continuities.]

Kosch, Franz. "Florian Leopold Gassmann als Kirchenkomponist," in *Studien zur Musikwissenschaft. Gesellschaft zur Herausgabe von Denkmälern der Tonkunst in Österreich,* vol. 14. Vienna, 1927.

Kracauer, Siegfried. *Von Caligari bis Hitler.* Hamburg: Rowohlt, 1958.

———. *From Caligari to Hitler, A Psychological History of the German Film.* Princeton: Princeton University Press, 1947.

———. *Orpheus in Paris: Offenbach and the Paris of His Time.* New York: Knopf, 1938.

Kralik, Heinrich. *Die Wiener Philharmoniker.* Vienna: W. Frick, 1938. [Very important.]

Kralik, Richard. *Altgriechische Musik*. Stuttgart: J. Roth, 1900. [Not very independent, little that is new.]

Kraus, Alexandre. *Ethnographie Musicale. La Musique au Japon*. Florence, 1879. [Not relevant, popular, no sources.]

Kreidler, Walter. *Heinrich Schütz und der Stile Concitato von Claudio Monteverdi*. Stuttgart: Graphische Werkstätten Fackel & Klein, 1934. [Only very little.]

Kreiser, Kurt. *Carl Gottlieb Reissiger*. Dresden: Druck von J. Pässler, 1918. [Riemann as *Referen*. Based on sources.]

Krenek, Ernst. *Selbstdarstellung*. Zurich: Atlantis, 1948.

XA   Kretzschmar, Hermann. "Die Denkmäler der Tonkunst," in *Studien zur Musikwissenschaft. Gesellschaft zur Herausgabe von Denkmälern der Tonkunst in Österreich*. Vienna, 1913–1934.

Kretzschmar, Hermann. *Geschichte der Oper*. Leipzig: Breitkopf & Härtel, 1919. [Has decisive section at the beginning. Information on the literature, which he often uses in detail in later notes; Occasionally directly quotes original texts of Gottsched and Mattheson and new editions, e.g., *Denkmäler der Tonkunst*.]

———. *Über den Stand der öffentlichen Musikpflege in Deutschland*. Sammlung Musikalischer Vorträge. Herausgegeben von Paul Graf Waldersee. Leipzig, 1879–1898.

XX   Kreutzhagen, Edward. *Hermann Goetz' Leben und sein Schaffen auf dem Gebiet der Oper*. Dissertation München. Leipzig: Breitkopf & Härtel, 1916.

Krohn, Ilmari. *Über die Art und Entstehung der Geistlichen Volksmelodien in Finland*. Helsingfors: Druckerei der Finnischen Litteratur-Gesellschaft, 1899. [Based on collections. Useful.]

Krohn, Kaarle. "Bärenlieder der Finnen," in *Festschrift. Publication d'hommage, offerte au Paul Wilhelm Schmidt*. Vienna, 1928, pp. 401–406.

Krone, Walter. *Wenzel Müller. Ein Beitrag zur Geschichte der Komischen Oper*. Dissertation Berlin. Berlin: E. Ebering, 1906, 86 pp.

Krüger, Liselotte. *Die Hamburgische Musikorganisation im XVII. Jahrhundert*. Strasbourg: Heitz, 1933. [Edited by Karl Nef.]

Krüger, Walther. *Das Concerto Grosso in Deutschland*. Wolfenbüttel: Georg Kallmeyer Verlag, 1932. [With detailed listing of old concerto grosso and the instruments in them, etc. Some sociological explanations.]

XA   Krüger-Riebow, Joachim. "Chopins Aufenthalt in Deutschland," in *Chopin Almanach*, Chopin-Komitee in Deutschland. Potsdam: Akademische Verlagsgesellschaft Athenaion, 1949, 164 pp.

Kruse, Georg Richard. *Albert Lortzing*. Leipzig: Breitkopf & Härtel, 1914. [Some things usable.]

Kühne, Alfred. *Handbuch für das Berufs und Fachschulwesen, im Auftrage des Zentralinstituts für Erziehung und Unterricht in Berlin*. Leipzig: Quelle & Meyer, 1929.

XA   Kulp, Johann. "Evangelische Radio Hörergemeinschaft," in *Provinzial Verband für innere Mission. Ziele und Wege*. August–September 1930.

Kunst, Jaap. *Music in Flores*. Leiden: Internationales Archiv für Ethnographie, 1942. [Follower of Sachs, problems of spread, praises "Fathers of the Divine World."]

———. "Music in Nias." *Internationales Archiv für Ethnographie*, 38(1–3). Leiden: Brill, 1939. [Follower of Sachs, based on travels and sources.]

———. *Expedition ot the Central Mountains (Nassau Range) in the Netherlands East Indies 1926.* Weltevreden: G. Kolff, 1931. [Based on Hornbostel in Grubner's sense.]

Kunz, Lucas. *Die Tonartenlehre des Römischen Theoretikers und Komponisten Pier Francesco Valentini. Münsterische Beiträge zur Musikwissenschaft,* no. 8. Kassel: Bärenreiter-Verlag, 1937, 136 pp. [Based on source material.]

Laban, Rudolf. *The Mastery of Movement on the Stage.* London: Macdonald & Evans, 1950.

Lachmann, Robert. *Jewish Cantillation and Song in the Isle of Djerba.* Jerusalem: Archives of Oriental Music, Hebrew University, 1940. [Arab influences; with Jewish milieu conservatory.]

———. *Die Musik der Aussereuropäischen Natur und Kulturvölker.* Wildpark: Akademische Verlagsgesellschaft Athenaion, m.b.h., 1929.

XX Lämmel, Rudolf. *Der moderne Tanz.* Berlin: Peter J. Oestergaard Verlag, n.d.

La Laurencie, Lionel de. *Les Créateurs de l'Opéra Français.* Paris, 1921. [Purely historical, not much that is new, some literature indicated.]

Laloy, Louis. *Aristoxène de Tarente et la Musique de l'Antiquité.* Paris: Société Française d'Imprimerie et de Libraire, 1904. [Fat volume based on sources and precursors; does not agree with Westphal.]

———. *La Musique Chinoise.* Paris: H. Laurens, 190—? [Some things useful.]

XX ———. *La dance à l'Opera.* Paris: Théo Bouquère, n.d.

Landau, Anneliese. *Das einstimmige Kunstlied Conradin Kreutzers und seine Stellung zum zeitgenössichen Lied in Schwaben.* Leipzig: Breitkopf & Härtel, 1930. [First chapter sociologically important. The Stuttgart music life of the time.]

Landau, Rom. *Ignace Paderewski, Musician and Statesman.* New York: Crowell, 1934.

Lange, Francisco Curt. *Los Estudios Musicales de la América Latina, Publicados Ultimamente.* Cambridge: Harvard University Press, 1938. [A lecture on why it is necessary to explore Latin American music, in order to promote its spread.]

Lasalle, Albert de. *Mémorial du Théâtre-Lyrique.* Paris: J. Lecuir, 1877. [Not relevant for us.]

Lassabathie, Théodore. *Histoire du Conservatoire Impérial de Musique et de Déclamation.* Paris: Michel Lévy frères, 1860. [Prints much about authors of the time of the Revolution.]

Launis, Armas, *Über Art, Entstehung und Verbreitung der Estnisch-Finnischen Runenmelodien.* Helsingfors: Druckerei der Finnischen Literatur-Gesellschaft, 1910. [Based on folk tunes that were collected in the Finnish-Estonian border region. Melodic variants are written down. Useful.]

Lawrence, Marjorie. *Interrupted Melody: The Story of My Life.* New York: Appleton-Century-Crofts, 1949.

Lawton, Mary. *Schumann-Heink, The Last of the Titans.* New York: Macmillan, 1928. [Largely an autobiography.]

Lederman, Minna. *Stravinsky in the Theatre.* New York: Pellegrini & Cudahy, 1949. [Many contributors. An expansion of Lederman. *Dance Index,* but essentially the same.]

Lehmann, Lilli. *My Path through Life.* New York: Putnam, 1914.

Lehmann, Lotte. *Wings of Song, An Autobiography.* London: K. Paul, Trench, Trubner & Co., 1938.

Leibowitz, René. *Schoenberg and His School.* New York: Philosophical Library, 1949.

XA Leichtentritt, Hugo. "Das Polnische in Leben und Werk Chopins," in *Chopin Almanach,* Chopin-Komitee in Deutschland. Potsdam: Akademische Verlagsgesellschaft Athenaion, 1949, 164 pp.

———. *Serge Koussewitzky, the Boston Symphony Orchestra and the New American Music.* Cambridge: Harvard University Press, 1946.

———. *Geschichte der Motette.* Leipzig: Breitkopf & Härtel, 1908. [At the end detailed sources and literature data concerning edition; no notes in the text, no special references. On the whole, book almost exclusively dealing with history of form, almost nothing on who, what, where performed, etc.]

Leitner, Franz Xaver. *Der gottesdienstliche Volksgesang im jüdischen und christlichen Altertum.* Freiburg im Breisgau: Herder, 1906, 283 pp. [Largely based on sources; but also the *Testallian* printed in Migne, etc.[

Lennartz, Werner. *Die Lieder und Leiche Tannhäusers im Lichte der neueren Metrik.* Dissertation Köln, 1932, 55 pp.

Lenz, Friedrich. *Einführung in die Soziologie des Rundfunks.* Lechte: Emsdetten, 1953.

Leroux, Charles. *La Musique Classique Japonaise.* Paris: Evette & Schaeffner, and Bibliotheque de la Société Franco-Japonaise, 1911. [Short explanation of the tonalities and musical notation based on the author's own stays in Japan as French military band leader.]

Leux, Irmgard. *Christian Gottlob Neefe (1748–1798).* Leipzig: Kistner & Siegel, 1925.

Levy, Josef. *Die Signalinstrumente in den Altfranzösischen Texten.* Halle: Hofbuchruckerei von C. A. Kaemmerer, 1910. [Based on thorough knowledge of the printed old French texts.]

Lewy, Heinrich. *Christian Gottlob Neefe.* Rostock: C. Hinstorffs Buchdruckerei, 1901. [On the whole not significant; based on source material in Rostock.]

Leyda, Jay, and Sergei Bertensson. *The Musorgsky Reader: A Life of Modeste Petrovich Musorgsky in Letters and Documents.* New York: Norton, 1947.

XX "Liebe, Luft, Leben." *Nachrichtenblatt der Arbeitsgemeinschaft der Bünde deutscher Lichtkämpfe,* vol. 19, no. 10. Dresden: Verlag der Schönheit. [Advocates nudism.]

XX Liebig, Bries R. "Die Musik im Kreisleben," in *Aus der Arbeit und dem Leben userer Neulandkreise.* 2nd. rev. ed., Neuland, no. 6. Eisenach, Neulandhaus: Neuland Verlag, n.d.

Lifar, Serge. *Giselle, Apothéose du Ballet Romantique.* Paris: A. Michel, 1942.

———. *Serge Diaghilev, His Life, His Work and His Legend.* New York: Putnam, 1940.

Lightwood, James Thomas. *The Music of the Methodist Hymn-Book.* London: The Epworth Press, 1935, 549 pp. [Almost exclusively description of the English hymns and of their origins. Introduction important because it shows all the directions from which the Methodists have borrowed.]

Linscott, Eloise Hubbard. *Folk Songs of Old New England.* New York: Macmillan, 1939.

Lisei, Cesare. *Giovanni Botteseine: Cenni Biografici. Estrati dalla Gazzetta Musicale di Milano.* Milan, 1886. [Anecdotal style.]

XA Lissa, Zofia. "Der Einfluss Chopins auf die Russische Musik," in *Chopin Almanach,* Chopin-Komitee in Deutschland. Potsdam: Akademische Verlagsgesellschaft Athenaion, 1949, 164 pp.

Liszt, Franz. *Correspondance de Liszt et de la Comtesse d'Agoult, 1833–1840*. Paris: B. Grasset, 1933.

———. *Souvenirs de Franz Liszt: Lettres Inédites*. Leipzig: Breitkopf & Härtel, 1913. [Letters in the forties during Liszt's recital travels in Southern Russia to the then Austrian Consul General in Odessa; edited by the latter's last son. Always within the extreme feudalism. No word on it by Liszt.]

———. *Franz Liszt's Briefe an Baron Anton Augusz, 1846–1878*. Budapest: F. Kilian's nachf., 1911.

XX ———. *Briefe hervorragender Zeitgenossen an Franz Liszt nach den Handschriften des Weimarer Liszt Museum mit Unterstützung von dessen Custos [sic] Geheimrat Gille. Herausgegeben von La Mara*, vols. 1–2. Leipzig: Breitkopf & Härtel, 1895–1905.

———. *Franz Liszt's Briefe*. Leipzig: Breitkopf & Härtel, 1893–1902. [The individual letters with subtitles added.]

———. *Briefwechsel zwischen Franz Liszt und Hans von Bülow*. Leipzig: Breitkopf & Härtel, 1898.

Liszt, Franz, and Carl Alexander. *Briefwechsel zwischen Franz Liszt und Carl Alexander, Grossherzog von Sachsen*. Leipzig: Breitkopf & Härtel, 1909.

Littlehales, Lillian. *Pablo Casals*. New York: Norton, 1948.

XX Lobo, Frank. "Herbert Former am Scheidewege." *Jugendvolksbühne*, 3(2), November 1932.

Lochner, Louis Paul. *Fritz Kreisler*. New York: Macmillan, 1950.

Loewe, Johann Carl Gottfried. *Dr. Carl Loewe's Selbstbiographie*. Berlin: W. Müller, 1870, 458 pp. [Some things usable; kings, Minister of Culture von Mühler, and the like. Protestant and freemason.]

Lomax, John Avery. *Adventures of a Ballad Hunter*. New York: Macmillan, 1947.

———. *Songs of the Cattle Trail and Cow Camp*. New York: Macmillan, 1919.

Lomax, John Avery, and Allan Lomax. *Our Singing Country*. New York: Macmillan, 1949.

———. *American Ballads and Folk Songs*. New York: Macmillan, 1934.

London, Kurt. *Film Music*. London: Faber & Faber, 1936.

Lootens, Louis. *La Théorie Musicale du Chant Grégorien*. Paris: Thorin et fils, 1895. [Does not give sources.]

Louis, Gustav. *Die Realschule. Im Auftrage des Zentralinstituts für Erziehung und Unterricht*. Leipzig: Quelle & Meyer, 1924.

Louis, Rudolf. *Die Deutsche Musik der Gegenwart*. Munich: G. Müller, 1912.

———. *Die Weltanschauung Richard Wagners*. Leipzig: Breitkopf & Härtel, 1898.

Lourié, Arthur. *Sergei Koussevitzky and His Epoch*. New York: Knopf, 1931.

XX Löwenberg, Bruno. "Kinder auf der Bühne." *Jugendvolksbühne*, 2(8), October 1931.

Lowinsky, Eduard. *Das Antwerpener Mottentenbuch Orlando di Lasso's und seiner Beziehungen zum Motettenschaffen der niederländischen Zeitgenossen*. The Hague: M. Nijhoff, 1937. [Based on sources.]

XX Lungershausen, (no initials). "Rundfunk und Schallplatte." *Mitteilungen der Carl Lindström A. G. Kulturabteilung Berlin*, 1(9), March 1930.

Luper, Albert T. *Music of Brazil*. Washington, D.C.: Music Division, Pan American Union, Music Series, no. 9, May 1943. [Usable details.]

XA Luserke, Martin. "Die besonderen Möglichkeiten der Jugendbühne in der Heimschule," in *Das Landerziehungsheim*, Alfred Andreesen. Leipzig: Quelle & Meyer, 1926, 125 pp.

XA ———. "Die Frage der körperlichen Erziehung an den Landerziehungsheimen," in *Das Landerziehungsheim*, Alfred Andreesen. Leipzig: Quelle & Meyer, 1926, 125 pp.

XA ———. "Bewegungsspiel und Schulbühne," in *Körperschulung Künstlerische*, Ludwig Pallat and Franz Hilker. Breslau: Ferdinand Hirt, 1925.

XX ———. "Körperliche Ausdruckskultur." *Die Schule der Gemeinshaft. Im Auftrage des Zentralinstituts für Erziehung und Unterricht. Herausgegeben von Heinrich Daters*. Leipzig: Quelle & Meyer, n.d.

Lütgendorff, Willibald Leo Freiherr von. *Die Geigen- und Lautenmacher vom Mittelalter bis zur Gegenwart*. 2 volumes, 5th and 6th rev. Frankfurt: Hans Schneider, 1922. [Large bibliography, but based largely on recent literature; evidently on studies in many libraries, also old pictures and manuscripts.]

Lynham, Deryck. *Ballet Then and Now*. London: Sylvan Press, 1947. [Historical.]

Lyra, Justus Wilhelm. *D. M. Luthers Deutsche Messe, etc.* Gütersloh: G. Bertelsmann, 1904. [Staunchly Lutheran, many special musical details; only little that is usable.]

MacDougall, Hamilton Crawford. *Early New England Psalmody: An Historical Appreciation, 1620–1820*. Brattleboro: Stephen Daye Press, 1940. [Music theoretical, history of the tonal systems. Important because of prohibition of use of organ by Methodists, spread to America.]

MacKenzie, Donald Richard. *Highland Dances: Illustrated Guide to the National Dances of Scotland*. Glasgow: A. MacLaren and Sons, 1939. [Entirely consisting of descriptions of particular dances, largely round dances. Nothing that is of sociological interest.]

Macleod, Joseph Todd Gordon. *The New Soviet Theatre*. London: Allen & Unwin, 1943, 242 pp. [Here, the new unchanged edition of 1944 used.]

Madeira, Louis Cephas. *Annals of Music in Philadelphia and History of the Musical Fund Society*. Philadelphia: J. B. Lippincott, 1896. [Prints some documents; short indication of other sources.]

Mahler, Alma. *Gustav Mahler: Memories and Letters*. London: J. Murray, 1946.

Mahler, Gustav. *Briefe*. Berlin: P. Zsolnay, 1924.

Mahrenholz, Christhard. *Samuel Scheidt, Sein Leben und Sein Werk*. Leipzig: Breitkopf & Härtel, 1924. [Based on knowledge of sources and on indication of sources, very important concerning organists and falsetto singers.]

Maine, Basil. *Elgar, His Life and Works*. London: G. Bell and Sons, 1933.

Malcolm, Charles Alexander. *The Piper in Peace and War*. London: J. Murray, 1927. [Evidently based on very accurate knowledge of locality. Relevant for us.]

Malherbe, Henry. *Richard Wagner Révolutionnaire*. Paris: A. Michel, 1938. [Very subjective; Wagner as revolutionary in every respect, also sexual customs. E.g., *Nibelungenring* as *Revolutionsangabe*.]

Malim, Arthur Warcup. *English Hymn Tunes from the Sixteenth Century to the Present Time*. London: W. Reeves, 189–? [Lecture, against innovations, especially against secular music. E.g., texts of today.]

Mandt, Heinrich. *Die Entwicklung des Romantischen in der Instrumentalmusik Felix Mendelssohn-Bartholdys*. Dissertation Köln. Cologne, 1927, 56 pp.

Mandyczewski, Eusebius. "Die Sammlung und Statuten," in *1 Zusatzbande. Geschichte der Kaiserlich-Königliche Gesellschaft der Musikfreunde in Wien.* Vienna: J. Herz, 1912.

Markov, Paul Aleksandrovich. *The Soviet Theater.* New York: Putnam, 1935.

XX   Martell, Paul. Über Tanzschrift." *Tonkünstlerzeitung,* **27**(23), December 5, 1929. [Particularly the *Laban* system.]

Martin, John Joseph. *Introduction to the Dance.* New York: Norton, 1939. [No sources, many pictures, goes back quite far; ends with modern America.]

———. *America Dancing: The Background and Personalities of the Modern Dance.* New York: Dodge, 1936.

Martynov, Ivan I. *Dimitri Shostakovich, The Man and His Work.* New York: Philosophical Library, 1947.

Mason, Lowell. *Address on Church Music.* Boston: Hilliard, Gray, Little and Wilkins, 1827. [Officially published by the Baptists; religious, for special church choir and for instruments as accompaniment.]

XX   Matallana, R. P. *Baltasar de Misionario Franciscano Capuchino. La Musica Indigena Taurepan.* Caracas, 1939. [Based on the author's own experience as missionary.]

Matida, Kasyo. *Odori.* (Japanese Dance). Tokyo: Board of Tourist Industry, Japanese Government Railways, 1938. [Short, panegyrical, no indication of sources, but with some usable materials.]

Maxwell, William Delbert. *An Outline of Christian Worship.* London: Oxford University Press, H. Milford, 1936.

Mayer, Jacob Peter. *British Cinemas and Their Audiences: Sociological Studies.* London: D. Dobson, 1948.

McCusker, Honor. *Fifty Years of Music in Boston.* Boston: Published by the Trustees of the Public Library, 1938. [Does not say much that is not known. New for chamber music.]

McDowell, Lucien L., and Flora Lassiter. *Folk Dances of Tennessee.* Ann Arbor: Edwards Brothers, 1938.

Medicus, Lotte. *Die Koloratur in der Italienischen Oper des 19. Jahrhunderts.* Wetzikon: Aktienbuchdruckerei, 1939. [Concerns castrates, important. Otherwise only history of technique.]

Mee, John Henry. *The Oldest Music Room in Europe: A Record of Eighteenth Century Enterprises of Oxford.* London: J. Lane, 1911.

Melba, Nellie. *Melodies and Memories.* New York: George H. Doran, 1926. [Tells much about receptions in high society.]

Mellers, Wilfred Howard. *François Couperin and the French Classical Tradition.* London: D. Dobson, 1950.

———. *Music and Society: England and the European Tradition.* London: D. Dobson, 1946, 1950.

XX   Melloff, Franz. *Richard Wagner und das Deutschtum.* Munich: Joseph Wurm, 1873. [Short, panegyrical, *im Ring der Nationalcharakteristik.*]

Mellor, Albert. *A Record of the Music and Musicians of Eton College.* Eton College: Spottiswoode, Ballantyne, 1929, 153 pp. [Short, panegyrical; description of the organ.]

Mendelssohn-Bartholdy, Felix. *Letters.* New York: Pantheon, 1945. [Not quite complete, therefore to be supplemented by Klingemann and Schubing collection.]

———. *Felix Mendelssohn-Bartholdys Briefwechsel mit Legationsrat Karl Klingemann in London*. Essen: G. D. Baedecker, 1909, 371 pp. [Some things important.]

Mendelssohn-Bartholdy, Felix, and Julius Schubring. *Briefwechsel*. Leipzig: Duncker & Humblot, 1892. [Only very little is usable.]

Mendl, Robert William Sigismund. *The Appeal of Jazz*. London: P. Allan, 1927. [Well grounded; largely going back to *Antik*.]

XA Mendlsohn, Ignz. "Zur Entwicklung des Walzers," in *Studien zur Musikwissenschaft. Gesellschaft zur Herausgabe von Denkmälern der Tonkunst in Österreich*. Vienna: 1913–1934.

Meng, Chih. *Remarks on Chinese Music and Musical Instruments*. New York: China Institute in America, 1932. [Very important.]

Menke, Werner. *History of the Trumpet of Bach and Handel*. London: W. Reeves, 1934. [Against Eichhorn; recommends his own new instruments, a modernized form of the clarinets used by Bach's orchestra.]

Mercy-Argenteau, La Comtesse de. *César Cui, Esquisse Critique*. Paris: Rischbacher, 1888. [Dedicated to the Tsarina.]

Messel, Oliver. *Stage Designs and Costumes*. London: J. Lane, 1933. [Expressionistic, mostly pictures, only about twenty pages of text.]

Messiter, Arthur Henry. *A History of the Choir and Music of Trinity Church, New York*. New York: E. S. Gorham, 1906. [Self-written with all historical material.]

XX *Méthode Jaques-Dalcroze*. Première Partie (2 vols.): *Gymnastique Rhythmique*. Paris: Sandoz, Jobin, n.d.

Milinowski, Marta. *Theresa Carreño*. New Haven: Yale University Press, 1940.

Millenkovich, Max von. *Cosima Wagner: ein Lebensbild*. Leipzig: Philipp Reclam, 1937. [Based on much letter material.]

Miller, Paul Eduard. *Miller's Yearbook of Popular Music*. Chicago: Pem Publications, 1943. [Some details important, gives list of innumerable recordings with his subjective value judgment, priced one to fifty dollars. Biography, etc.]

XX "Mission play special." *California Life*, 17(29), December 25, 1920. [Panegyrical, many illustrations.]

Möckel, Otto. *Die Kunst des Geigenbaues*. Leipzig: Bernhard Friedrich Voigt, 1930. 397 pp. [Purely technical.]

XX Mohn, Joseph. *Anleitung zur Kirchlichen Psalmodie*. Regensburg: Friedrich Purfet, 1878. [Mostly technical instructions for singing.]

Mohr, Ernst. *Die Allemande, Eine Untersuchung ihrer Entwicklung von den Anfängen bis zu Bach und Händel*. Zurich: Kommissions-Verlag von Gebr. Hug & Co., 1932.

Mohr, Wilhelm. *Das Gründerthum in der Musik*. Cologne: M. Du Mont-Schauberg, 1872. [Anti-Wagner; stresses Jewish advertising activities.]

Moisenco, Rena. *Realist Music: 25 Soviet Composers*. London: Meridian Books, 1949.

———. *Twenty Soviet Composers*. London: Workers' Music Association, 1943. [Official.]

Moldenhauer, Hans. *Duo-Pianism*. Chicago: Chicago Musical College Press, 1950. [Half of the book is purely technical, with practical instructions.]

Molitor, Raphael. *Die Nach-tridentinische Choralreform zu Rom*. Leipzig: F. E. C. Leuckart, 1901–1902. [Benedictine from Beuron congregation, from very exact sources and studies.]

Montagu-Nathan, Montagu. *Glinka*. London: Constable, 1916.

————. *A History of Russian Music*. London: W. Reeves, 1914. [Few words on the time before 1800. Details on the *Nationalliste*, Rimsky-Korsakoff, Mussorgsky, etc., to beginning 1914. Not relevant.]

Mooser, Robert Aloys. *Annales de la Musique et des Musiciens en Russie au XVIIIᵉ Siècle*. Geneva: Mont-Blanc, 1948–1951. [Based on source materials from archives.]

Moresby, Emily Isabelle. *Australia Makes Music*. London: Longmans, 1948. [With short bibliography, also list of all recorded new Australian musicians.]

Morgenstern, Otto. *Das Gymnasium*. Leipzig: Quelle & Meyer, 1926, 271 pp.

Morneweck, Evelyn Foster. *Chronicles of Stephen Foster's Family*. Pittsburgh: University of Pittsburgh Press, 1944. [Prints worthwhile documents; also musical life in well-to-do farming families in Pennsylvania, published in 1917.]

Morris, Alton Chester. *Folk Songs of Florida*. Gainesville: University of Florida Press, 1950.

Morris, William Meredith. *British Violin Makers Classical and Modern*. London: R. Scott, 1920. [Many examples; no sources; based on travels to workshops of violin makers; alphabetic report on the latter.]

————. *British Violin Makers*. 2nd ed. London: R. Scott, 1920. [A biographical dictionary of British makers of stringed instruments and bows and a critical description of their work. (Probably the same work referred to above. Eds.)

Moscheles, Charlotte. *Life of Moscheles, with Selections from His Diaries and Correspondence*. London: Hurst and Blackett, 1873. [The same also exists in another edition. Amateur Series, Recent Music, and . . . as described in the diaries and correspondence of Ignatz Moscheles. Edited by his wife and adapted from the original German by A. D. Coleridge. New York: Holt, 1879.]

Moser, Andreas. *Geschichte des Violinspiels*. Berlin: M. Hesse, 1923. [The author is professor (?) at the Berlin Staatliche Hochschule für Musik. Without detailed indication of sources, but according to the preface, based on studies in libraries and archives.]

Moser, Hans Joachim. *Tönende Volksaltertümer*. Berlin: Max Hesses Verlag, 1935. [With many musical examples in the text; detailed and systematic collection.]

————. *Paul Hofhaimer, Ein Lied und Orgelmeister des Deutschen Humanismus*. Stuttgart: Colta, 1929. [More than half of the book consists of musical examples and documents.]

XX Moser, J. J. *Das deutsche Lied seit Mozart*.

Moser, Max. *Richard Wagner in der Englischen Literatur des XIX. Jahrhunderts*. Bern: A. Francke ag., 1938. [Some things, concerning Wagner and socialism, are relevant.]

Moses, Montrose Jonas, and John Mason Brown. *The American Theater as seen by its Critics, 1752 to 1934*. New York: Norton, 1934. [Collection of reviews by various critics on diverse productions.]

Mosoriak, Roy. *The Curious History of Music Boxes*. Chicago: Lightner, 1943. [Popular, often almost silly.]

XX Mostimer, P. *Der Choralgesang zur Zeit der Reformation*. Berlin: Georg Reiner, 1821. [Primarily musical; looks upon present as decadent.]

Mozart, Johann C. W. A. *The Letters of Mozart and His Family, Chronologically Arranged, Translated and Edited with an Introduction, Notes and Indices by Emily Anderson*. London: Macmillan, 1938.

Mufaddal ibn Salamah, Abu Talib. *Ancient Arabian Musical Instruments*. Trans. James Robson. Glascow: The Civic Press, 1938. [Based on original source studies. Some of it important for us.]

XA   Mühlemann, Karl. "Sonderfachschulen," in *Handbuch für das Berufs-und Fachschulwesen*, Alfred Kühne. Leipzig: Quelle & Meyer, 1929.

Müller, C. J. "Körperpflege und Musik." *Musik im Leben*, 1:97–100, 1925. [The usual, especially pro-Dalcrose.]

Müller, Georg Hermann. *Richard Wagner in der Mai-Revolution 1849*. Dresden: O. Laube, 1919. [Objective; based on memoirs.]

Müller, Gottfried. *Daniel Steibelt, sein Leben und seine Klavierwerke*. Strasbourg: Heitz, 1933.

Müller, John Henry. *The American Symphony Orchestra*. Bloomington: Indiana University Press, 1951.

Müller, John Henry, and Kate Hevner. *Trends in Musical Taste*. Bloomington: Indiana University Press, 1942.

XX   Müller, Joseph Edmund. "Jugend und Musik." *Die zweite Freusburger Singwoche*. *Musik im Leben*, 1(7–9):120–21, July-September 1925.

XX   Münnich. *Musik. Die Realschule. Im Auftrage des Zentralinstituts für Erziehung und Unterricht. Herausgegeben von Gustav Louis*. Leipzig: Quelle & Meyer, 1926.

Müry, Albert Louis Ernst. *Die Instrumentalwerke Gaetano Pugnanis; Ein Beitrag zur Erforschung der frühklassischen Instrumentalmusik*. Basel: Buckdruckerei G. Krebs, 1941.

XX   *Musik im Leben. Eine Musikpolitische Gesamtschau*. Herausgegeben von Walter Berten. Augsburg: Filser.

Mussik, F. A. *Skizzen aus dem Leben des sich in Amerika befindenden deutschen Tondichters Anton Phillip Heinrich*. Prague: Druck von G. Haase Söhne, 1843.

Myers, Rollo Hugh. *Music in the Modern World*. London: E. Arnold, 1939.

Nabokov, Nicolas. "Russian Music after the Purge." Partisan Review, 16(8):842–51, 1949.

Neel, Boyd. *The Story of an Orchestra*. London: Vox Mundi, 1950. [History of his own small orchestra.]

Nef, Karl. *Geschichte der Sinfonie und Suite*. Leipzig: Breitkopf & Härtel, 1921. [Has many musical illustrations, but also at the beginning only within the particular sections, which do *not* bear chapter numbers. Data on special literature and occasionally also on editions.]

XX   Nenninger, Rudolf. "Die Musik und unser Bund," in *Das Gothabuch des Bundes deutscher Jugendvereine*, Walter Kabbe, ed. Sollstedt: Buchverlag des B.D.J., n.d.

Nest'ev, Izrail' Vladimirovich. *Sergei Prokofiev, His Musical Life*. New York: Knopf, 1946.

Nettel, Reginald. *The Orchestra in England, A Social History*. London: J. Cape, 1946.

Nettl, Paul. "Zur Geschichte der kaiserlichen Hofmusikkapelle 1636–1680," in *Studien zur Musikwissenschaft. Gesellschaft zur Herausgabe von Denkmälern der Tonkunst in Österreich*, vols. 16–19. Vienna: 1929–1932.

Neumann, Werner. *J. S. Bachs Chorfuge. Schriftenreihe des staatlichen Instituts für Deutsche Musikforschung*, vol. 4. Leipzig: Kistner & Siegel, 1938, 30 pp. [Only very little is usable.]

Neupert, Hans. *Das Cembalo, Eine geschichtliche und technische Betrachtung der Kielinstrumente.* Kassel: Bärenreiter-Verlag, 1933. [Knowledgeable on the subject, without much documentation.]

Newman, Ernest. *The Life of Richard Wagner.* New York: Knopf, 1933.

———. *Facts and Fictions about Wagner.* New York: Knopf, 1931. [Chiefly against Hurn and Ruth; defends Cosima; also against Turner, in whom he proves contradictions, and likewise against Fink, in whom he proves chronological contradictions.]

Newmarch Rosa Harriet. *Jean Sibelius.* Boston: C. C. Birchard Co., 1939. [Chiefly analysis of his symphonies.]

Nicholson, Sydney Hugo. *Quires and Places Where They Sing.* London: G. Bell and Sons, 1932. [Few sources; largely practical; some things usable; Episcopalian.]

Nicolais, Otto. *Tagebücher nebst biographischen Ergänzungen.* Leipzig: Breitkopf & Härtel, 1892, 166 pp. [Only some things usable; accurate edition.]

Nicoll, Allardyce. Stuart Masques and the Renaissance Stage. London. Harrap, 1937, 223 pp. [Based on special sources, which are quoted.]

Niedecken, Hans. *Jean Georges Noverre, (1727–1810); Sein Leben und seine Beziehung zur Musik.* Halle a.d.s., 1914. [Based on sources.]

Niemann, Walter. *Die Virginalmusik.* Leipzig: Breitkopf & Härtel, 1919. [Always without indication of sources; many historical details.]

———. *Die Musik Skandinaviens.* Leipzig: Breitkopf & Härtel, 1906. [On the whole indifferent. Stories of performances, virtuosos, playing of continental music, etc.]

XA Niessen, Carl. "Das Theaterwesen," in *Köln als Stätte der Bildung,* Joseph Theele and Adam Wrede. Cologne: Gonski, 1922.

Nissen, Frau Constance Maria. *Briefe, Aufzeichnungen, Dokumente, 1782–1842, im Auftrage des Mozarteums zu Salzburg mit einem biographischen Essay hrsg. von Arthur Schurig.* Dresden: Opal-Verlag, 1922. [Particularly important the correspondence with Breitkopf & Härtel.]

Noli, Bishop Fan Stylian. *Beethoven and the French Revolution.* New York: International Universities Press, 1947.

Nordin, Dayton W. *The Choirmaster's Workbook.* Rock Island, Ill.: Augustana Book Concern, 1947.

North, Louise McCoy. *The Psalms and Hymns of Protestantism from the Sixteenth to the Nineteenth Century.* Madison, N.J.: The Universiy, 1936. [Very short but good. Coherent with full illustrations. In the library of Drew University.]

Northcote, Sydney. *The Songs of Henri Duparc.* London: D. Dobson, 1949.

Nowak, Leopold. *Joseph Haydn: Leben, Bedeutung und Werke.* Zurich: Amalthea-Verlag, 1951.

———. "Das deutsche Gesellschaftslied in Österreich von 1480 bis 1550," in *Studien aur Musikwissenschaft. Gesellschaft zur Herausgabe von Denkmälern der Tonkunst in Österreich,* vol. 17. Vienna, 1930.

XA Nowothy, Gerhard, and Carl Hannemann. "Volksmusikalische Abende," in *Music im Volk,* Wolfgang Stumme. Berlin: C. F. Vieweg, 1939.

Obreschkoff, Khristo. *Das Bulgarische Volkslied.* Berner Veröffentlichungen zur Musikforschung, no. 9. Bern: Haupt, 1937, 106 pp. [Especially important Part I, pp. 15–16, because of attitude of church fathers to folksongs. Based on sources.]

Odell, Mary Theresa. *More About the Old Theatre Worthing.* Worthing, Sussex: Published under the Worthing Art Development Scheme by Aldridge Bros., 1945. [History of a local theater with some pictures of the one barn theater.]

———. *The Old Theatre, Worthing: The Theatre Royal, 1807–1855.* Aylesbury: G. W. Jones, under the Worthing Art Development Scheme, 1938. [History of a local theater.]

Odum, Howard Washingon. *Negro Workaday Songs.* London: Oxford University Press, H. Milford, 1926.

———. *The Negro and His Songs.* Chapel Hill: University of North Carolina Press, 1925.

XX O'Keeffe, J. C., and A. O'Brien. *A Handbook of Irish Dances.* Dublin: O'Donoghue & Co., n.d. [Short, panegyrical, practical learning; some things relevant concerning sources.]

Oliver, Alfred Richard. *The Encyclopedists as Critics of Music.* New York: Columbia University Press, 1947.

Olrik, Axel. *A Book of Danish Ballads.* Princeton: Princeton University Press, 1939. [Derives from Grundeg's impulse for collecting.]

Opieński, Henryk, and G. Koeckert. *La Musique Polonaise.* Paris: C. Crès, 1918. [Luxury edition, biased for Poland. No indication of sources.]

Osgood, Henry Osborne. *So This Is Jazz!* Boston: Little, Brown, 1926. [Very journalistic, many details concerning instruments. But on the whole, little that is not known.]

Österley, W. O. E. "Music of the Hebrews," in *The Oxford History of Music,* introductory volume, Percy C. Buck, ed. London: Oxford University Press, 1929.

Osthoff, Helmuth. *Adam Krieger (1634–1666), Neue Beiträge zur Geschichte des deutschen Liedes im 17. Jahrhundert.* Leipzig: Breitkopf & Härtel, 1929. [Sources lacking.]

———. *Der Lautenist Santino Garsi da Parma.* Leipzig: Breitkopf & Härtel, 1926. [Based on manuscripts.]

Ottzen, Curt. *Telemann als Opernkomponist.* Berlin: E. Ebering, 1902.

Paderewski, Ignacy Jan. *The Paderewski Memoirs.* New York: Scribner, 1938.

Pallat, Ludwig, and Franz Hilker. *Körperschulung Künstlerische.* Breslau: Ferdinand Hirt, 1925, 168 pp.

Panassié, Hugues. *Hot Jazz: The Guide to Swing Music.* New York: M. Witmark & Sons, 1934.

Panov, Petŭr. *Militärmusik in Geschichte und Gegenwart.* Berlin: K. Siegismund, 1938. [Without indication of sources. But on new developments prints regulations, etc. National Socialist, his thinking strongly Hitlerian. No numbering of the chapters.]

Panum, Hortense. *The Stringed Instruments of the Middle Ages.* London: W. Reeves, 1939? [With many illustrations, analysis of monuments; not many references to sources, e.g., inexact quoting of Leges Wallicae, etc.]

Parry, Charles Hubert Hastings. *The Music of the Seventeenth Century.* London: Oxford University Press, 1938. [Pp. 337–357, details concerning violin concerto.]

XX Party, Otto. "Wandertheater." *Freie Bildung,* 1(2), 1919.

Pastene, Jerome. *Three Quarter Time: The Life and Music of the Strauss Family of Vienna.* New York: Abeland Press, 1951.

Pastor, Willy. *The Music of Primitive Peoples.* Washington, D.C.: Annual Report of the Smithsonian Institution, 1912.

Patrick, Millar. *Four Centuries of Scottish Psalmody.* London: Oxford University Press, 1949. [History of the psalters, criticism of the present one, suggestions for changes.]

Pattison, Bruce. *Music and Poetry of the English Renaissance.* London: Methuen, 1948.

Paul, Oskar. *Geschichte des Claviers vom Ursprunge bis zu den modernsten Formen dieses Instruments nebst einer Übersicht über die musikalische Abtheilung der Pariser Weltausstellung im Jahr 1867.* Leipzig: A. H. Payne, 1868. [No bibliography, almost exclusively a purely technically-considered history of the construction of the instrument.]

Pearce, Charles William. *The Priest's Part of the Anglican Liturgy.* London: Church Music Monographs, no. 6, 1922. [Author at the Trinity College of Music; popular, many music examples.]

XX Peirce, Rev. "A Treatise on Church Music," in *Übereinstimmung mit Dissentus für Erhaltung des Alters.* London, 1786. [Very short; against introduction of instruments at services; based on the Bible.]

Pereira de Mello, Guilherme Theodoro. *A Musica no Brasil desde os Tempos Coloniaes até o Primeiro decenio da Republica.* Bahia: Typ. de S. Joaquim, 1908. [The author himself a musician. Enumeration, without much analysis or indication of sources.]

Pereira Salas, Eugenio. *Notes on the History of Music Exchange between the Americas before 1940.* Washington, D.C.: Music Division, Pan American Union. 1943.

Perger, Richard von, and Robert Hirschfeld. *Geschichte der K. K. Gesellschaft der Musikfreunde in Wien.* Vienna: Kaiserlich-Königliche Gessellschaft der Musikfreunde, 1913. [Chronological, panegyrical, ruses of the instructors, students, performances. Of interest concerning the changed interest in instruments, composers, etc.]

Petitpierre, Jacques. *The Romance of the Mendelssohns.* London: D. Dobson, 1947.

Pfäfflin, Clara. *Pietro Nardini, Seine Werke und Sein Leben: Ein Beitrag zur Erforschung vorklassischer Instrumentalmusik.* Plieningen: Druck von F. Find Söhne, 1935. [Hause as *Referent.* Based on sources.]

XX Pfleiderer, Wolfgang. *Unser Heutiges Musikleben in Musikerziehung.* Kassel: Bärenreiter-Verlag, 1929.

XX *Philharmonic Symphony Faces.* For subscribers and radio members. New York: Philharmonic Symphony Society of New York, 1937–1938 season. [Photographs with biography.]

Phillips, Charles Joseph MacConaghy. *Paderewski, The Story of a Modern Immortal.* New York: Macmillan, 1934.

Phillips, William J. *Carols: Their Origin, Music and Connection with Mystery Plays.* London: Routledge; New York: Dutton, 1921. [Popular, no source references, prints many carols.]

Pickard-Cambridge, Arthur Wallace. *The Theatre of Dionysus in Athens.* Oxford: Clarendon Press, 1946, 288 pp. [Mostly history of construction, nothing on the sociological position of actor and spectators. Only one article is relevant.]

Pierik, Marie. *The Spirit of Gregorian Chant.* Boston: McLaughlin and Reilly, 1939. [Popular, Catholic; no bibliography. Occasionally reference to official literature, etc.]

Piersig, Fritz. *Die Einführung des Hornes in die Kunstmusik und Seine Verwendung bis zum Tode Johann Sebastian Bachs.* Halle: A. S. M. Niemeyer, 1927. [On p. 2 appear the *"Berichterstatter,"* thus apparently a doctoral dissertation. The university not indicated. Refers to F. L. Schubert, *Die Blechinstrumente in der Musik,* 2nd ed., Leipzig, 1883.]

Pinthus, Gerhard. *Das Konzertleben in Deutschland, Ein Abriss seiner Entwicklung bis zum Beginn des 15. Jahrhunderts.* Strasbourg: Heitz, 1932. [Literary, excellent; based on Tönnies; truly sociological. With bibliography; often secondhand quotations.]

Pirro, André. *La Musique à Paris Sous le Règne de Charles VI.* Strasbourg: Heitz, 1930. [Refers to source materials, important for music in the home.]

Poladian, Sirvart. *Armenian Folk Songs.* Berkeley: University of California Press, 1942. [Collected by Prestus Comitas Vartabed between 1890 and 1914 in villages towards border of Caucasia, p. 1.]

Pougin, Arthur. *Le Violin, les Violinistes et la Musique de Violin du XVIe au XVIIIe Siècle.* Paris: Fischbacher, 1924. [No direct source references; rich bibliography; much is secondhand, but sometimes something is firsthand; catalogues of collections.]

―――. *The Music of India.* London: Oxford University Press, 1921. [On intervals, etc. Also Dravidic music.]

―――. *Marie Malibran: The Story of a Great Singer.* London: F. Nash, 1911. [Narrative, but worthwhile documents in the appendix, also some letters in the text.]

―――. *Essai Historique sur la Musique en Russie.* Paris: Fischbacher, 1904. [On Middle Ages, National School, cadet, about 1900. Survey of composers, virtuosos, conservatories.]

Powell, Dora M. *Edward Elgar: Memories of a Variation.* London: Oxford University Press, 1937.

Pratt, Waldo Selden. *The Music of the Pilgrims.* Boston: Oliver Ditson, 1921. [With detailed musical examples.]

Pretzsch, Paul. *Die Kunst Siegfried Wagners: Ein Führer durch seine Werke.* Leipzig: Breitkopf & Härtel, 1919. [Detailed; especially musical analysis, but also texts.]

Preussner, Eberhard. *Die bürgerliche Musikkultur.* Hamburg: Hanseatische Verlagsanstalt, 1935.

XX Preussner, Eberhard. "Musikpolitische Zeitschau." *Deutsche Tonkünstler Zeitung,* **27** (23), December 5, 1929.

Prod'homme, Jacques Gabriel. *L'Opéra (1669–1925).* Paris: Delagrave, 1925. [History of founding. Not relevant.]

Prüfer, Arthur. *Das Werk von Bayreuth.* Leipzig: Siegel's Musikalienhandlung (R. Linnemann), 1909. [A completely rewritten and considerably augmented edition of the *Vorträge der Bühnenfestspiele in Bayreuth.* Pro-Wagner, Germany, etc.]

Prunières, Hènry. *Le Ballet de Cour en France avant Benserade et Lully.* Paris: H. Laurens, 1914. [Based on accurate contemporary sources.]

Puttkammer, Albert von. *50 Jahre Bayreuth.* Berlin: Schlieffen-Verlag, 1927, 192 pp.

Quatrelles L'Epine, Maurice. *Chérubini (1760–1842), Notes et Documents Inédits.* Paris: Fischbacher, 1913. [Especially diaries, notes, bills, etc.]

Quelline, Narcisse. *Chansons et Danses des Bretons.* Paris: J. Maisonneuve et C. Leclerc, 1889. [Government-ordered, collected tunes in Breton Language.]

Raabe, Peter. "Kulturwille im Deutschen Musikleben," in *Kulturpolitische Reden und Aufsätze*, vol. 2, Regensburg: Bosse, 1936.

———. "Die Musik im Dritten Reich," in *Kulturpolitische Reden und Aufsätze*. Regensburg: Bosse, 1935, p. 93.

Rachmaninoff, Sergei. *Rachmaninoff's Recollections, Told to Oscar von Riesemann*. London: Allen & Unwin, 1934.

Ram Gopal and Sarosh Dādāchānjī. *Indian Dancing*. London: Phoenix House, 1951, 119 pp.

Ramsey, Frederic, and Smith, Charles Edward. *Jazzmen*. New York: Harcourt, Brace, 1939. [Many biographies, some things on slavery period.]

Ramuz, Charles Ferdinand. *Souvenirs sur Igor Strawinsky*. Paris: Gallimard, Editions de la Nouvelle Revue Française, 1929.

Rau, Carl August. *Loretto Vittori: Beiträge zur historischen-kritischen Würdigung seines Lebens*. Munich: Verlag für Moderne Musik, 1916. [Froyer and Vossler as Referenten. Important on Papal music, castrates, and falsetto singing.]

Ravel, Maurice. *Maurice Ravel par Quelques-Uns de Ses Familiers*. Paris: Editions du Tambourinaire, 1939. [Many collaborators.]

Rayner, Robert Macey. *Wagner and die Meistersinger*. London: Oxford University Press, 1940. [Matter-of-fact, usable.]

Rearick, Elizabeth Charlotte. *Dances of the Hungarians*. New York: Teachers College Press, 1939. [Based on Hungarian sources, with musical examples and drawings. Important on Gypsies, military recruitment dances, etc. Winds up with recommendation of folk dancers.]

Redway, Virginia Larkin. *Music Directory of Early New York City*. New York: New York Public Library, 1941. [An important short introduction; the rest chiefly addresses. Painstakingly collected.]

Reed, Edward Bliss. *Christmas Carols printed in the Sixteenth Century*. Cambridge: Harvard University Press, 1932. [With many references to new printings of old carols.]

Reed, William Henry. *Elgar*. London: Dent; New York: Dutton, 1939.

———. *Elgar as I Knew Him*. London: V. Gollancz, 1936. [Anecdotal, not relevant.]

Reese, Gustave. *Music in the Middle Ages, with an Introduction on the Music of Ancient Times*. New York: Norton, 1940. [With lots of details, bibliographies, and accurate quotations.]

Rehm, Hermann Siegfried. *Das Buch der Marionetten*. Berlin: E. Frensdorff, 1905. [Some of it important.]

Reichenburg, Louisette Eugénie. *Contribution à L'Histoire de la "Querelle des Bouffons."* Philadelphia, 1937. [With many sources, but not relevant for us.]

Reichwein, Leopold. *Bayreuth: Werden und Wesen der Bayreuther Bühnenfestspiele*. Bielefeld: Velhagen & Klasing, 1934. [Wagnerian and Hitlerian. Dedicated to Goebbels.]

XA   Rein, Walter. "Wende," in *Der Wegwart*, Arnold Eberhard, Adolf Braun, and Gertrud Dalgas. Wolfenbüttel, 1926–1928.

Reinach, Theodore. *La Musique Grecque*. Paris: Payot, 1926.

XX   Reisch, Erich. "Gefahren des Rundfunks." *Blätter der Volkshochschule Breslau*, 6, 1927–1928.

XX Remmert, Otto. *Von Festen und Feiern im Kinderdorf.* Staumühle: Selbstverlag Kindersdorf Staumühle, n.d.

Renton, Edward. *The Vaudeville Theater, Building, Operation, Management.* New York: Gotham Press, 1918. [Wholly practical; technical instructions concerning advertising, uniforms of musicians, etc.]

Rentzow, Hans. *Die Mecklenburgischen Liederkomponisten des 18. Jahrhunderts.* Hannover: A. Nagel, 1938. [Some of it important.]

XX Resch, Johannes. "Von der Gemeinschaft als Grundlage der Kommenden Schaubühne." *Junge Menschen,* 6(2), February 1925.

XX ———. "Der Tag des Proletariats." *Kommunistisches Sonderheft der Zeitschrift "Die Tat,"* 15, 1923

XX *Retrospect. The Philharmonic Society of New York and Its Seventy-fifth Anniversary.* New York, 1917. [Anonymous, popular, retrospective. Detailed list of everything that has ever been played there.]

Ribera y Tarragó, Julian. *La Música Andaluza Medieval en las Canciones de Trovadores.* Madrid: Tip. de la "Revista de Archivos," 1923–1925. [With detailed documentation down to *Jenaer Liederhandschrift.*]

Rice, William Gorham. *The Carillon in Literature.* New York: J. Lane, 1916. [All kinds of romantic sentimental descriptions, but very accurate knowledge of *Beffroy.*]

Richter, Raoul Hermann Michael. *Kunst und Philosophie bei Richard Wagner.* Leipzig: Quelle & Meyer, 1906.

Riedinger, Lothar. "Karl von Dittersdorf als Opernkomponist," in *Studien zur Musikwissenschaft. Gesellschaft zur Herausgabe von Denkmälern der Tonkunst in Österreich,* vol. 2. Vienna, 1914.

Riemann, Hugo. *Studien zur Byzantinischen Musik.* Leipzig: Breitkopf & Härtel, 1915, 17 pp. [Purly of reference to study of notation.]

———. *Die Byzantinische Notenschrift im 10. bis 15. Jahrhundert.* Leipzig: Breitkopf & Härtel, 1909.

Riemenschneider, Albert. *Some Aspects of the Use of the Flutes in the Sacred Choral and Vocal Works of Johann Sebastian Bach.* Washington, D.C.: Musical Division, Dayton C. Miller Fund, Library of Congress, 1950.

Riesemann, Oskar von. *Monographien zur Russischen Musik.* Munich: Drei Masken Verlag, 1923–   [Very much detail, going back very far. Greek Orthodox, Peter the Great, etc. But usually without source references.]

Riess, Karl. *Musikgeschichte der Stadt Eger im 16. Jahrhundert.* Brünn: R. M. Rohrer, 1935. [Criticism of sources, a few things usable.]

Rimskiĭ-Korsakov, Nikolaĭ Andreevich. *My Musical Life.* New York: Knopf, 1942.

Rittelmeyer, F. "Musik und Kultus in der Christengemeinschaft." *Tonkünstler-Zeitung,* 29:21, 1931.

Ritter, Frédéric Louis. *Music in America.* New York: Scribner, 1883. [Mostly secondhand sources; prints some records; popular, not very important.]

Ritter, Frédéric Louis. *Music in England.* New York: Scribner, 1883. [Same note as above.]

Robert, Grace. *The Borzoi Book of Ballets.* New York: Knopf, 1946. [Alphabetic listing of the particular ballets.]

Roberts, Helen Heffron. *Form in Primitive Music: An Analytical and Comparative Study of the Melodic Form of Some Ancient Southern California Indian Songs.* New York: American Library of Musicology, Norton, 1933. [With example of the Pantavoniks.]

Robertson, Alec. *Dvořák.* London: Dent, 1945.

Robinson, Geroid Tanquary. *Rural Russia under the Old Regime: A History of the Landlord-Peasant World and a Prologue to the Peasant Revolution of 1917.* London: Longmans, 1932.

Röckl, Sebastian. *Ludwig the II. und Richard Wagner,* vols. 1 and 2. Munich: Beck, 1913–1920. [Prints very much material.]

Roedemeyer, Friedrich Karl. *Vom Wesen des Sprech-Chores.* Augsburg: Bärenreiter-Verlag, 1926, 112 pp.

Roeder, Martin. *Über den Stand der Öffentlichen Musikpflege in Italien. in Sammlung Musikalischer Vorträge; Herausgegeben von Paul Graf Waldersee.* Leipzig, 1881. [Much is usable.]

XX   Roeseling, Kaspar. *Beiträge zur Untersuchung der Grundhaltung romantischer Melodik.* Dissertation Köln, 1928. Oberassel Düppen, 1928.

Rohrer, Gertrude Martin. *Music and Musicians of Pennsylvania.* Philadelphia: Theodore Presser Co., 1940. [Many individual articles; some of its usable.]

Roig, Gonzalo. *Apuntes Históricos sobre Nuestras Bandas Militares y Orquestas.* Havana: Molina y Compañía, 1936.

XX   Roland, Manuel. *Maurice Ravel.* London: Dennis Dobson, 1957.

Rolland, Romain. *Goethe and Beethoven.* New York: Harper, 1931.

———. *A Musical Tour Through the Land of the Past.* New York: Holt, 1927.

———. *Händel.* London: K. Paul, Trench, Trubner & Co., 1916.

———. *Musicians of Today.* New York: Holt, 1915. [Mostly former periodical articles and reviews.]

———. *Some Musicians of Former Days.* New York: Holt, 1915.

Roller, Alfred. *Die Bildnisse von Gustav Mahler.* Leipzig: Tal, 1922.

Rossat, Arthur. *La Chanson Populaire dans la Suisse Romande.* Basel: Société Suisse de Traditions Populaires, 1917. [On basis of detailed results. Much material on relationship to France, content, etc.]

Rothe, Hans. *Max Reinhardt: 25 Jahre Deutsches Theater.* Munich: R. Piper, 1930. [Panegyrical, but written with knowledge.]

Rubio, Piqueras Felipe. *Música y Músicos Toledanos.* Toledo: Sucs. de J. Pelayo, 1923. [In particular, among other things, on continuation of Gothic church music under Arab rule. Refers to printed sources of the eighteenth century.]

Ruelle, Charles Emile. *Le Congrès Européen d'Arezzo pour l'Etude et l'Amélioration du chant liturgique.* Paris: F. Didot, 1884. [With short bibliography.]

Ruggles, Eleanor. *Prince of Players: Edwin Booth.* London: Peter Davies; New York: Norton, 1953.

Rühlemann, Martin. *Etymologie des Wortes Harlequin und verwandter Wörter.* Dissertation Halle, 1912, 112 pp.

XX   *Rundfunkjahrbuch. Herausgegeben von der Reichsrundfunkgesellschaft.*

XX *Rundfunk und Volksbildung. Tagung des Berliner Ausschusses der Schmutz und Schundliteratur und des Unwesens im Kino am Fünfzehnten und Sechszehnten.* October 1926. [No indication of place of publication and publisher.]

Runge, Paul. *Die Lieder und Melodien der Geissler des Jahres 1349 Nach der Aufzeichnung Hugos von Reuteingen.* Leipzig Breitkopf & Härtel, 1900. [With many details on rules of citation; e.g., knee-bending when singing the songs.]

Rupp, Emile. *Die Entwicklungsgeschichte der Orgelbaukunst.* Einsiedeln: Benziger, 1929. [The author himself an organist of the classical school.]

Rützow, Sophie. *Richard Wagner und Bayreuth.* Munich: Knorr & Hirth, 1943. [Journalistic, based on interviews of contemporaries who were still living.]

Saam, Joseph. *Zur Geschichte des Klavierquartetts bis in die Romantik.* Strasbourg: Heitz, 1933.

Sabaneev, Leonid Leonidovich. *Modern Russian Composers.* New York: International Publishers, 1927.

———. *Geschichte der Russischen Musik.* Leipzig: Breitkopf & Härtel, 1926. [Goes back far, Tartars, also recognizes problem of influence; wholly modern, operates with classes, very important.]

Sachs, Curt. *The Rise of Music in the Ancient World East and West.* New York: Norton, 1943.

———. *The History of Musical Instruments.* New York: Norton, 1940.

———. *Les Instruments de Musique de Madagascar.* Paris: Institut d'Ethnologie, 1938. [Based on materials of the Trocadéro museums. Knowledge of the same museums and their literature. Bibliography; primarily on musical instruments.]

———. "Die Musik der Antike," in *Handbuch der Musikwissenschaft,* Ernst Bücken. Lfg. 19. Wildpark: Athenaion, 1928, 34 pp.

———. *Der Ursprung der Saiteninstrumente.* St. Gabriel-Mödling, 1928?

———. *Musik des Altertums.* Breslau: Ferdinand Hirt, 1924, 96 pp. [A short survey.]

———. *Die Musikinstrumente des alten Ägyptens. Mitteilungen aus der ägyptischen Sammlung der Staatlichen Museen zu Berlin,* vol. 3. Berlin: K. Curtius, 1921, 92 pp.

XX ———. "Altägyptische Musikinstrumente." *Der alte Orient,* 21(3–4), 1920.

———. "Die Musikinstrumente der Minneregel." *Sammelbände der internationalen Musikgesellschaft,* 14:484–486, 1912–1913. [Linguistic interpretation of a *Minneregel* completed in 1404 by a Westphalian; details on instruments.]

———. *Musik und Oper am Kurbrandenburgischen Hof.* Berlin: J. Bard, 1910, 299 pp.

———. *Musikgeschichte der Stadt Berlin bis zum Jahre 1800.* Berlin: Gebr. Paetel, 1908, 325 pp.

Saint-Victor, Adam de. *Les Proses d'Adam de Saint Victor.* Paris: Welter, 1900.

Salas Viu, Vicente. *Músicos Modernos de Chile.* Washington, D.C.: Music Division, Pan American Union, 1944.

Salazar, Adolfo. *La Música en la Sociedad Europea.* Mexico El Colegio de México 1942–

———. *La Música Contempoánea en España.* Madrid: Ediciones La Nave, 1930. [Individual composers, etc.]

XX Salvidar, Gabriel. *Historia de la Música en México.* Publicationes del Departamento de Bellos Artes. Mexico, 1934. [With very detailed bibliography on all branches of Latin American music; with detailed reference to Aztec codices.]

Sanborn, Pitts. *The Metropolitan Book of the Opera.* New York: Simon and Schuster, 1937. [Contents of the operas performed with biographic sketch of the composers. Indifferent. Important only the introduction by Edward Johnson, which includes a short history of the Metropolitan Opera and the language of musical performance employed there, etc.]

Saminsky, Lazare. *Music of Our Day.* New York: Crowell, 1932. [Contains, among others, New Russians and their alma maters.]

———. *Consideraciones sobre la Música Cubano.* Havana: Academia Nacional de Artes y Letras, 1936, 20 pp. [—Schwartzen, traced back to Indian rhythm on Cuba. Spanish tunes, some things relevant.]

Sanchez de Fuentes, Eduardo. *Viejos Ritmos Cubanos.* Havana: Academia Nacional de Artes y Letras, 1937, 34 pp. [Some things relevant.]

Sand, Maurice. *The History of the Harlequinade.* London: M. Secker, 1915.

Sandberger, Adolf. *Beiträge zur Geschichte der bayerischen Hof-Kapelle unter Orlando di Lasso.* Leipzig: Breitkopf & Härtel, 1894. [Prints many documents for the first time, accounts of the Bavarian Court Comptroller's Office, for which old sources are used. Very specialized archive studies on origin of many musical pieces. Some things relevant.]

Sargeant, Winthrop. *Jazz, Hot and Hybrid.* New York: Arrow Editions, 1938. [Some of it usable.]

Sauerlandt, Max. *Die Musik in Fünf Jahrhunderten der Europäischen Malerei.* Königsstein-im-Taunus: K. R. Langewiesche, 1922. [Almost exclusively pictures, with eight pages introductory texts; not much that is not known.]

Sayler, Oliver Martin. *Our American Theater.* New York: Brentano's, 1923. [Only problems of the present, almost wholly on dramatic plays.]

Scarborough, Dorothy. *A Song Catcher in Southern Mountains.* New York: Columbia University Press, 1937.

Schaeffner, André. *Origine des Instruments de Musique.* Paris: Payot, 1936. [Based on Marcel Mauss, among others.]

———. *Strawinsky.* Paris: Rieder, 1931.

Schauffler, Robert Haven. *Music as a Social Force in America.* New York: The Caxton Institute, 1927.

Schemann, Ludwig. *Meine Erinnerungen an Richard Wagner.* Stuttgart: F. Frommanns Verlag, (E. Hauff), 1902. [Short, racist, anti-Semitic.]

XA Schenk, Johann Baptist. "Autobiographische Skizze," in *Studien zur Musikwissenschaft. Gesellschaft zur Herausgabe von Denkmälern der Tonkunst in Österreich.* Vienna: 1913–1934.

Schering, Arnold. *Geschichte des Instrumentalkonzerts.* Leipzig: Breitkopf & Härtel, 1927.

———. *Die Niederländische Orgelmesse im Zeitalter des Josguin.* Leipzig: Breitkopf & Härtel, 1912. [Based on studies of the new editions of sources. Usable.]

———. *Geschichte des Oratoriums.* Leipzig: Breitkopf & Härtel, 1911.

Scheuer, Oskar F. *Richard Wagner als Student.* Vienna: Neuer Akademischer Verlag, 1920.

Schick, Joseph Schlueter. *The Early Theater in Eastern Iowa: Cultural Beginnings and the Rise of the Theater in Davenport and Eastern Iowa, 1836 to 1863.* Chicago: University of Chicago Press, 1939.

Schiedermair, Ludwig Ferdinand. *Die Gestaltung weltanschaulicher Ideen in der Vokalmusik Beethovens.* Veröffentlichungen des Beethovenhauses in Bonn, no. 10. Leipzig: Quelle & Meyer, 1934, 56 pp.

———. *Beethovens Beiträge zum Leben und Schaffen nach Dokumenten des Beethovenhauses.* Leipzig: Quelle & Meyer, 1930.

———. "Die Oper an den badischen Höfen des 17. und 18. Jahrhunderts." *Sammelbände der internationalen Musikgesellschaft,* 14:191–207, 369–449, 510–550, 1912–1913. [Usable.]

———. "Die Blütezeit der Öttingen-Wallerstein'schen Hofkapelle." *Sammelbände der internationalen Musikgesellschaft,* 9:83–130, 1907–1908. [Many details usable.]

XX Schieffelin, Samuel B. *Music in Our Churches. A Letter to the Elder of the Reformed Church.* New York: Board of Publication of the Reformed Churches in America, 1881. [Short, without material. It is against God's, etc.]

Schiffer, Lei. *Johann Ladislaus Dussek, Seine Sonaten und Seine Konzerte.* Borna: Druck von R. Noske, 1914. [First part biography, somewhat usable.]

Schild, Emilie. *Geschichte der Protestantischen Messenkomposition im 17. und 18. Jahrhundert.* Wuppertal: Gedruckt bei F. W. Köhler, g.m.b.h., 1934.

Schindler, Kurt. *Folkmusic and Poetry of Spain and Portugal.* New York: Hispanic Institute in the United States, 1941.

Schletterer, Hans Michel. *Studien zur Geschichte der Französischen Musik.* Berlin: R. Damköhler, 1884–1885. [With much material of contributions, very usable. Order.]

———. *Die Entstehung der Oper.* Nördlingen: C. H. Beck, 1873. [Apparently a musician by profession. Not relevant.]

XX Schmidt, Görg. *Nicolaus Gambert, Kapellmeister Kaiser Karl V. Leben und Werk.* Bonn: Ludwig Röhrscheid, 1938.

Schmidt, Hans Georg. *Das Männerchorlied Franz Schuberts.* Hildburghausen: Gadow, 1931, 84 pp. [Very important because of introduction Nageli and Zelter and the various social backgrounds and bases.]

Schmidt, Heinrich. *Johann Mattheson, Ein Förderer der Deutschen Tonkunst im Lichte Seiner Werke.* Leipzig: Breitkopf & Härtel, 1897. [With many musical appendixes; not much is said about his other sources.]

Schmidt, Heinrich, and Ulrich Hartmann. *Richard Wagner in Bayreuth.* Leipzig: C. Klinner (H. Kittenberg), 1909. [Anecdotal, some things on instruments usable.]

Schmidt, Joseph. *Unbekannte Manuskripte zu Beethovens Weltlicher und Geistlicher Gesangsmusik.* Leipzig: Quelle & Meyer, 1928.

Schmitz, Eugen. *Geschichte der Kantate und des Geistlichen Konzerts.* Leipzig: Breitkopf & Härtel, 1914–

Schneider, Constantin. *Geschichte der Musik in Salzburg von der Ältesten Zeit bis zur Gegenwart.* Salzburg: R. Kiesel, 1935.

————. "Die Oratorien und Schuldramen Anton Cajetan Adlgassers," in *Studien zur Musikwissenschaft. Gesellschaft zur Herausgabe von Denkmälern der Tonkunst in Österreich*, vol. 18. Vienna, 1929.

Schneider, Louis. *Das Französische Volkslied*. Berlin: Marquardt, 1908. [Popular, based on Tisserant. Drinking songs, pp. 76–92; songs of spinning and sewing women, p. 72. Influence of folksong on modern composers, p. 113 ff., etc.]

Schneider, Marius. *Geschichte der Mehrstimmigkeit: historische und phänomenologische Studien*. Berlin: J. Bard, 1934–

XX Schoen, Egmont. *Die Guitarre und ihre Geschichte. Ein Vortrag gehalten im Leipziger Guitarren-Club*. Leipzig: C. A. Klemm, 1879. [Philosophic studies. Short, panegyrical for his *Verein*.]

Scholes, Percy Alfred. *The Puritans and Music in England and New England*. London: Oxford University Press, H. Milford, 1934.

Schönberg, Jakob. *Die traditionellen Gesänge des Israelitischen Gottesdienstes in Deutschland*. Dissertation Erlangen, 1926, 26 pp. [Still to be looked through.]

XX Schönlak, Bruno. "Schafft Sprechchöre." *Junge Menschen*, 6(2), February 1925.

Schopenhauer, Arthur. *Schriften über Musik, Im Rahmen seiner Aesthetik herausgegeben von Karl Stabenow*. Regensburg: G. Bosse, 1924. [With excerpts and source references from Griesebach's Reclam edition and from the edition of posthumous papers, also by Griesebach at Reclam.]

Schrade, Leo. *Monteverdi, Creator of Modern Music*. New York: Norton, 1950. [On the whole not much that is not known.]

Schramm, Willi. *Johannes Brahms in Detmold*. Leipzig: Kistner & Siegel, 1933, 64 pp.

Schröder, Fritz. *Bernhard Molique und Seine Instrumentalkompositionen*. Stuttgart: Berthold und Schwerdtner, 1923. [Some things relevant on the nineteenth century; also London concerts.]

Schroeder, Leopold von. *Die Vollendung des Arischen Mysteriums in Bayreuth*. Munich: J. F. Lehmann, 1911. [Shows that everything was already there in old (*uralten*) Aryan myths, including the Grail-Parzifal.]

Schubert, Karl. *Spontinis Italienische Schule*. Strasbourg: Heitz, 1932.

Schullian, Dorothy May, and Max Schoen. *Music and Medicine*. New York: Schumann, 1948. [Many collaborators, exact bibliography, some things important.]

Schumann, Eugenie. *Memoirs*. Trans. Marie Busch. London: Heinemann, 1927. [Apparently by very old woman. Also details on the three brothers who either turned mad or morphinist or died early. Apparently an attempt to spread legend on the two.]

Schumann, Robert Alexander. *The Letters of Robert Schumann*. Selected and edited by Dr. Karl Storck, trans. Hannah Bryant. London: J. Murray, 1907.

Schünemann, Georg. *Geschichte der Deutschen Schulmusik*. Leipzig: Kistner & Siegel, 1928. [Very short. Youth movement.]

Schur, Gustav. *Erinnerungen an Hugo Wolf*. Regensburg: G. Bosse, 1922.

Schuré, Edouard. *Erinnerungen an Richard Wagner*. Leipzig: Breitkopf & Härtel, 1900. [Anecdotal.]

Schütz, Heinrich. *Gesammelte Briefe und Schriften, Herausgegeben im Auftrag der Heinrich-Schütz Gesellschaft*. Regensburg: G. Bosse, 1931.

Schweitzer, Albert. *J. S. Bach*. New York: Macmillan, 1950. [Bibliography.]

Séchan, Louis. *La Dance Grecque Antique*. Paris: E. de Boccard, 1930.

XX Seeger, Charles. *Music in Latin America. A Brief Survey*, vol. 3, Series Literature, Art, Music. Washington, D.C.: Pan American Union, 1942. [Does not purport to be more than a compilation.]

XX Seelig, Ludwig. *Geschäfstheater und Kulturtheater*. Berlin: Genossenschaft deutscher Bühnenangehöriger, n.d. [What is known.]

Seligman, Vincent Julian. *Puccini Among Friends*. London: Macmillan, 1938.

Sellers, Ovid Rogers. "Intervals in Egyptian Music." *The American Journal of Semitic Language*, 41:11–16, October 1924. [Largely based on Curt Sachs. Ancient Egyptian musical instruments. The ancient East. Vol. 21, no. 3–4. Leipzig, 1920.]

Sellmann, Adolf Wilhelm. *Der Cinematograph als Volkserzieher*. Langensalza: H. Beyer & Söhne, 1912.

Serauky, Walter. "Musikgeschichte der Stadt Halle," in *Beiträge zur Musikforschung*, Max Schneider. Halle: Waisenhaus, 1932.

Seroff, Victor Ilyitch. *Rachmaninoff*. New York: Simon and Schuster, 1950.

–––. *Dimitri Shostakovich*. New York: Knopf, 1943.

Shaliapin, Fedor Ivanovich. *Man and Mask: Forty Years in the Life of a Singer*. Garden City, N.Y.: Garden City Publishing Co., 1935.

Sharp, Thomas. *A Dissertation on the Pageants or Dramatic Mysteries Anciently Performed at Coventry, by the Trading Companies of that City*. Coventry: Merridew and Son, 1825. [Immeasurably long title. Detailed description with illustrations; especially important on what the guilds produced, also the occasions: Corpus Christi, processions, also with instruments indicated. All on thirteenth and fourteenth centuries especially.]

Shawn, Ted. *The American Ballet*. New York: Holt, 1926. [Includes ethnological material: Indians and Negroes. Some things usable.]

Shay, Frank. *American Sea Songs and Chanteys from the Days of Iron Men and Wooden Ships*. New York: Norton, 1948.

Shoemaker, Henry Wharton. *Mountain Minstrelsy of Pennsylvania*. Philadelphia: N. F. McGirr, 1931. [Apparently a population living very isolated. Includes some things German.]

Sieber, Paul. *Johann Friedrich Reichardt als Musikästhetiker: Seine Anschauung über Wesen und Wirkung der Musik*. Strasbourg: Heitz, 1930. [Sociology seems to be completely lacking in Reichardt's theory of music.]

Siegmeister, Elie. *Musik und Gesellschaft*. Berlin: Dietz Verlag, 1948.

Simbriger, Heinrich. *Gong und Gongspiele*. Internationales Archiv für Ethnographie, no. 36. Leiden: Brill, 1939, 180 pp.

Simon, James. *Abt Voglers Kompositorisches Wirken mit Besonderer Berücksichtigung der Romantischen Momente*. Berlin: Universitäts-Buchdruckerei von G. Schade, 1904. [Sandberger as *Referent*. Some things quite usable. Based on sources.]

Singer, Kurt. "Das Publikum." *Musik im Leben*, vol. 5:81ff, 1929.

Sirp, Herman. *Anton Dvořák*. Potsdam: Athenaion, 1939, 132 pp.

Slonimskii, Iurii Iosifovich, et al. *The Soviet Ballet*. New York: Philosophical Library, 1947. [Some things usable.]

Slonimsky, Nicolas. *Music of Latin America*. New York: Crowell, 1945. [Based on his own travels, description by countries.]

Smijers, Albert. "Die Kaiserliche Hofmusik-Kapelle von 1543–1619," in *Studien zur Musikwissenschaft*. *Gesellschaft zur Herausgabe von Denkmälern der Tonkunst in Österreich*, vols. 6-9. Vienna: 1920.

Smith, Cecil Michener. *Musical Comedy in America*. New York: Theatre Arts Books, 1950. [With many details on pantomime and Marx brothers.]

Smith, Moses. *Koussevitsky*. New York: Allen, Towne & Heath, 1947, 400 pp.

Smith, William Charles. *Concerning Handel*. London: Cassel, 1948.

Smith, Winifred. *Italian Actors of the Renaissance*. New York: Coward-McCann, 1930. [Based on printed Italian sources, with detailed source references.]

Soibelman, Doris. *Therapeutic and Industrial Uses of Music*. New York: Columbia University Press, 1948. [Primarily psychological.]

Sonneck, Oscar George Theodore. *A Survey of Music in America*. Washington, D.C.: The McQueen Press (private printing for author), 1913. [Subjective.]

——. *Early Concert-Life in America (1731–1800)*. Leipzig: Breitkopf & Härtel, 1907.

Sorensen, Margot Ida Sigrid. *Musik und Gesang im Mittelhochdeutschen Epos*. Dissertation Philadelphia, 1939.

Soriano Fuertes, Mariano. *Historia de la Música Española*. Madrid, 1855–1859. [Not relevant; does not indicate sources; a few things on opera performance for traveling Spaniards, kings.]

Soubies, Albert. *Le Théâtre-Italien de 1801 à 1913*. Paris: Fischbacher, 1913. [Based on knowledge of material, but mostly narrative.]

——. *Histoire du Théâtre-Lyrique 1851–1870*. Paris: Fischbacher, 1899. [Essentially enumeration of the operas performed; nothing basic.]

——. *Histoire de la Musique, Espagne*. Paris: Librairie des Bibliophiles, Flammarion, 1898. [Three short volumes, popular, without material or source references. Enumeration of all virtuosos, composers, quartets, etc.]

——. *Histoire de la Musique, Portugal*. Paris: Librairie des Bibliophiles, Flammarion, 1898. [No quotes or sources. Author claims he read all available books in the languages concerned. Enumerations without any historical documentation.]

——. *Soixante-sept ans à l'Opéra en Une Page*. Paris: Fischbacher, 1893. [Only panegyrical enumeration.]

——. *Histoire de l'Opéra-Comique*. Paris: Flammarion, 1892–1893. [Not relevant.]

Soulié, Charles Georges. *Théâtre et Musique Modernes en Chine, avec une Etude Technique de la Musique Chinoise et Transcriptions pour Piano par André Gailhard*. Paris: P. Geuthner, 1926. [French consul, who is in China, much on the Chinese school. Many musical examples, transcribed for piano. Many new Chinese source books, does not go back historically. Much is usable.]

——. *La Musique en Chine*. Paris: Leroux, 1911. [Constructs a theory of the *Pentatonic* mode.]

Spaeth, Sigmund Gottfried. *Dedication, the Love Story of Clara and Robert Schumann*. New York: Holt, 1950. [Not much that is new.]

——. *The Facts of Life in Popular Song*. New York: Whittlesey House, McGraw-Hill, 1934. [Essentially sex is the hit song.]

Spalding, Walter Raymond. *Music at Harvard*. New York: Coward-McCann, 1935. [Goes back to colonial period, development of the diplomas, etc.]

Specht, Richard. *Gustav Mahler*. Berlin: Schuster & Loeffler, 1922.

————. *Das Wiener Operntheater von Dingelstedt bis Schalk und Strauss*. Vienna: P. Knepler, 1919. [Panegyrical, popular, not relevant.]

Speck, Frank Gouldsmith. *Ceremonial Songs of the Creek and Yuchi Indians*. Philadelphia: University Museum, 1911.

Spillane, Daniel. *History of the American Pianoforte, Its Technical Development and the Trade*. New York: D. Spillane, 1890. [Especially history of the individual factories (p. 363 ff.), list of patents. On the whole not very scholarly, no notes, no bibliography.]

Spohr, Louis. *Ludwig Spohr's Autobiography*. London, 1865.

Stahl, Wilhelm. *Dietrich Buxtehude*. Kassel: Bärenreiter-Verlag, 1937.

Stainer, Sir John. *The Music of the Bible*. London: Novello, 1879.

Stauch, Adolf. *Muzio Clementi's Klavier-sonaten im Verhältnis zu den Sonaten von Haydn, Mozart und Beethoven*. Dissertation Oberkassel, 1930.

Stefan-Gruenfeldt, Paul. *Anton Dvořák*. Trans. Y. W. Vance. New York: Greystone Press, 1941.

————. *Arturo Toscanini*. Trans. Eden Paul and Cedar Paul. New York: Viking, 1936.

————. *Tanz in dieser Zeit*. Vienna: Universal Edition, 1926, 113 pp. [Many individual articles by Wiegmann, Luserke, Hugo von Hofmannstal, etc.]

————. *Gustav Mahler: Eine Studie über Persönlichkeit und Werk*. Munich: R. Piper, 1912.

XA Stehle, Anton. "Die öffentliche Musikpflege," in *Köln als Stätte der Bildung*, Joseph Theele and Adam Wrede. Cologne: Gonski, 1922.

Stein, Leon. *The Racial Thinking of Richard Wagner*. New York: Philosophical Library, 1950. [Winds up with theory that there is no Jewish race; Germans not the most productive in music. P. 21.]

Steinecke, Wolfgang. *Die Parodie in der Musik. Kieler Beiträge zur Musikwissenschaft*, no. 1. Wolfenbüttel: Kallmeyer, 1934, 208 pp.

Steinhardt, Milton. *Jacobus Vaet and His Motets*. East Lansing: Michigan State College Press, 1951. [Strongly underpinned by philosophic discussions.]

Steinkrüger, August. *Die Asthetik! der Musik bei Schelling und Hegel*. Bonn: Verein Studentenwohl, 1927.

Stellfeld, J. A. *Bronnen Tot de Geschiedenis der Antwerpsche Clavecimbelen Orgelbouwers in XVI en XVII eeuwen*. Antwerp: Drukkerij Resseler, 1942. [With bibliography, alphabetic enumeration.]

Stengel, Theo, and Herbert Gerigk. *Lexikon der Juden in der Musik*. Berlin: B. Hahnefeld, 1940.

XX Stephun, Fedor. *Theater und Kino*. Berlin: Verlag des Bühnenvolksbundes, n.d.

Stier-Somto, Helene. *Das Grimmsche Märchen als Text für Oper und Spiele*. Dissertation Köln, 1925. Berlin: De Gruyter, 1926, 193 pp. [With detailed analysis of all texts.]

Stock, Richard Wilhelm. *Richard Wagner und seine Meistersinger*. Nuremberg: K. Ulrich, 1943. [Entirely Hitlerian, anti-Semitic, of interest in that respect, extols Ley, etc.]

Stoeving, Paul. *The Story of the Violin*. London: The Walter Scott Publishing Co.; New York: Scribner, 1904. [Without much documentation in the details, but mentions many source books, also older ones.]

Stokes, Adrian. *Russian Ballets*. New York: Dutton, 1936, 213 pp. [Without anything basic, only admiring description of individual ballets.]

Stone, James. "War music and War psychology in the Civil War." *Journal of Abnormal and Social Psychology*, 36(4):543–60, 1940.

Straeten, Edmund Sebastian. *History of the Violin*. London: Cassell, 1933. [Particular details, not many source references.]

Strangways, A. H. Fox. "The Hindu Scale." *Sammelbände der internationalen Musikgesellschaft*, 9:449–511, 1907–1908. [Some things concerning Greeks and Hindu links.]

Stravinskiĭ, Igór Fedorovich. *Chronicle of My Life*. London: V. Gollancz, 1936.

XA Stravinsky, Igor. "Meine Stellung zur Schallplatte," in *Kultur und Schallplatte*, Carl Lindström. Berlin: C. Lindström A.-G. Kultur-Abt., 1930, 124 pp.

Strunk, William Oliver. *State and Resources of Musicology in the United States*. Washington, D.C.: American Council of Learned Societies, 1932, 76 pp. [Details on teaching, examinations, etc., in musicology.]

XA Stumme, Wolfgang. "Musik in der Hitlerjugend," in *Musik im Volk*, Wolfgang Stumme. Berlin: C. F. Vieweg, 1939.

———. *Musik im Volk*. Berlin: C. F. Vieweg, 1939. [Quite official; almost all collaborators are *Reichsmusikkammer* or Hitler youth.]

Subirá, José. *El Compositor Iriarte (1750–1791) y el Cultivo Español del Melólogo* (Melodrama). Barcelona, 1949–1950.

———. *La Tonadilla Escénica, Sus Obras y Sus Autores*. Barcelona: Editional Labor, 1933. [Chiefly based on his own data; the book is without source references.]

———. *Tonadillas Teatrales Inéditas: Libretos y Partituras, con una Descripción Sinóptica de Nuestra Música Africa*. Madrid: Tip. de Archivos, 1932.

Sugiyama, Makoto. *An Outline History of the Japanese dance*. Tokyo: Kokusai Bunka Shinkokai (The Society for International Cultural Relations), 1937. [Short, with many pictures, no sources, but useful because of the different types of dances.]

Sunaga, Katsumi. *Japanese Music*. Tokyo: Tourist Library, no. 15, 1936. [Quite popular, especially modern music, taking over of violins, Beethoven, etc.]

Suñol, Gregorio Maria. *Textbook of Gregorian Chant According to the Solesmes Method*. Tournai: Society of St. John Evangelist, Desclée & Co., 1930. [Introduction is historically well founded, is usable.]

Swalin, Benjamin Franklin. *The Violin Concerto*. Chapel Hill: University of North Carolina Press, 1941. [Mostly analyses of concerts; bibliography, enumeration of concerts, also much detail on virtuosos, concerts by second-rank composers, Paganini.]

Swan, Alfred Julius. *Music, 1900–1930*. New York: Norton, 1929. [Moscow school, among other things.]

XX Szendrei, Alfred. *Tonkünstler und Rundfunk*. Berlin: Wegner & Flemming, 1928.

Tansman, Alexandre. *Igor Stravinsky*. Paris: Amiot-Dumont, 1948.

XX Tappert, Wilhelm. "Sebastian Bachs Kompositionen für Laute." *Sonderabdruck aus der Redende Kunst*, 6(36–40), 1901. [According to the book, he composed more for lute than had hitherto been assumed. Not relevant for us.]

Tappolet, Willy. *Maurice Ravel*. Olten: O. Walter, 1950.

Taubman, Hyman Howard. *Music as a Profession*. New York: Scribner, 1939. [Popular, practical.]

XX   Tauren, Hjalmar. *Folkesangen pa Faeroerne*. Kobenhagn: And Fred Host & Sons, 1908. [Based on disc recordings made by himself and archive materials. With German summary at the end.]

Taut, Kurt. *Beiträge zur Geschichte der Jagdmusik*. Leipzig: Gedruckt bei Radelli & Hille, 1927. [Begins with prehistorical times (Urzeit), quotes primary sources, detailed bibliographies; not much usable for us.]

XX   Tchaikovsky, Peter. *The Diaries of Tchaikovsky*. Trans. from the Russian with notes by Wladimir Lakond. New York: Norton. [Always stichwortartig, encounters, dinners.]

Techritz, Hermann. *Sächsische Stadtpfeifer. Zur Geschichte des Stadtmusikwesens im chemaligen Königsreich Sachsen*. Dissertation Leipzig, 1932. Dresden, Bufra, 1932, 34 pp. [Very specialized details. Usable.]

Tepp, Max. "Körperkultur als Grundlage einer proletarischen Kultur." *Die Tat*, 15: 617, 1923.

Theele, Joseph, and Adam Wrede. *Köln als Stätte der Bildung*. Cologne: Gonski, 1922.

Thierfelder, Albert. "Altgriechische Musik." *Sammelbände der internationalen Musik-Gesellschaft*, 7:485–507, 1905–1906. [Deals exclusively with *Einharmonik;* not usable for us.]

Thomas, Jeannette. *Ballad Makin' in the Mountains of Kentucky*. New York: Holt, 1939.

Thompson, Oscar. *The American Singer: A Hundred Years of Success in Opera*. New York: Dial, 1937. [Almost all individual biographies.]

Thompson, Virgil. *The State of Music*. New York: Morrow, 1939.

Thorp, Willard. *Songs from the Restoration Theater*. Princeton: Princeton University Press, 1934.

Tiersot, Julien. *Notes d'Ethnographie Musicale*. No. 7, *La Musique de Arabes*. Paris: Fischbacher, 1905. [Sharply against Salvador Daniels, esp. pp. 105–106, note 2.]

———. *Notes d'Ethnographie Musicale*. No. 5, *La Musique dans l'Inde*. Paris: Fischbacher, 1905. [Based on printed collection of songs.]

———. *Notes d'Ethnographie Musicale: Quelques Mots sur les Musiques de l'Asie Centrale, les chantes de l'Arménie*. Paris: Fischbacher, 1905. [Details on American customs, one-sided, especially on religious ones.]

———. *Ronsard et la Musique de Son Temps*. Leipzig: Breitkopf & Härtel, 1903. [No source references.]

———. *Histoire de la Chanson Populaire en France*. Paris: Plon, 1889. [With very many texts, musical examples; classified: love songs; dance songs; work songs (140–169); soldiers' songs (170–186); drinking songs (216–225); details on rhythm, tunes, and patriotic songs on Henry IV (276).]

Tillyard, Henry Julius Wetenhall. *Byzantine Music and Hymnography*. London: The Faith Press, 1923. [Exact bibliography, mostly secondary. Reference to editions of primary sources. Popular, many musical examples, detailed explanation of notation systems.]

Titterton, William Richard. *From Theatre to Music Hall*. London: Stephen Swift, 1912. [Superficial, no source references.]

Tolman, Beth, and Ralph Page. *The Country Dance Book*. Weston, V.: The Countryman Press, 1937.

Tomars, Adolph Siegfried. *Introduction to the Sociology of Art*. Mexico City, 1940.

Towse, John Ranken. *Sixty Years of the Theater: An Old Critic's Memories.* New York: Funk and Wagnalls, 1916. [Mostly reviews, collected at random, dealing almost exclusively with American plays.]

XA   Trautwein, Susanne. "Musik. Lyzeum und Oberlyzeum," in *Auftrage des Zentralinstituts für Erziehung und Unterricht,* Friedrich Cauer and Agnes Moltan. Leipzig: Quelle & Meyer, 1925.

Treder, Dorothea. *Die Musikinstrumente in den Höfischen Epen der Blütezeit.* Greifswald: L. Bamberg, 1933. [Wolfgang Stammler as *Referent.* Survey of existing instrument combinations and festival occasions; everything dealt with by classification by instruments; influence of Curt Sachs.]

Trend, John Brande. *The Music of Spanish History to 1600.* New York: Oxford University Press, H. Milford, 1926. [Many details about the Moors; in Hispanic Notes and Monographs, Essays, Studies and Biographies issued by the Hispanic Society of America, vol. 10.]

Truinet, Charles Louis Etienne. *Les Origines de l'Opéra Française.* Paris: Plon, 1886. [Says it is based on very much archive material.]

Tucker, Archibald Norman. *Tribal Music and Dancing in the Southern Sudan (Africa) at Social and Ceremonial Gatherings.* London: William Reeves, 1933. [Based on his own experiences and commissioned by the Sudan government between 1929 and 1931. Important on myth of dance.]

Udall, Hans. *Das Klavierkonzert der Berliner Schule mit kurzem Überblick über seine allgemeine Entstehungsgeschichte und spätere Entwicklung.* Sammlung musikwissenschaftlicher Einzeldarstellungen, vol. 10. Leipzig: Breitkopf & Härtel, 1928, 119 pp. [Detailed discussion based on sources. Only little for us.]

Umble, John Sylvanus. *Goshen College.* Goshen College, 1955. [With history of internal Mennonite conflicts on music.]

Unger, Max. *Muzio Clementis Leben.* Langensalza: H. Beyer & Söhne, (Beyer & Mann), 1914. [Much detailed piano stuff, piano history, etc. Based on source material. Only some things usable for us.]

XX   Union Académique Internationale. *Monumenta Musicae Byzantinae,* Carsten Hoeg, H. J. W. Tillyard, and Egon Wellesz, eds. Vol. 1: *Die Hymnen des Sticherarium für Sept,* E. Wellesz, 1936. Vol. 2: *The Hymns of the Sticherarium for November,* H. J. W. Tillyard, 1938. Vol. 3: *The Hymns of the Octoechus,* Part 1, H. J. W. Tillyard, 1940. Copenhagen: Levin & Munksgaard, 1936–

XX   ———. *Monumenta Musical Byzantinae Subordia,* Carsten Hoeg, H. J. W. Tillyard, and Egon Wellesz, eds. Copenhagen: Levin & Munksgaard, 1935. Vol. 1, fasc. 1. [Tillyard, H. J. W. *Handbook of the Middle Byzantine Notation,* vol. 1, fasc. 2. Carsten Hoeg. *La Notation Ekphonetique.* I. *ibid.,* 1935. Both purely on history of notation with extensive apparatus.]

XX   Upham, J. Baxter. "Music in our Public School." *Boston Evening Traveller,* April 22, 1871. [Deals chiefly with singing. Very short, popular.]

Ursprung, Otto. *Münchens Musikalische Vergangenheit.* Munich: Bayerland-Verlag, 1927. [With much secondhand quoting, but also based on the new critical editions. Some things important.]

Vadding, M. *Das Violincello und Seine Literatur.* Leipzig: C. Merseburger, 1920. [Description of its structures, only little on origin. Detailed, systematic references to literaure. No relevant for us.]

Valentin, Caroline. *Geschichte der Musik in Frankfurt am Main vom Anfang des XIV. bis zum Angange des XVIII. Jahrhunderts.* Frankfurt: Voelcker, 1906.

Vallas, Léon. *Un Siècle de Musique et de Théâtre à Lyon.* Lyons: P. Masson, 1932. [Very detailed; on knowledge of archives.]

Van Aalst, J. A. *Chinese Music.* Published by order of the Inspectorate General of Peking. Reissued and sold by the French bookstore, 1933. [To some extent historical. Description of instruments; chiefly on present time; not much that is new.]

Vanderstraeten, Edmond. *La Musique aux Pays-Bas avant le XIX*^e *Siècle.* Brussels: Van Trigt, 1867–1888. [Eight volumes.]

Van de Wall, Willem. *The Music of the People.* New York: American Association for Adult Education, 1938.

Van Doren, Dom Rombaut. *Etude sur l'Influence Musicale de l'Abbaye de Saint-Gall, (VIII*^e *au XI*^e *Siècles).* Brussels: Lamertin, 1925. [Based on very accurate knowledge of primary sources. Useful for details.]

Van Lelyveld, T. B. *La Danse dans le Théâtre Javanais.* Paris: H. Floury, 1931. [With many illustrations; based on Malayan sources translated into French or Dutch and on translation of . . . texts. Traces much of the Malayan to . . . influence.]

Vaughan Williams, Ralph. *National Music.* London: Oxford University Press, 1934.

Veinus, Abraham. *The Concerto.* Garden City, N.Y.: Doubleday, 1944. [Without notes. Detailed list of all concerti extant in records (including *B. Konz.*, etc.), but deals with all types of concerti.]

Velten, Rudolf. *Das Ältere deutsche Gesellschaftslied unter dem Einfluss Italienischer Musik.* Heidelberg: C. Winter, 1914. [Some of it important.]

Ver, J. *La Cantilène Huguenote de XVI*^e *Siècle.* Réalville: Chez l'auteur, 1918. [With only a few quotations, which are exact.]

Verdi, Giusseppe. *Verdi, The Man in His Letters.* Edited and selected by Franz Werfel and Paul Stefan. Trans. by Edward Downes. New York: L. B. Fischer, 1942.

XX Virdleaud, C., and F. Pellagand. "La Musique Assyro-Babylonienne," in *Encyclopédie de la Musique,* Part 1. [Strictly scholarly.]

Visan, Tancrède de. *Le Guignol Lyonnais.* Paris: Bloud, 1910.

Viski, Károly. *Hungarian Dances.* London: Simpkin Marshall; Budapest: G. Vajna, 1937. [With a short but good source bibliography; very sociological. Also on *Rekrutenmusik*, Gypsies, etc.]

Vogel, Emil. *Claudio Monteverdi. Leben, Wirken im Lichte der Zeitgenössischen Kritik und Verzeichniss seiner im Druck erschienen Werke.* Dissertation Berlin, 1887. Leipzig: Breitkopf & Härtel, 1887. [Some things important because of ducal orchestras in Mantua.]

Vogl, Hertha. "Zur Geschichte des Oratoriums in Wien von 1725 bis 1740," in *Studien zur Musikwissenschaft. Gesellschaft zur Herausgabe von Denkmälern der Tonkunst in Österreich,* vol. 14. Vienna, 1927.

Vojan, Jaroslav Egon Salaba. *Antonin Dvořák.* Chicago: The Antonin Dvořák Centennial Committee of the Czechoslovak National Council, 1941.

XX Völsing, Erwin. *G. F. Händels englische Kirchenmusik.* Schriftreihe des staatlichen Instituts für deutsche Musikforschung, no. 6. Leipzig, 1940.

XX   Von der Heidt, Johann Daniel. *Geschichte der evangelischen Kirchenmusik*. Baden: Trowitzsch & Sohn, 1926. [Popular, based on secondary sources only.]

XX   Von Jan, Karl. "Die Griechischen Saiteninstrumente." Wissensch. Beitrag zum Jahres-bericht des Gymnasiums zu Saargemünde für das Schuljahr 1881–1882. Leipzig: Dunk, Commissionsverlag von B. G. Teubner, 1882. [Based on much quoting of sources, but chiefly dealing with structure of instruments.]

XA   Wackernagel, Peter. "Handschriften Chopins," in *Chopin Almanach*, Chopin-Komitee in Deutschland. Potsdam: Akademischer Verlagsgesellschaft Athenaion, 1949, 164 pp.

Wagner, Cosima, and Fürst, Ernst. *Briefwechsel zwischen Cosima Wagner und Fürst Ernst zu Hohenlohe-Langenburg*. Stuttgart: Cotta, 1937.

Wagner, Peter. *Geschichte der Messe*. Leipzig: Breitkopf & Härtel, 1913–   . [Without bibliography; but much quotation in detail of his new data.]

———. *Einführung in die Gregorianischen Melodien; Ein Handbuch der Choralwissen-schaft*. Leipzig: Breitkopf & Härtel, 1911–1921. [Based on sources, volume almost exclusively paleographic.]

Wagner, Richard. *My Life*. New York: Dodd, Mead, 1924.

———. *Richard Wagner's Prose Works*. Trans. William Ashton Ellis. London: K. Paul, Trench, Trübner & Co., 1893–1899. [Vol. 1, 2nd ed., 1895. Vol. 2, 2nd ed., 1900 (1st ed., 1895). Vol. 3, theater, 1895. Vol. 4, his art and politics, 1895. Vol. 5, no title, also 1895. Vol. 6, religion and his art, 1897. Vol. 7, also no title, 1898. Vol. 8, posthumous works, 1899.]

Wagner, Siegfried. *Erinnerungen*. Stuttgart: Engelhorns, nachf., 1923. [Short.]

Walker, Joseph Cooper. *Historical Memoirs of the Irish Bards*. London: Printed for the author by L. White, 1786. [Refers to *Quellen Zeiten Reihen*. Based on contem-porary oral reports from Limerick.

Wallaschek, Richard. *Primitive Music*. London: Longmans, 1893.

Walter, Bruno. *Theme and Variations, An Autobiography*. Trans. from the German by James A. Galston. New York: Knopf, 1946. [Very much on culture, philosophy, Nietzsche, etc. Without table of contents and without chapter titles.]

———. *Gustav Mahler*. London: Kegan Paul, 1937.

XX   Walter, Howard. "Sozialismus und Musik." Vortrag gehalten für den Bund freier Musiklehrkräfte eingel. Verch. Berlin, April 2, 1930. Berlin-Hermsdorf: Verlag für Kunst und Kultur, n.d. [Has little to do with the subject.]

Walters, Raymond. *The Bethlehem Bach Choir*. Boston: Houghton Mifflin, 1923. [His-tory of the choir of the Moravian Brethren; without giving much stress in rela-tion to facts, that from a religious communal it became a much more worldy affair.]

Waltz, Heinrich Jakob. *Die Lage der Orchestermusiker in Deutschland mit besonderer Berücksichtigung der Musikgeschäfte (Stadtpfeifereien)*. Karlsruhe: Druck der G. Braunschen Hofbuchdruckerei, 1906. [Very important.]

Wangemann, Otto. *Die Orgel, Ihre Geschichte und Ihr Bau*. Leipzig: Verlags-institut R. Kuhn, 1895. [History of construction; not relevant for us.]

XX   Wanters, E. *Jean Guyot de Chatelet, Musique de la Renaissance, sa Vie et son Oeuvre*. Brussels: A. de Boeck, 1944. [Short, popular, but based on works of Guyot. Secondary sources.]

Warsage, Rodolphe de. *Histoire du Célèbre Théâtre Liégeois de Marionettes.* Brussels: Van Oest, 1905. [With very rich and critical bibliography.]

————. *Au Royaume des Marionettes.* Liege: Imprimerie La Meuse, 1903. [On the whole similar to his great book on Liège marionettes.]

Wasielewski, Wilhelm Joseph von. *Das Violincell und Seine Geschichte.* Leipzig: Breitkopf & Härtel, 1911. [Introduction on Viola da Gamba and Gamba players. Detailed history of the lives of the virtuosos. Not relevant for us.]

————. *Die Violine und ihre Meister.* Leipzig: Breitkopf & Härtel, 1904. [Largely based on secondary materials.]

————. *Aus Siebzig Jahren.* Stuttgart: Deutsche Verlagsanstalt, 1897.

Wassermann, Rudolf. *Ludwig Spohr als Opernkomponist.* Dissertation München, 1909. [Thierfelder as *Referent.* Only a few things concerning the court at Kassel.]

Waugh, Jennie. *Das Theater als Spiegel der Amerikanischen Demokratie.* Berlin: Junker, 1936. [Especially important the concluding article; history of the American national theater, i.e., school theater, children's theater, government support.]

Weber, Carl Maria von. *Sämtliche Schriften. Kritische Ausgabe von George Kaiser.* Berlin: Schuster & Loeffler, 1908.

————. *Briefe von Carl Maria von Weber an seine Gattin Carolina. Hersg. von seinem Enkel.* Leipzig: A. Dürr, 1886, 224 pp.

Weber, Max. *Die Rationalen und Soziologischen Grundlagen der Musik.* Munich: Drei Masken Verlag, 1924.

Weber, Wilhelm. *Beethovens Missa Solemnis.* Leipzig: F. E. C. Leuckart, 1908. [No source references or bibliography, but usable only because of observations on Beethoven and Cardinal Archbishop Rudolf von Olmütz.]

Weckerlin, Jean Baptiste Théodore. *L'Ancienne Chanson Populaire en France XVIe– XVIIIe Siècles.* Paris: Garnier, 1877. [Based on old popular printings; with exact bibliography; With all variants; many drastically sexual.]

XX Weidemann, Magnus. "Von deutschen Tänzen." *Die Freude,* 2(9), September, 1925.

Weil, Rudolf. *Das Berliner Theaterpublikum unter A. W. Ifflands Direktion. (1796– 1814).* Berlin: Selbstverlag der Gesellschaft für Theatergeschichte, 1932.

Weilen, Alexander von. "Geschichte des Wiener Theaterwesens von den ältesten Zeiten bis zu den Anfängen der Hoftheater," in *Die Theater Wiens,* vol. 1, 1899. Vienna: Gesellschaft für Vervielfältig, 1899.

Weingartner, Felix. *Lebenserinnerungen.* Zurich: Orell Füssli, 1928–1929.

Weiser, Theresa. *Music for God.* New York: Philosophical Library, 1951.

Weismann, Adolf. *Berlin als Musikstadt.* Berlin: Schuster & Loeffler, 1911. [Chiefly small talk and biographies, without quotes or notes; with some literature; some things are usable for us. Popular; many personalities described, some things simply untrue.]

Weitzel, Wilhelm. *Kirchenmusik und Volk.* Freiburg: Herder, 1923, 118 pp. [Collected lectures; Catholic; modern; not friendly to liturgical movement.]

Welch, Christopher. *Six Lectures on the Recorder and Other Flutes in Relation to Literature.* London: H. Frowde, 1911. [Some historical things usable. Details based on older printed sources.]

————. *History of the Boehm-Flute.* London: Rudall, Carte, 1896. [For Boehm, many documents; not usable for us.]

Welch, Roy Dickinson. *The Study of Music in the American College.* Northampton, Mass.: Smith College, 1925, 116 pp.

Wellesz, Egon. *Essays on Opera.* New York: D. Dobson, 1950, 158 pp. [With several historical articles concerning baroque, text his own operas, etc.]

——. *Trésor de Musique Byzantine.* Paris: Editions de l'Oiseau Lyre, chez I. B. M. Dyer, 1934–

XA ——. "Eastern Church Music," in *Grove's Dictionary of Music and Musicians,* Sir George Grove. New York: Macmillan, 1927–1928.

——. *Byzantinische Musik.* Breslau: Ferdinand Hirt, 1927, 96 p. [Short, popular, but quite worthwhile for excursions, etc.]

XX ——. "Musikalisches Barok und die Anfänge der Wiener Oper," in *Theater und Kultur.* Zurich, Amalthea Verlag, 1922. [Important concerning courtly society, ballet, etc.]

——. *Arnold Schönberg.* Vienna: Tal, 1921, 154 pp.

Wendel, Hermann. *Die Marseillaise: Biographie einer Hymne.* Zurich: Europa-Verlag, 1936.

Wenz, Josef. *Kinderlied und Kindesseele.* Kassel: Bärenreiter-Verlag, 1929.

Werner, Arno. *Vier Jahrhunderte im Dienste der Kirchenmusik.* Leipzig: C. Merseburger, 1933.

Westby, David L. "The Career Experience of the Symphony Musician." *Social Forces,* 38(3):223–230, March 1960.

Westermeyer, Karl. *Die Operette im Wandel der Zeitgeistes: von Offenbach bis zur Gegenwart.* Munich: Drei Masken Verlag, A. G., 1931. [Very important, with much analysis of Viennese society and related changes.]

Westphal, Rudolph. *Die Musik des Griechischen Alterthumes.* Leipzig: Veit, 1883. [Almost exclusively history of rhythm.]

——. *Allgemeine Theorie der Musikalischen Rhythmik seit J. S. Bach.* Leipzig: Breitkopf & Härtel, 1880. [Entirely rhythmic; printed upon Spitta's recommendation, dedicated to the Russian minister Katkow.]

——. *Geschichte der Alten und Mittelalterlichen Musik.* Breslau: F. E. C. Leuckart, 1865.

——. *System der antiken Rhythmik.* Leipzig: Leuckart, 1865, 195 pp. [Almost exclusively on history of rhythm.]

White, Newman Ivey. *American Negro Folk-songs.* Cambridge: Harvard University Press, 1928.

Whiteman, Paul, *Jazz.* New York: J. H. Sears & Co., 1926. [Very anecdotal.]

Whitfield, Irène Thérèse. *Louisiana French Folk Songs.* Baton Rouge: Louisiana State University Press, 1939.

Whitworth, Reginald. *The Electric Organ.* London: Musical Opinion, 1930. [Largely technical.]

Wichmann, Heinz. *Grétry und das Musikalische Theater in Frankreich.* Dissertation Berlin, 1929. Halle: Niemeyer, 1929, 131 pp. [Especially the introduction with observation on sociological contrasts, opera lyrics, and the comic opera at that time is sociologically important; Part 1 likewise.]

XX Widera, Friedl. "Ich geh ins Konzert." *Jugendvolksbühne,* 3(2), February 1933.

Wieninger, Gustav. *Immanuel Kants Musikästhetik.* Berlin: Reuther & Reichard, 1931, 76 pp.

Wier, Albert Ernst. *The Piano: Its History, Makers, Players, and Music.* London: Longmans, 1940.

Wieschhoff, Heinrich Albert. *Die Afrikanischen Trommeln und ihre ausserafrikanischen Beziehungen.* Stuttgart: Strecker & Schroeder, 1933.

Williams, Charles Francis Abdy. *The Story of the Organ.* London: The Walter Scott Publishing Co.; New York: Scribner, 1905. [Without sources, but with detailed description of *Figuren der Cathedralplants.*]

XX   Williams, Landa. "Arabic Music." Reprinted from the *Open Count,* August 1934. [A side thesis: Greek music not dependent on Persian.]

XX   Williams, Lloyd. "Welch National Melodies and Folksongs," in *Cymmrodion Society Publication Transaction Sessions 1907–1908.* London: Issued by the society. [Popular, no sources.]

Williamson, Audrey. *The Art of Ballet.* New York: Elek, 1950.

Willis, Richard Storrs. *Our Church Music.* New York: Dana & Co., 1856. [Not evident which denomination; against specialized choirs; for folk singing; for children's choir.]

XX   Wilmart, André, O.S.B. *L'Ancien Cantatorium de l'Eglise de Strasbourg.* Manuscript additionel 23.922 du Musée Britannique. Avec un mémoire de l'abbé J. Walters. Conservatum de la Bibliotèque de Séleste. Colmar: Alsa Fia, 1928. [Printed text eighteenth century. Details of the music for each feast; with appendix by Walter on processions, pp. 91–115.]

Wilson, Archibald Wayet. *The Chorals: Their Origin and Influence.* London: The Faith Press, 1920. [Organist at Manchester Cathedral. Popular; with little by way of sources; but many examples of music; somewhat usable.]

Wingender, Hans. *Erfahrungen im Kampfe gegen Schund-und Schmutzschriften.* Düsseldorf: Landesrat H. Wingender, 1929, 97 pp.

Winnington-Ingram, Reginald Pepys. *Mode in Ancient Greek Music.* Cambridge: The University Press, 1936.

Winter, Carl. *Ruggiero Giovanelli (c. 1560–1625), Palestrinas St. Peter In Rom.* Munich: Musikwissenschaftliches Seminar der Universität München, 1935.

Winterfeld, Carl von. *Der Evangelische Kirchengesang und sein Verhältniss zur Kunst des Tonsatzes.* Leipzig: Breitkopf & Härtel, 1843–1847.

Winzheimer, Bernhard. *Das musikalische Kunstwerk in elektrischer Fernübertragung.* Augsburg: Dr. B. Filser, 1930, 120 pp.

XX   Wissig, Otto. *Franz Schuberts Messen.* Dissertation Leipzig, 1909. Leipzig: Poeschel & Trepte, 1909. [*Referenten* Riemann and Köster. Only very little that is important for us.]

Wister, Frances Anne. *Twenty Five Years of the Philadelphia Orchestra.* Philadelphia: 1925. [With details concerning financing, conductor, and members of the orchestra.]

Wolf, Bodo. *Heinrich Valentin Beck (1698–1758).* Dissertation München, 1911, 139 pp. [Some things usable, on salary stipend, etc.]

Wolf, Hugo. *Briefe an Heinrich Potpeschnigg.* Stuttgart: Union Deutsche Verlagsgesellschaft, 1923.

———. *Briefe an Rosa Mayreder*. Vienna: Rikola-Verlag, 1921.

———. *Hugo Wolf, Eine Persölichkeit in Briefen: Familienbriefe herausgegeben von Edmund von Hellmer*. Leipzig: Breitkopf & Härtel, 1912. [Not relevant for us.]

———. *Hugo Wolf's Briefe an Oskar Grohe: Im Auftrage des Hugo Wolf-Vereins in Wien*. Berlin: C. Fischer, 1905.

———. *Hugo Wolf's Briefe an Emil Kauffmann: Im Auftrage des Hugo Wolf-Vereins in Wien*. Berlin: C. Fischer, 1903.

XX Wolf, Max. *Geschichte der Mensuralnotation von 1250–1460*. Leipzig: Breitkopf & Härtel, 1904.

Wolff, Hellmuth Christian. *Die Venezianische Oper in der Zweiten Hälfte des 17. Jahrhunderts*. Berlin: O. Elsner, 1937. [P. 42. Very usable. Especially sociological concerning publications. Von Wiese quoted often. On many sources and detailed literature.]

Wolfurt, Kurt von. *Mussórgskij*. Stuttgart: Deutsche Verlagsanstalt, 1927. [The author apparently Baltic.]

XX Wunsch, Karl. "Neugestaltung der Erziehung zur Musik." Einleitung zu: Musik der neuen Jugend. Ein Führer durch die Musikveröffentlichungen des Georg Kallmeyer Verlages. Wolfenbüttel: Georg Kallmeyer, 1925. [The known things, especially on Jöde.]

Wünsch, Walther. *Die Geigentechnik der südslavischen Guslaren*. Brünn: Rohrer, 1934. [On basis of reports of own travels, with bibliography.]

Würz, Anton. *Franz Lachner als Dramatischer Komponist*. Munich: Druck von Knorr & Hirth, g.m.b.h., 1927. [Alfred Lorenz and Förster as *Referenten*. Also in German Romantic opera texts. Relevant.]

Young, Percy Marshall. *The Oratorios of Handel*. London: D. Dobson, 1949.

Zanzig, Augustus Delafield. *Music in American Life, Present and Future*. London: Oxford University Press, 1932, 560 pp.

Zelle, Friedrich. *Johann Wolfgang Franck*. Berlin: R. Gärtner, 1889. [Some things usable.]

———. *J. Theile und N. A. Strungk*. Berlin: R. Gärtner, 1891. [Some things usable.]

Zimmern, Helen. *Schopenhauer*. London: Allen & Unwin, 1932. [Wagner obtained no actual philosophy from Schopenhauer but simply the request ideas and terms whereby to present his own individual principles clearly and succinctly.]

Zingel, Hans Joachim. *Harfe und Harfenspiel vom Beginn des 16. bis ins zweite Drittel des 18. Jahrhunderts*. Halle: (Saale) M. Niemeyer, 1932. [Often with exact source reference. Usable. List of contemporary pictures. Indicates manuscripts of harp compositions in library.]

Zoete, Beril de, and Walter Spies. *Dance and Drama in Bali*. London: Faber & Faber, 1938, 343 pp. [Illustrated volume, based on travels; apparently knows language; detailed description of all the particular dances; some things very usable.]

Zosel, Alois. *Heinrich Schulz-Beuthen 1838–1915. Leben und Werke. Ein Beitrag zur Geschichte der neueren Programmusik*. Dissertation Leipzig, 1931. Würzburg: Triltsch, 1931, 85 pp. [Only a few things usable.]

SOCIOLOGY AND MUSIC: ADDITIONAL AND RECENT BIBLIOGRAPHIC ENTRIES

Abrahams, Roger D. "Public drama and common values in two Caribbean islands." *Trans-Action,* **5**(8):62–71, 1968.

———. "Patterns of structure and role relationships in the child ballad in the United States." *Journal of American Folklore,* **79**(313):448–462, 1966.

Adorno, Theodor Wiesengrund. *Impromptus—Zweite Folge neu gedruckter musikalischer Aufsätze.* Frankfurt: Edition Suhrkamp, 1968.

———. *Moments musicaux—Neu gedruckte Aufsätze,* 1928–1962. Frankfurt: Edition Suhrkamp, 1964.

———. *Der getreue Korrepetitor.* Frankfurt: S. Fischer, 1963.

———. *Einleitung in die Musiksoziologie.* Frankfurt: Edition Suhrkamp, 1962.

———. "A social critique of radio music." *Kenyon Review,* **7**, 1945. Reprinted in *Reader in Public Opinion and Communication,* Bernard Berelson and Morris Janowitz (eds.). Glencoe: Free Press, 1950, pp. 309–316.

———. *Philosophie der neuen Musik.* Tübingen: Mohr, 1949.

———. "On popular music." *Zeitschrift für Sozialforschung,* **9**:17–49, 1941.

———. "Über den Fetischcharakter und die Regression des Hörens." *Zeitschrift für Sozialforschung,* **7**:321–356, 1939.

———. "Zur gesellschaftlichen Lage der Musik." *Zeitschrift für Sozialforschung,* **1**:103–124, 356–378, 1932.

Agarkar, A. J. "The Social Background of Physical Education with Special Reference to the Folk-Dances of Maharashtra." Ph.D. Thesis, Bombay, 1947.

Albrecht, Milton C., James H. Barnett, and Mason Griff. *The Sociology of Art and Literature: A Reader*. New York: Praeger, 1970.

———. "Art as an institution," *American Sociological Review*, 33:383–397, 1968.

Aler, Jan (Ed.). *Proceedings of the Fifth International Congress of Aesthetics*, Amsterdam, 1964. The Hague: Mouton, 1968.

Ambros, August Wilhelm. *Geschichte der Musik*, 2nd ed. Leipzig, 1881.

Anderson, Simon V. "Adolescent musical preferences: Two commentaries. The role of rock." *Music Educators Journal*, 54(5):37, 39, 41, 85–87, 1968.

Anonymous. "Understanding the jazz musicians: The artist and his problems." *Jazz Today*, 2:41–56, March 1956.

Azbill, Henry. "Native dances: A basic part of culture, tradition, religion." *Indian Historian*, 1(1):16–17, 20, 1967.

Baldwin, James A. "Mass culture and the creative artist: Some personal ideas." *Daedalus*, 89:373–376, 1960.

Ballinger, Thomas O. "Nepalese musical instruments." *Southwestern Journal of Anthropology*, 16(4):398–416, 1960.

Barbour, J. Murray. *Tuning and Temperament*. East Lansing: Michigan State University Press, 1951.

Barker, John Wesley. "Sociological influences upon the emergence of Lutheran music." *Miscellanea Musicologica* (Adelaide), 4:157–198, 1969.

Bartenieff, Irmgard, and Forrestine Paulay. "Dance as cultural expression," in *Dance: An Art in Academe*, Martin Haberman and Tobie Garth Meisel. New York: Teachers College Press, 1970, pp. 23–31.

———. "Research in anthropology: A study of dance styles in primitive cultures," in *Research in Dance: Problems and Possibilities, Proceedings of the Preliminary Conference on Research in Dance*, New York, 1967, Richard Bull, ed. New York: CORD, New York University, 1968, pp. 91–104.

Bascom, W. R., and M. J. Herskovits. *Continuity and Change in African Cultures*. Chicago: University of Chicago Press, 1959.

Battock, Gregory (Ed.). *The New American Cinema: A Critical Anthology*. New York: Dutton, 1968.

Baumgarten, Eduard. *Max Weber: Werk und Person, Dokumente Ausgewählt und Kommentiert, mit Zeittafel und 20 Bildertafeln*. Tübingen: Mohr, 1964.

Baumol, William J., and William G. Bowen. *Performing Arts: The Economic Dilemma: A Study of Problems Common to Theater, Opera, Music, and Dance*. New York: Twentieth Century Fund, 1966.

Becker, Howard S. (Ed.). *The Other Side*. New York: Free Press, 1964.

———. *Outsiders: Studies in the Sociology of Deviance*. New York: Free Press, 1963.

———. "Notes on the concept of comitment." *American Journal of Sociology*, 66:32–40, 1960.

Beegle, Allan, and Rolf Schulze. "Paul Honigsheim (1885–1963)." *Kölner Zeitschrift für Soziologie und Sozialpsychologie*, 15(1):1–5, 1963.

Belz, Carl I. "Popular music and the folk tradition." *Journal of American Folklore*, 80:130–142, 1967.

Bensman, Joseph. "Classical music and the status game." *Trans-Action*, 4(9):54–59, 1967.

Bentley, Eric. *The Theatre of Commitment, and Other Essays on Drama in Our Society*. New York: Atheneum, 1967.

Berger, Donald Paul. "Ethnomusicology past and present." *Music Educators Journal*, 54(7):77–79, 127–131, 1968.

Bhattacharya, Sudhibhushan. "Role of music in society and culture." *Folklore* (Calcutta), 11(6):202–211, 1970.

———. "Ethnomusicology and India." *Folklore* (Calcutta), 9(1):1–6, 1968.

Bigsby, C. W. E. *Confrontations and Commitment: A Study of Contemporary American Drama, 1959–66*. Columbia: University of Missouri Press, 1968.

Blacking, John. "The value of music in human experience." *Yearbook of the International Folk Music Council*, 1:33–71, 1969.

———. *Venda Children's Songs: A Study in Ethnomusicological Analysis*. Johannesburg: Witwatersrand University Press, 1967.

Blass, Joseph Herring. "Indeterminacy as a Factor in Scientific and Artistic Attitudes of the Twentieth Century." Ph.D. Thesis (Humanities), Florida State University, 1968.

Blaukopf, Kurt. "Musik," in *Wörterbuch der Soziologie*, W. Bernsdorf and Fr. Bülow, eds. Stuttgart: Enke, 1955, pp. 342–346.

———. *Musiksoziologie: Eine Einführung in die Grundbegriffe mit besonderer Berücksichtigung der Soziologie der Tonsysteme*. St. Gallen: Zollikopfer, 1950.

Botkin, Benjamin A. "The folksong revival, cult or culture?" *Folk Music and Dance*, 4:1–4, April 1964.

Brandel, Rose. The Music of Central Africa—An Ethnomusicological Study—French Equatorial Africa, the Belgian Congo and Ruanda-Urundi, Uganda, Tanganyika. Ph.D. Thesis (Music), New York University, 1959.

Braun, D. Duane. *Toward a Theory of Popular Culture: The Sociology and History of American Music and Dance, 1920–1968*. Ann Arbor: Ann Arbor Publishers, 1969.

Briegleb, Ann. "Ethnomusicological collections in Western Europe—A selective study of seventeen archives." *Selected Reports*, (Los Angeles, Institute of Ethnomusicology of the University of California), 1(2):77–148, 1968.

Broere, Bernard J., and Sylvia Moore. "Ethnomusicology in the Netherlands." *Recorded Sound* (London), 36:545–559, 1969.

Browne, John Paddy. "Christmas carols and customs." *English Dance and Song* (London), 30(4):121–123, 1968.

Bruford, W. H. *Culture and Society in Classical Weimar, 1775–1806*. London: Cambridge University Press, 1962.

Bucci, Jerry Michael. Love, Marriage, and Family Life Themes in the Popular Song: A Comparison of the Years 1940 and 1965. Ph.D. Thesis (Sociology), Columbia University, 1968.

Buhociu, Octavian, "Folklore and ethnography in Rumania." *Current Anthropology*, 7(3):295–314, 1966.

Bush, P. A., and K. G. Pease. "Pop records and connotative satiation: Test of Jakobovits' theory." *Psychological Reports*, 23(3):871–875, 1968.

Butcher, Vada E., et al. *Development of Materials for a One-Year Course in African music for the General Undergraduate Student (Project in African Music).* Washington: U.S. Department of Health, Education, and Welfare, Office of Education, Bureau of Research, 1970. "Music in Yoruba society," pp. 107–111; "Social organization of Yoruba musicians," pp. 115–118.

Butler, Janet W., and Paul G. Daston. "Musical consonance as musical preference: A cross-cultural study." *Journal of General Psychology,* 79(1):129–142, 1968.

Cage, John. *Notations.* New York: Something Else, 1969.

———. *Silence. Lectures and Writings by the Author.* Middletown, Conn.: Wesleyan University Press, 1967.

———. *A Year from Monday.* Middletown, Conn.: Wesleyan University Press, 1967.

Calabria, Frank M. "Experimentally induced psyche and socio-process in small groups." *Journal of Social Psychology,* 60:57–69, 1963.

Cambor, Glenn C., Gerald M. Lisowitz, and Miles D. Miller. "Creative jazz musicians: A clinical study." *Psychiatry,* 25(1):1–15, 1962.

Cameron, William Bruce. *Informal sociology.* New York: Random House, 1963.

Cantrick, Robert P. "The blind men and the elephant: Scholars on popular music." *Ethnomusicology,* 9(2):100–114, May 1965.

Carawan, Guy, and Candie Carawan. *Freedom Is a Constant Struggle: Songs of the Freedom Movement.* New York: Oak Publications, 1968.

Carey, James T. "Changing courtship patterns in the popular song." *American Journal of Sociology,* 74(6)720–731, 1969.

Chanan, Michael. "The language of music." *Music and Musicians* (London), 16(10):30–31, June 1968.

Chase, Gilbert. "An approach to Latin American music: Notes toward a theory of values." *Studies in Ethnomusicology* (New York), 1:23–28, 1961.

Chen, Marjory Liu. "Music education and community life in Taiwan China." *Musart* (Washington, D.C.), 20(5):38–39, 60, 1968.

Chenoweth, Vida, and Darlene Bee. "On ethnic music." *Practical Anthropology,* 15(5):205–212, 1968.

Chu Liu-yi. "Folk opera flowers among national minorities." *China Reconstructs,* 11(9):37–39, 1962.

Churchill, Allen. *The Improper Bohemians: A Re-creation of Greenwich Village in Its Heyday.* New York: Dutton, 1959.

Clausen, Raymond. "The ethnomusicology committee of the Royal Anthropological Institute." *Ethnomusicology,* 2(1):22–26, 1958.

———. A Musicological Study of the Layard Collection of Recorded Malekulan Music in Its Sociological and Ritual Setting. B. Litt. Thesis, Oxford (Exeter), n.d.

Cohen, Joel E. "Information theory and music." *Behavioral Science,* 7(2):137–163, 1962.

Cohen, Norman. "Urban vs. rural values in country and pop songs: A review essay." *John Edwards Memorial Foundation Quarterly,* 6:62–65, Summer 1970.

Coles, Robert. "The words and music of social change." *Daedalus,* 98:684–689, 1969.

Combarieu, Jules. *La Musique et la Magic: Etude sur les Origines Populaires de l'Art Musical, son Influence et Sa Fonction dans les Sociétés.* Paris: 1909.

Conyers, James E. "An exploratory study of musical tastes and interests of college students." *Sociological Inquiry,* 33(1):58–66, Winter 1963.

Cray, Ed. "An acculturative continuum for Negro folk song in the United States." *Ethnomusicology*, 5(1):10–15, January 1961.

Crossley-Holland, Peter (Ed.). *Proceedings of the Centennial Workshop in Ethnomusicology*, University of British Columbia, Vancouver, June 19 to 23, 1967. Victoria: Government of the Province of British Columbia, 1968.

Cutter, Charles. "The politics of music in Mali." *African Arts*, 1(3):38–39, 74–77, 1968.

Daniélou, Alain. "Cultural genocide." *World of Music* (Paris), 11(1):6–16, 1969.

———. "Values in music," in *Artistic Values in Traditional Music: Proceedings of a Conference*, Berlin, July 14 to 16, 1965, Peter Crossley-Holland, ed. Berlin: International Institute for Comparative Music Studies and Documentation, 1966, pp. 10–21.

Davis, Ronald G. "Radical theatre versus institutional theatre." *Studies on the Left*, 4:28–38, 1964.

Dees, David R. "Art as an event: An interpretation from structuralism." Paper presented at the XIII Congreso, Institut International de Sociologie, Caracas, Venezuela, 1972.

DeLeeuw, Ton. "Music in orient and occident—A social problem." *World of Music* (Paris), 11(4):6–17, 1969.

de Lerma, Dominique-René (Ed.). *Black Music in our Culture: Curricular Ideas on the Subjects, Materials and Problems*. Kent, Ohio: Kent State University Press, 1970.

Denisoff, R. Serge. *Sing a Song of Social Significance*. Bowling Green: University Popular Press, 1972.

———. *Folk Consciousness. The People's Music and American Communism*. Urbana: University of Illinois Press, 1971.

Denisoff, R. Serge, and Richard A. Peterson (Eds.). *The Sounds of Social Change*. Chicago: Rand McNally, 1972.

Denney, Reuel, and Mary Lea Meyersohn. "A preliminary bibliography on leisure." *American Journal of Sociology*, 62:602–615, 1957.

Deva, Indra. "Modern social forces in Indian folk songs." *Diogenes*, 15:58–65, 1956.

Dilthey, Wilhelm. *Von Deutscher Dichtung und Musik: Aus den Studien zur Geschichte des deutschen Geistes*. Leipzig: 1933.

———. *Der Aufbau der geschichtlichen Welt in den Geisteswissenschaften*. Leipzig: 1927.

———. *Einführung in die Geisteswissenschaften*, 2nd ed., 1923. Here quoted from T. A. Hodges, *Wilhelm Dilthey: An Introduction*. London: 1944.

Dingle, P. "Israel Young: The music belongs to the people." *Rat: Subterranean News* (New York), 1(32)14–16, March 7–13, 1969.

Dobryn, Henry F., and Robert C. Euler. *The Ghost Dance of 1889 among the Pai Indians of Northwestern Arizona*. Prescott, Ariz.: Precott College Press, 1967. (Prescott College Studies in Anthropology, no. 1.)

Downey, James Cecil. "The Music of American Revivalism." Ph.D. Thesis (Music), Tulane University, 1968.

———. "Revivalism, the gospel songs, and social reform." *Ethnomusicology* 9(2): 115–125, 1965.

Duncan, Hugh Dalziel. *Language and Literature in Society*. New York: Bedminister, 1961.

————. "Sociology of art, literature and music: Social contexts of symbolic experience," in *Modern Sociological Theory in Continuity and Change,* Howard Becker and Alvin Boskoff, eds. New York: The Dryden Press, 1957.

Duvignaud, Jean. *Sociologie du Théâtre.* Paris: Presses Universitaires, 1965.

Eisen,Jonathan (Ed.). *The Age of Rock: Sounds of the American Cultural Revolution.* New York: Random House, 1969.

Elder, J. D. "Color, music and conflict A study of aggression in Trinidad with reference to the role of traditional music." *Ethnomusicology,* 8(2):128–136, 1964.

Ellis, Alexander J. "On the musical scales of various nations," *Journal of the Society of Arts,* 1885.

Ellis, Catherine J. "Central and South Australian song styles." *Journal of the Anthropological Society of South Australia* (Adelaide), 4(7):2–11, 1966.

Erdely, Stephen. *Methods and Principles of Hungarian Ethnomusicology.* Bloomington: Indiana University Publications, 1965. Uralic and Altaic Series, vol. 52.

Etzioni, Amitai. *The Active Society. A Theory of Societal and Political Process.* New York: Free Press, 1968.

Etzkorn, K. Peter. "A sociological look at African art," in *The Traditional Artist in West African Societies,* Warren d'Azevedo, ed. Bloomington: Indiana University Press, 1972.

————. "Die Verwundbarkeit von Berufen und der soziale Wandel," *Kölner Zeitschrift für Soziologie,* 21:529–542, 1969.

————. *Georg Simmel: The Conflict in Modern Culture.* New York: Teachers College Press, 1968.

————. "On esthetic standards and reference groups of popular songwriters." *Sociological Inquiry,* 36(1):39–47, 1966.

————. "Non-rational elements in the sociology of arts." *Indian Sociological Bulletin,* 3(4):279–285, 1966.

————. "Georg Simmel and the sociology of music." *Social Forces,* 43(1):101–107, 1964.

————. "The relationship between musical and social patterns in American popular music." *Journal of Research in Music Education,* 12:279–286, 1964.

————. "Social context of songwriting in the United States." *Ethnomusicology,* 7(2):96–106, 1963.

Evans, James F. "What the church tells children in story and song." *Journalism Quarterly,* 44(3):513–519, 1967.

Fallico, Arturo B. *Art and Existentialism.* Englewood Cliffs, N.J.: Prentice-Hall, 1962.

Farnsworth, Paul R. *The Social Psychology of Music,* 1958. Reprint. Ames: Iowa State University Press, 1969.

Faulkner, Robert Roy. "Studio Musicians: Their Work and Career Contingencies in the Hollywood Film Industry." Ph.D. Thesis (Sociology), University of California, Los Angeles, 1968.

Ferris, William R., Jr. "Racial repertoires among blues performers." *Ethnomusicology,* 14(3):439–449, 1970.

Fletcher, Colin. "Beat and gangs on Merseyside." *New Society,* 73:11–14 February 20, 1964.

Foreman, Ronald Clifford. "Jazz and Race Records, 1920–32; Their Origins and Their Significance for the Record Industry and Society." Ph.D. Thesis (Communications), University of Illinois, 1968.

———. "Jazz and race records, 1920–32; Their origins and their significance for the record industry and society." *John Edwards Memorial Foundation Newsletter* **4** (part 3, no. 11):97–99, September 1968.

Fowke, Edith. "Labor and industrial protest songs in Canada." *Journal of American Folklore*, **82**(323):34–50, 1969.

Fox, Daniel M. "Artists in the modern state: The nineteenth-century background." *Journal of Aesthetics and Art Criticism*, **22**:135–148, 1963.

Fox, Lilla M. *Instruments of Religion and Folklore*. New York: Roy Publishers; London: Lutterworth Press, 1969.

Freedman, Alex S. "The sociology of country music." *Southern Humanities Review*, **3**(4):358–362, 1969.

———. "The folksinger: A note on ethnocentrism." *Ethnomusicology*, **9**(2):154–156, 1965.

Freeman, Linton D., and Alan P. Merriam. "Statistical classification in anthropology: An application to ethnomusicology." *American Anthropologist*, **58**(3):464–472, June 1956.

Friedman, Estelle R. "Psychological aspects of folk music." in *Proceedings of the 76th Annual Convention of the American Psychological Association*, 1968, pp. 449–450.

Fubini, Enrico. "Music aesthetics and philosophy." *International Review of Music Aesthetics and Sociology*, **1**(1):94–97, 1970.

Fukač, J., L. Mokrý, and V. Karbusický. *Die Musiksoziologie in der Tschechoslowakai*. Prague: Tschechoslowakisches Musikinformationszentrum, 1967, (Bibliography.)

Garon, Paul. "Blues and the church: Revolt and resignation." *Living Blues* (Chicago), **1**(1):18–23, 1970.

Gehring, Axel. *Genie und Verehrergemeinde: Eine Soziologische Analyse des Genieproblems*. Bonn: Bouvier, 1968. (*Abhandlungen zur Philosophie, Psychologie und Pädagogik*, vol. 46.)

Gehuld, Harry M. *Film Makers on Film Making*. Bloomington: Indiana University Press, 1967.

Gillett, Charlie. *The Sound of the City*. New York: Outerbridge and Dienstfrey, 1970.

Gillis, Frank, and Alan P. Merriam. *Ethnomusicology and Folk Music: An International Bibliography of Dissertations and Theses*. Middletown, Conn.: Wesleyan University Press for the Society of Ethnomusicology, 1966.

Glavan, Joyce. "Sorority tradition and song." *Journal of the Ohio Folklore Society*, **3**(3):192–198, 1968.

Gleason, Ralph J. "Like a rolling stone." *The American Scholar*, **36**(3):555–563, Autumn 1967.

Goldberg, Herbert. "Contemporary popular music." *Journal of Popular Culture*, **4**(3): 572–589, 1971.

Goldman, Albert. *Freakshow: The Rocksoulbluesjazzsickjewblackhumorsexpoppsych Gig and Other Scenes from the Counter-Culture*. New York: Atheneum, 1971.

Gottlieb, Adolph. "Artist and society: A brief case history." *College Art Journal*, **14**: 96–101, 1955.

Gotshalk, D. W. *Art and the Social Order*. New York: Dover, 1962.

Grana, Cesar. *Bohemian versus Bourgeois: French Society and the French Man of Letters in the Nineteenth Century*. New York: Basic Books, 1963.

Grass, Günter. *Über des Selbstverständliche. Reden. Aufsätze. Offene Briefe. Kommentare*. Berlin: Luchterhand, 1968.

Gray, Philip H., and Gloria E. Wheeler. "The semantic differential as an instrument to examine the recent folksong movement." *Journal of Social Psychology,* **72**(2): 24–47, 1967.

Greenway, John. "American Folksongs of Social and Economic Protest." Ph.D. thesis (English Literature), University of Pennsylvania, 1951.

Griff, Mason. "The recruitment and socialization of artist," in *International Encyclopedia of the Social Sciences,* David L. Sills, ed. New York: Macmillan and Free Press, 1968, vol. 5, pp. 447–455.

———. *The Commercial Artist: A Study in Role Conflict and Career Development.* Chicago: University of Chicago Press, 1958.

Grotts, Pearl Irene. "Sociological Aspects of the Crow Indian Dance." M. A. Thesis (Physical Education), Iowa, 1942.

Guild, Elliott William. "The Sociological Role of Music in Primitive Cultures." M. A. Thesis (Economics), Stanford University, 1931.

Habermas, Jürgen. *Strukturwandel der Öffentlichkeit. Untersuchungen zur Kategorie der bürgerlichen Gesellschaft.* Berlin: Luchterhand, 1968.

———. *Theorie und Praxis: Sozialphilosophische Studien.* Berlin: Luchterhand, 1968.

Hall, James W. "Concepts of liberty in American broadside ballads, 1850–1870: A study of the mind of American mass culture." *Journal of Popular Culture,* **2**(2): 252–277, 1968.

Hamburger, Ludwig. "Fragmented society: The structure of Thai music." *Sociologus* (Berlin), **17**(1):54–71, 1967.

Hand, Wayland D. "American occupational and industrial folklore: The miner," in *Kontakte und Grenzen: Probleme der Volks-, Kultur- und Sozialforschung: Festschrift für Gerhard Heilfurth zum 60.* Geburtstag, Göttingen: Otto Schwartz, 1969, pp. 453–460,

Haney, James E. *Ethnomusicology: The World of Music Cultures.* Ann Arbor: University of Michigan, Office of Research Administration, August, 1970. (*Research News,* vol. 21, no. 2.)

Hanna, Judith Lynne. "Dance and the social sciences: An escalated vision," in *Dance: An Art in Academe,* Martin Haberman and Tobie Garth Meisel, eds. New York: Teachers College Press, 1970, pp. 32–38.

Hansen, Chadwick Clarke. "The Ages of Jazz: A Study of Jazz in Its Cultural Context." Ph.D. Thesis (American Studies), University of Minnesota, 1956.

Harap, Louis. "The case for hot jazz." *The Musical Quarterly,* **27**:47–61, 1941.

Harris, Neil. *The Artist in American Society: The Formative Years 1790–1860.* New York: Braziller, 1966.

Harvey, Edward. "Social change and the jazz musician." *Social Forces,* **46**(1):34–42, 1967.

Haskell, Francis. *Patrons and Painters: A Study in the Relations Between Italian Art and Society in the Age of the Baroque.* New York: Knopf, 1963.

Hatterer, Lawrence J. *The Artist in Society: Problems and Treatment of the Creative Personality.* New York: Grove, 1965.

Heckman, Don. "Black music and white America," in *Black America,* John F. Szwed, ed. New York: Basic Books, 1970, pp. 158–170.

Helmholtz, Hermann L. F. *On the Sensations of Tone,* 2nd rev. ed. New York: Dover, 1954.

Hemphill, Paul. *The Nashville Sound*. New York: Simon & Schuster, 1970.

Hennenberg, Fritz. *Deassau-Brecht: Musikalische Arbeiten*. Berlin: Henschelverlag, 1963.

Hentoff, Nat. *The Jazz Life*. New York: The Dial Press, 1961.

Herbert, Robert L. (Ed.). *Modern Artists on Art*. Englewood Cliffs, N.J.: Prentice-Hall, 1968.

Herring, Paul D., and James E. Miller, Jr. *The Arts and the Public*, Chicago: University of Chicago Press, 1967.

Herrmann, Rolf-Dieter. *Der Künstler in der Modernen Gesellschaft*. Frankfurt: Athenäum, 1971.

————. "Über das gesellschaftliche Sein des Künstlers." *Zeitschrift für Ästhetik und Allgemeine Kunstwissenschaft*, 13:113–139, 1968.

Hertzler, Joyce O. *A Sociology of Language*. New York: Random House, 1965.

Herzog, George. "Music at the Fifth International Congress of Anthropological and Ethnological Sciences, Philadelphia, U.S.A." *Journal of the International Folk Music Council*, 9:71–73, 1957.

Hill, John D. "A Study of the Musical Achievement of Culturally Deprived Children and Culturally Advantaged Children at the Elementary School Level." Ph.D. Thesis (Music), University of Kansas, Lawrence, 1968.

Hitchcock, H. Wiley. *Music in the United States*. Englewood Cliffs, N.J.: Prentice-Hall, 1969.

Honigsheim, Paul. *On Max Weber*. Trans. Joan Rytina. New York: Free Press, 1968.

————. "Max Weber in Heidelberg," in Sonderheft 7, *Kölner Zeitschrift für Soziologie und Sozialpsychologie, Max Weber zum Gedächtnis*, René König and Johannes Winckelmann, eds. Cologne: Westdeutscher Verlag, 1963, pp. 161–271.

————. "Sociology of Literature, Theater, Music, and the Arts: A Working Outline." East Lansing, Michigan State University, 1962, (Mimeograph.)

————. *Über Objekt, Methode und wissenschaftliche Stellung der Soziologie*. Cologne: Westdeutscher Verlag, 1961.

————. "Aus den Erinnerungen eines alten Volksbildners," in *Festschrift für Rudolf Reuter: Im Dienste der Erwachsenenbildung*, Franz Pöggeler, Ludwig Langenfeld,, and Gotthard Welzel, eds. Bonn: Bund der Theatergemeinden, 1961, pp. 2–16.

————. "Soziologie der Kunst, Musik und Literatur," in *Die Lehre von der Gesellschaft*, Gottfried Eisermann, ed. Stuttgart: Enke, 1958, pp. 338–373.

————. *Three Lectures on Anthropology for RIAS* (Radio im Amerikanischen Sektor): "Die Altindianischen Hochkulturen I, II"; "Indianerleben im heutigen Amerika." Berlin, RIAS, 1957.

————. "Musikformen und Gesellschaftsformen," in *Die Einheit der Sozialwissenschaften*, W. Bernsdorf and G. Eisermann, eds. Stuttgart: Enke, 1955, pp. 214–225.

————. "The problem of diffusion and parallel evolution," *Papers of the Michigan Academy of Sciences*, vol. 35, 1941.

————. *La Teoría de los Circulos de Cultura y el Evoluciónism*. Lima: Letras de la Facultad de Letras de la Universidad de San Marcos, 1937.

————. "Psychoanalyse, Ethnologie und Primitive Kunst." *Jahrbuch für Prähistorische und Ethnographische Kunst*, Leipzig, vol. 4, 1930.

————."Die Wanderung vom historisch-ethnologischen Standorte aus betrachtet," in *Verhandlungen des 6. deutschen Soziologentages, Zürich 1928, Schriften der deutschen Gesellschaft für Soziologie*, series 1, vol. 6, pp. 127–147, 1929.

Hood, Mantle. *The Ethnomusicologist*. New York: McGraw Hill, 1971.

————."Program of the Institute of Ethnomusicology, University of California, Los Angeles," in *Artistic Values in Traditional Music: Proceedings of a Conference*, Berlin, July 14 to 16, 1965, Peter Crossley-Holland, ed. Berlin: International Institute for Comparative Music Studies and Documentation, 1966, pp. 108–114.

————."The quest for norms in ethnomusicology." *Inter-American Music Bulletin*, 35:1–5, May 1963.

Horowitz, Irving L. "Rock, recordings and rebellion," in *American Music from Storyville to Woodstock*, Charles Nanry, ed. New Brunswick: Trans-Action Books, 1972, pp. 267–288.

Horton, Donald. "The dialogue of courtship in popular songs." *American Journal of Sociology*, 62(6):569–578, 1957.

Huaco, George A. *The Sociology of Film Art*. New York: Basic Books, 1965.

Hughes, H. Stewart. *Consciousness and Society: The Reorientation of European Social Thought, 1890–1930*. New York: Random House, Vintage Book, 1958.

Hunt, David C. "Today's jazz artist: His communication and our technological age." *Jazz and Pop* (New York), 8(9):19–20, September 1969.

Hunt, Irmgard. 'Towards soul: The American hippie—a German romantic?" *Journal of Popular Culture*, 3(4):736–748, 1970.

Huskisson, Yvonne. "The social and ceremonial music of the Pedi." *Journal of Social Research*, 10:129–130, 1959.

Hutchings, Patrick A. "Privacy and musical experience." *Studies in Music* (Nedlands, Western Australia), 2:98–103, 1968.

Inglefield, Howard Gibbs. "The Relationship of Selected Personality Variables to Conformity Behavior Reflected ⁱn the Musical Preferences of Adolescents when Exposed to Peer Group Leader Influences." Ph.D. Thesis (Music), Ohio State University, 1968.

Iyer, M. Subramania. "Classical music under the impact of industrial change," in *Music East and West*, Róger Ashton, ed. New Delhi: Indian Council for Cultural Relations, 1966, pp. 143–145.

Jackson, Anthony. "Sound and ritual." *Man*, 3(2):293–299, 1968.

Jacobs, Norman (Ed.). *Culture for the Millions: Mass Media in Modern Society*. Boston: Beacon, 1964.

Jay, Martin. "The *Institut für Sozialforschung* and the origin of critical sociology." *The Human Factor*, 8(2):6–18, n.d.

"Jazz and revolutionary black nationalism—A panel discussion." *Jazz* (New York), 5(4): April 1966; 6(7):July 1967. (Thirteen installments.)

Jenne, Michael. "The role of tradition in musical education." *The World of Music*, 10(2):8–16, 1968.

Johnson, Guy B. "The Negro Spiritual." *American Anthropologist*, 33:170, 1931.

Johnson, Priscilla. *Khrushchev and the Arts: The Politics of Soviet Culture, 1962–1964*. Cambridge: M.I.T. Press, 1965.

Johnstone, John, and Elihu Katz. "Youth and popular music: A study in the sociology of taste." *American Journal of Sociology*, 62(6):563–68, May 1957.

Jolly, Howard Delcour. "Popular Music: A Study in Collective Behavior." Ph.D. Thesis (Sociology), Stanford University, 1967.

Kadushin, Charles. "The professional self-concept of music students." *American Journal of Sociology*, 75(3):389–404, 1969.

Kaeppler, Adrienne L. "The Structure of Tongan Dance." Ph.D. Thesis (Anthropology), University of Hawaii, Honolulu, 1967.

Kaplan, Arthur Abraham. "Popular Music as a Reflection of the Depression Era." M.A. Thesis (Music), University of Southern California, 1949.

Kaplan, Max. "The Musician in America: A Study of His Social Roles." Ph.D. Thesis (Sociology), University of Illinois, 1951.

———. "Teleopractice: A symphony orchestra as it prepares for a concert." *Social Forces*, 33(4):352–355, 1955.

Karbusický, V., and J. Kasan. *Výzkum Současné Hudebnosti*. Prague: 1964.

Karpeles, Maud. "The distinction between folk and popular music." *Journal of the International Folk Music Council*, 20:9–12, 1968.

Kasdan, Leonard, and Jon H. Appleton. "Tradition and change: The case of music." *Comparative Studies in History and Society*, 12:50–58, 1970.

Katz, Bernard (Ed.). *The Social Implications of Early Negro Music in the United State (1862–1939)*. New York: Arno Press, 1969.

Katz, Ruth. "Mannerism and cultural change: An ethnomusicological example." *Current Anthropology*, 11(4–5):465–475, 1970.

Kautzenbach, George. "The aristocratic profession of music." *Journal of Popular Culture*, 2(2):242–251, 1968.

Kavolis, Vytautas. *Artistic Expression: A Sociological Analysis*. Ithaca, N.Y.: Cornell University Press, 1968.

Kiefer, Thomas M. "Continuous geographical distributions of musical patterns: A test case from the Northwest coast." *American Anthropologist*, 71(4):701–705, 1969.

———. "A note on cross-sex identification among musicians." *Ethnomusicology*, 12(1): 107–109, 1968.

Kirchheimer, Otto. "Private man and society." *Political Science Quarterly*, 81:1–24, 1966.

Kishibe, Shigeo. "Means of preservation and diffusion of traditional music in Japan, 1967. Reprint. *Asian Music* (New York), 2(1):8–13, 1971.

Kitahara, Michio. "Acculturation, survival, and syncretism in Blackfoot, Flathead, and Dakota music." *Japanese Journal of Ethnology*, 26(3):45–48, 1962.

Kleinheksel, John R. "The role of the choir in reformed church worship: Past, present, and future." *Reformed Review*, 17:13–24, 1964.

Klymasz, Robert B. "Social and cultural motifs in Canadian Ukrainian lullabies." *Slavic and East European Journal*, 12(2):176–183, 1968.

Kneif, Tibor. *Musiksoziologie*. Cologne: Hans Gerig, 1971.

Kofsky, Frank. *Black Nationalism and the Revolution in Music*. New York: Pathfinder Press, 1970.

Konz, Stephen and David McDougal. "The effect of background music on the control activity of an automobile driver." *Human Factors* 10(3):233–244, 1968.

Korall, Burt. "The music of protest." *Saturday Review*, 51(46):36–39, 126, November 16, 1968.

Kostelanetz, Richard (Ed.). *The Theatre of Mixed Means. An Introduction to Happenings, Kinetic Environments, and Other Mixed-Means Performances.* New York: Dial, 1968.

Kremenliev, Boris. "Some social aspects of Bulgarian folksongs." *Journal of American Folklore,* **69**:310–319, 1956.

Kresánek, Josef. *Sociálna Funkcia Hudby.* Bratislava: 1961.

Kunst, Jaap. "Some sociological aspects of music," in *Lectures on the History and Art of Music: The Louis Charles Elson Memorial Lectures at the Library of Congress, 1946–1963.* New York: Da Capo Press, 1968, pp. 139–165.

———. *Ethnomusicology: A Study of Its Nature, Its Problems, Methods and Representative Personalities to Which Is Added a Bibliography.* 3rd ed. The Hague: Nijhoff, 1959.

Kurath, Gertrude P. "Dance, music and the daily bread." *Ethnomusicology,* **4**(1):1–8, 1960.

———. Catholic hymns of Michigan Indians." *Anthropological Quarterly,* **30**(2):31–44, 1957.

Laade, Wofgang. "The situation of music and music research in the Pacific—A call for increased activity." *Bulletin of the International Committee on Urgent Anthropological and Ethnological Research,* **10**:53–60, 1968.

Ladner, Robert, Jr. "Folk music, pholk music and the angry children of Malcolm X." *Southern Folklore Quarterly,* **34**(2):131–145, 1970.

Larmin, O. "Soviet society and the aesthetic ideal," in *Art and Society: Collection of Articles.* Moscow: Progress Publishers, 1968, pp. 44–53.

Laskowski, W. T. "Music and maximum participation." *Practical Anthropology,* **15**(1): 37–39, 1968.

Leblond, Richard Emmett, Jr. "Professionalization and Bureaucratization of the Performance of Serious Music in the United States." Ph.D. Thesis (Sociology), University of Michigan, 1968.

Lee, Edward. *Music of the People: A Study of Popular Music in Great Britain.* London: Barrie & Jenkins, 1970.

Lees, Gene. "Rock Symptom of today's sociological disturbances." *High Fidelity,* **17**(11): 57–61, November 1967.

Leiter, Robert D. *The Musicians and Petrillo.* New York: Bookman Associates, 1953.

Leonard, Neil. *Jazz and the White Americans: The Acceptance of a New Art Form.* Chicago: University of Chicago Press, 1962.

Lesure, François. *Music and Art in Society.* University Park: Pennsylvania State University Press, 1968.

Leventman, Seymour. "Sociological Analysis of Musical Taste." M.A. Thesis (Sociology), Indiana University, 1953.

Lévi-Strauss, Claude. *Le Cru et le Cui.* Paris: Plon, 1964.

———. *Le Totémisme Aujourd'hui.* Paris: Presses Universitaires, 1963. Trans. by Rodney Needham. *Totemism.* Boston: Beacon Press, 1963.

———. *Anthropologie Structurale.* Paris: Plon, 1958. Trans. by Claire Jacobson and Brooke Grundfest Schoepf. *Structural Anthropology.* New York: Basic Books, 1967.

Lieberman, Fredric. "Relationships of musical and cultural contrasts in Java and Bali." *Asian Studies* (Quezon City), **5**(2):274–281, 1967.

Lipset, Seymour Martin, and Leo Lowenthal (Eds.). *Culture and Social Character*. New York: Free Press, 1961.

Lissa, Zofie. "Prolegomena to the theory of musical tradition." *International Review of Music Aesthetics and Sociology*, 1(1):35–54, 1970.

List, George. "Acculturation and musical tradition." *Journal of the International Folk Music Council*, 16:18–21, 1964.

———. "Ethnomusicology in higher education." *Music Journal*, 20(8):20–26, 95, 1962.

List, George, and Juan Orrego-Salas (Eds.). *Music in the Americas*. Bloomington: Indiana University Research Center in Anthropology, Folklore, and Linguistics, 1967. (Inter-American Music Monograph Series, vol. 1.)

Lloyd, Albert Lancaster. "Towards distinction between 'popular' and 'folk': A bit of history." *Club Folk* (London), 3(2):8–11, 1970.

Lomax, Alan (Ed.). *Folk Song Style and Culture: A Staff Report on Cantometrics*. Washington, D.C.: American Association for the Advancement of Science, 1968.

Lomax, Alan. "Song structure and social structure." *Ethnology*, 1(4):425–451, 1962.

———. "Folk song style." *American Anthropologist*, 61(6):927–954, 1959.

Lomax, Alan, Irmgard Bartenieff, and Forrestine Paulay. "Choreometrics: A method for the study of cross-cultural pattern in film." *Research Film*, 6(6),505–517, 1969.

Lowenthal, Leo. *Literature, Popular Culture and Society*. Englewood Cliffs, N.J.: Prentice-Hall, 1961.

———. *Literature and the Image of Man: Sociological Studies of the European Drama and Novel, 1600–1900*. Boston: Beacon, 1957.

Lukas, Victor Thomas. "The Traditionally Oriented Urban Folk Musician: Revitalistic Aspects of a Subculture." M.A. Thesis (Anthropology), University of Illinois, Urbana, 1967.

Luthe, Heinz Otto. "Recorded music and the record industry: A sector neglected by sociological research." *International Social Science Journal*, 20(3):656–666, 1968.

MacCann, Richard Dyer (Ed.). *Film and Society*. New York: Scribner, 1964.

Maceda, José: "Means of preservation and diffusion of traditional music: The Phillippine situation," 1967. Reprint. *Asian Music*, 2(1):14–23, 1971.

MacGilvray, Dan. "Topical song and the American radical tradition," in *Newport Folk Festival*, Henry Glassie and Ralph Rinzler, eds. 1967, pp. 11, 36–37.

MacIver, Robert M. *Politics and Society*. New York: Atherton, 1969.

Madsen, Clifford K., and Charles H. Madsen, Jr. "Music as a behavior modification technique with a juvenile delinquent." *Journal of Music Therapy*, 5(3):72–76, 1968.

Manheim, Henry L., and Alice Cummins. "Selected musical traits among Spanish, Negro, and Anglo-American girls." *Sociology and Social Research*, 45(1):56–64, 1960.

McAllester, David P. "Ethnomusicology, the field and the society." *Ethnomusicology*, 7(3):182–186, 1963.

———. "The role of music in western Apache culture," in *Selected Papers of the Fifth International Congress of Anthropological and Ethnological Sciences, 1956*. Philadelphia: University of Pennsylvania Press, 1960, pp. 468–472.

McKissick, Marvin Leo. "A Study of the Function of Music in the Major Religious Revivals in America since 1875." MM. Thesis, University of Southern California, 1957.

McLean, Mervyn. "Song loss and social context among the New Zealand Maori." *Ethnomusicology*, 9(3):296–304, 1965.

McLeod, N. "The Social Context of Music in a Polynesian Community." M.A. Thesis (Anthropology), London School of Economics, 1956–1957.

McPhee, William N. "When culture becomes a business," in *Sociological Theories in Progress*, Joseph Berger, ed. New York: Houghton Mifflin, 1966, pp. 227–243.

Means, Richard L., and Bertha Doleman. "Notes on Negro jazz. 1920–1950; The use of biographical materials in sociology." *Sociological Quarterly*, 9(3):332–342, 1968.

Meltzer, R. *The Aesthetics of Rock.* New York: Something Else, 1970.

Merriam, Alan P. "Ethnomusicology revisited." *Ethnomusicology* 13(2):213–229, May 1969.

———. 'Ethnomusicology," in *International Encyclopedia of the Social Sciences*, David L. Sills, ed. New York: Macmillan and Free Press, 1968, vol. 10, pp. 562–66.

———. 'Ethnomusicology." *The Review* (Indiana University, Alumni Association of the College of Arts and Sciences—Graduate School), 9(3):1–9, 1967.

———. *Ethnomusicology of the Flathead Indians.* Chicago: Aldine, 1967.

———. "Music and the origin of the Flathead Indians—A problem in culture history," in *Music in the Americas*, George List and Juan Orrego-Salas, eds. Bloomington: Indiana University Research Center in Anthropology, Folklore, and Linguistics, 1967, pp. 129–138. (Inter-American Music Monograph Series, vol. 1.)

———. "The use of music as a technique of reconstructing culture history in Africa," in *Reconstructing African Culture History*, Creighton Gabel and Norman R. Bennett, eds. Boston: Boston University Press, 1967, pp. 83–114. (Boston University African Research Studies, no. 8.)

———. "Music and the dance," in *The African World: A Survey of Social Research*, Robert A. Lystad, ed. New York: Praeger, 1965, pp. 452–468.

———. *The Anthropology of Music.* Evanston: Northwestern University Press, 1964.

———. "The arts and anthropology," in *Horizons of Anthropology*, Sol Tax, ed. Chicago: Aldine, 1964, pp. 224–236.

———. 'The purposes of ethnomusicology, An anthropological view." *Ethnomusicology*, 7(3):206–213, 1963.

———. "Ethnomusicology—Discussion and definition of the field." *Ethnomusicology*, 4(3):107–114, 1960.

———. "Ethnomusicology in our time." *American Music Teacher*, 8:6–7, 27–32, 1959.

———. "Music in American culture." *American Anthropologist*, 57(6):1173–1181, 1955.

Merriam, Alan P., and Warren L. D'Azevedo. "Washo Peyote songs." *American Anthropologist*, 59:615–641, 1957.

Merriam, Alan P., and Raymond W. Mack. "The jazz community." *Social Forces*, 38:211–222, 1960.

Merrill, Francis E. "Art and the self." *Sociology and Social Research*, 52:185–194, 1968.

Mersmann, Hans. "Soziologie als Hilfswissenschaft der Musikgeschichte." *Archiv für Musikwissenschaft*, 10:1–15, 1953.

Meyer, Ernst Hermann. *Musik im Zeitgeschehen.* Berlin: Henschel, 1952.

———. *English Chamber Music.* London: Lawrence and Wishart, 1946.

———. *Die Mehrstimmige Spielmusik des 17. Jahrhunderts in Nord und Mitteleuropa.* Kassel: Bärenreiter, 1934.

Meyer, Leonard B. *Music, the Arts, and Ideas.* Chicago: University of Chicago Press, 1967.

———. "Meaning in music and information theory." *Journal of Aesthetics and Art Criticism,* 15:412–424, 1957.

Miller, Lloyd. "The sound of protest." *Case Western Reserve Journal of Sociology,* 1:41–52, 1967.

Mooney, H. F. "Popular music since the 1920s: The significance of shifting taste." *American Quarterly,* 20(1):67–85, 1968.

Moore, Thomas Gale. *The Economics of the American Theater.* Durham, N.C.: Duke University Press, 1968.

Moore, Wilbert E. *Man, Time, and Society.* New York: Wiley, 1963.

Morgen, Sandi. "Antiwar protest songs: Folklore in a modern age." *Folklore Annual of the University Folklore Association,* 2:73–80, 1970.

Morton, David. *The Traditional Music of Thailand: Introduction, Commentary, and Analyses.* Los Angeles: UCLA Institute of Ethnomusicology, 1968.

Mueller, John H. "A sociological approach to musical behavior." *Ethnomusicology,* 7(3):216–220, 1963.

Mullen, Patrick B. "A Negro street performer: Tradition and innovation." *Western Folklore,* 29(2):91–103, 1970.

Müller, John H. "Review of Alphons Silbermann, *The Sociology of Music.*" *Kölner Zeitschrift für Soziologie und Sozialpsychologie,* 16(1):196–198, 1964.

Murphy, Robert F. "Social structure and sex antagonisms." *Southwestern Journal of Anthropology,* 15(1):89–98, 1959.

Murphy, William Robert. Melodic Contour in White Anglo-American Traditional Narrative Song in North America. Ph.D. Thesis (Music), University of Pennsylvania, 1969.

Mursell, James L. *The Psychology of Music,* 1937. Reprint. New York: Johnson Reprint, 1970.

Nanry, Charles (Ed.). *American Music: From Storyville to Woodstock.* New Brunswick, N.J.: Dutton, 1972.

Naroll, Roal, with appendixes by Alan Lomax and Edwin Erikson. "What have we learned from cross-cultural surveys?" *American Anthropologist,* 72(6);1227–1288, 1970.

Nash, Dennison. "The role of the composer." *Ethnomusicology,* 5:81–94, 187–205, 1961.

———. "The socialization of an artist: The American composer." *Social Forces,* 35(4): 307–313, 1957.

———. "The American Composer: A Study in Social-Psychology." Ph.D. Thesis (Sociology), Pennsylvania, 1954.

Needham, Joseph. "Science and society in East and West," *Science and Society,* 28(4): 385–408, Fall 1964.

Nettel, Reginald. Sing a Song of England: A Social History of Traditional Song. Denver: Alan Swallow, 1954.

———. *A Social History of Traditional Song,* 1954. Reprint. London: Adams and Dart; New York, Augustus M. Kelley, 1969.

Nettl, Bruno. "The place of ethnomusiciology in American education: Background for discussion," in *Yugoslav-American Seminar on Music*. Su. Stefan, Yugoslavia, July 6 to 14, 1968, pp. 321–330.

———. *Reference Materials in Ethnomusicology. A Bibliographic Essay*. 2nd rev. ed. Detroit: Information Coordinators, 1967.

———. *Theory and Method in Ethnomusicology*. New York: Free Press, 1964.

———. "Speculations on musical style and musical content in acculturation." *Acta Musicologica*, 35(1):35–37, 1963.

———. "Musical cartography and the distribution of music." *Southwestern Journal of Anthropology*, 16(3):338–347, 1960.

———. "Historical aspects of ethnomusicology." *American Anthropologist*, 60:518–532, 1958.

———. "The Hymns of the Amish: An example of marginal survival." *Journal of American Folklore*, 70:323–328, 1957.

———. "Change in folk and primitive music A survey of methods and studies." *Journal of American Musicological Society*, 8:101–109, Summer 1955.

Nketia, J. H. Kwabena. "The arts in traditional society." *Ghana News* (Washington, D.C., Embassy of Ghana) 2(5):4–6, 8, 1970.

Noebel, David A. *Rhythm, Riots and Revolution: An Analysis of the Communist Use of Music—The Communist Master Music Plan*. Tulsa: Christian Crusade Publications, 1966.

Nurse, George T. "Popular songs and national identity in Malawi." *African Music, 3*(3): 101–106, 1964.

O'Connor, Francis V. *Federal Art Patronage, 1933–1943*. College Park: University of Maryland Press, 1966.

Ocsiannikov, Michail F. "Creative freedom and moral responsibility," in *Art and Society: Collection of Articles*. Moscow: Progress Publishers, 1968, pp. 114–120.

Onion, Charles Clary. "The Social Status of Musicians in Seventeenth Century France." Ph.D. Thesis (History), Minnesota, 1959.

Orring, Elliott. "Whalemen and their songs: A study of folklore and culture." *New York Folklore Quarterly*, 23(1):30–52, 1971.

Osman, Mohd, Taib. "Some observations on the socio-cutural context of traditional Malay music." *Tenggara*, 5:121–128, 1969.

Osvětový Ústav V Praze, Otázky Hudebni Sociologie: Sbornik Přiscpěvků z Hudebné Sociologického Semináře. Svazu Československých Skladatelů 6. -8. Dubna 1966. Prague: 1967. (With English summary.)

Owen, Roger C., Nancy E. Walstrom, and Ralph C. Michelsen. "Musical culture and ethnic solidarity: A Baja California case study." *Journal of American Folklore*, 82(324):99–111, 1969.

Parmar, Shyam. "Prelude to ethnomusicology in India." *Folklore*, 12(1):20–29, 1971.

Peacock, James L. *Rites of Modernization, Symbolic and Social Aspects of Indonesian Proletarian Drama*. Chicago: University of Chicago Press, 1968.

The Performing Arts, Problems and Prospects, Rockefeller Panel Report of the Future of Theatre, Dance, Music in America. New York: McGraw-Hill, 1965.

Peterson, Richard A. "Taking popular music too seriously." *Journal of Popular Culture*, 4(3):590–594, 1971.

————. "Artistic creativity and alienation: The jazz musician vs. his audience." *Arts in Society*, 3:244–248, 1965.

Peterson, Richard A., and David G. Berger. "Entrepreneurship in organizations: Evidence from the popular music industry." *Administrative Science Quarterly*, 16: 97–106, March 1971.

Petrovic, Radmila. "Ethnomusicology in Yugoslavia." *Zvuk*, 77–78:20–30, 1967.

Phillips, Bruce. "Writing people's songs." *Sing Out!*, 20(2):6–9, November 1970.

Piaget, Jean. "The place of the sciences of man in the system of sciences," in *Main Trends of Research in the Social and Human Sciences, Part I: Social Sciences*, René Maheu, ed. The Hague: Mouton, 1970, pp. 1–57.

Pinthus, Gerhard. *Das Konzertleben in Deutschland*. Strasbourg: Heitz, 1932.

Podvin, Mary Grace. "The influence of music on the performance of a work task." *Journal of Music Therapy*, 4(2):52–56, 1967.

Polunin, Ivan. "Visual and sound recording apparatus in ethnographic fieldwork." *Current Anthropology*, 11(1):3–22, 1970.

Powdermaker, Hortense. *Hollywood, The Dream Factory: An Anthropologist Looks at the Movie-makers*. Boston: Little, Brown, 1950.

Pratt, Carroll C. *The Meaning of Music: A Study in Psychological Aesthetics*, 1931. Reprint. New York: Johnson Reprint, 1968.

————. "Music as the language of emotion," in *Lectures on the History and Art of Music: The Louis Charles Elson Memorial Lectures at the Library of Congress, 1946–1963*. New York: Da Capo Press, 1968, pp. 41–64.

Pritchard, B. W. "Societies in Society: A Case Study in the Historical Sociology of Music." M.A. Thesis (Folklore), Indiana University, 1965.

Ramachandran, N. S. "Classical music and the mass-media (with special reference to South India)," in *Music East and West*, Roger Ashton, ed. New Delhi: Indian Council for Cultural Relations, 1966, pp. 166–170.

Randall, Richard S. *Censorship of the Movies*. Madison: University of Wisconsin Press, 1968.

Reid, Lawrence. "Dancing and music." *Philippine Sociological Review*, 9(3–4):55–82, 1961.

Rhodes, Willard. "Music as an agent of political expression." *African Studies Bulletin*, 5:14–22, 1962.

————. "Society of ethnomusicology." *African Music*, 1(3):70–71, 1956.

Ricks, George Robinson. "Some Aspects of the Religious Music of the United States Negro: An Ethnomusicological Study with Special Emphasis on the Gospel Tradition." Ph.D. Thesis (Anthropology), Northwestern University, 1960.

Rihtman, Cvjetko. "The philosophy of traditional folk music," in *Yugoslav-American Seminar on Music*, Su. Stefan, Yugoslavia, July 6 to 14, 1968, pp. 309–320.

Rodman, Selden. *Conversation with Artists*. New York: Braziller, 1967.

Rodnitzky, Jerome L. "The evolution of the American protest song." *Journal of Popular Culture*, 3(1):35–45, 1969.

Rogers, M. Robert. "Jazz influence on French music." *The Musical Quarterly*, 21:53–68, 1935.

Rosenberg, Bernard, and Norris Fliegel. *The Vanguard Artist: Portrait and Self-portrait*. Chicago: Quadrangle, 1965.

Rosenberg, Bernard, and David M. White (Eds.). *Mass Culture: The Popular Arts in America*. Glencoe, Free Press, 1957.

Rosenberg, Neil V. "Taking popular culture seriously: The Beatles." *Journal of Popular Culture*, 4(1):53–56, 1970.

Rosenstone, Robert A. "The times they are a-changing': The music of protest," in *Protest in the Sixties*, Joseph Boskin and Robert A. Rosenstone, eds. Philadelphia: Annals of the American Academy of Political and Social Science, vol. 382, March 1969, pp. 131–144.

Ross, James. "Folk song and social environment." *Scottish Studies*, 5(1):18–39, 1961.

Rout, Leslie B., Jr. "Economics and race in jazz," in *Frontiers of American Culture*, Bay B. Browne, Richard H. Crowder, Virgil L. Lokke, and William T. Stafford, eds. West Lafayette: Purdue University Studies, 1968, pp. 154–171.

Rubin, Ruth. *Yiddish Folksongs of Social Significance*. New York: Education Department of the Workmen's Circle, 1968.

———. "A comparative approach to a Yiddish song of protest." *Studies in Ethnomusicology*, 2:54–74, 1965.

———. "Yiddish folksongs of immigration and the melting pot." *New York Folklore Quarterly*, 17:173–182, 1961.

Ruby, Jay. "Censorship, nudity and obscenity in American popular music." *Jazz and Pop* (New York), 8(1):22–25, 1969.

Russel, Ross. *Jazz Style in Kansas City and the South West*. Berkeley: University of California Press, 1971.

Rust, Frances. *Dance in Society: An Analysis of the Relationship Between the Social Dance and Society in England from the Middle Ages to the Present Day*. London: Routledge and Kegan Paul, 1969.

Ruwet, Nicolas. "Musicology and linguistics." *International Social Science Journal*, 19 (1):79–87, 1967.

Sakuma, Arline Fuju. "Education and Styles of Innovation: The Socialization of Musicians." Ph.D. Thesis (Sociology), University of Washington, 1968.

Šamko, Josef. *Hudba a Hubnisľ v Spoločnosti*. Bratislava, 1947.

Sandvoss, Joachim. "A Study of the Musical Preferences, Interests, and Activities of Parents as Factors in Their Attitude Toward the Musical Education of Their Children." Ed.D. Thesis (Music), University of British Columbia, 1969.

Schapiro, Meyer. "On the relation of patron and artist. Comments on a proposed model for the scientist." *American Journal of Sociology*, 70:363–369, 1964.

Schenk, Erich (Ed.). *Musik als Gestalt und Erlebnis: Festschrift Walter Graf zum 65. Geburtstag*, Vienna: Hermann Bohlaus Nachf., 1970.

Schering, Arnold. "Musik," in *Handwörterbuch der Soziologie*, Alfred Vierkandt, ed. Stuttgart: Enke, 1931, pp. 393–399.

Schlesinger, Arthur, Jr. "Notes on a national cultural policy." *Daedalus*, 89(2):394–400, 1960.

Scholl, Sharon, and Sylvia White. *Music and the Culture of Man*. New York: Holt, Rinehart and Winston, 1970.

Schuessler, Karl F. "Social background and musical taste." *American Sociological Review*, 13(3):330–335, 1948.

Schuller, Gunther. *Early Jazz, Its Roots and Musical Development*. New York: Oxford University Press, 1968.

Schütz, Alfred. "Making music together: A study in social relationship," in *Collected Papers, Studies in Social Theory (Schütz)*, Arvid Brodessen, ed., The Hague: Martinus Nijhoff, 1964, vol. 2, pp. 159–178.

Seeger, Charles. "Toward a unitary field theory for musicology." *Selected Reports* (Los Angeles, Institute for Ethnomusicology of the University of California), 1(3):172–210, 1970.

———. "The folkness of the non-folk vs. the non-folkness of the folk," in *Folklore and Society: Essays in Honor of Benjamin A. Botkin*, Bruce Jackson, ed. Hatboro, Pa.: Folklore, Associates, 1966, pp. 1–9.

———. "Music as a tradition of communication, discipline, and play." *Ethnomusicology*, 6(3):156–163, 1962.

———. "The cultivation of various European traditions in the Americas," in *Report of the 8th Congress of the International Musicological Society*. Kassel: Bärenreiter, 1961, pp. 364–375.

———. "Music and class structure in the United States." *American Quarterly*, 9(3):281–294, Fall 1957.

Seeger, Pete. "The popularisation of folk songs in the U.S.A." *Folkmusic and Folklore*, 1:139–142, 1967.

Sellers, Mary Josephine. "The Role of the Fine Arts in the Culture of Southern Baptist Churches." Ph.D. Thesis (Humanities), Syracuse University, 1968.

Sendrey, Alfred. *The Music of the Jews in the Diaspora (up to 1800): A Contribution to the Social and Cultural History of the Jews*. New York: Thomas Yoseloff, 1970.

Serauky, Walter. "Wesen und Aufgabe der Musiksoziologie." *Zeitschrift für Musikwissenschaft*, 16:232–244, 1934.

Seymour, Margaret R. "Music in Lincoln, Nebraska in the Nineteenth Century: A Study of the Musical Culture of a Frontier Society." M.A. Thesis, University of Nebraska, 1968.

Shaw, Arnold. "Rocks in their heads: What will the protest generation listen to now that the professors have taken over the rock?" *High Fidelity*, 19(4):49–51, April 1969.

Silbermann, Alphons. "Schwächen und Marotten der Massenmedienforschung." *Kölner Zeitschrift für Soziologie und Sozialpsychologie*, 24:118–131, 1972.

———. "Situation et vocation de la sociologie de l'art." *Revue Internationale des Sciences Sociales*, 20(4):617–639, 1968.

———. *Vorteile und Nachteile des kommerziellen Fernsehens, Eine Soziologische Studie*. Düsseldorf: Econ, 1968.

———. *Bildschirm und Wirklichkeit*. Berlin: Ullstein, 1966.

———. "Réflexions sur les conflits des groupes dans les milieux musicaux," in *Soziologische Arbeiten*, Peter Atteslander and Roger Girod, eds. Bern: Verlag Hans Huber, 1966, pp. 1–19.

———. "Theater und Gesellschaft," in *Atlantisbuch des Theaters*. Zürich: Atlantis Verlag, 1966, pp. 387–406.

———. "Max Weber's musikalischer Exkurs," in Sonderheft 7, *Kölner Zeitschrift für Soziologie und Sozialpsychologie, Max Weber zum Gedächtnis*, René König and Johannes Winckelmann, eds., Cologne: Westdeutscher Verlag, 1963, pp. 448–469.

———. "Schallplatte und Gesellschaft." *Bertelsmann Briefe*, 24:1–8, 1963.

———. *The Sociology of Music*. London: Routledge and Kegan Paul, 1963.

———. *Wovon lebt die Musik: Die Prinzipien der Musiksoziologie.* Regensburg: Bosse, 1957.

———. *Introduction à une Sociologie de la Musique.* Paris: Presses Universitaires, 1955.

———. "Sociological aspects of radio music." *Transactions of the 2nd World Congress of Sociology,* 1953, vol. 1, pp. 129–131.

Silbermann, Alphons and Ernest Zahn. *Die Konzentration der Massenmedien und ihre Wirkungen.* Düsseldorf: Econ, 1970.

Simmel, Georg. "Psychologische und ethnologische Studien über Musik." *Zeitschrift für Völkerpsychologie und Sprachwissenschaft,* 13:261–305, 1882. Trans. in K. Peter Etzkorn, *Georg Simmel: The Conflict in Modern Culture.* New York: Teachers College Press, 1968, pp. 98–140.

Slotkin, J. S. "Jazz and its forerunners as an example of acculturation." *American Sociological Review,* 8(5):570–575, 1943.

Smalley, William A. "Music, church, and ethnocentrism." *Practical Anthropology,* 9:272–273, 1962.

Smith, Don Crawmer. "Music programming of thirteen Los Angeles AM radio stations." *Journal of Broadcasting,* 8(2):173–184, 1964.

Smith, Lucy Harth. "Negro Musicians and Their Music." *The Journal of Negro History,* 20:430, 1935.

Smith, Michael G. "The social functions and meaning of Hausa praise-singing." *Ibadan,* 21:81–92, 1965.

Soderberg, Bertil. "Field research in ethnomusicology." *Ethnos* (Stockholm), 31:83–88, 1966.

Sorokin, Pitirim A. *Social and Cultural Dynamics,* vol. 1, New York: American Book Co., 1937.

Spellman, A. B. *Four Lives in the Bebop Business.* New York: Pantheon Books, 1966.

Stafford, Peter. "Rock as politics." *Crawdaddy* (New York), 19:31–33, 1968.

Stanislav, Jozef. *Hudebni Kultura, Uméní a Život,* n.p. 1940.

———. "Ideologie a hudba." *Rytmus,* 1936–1937.

Staples, Sylvia M. "A paired-associates learning test utilizing music as the mediator: An exploratory study." *Journal of Music Therapy,* 5(2):53–57, 1968.

Stebbins, Robert A. "Role distance, role distance behavior and jazz musicians." *British Journal of Sociology,* 20(4):406–415, 1969.

———. "A theory of the jazz community." *Sociological Quarterly,* 9(3):318–331, 1968.

———. "Class, status, and power among jazz and commercial musicians." *The Sociological Quarterly,* 7(2):197–213, 1966.

———. "The Jazz Community: The Sociology of a Musical Sub-Culture." Ph.D. Thesis (Sociology), University of Minnesota, 1964.

———. "The Conflict between Musical and Commercial Values in the Minneapolis Jazz Community," *Proceedings of the Minnesota Academy of Science,* 30:75, 1962.

Steele, Anita Louis. "Effects of social reinforcement on the musical preference of mentally retarded children." *Journal of Music Therapy,* 42(2):57–62, 1967.

Stekert, Ellen Jane. "Two Voices of Tradition: The Influence of Personality and Collecting Environment upon the Songs of Two Traditional Folk Singers. Ph.D. Thesis (Folklore), University of Pennsylvania, 1965.

Stockhausen, Karlheinz. *Texte zur Elektronischen und Instrumentalen Musik 1.* Cologne: DuMont Schauberg, 1963.

Stumpf, Carl. *Die Anfänge der Musik.* Leipzig, 1911.

——. "Lieder der Bellakula-Indianer." *Viertel Jahreshcrift für Musikwissenschaft, 11,* 1886. Reprinted in *Sammelbände für Vergleichende Musikwissenschaft, I,* 1922.

Supičić, Ivo. *Musique et Société: Perspectives pour une Sociologie de la musique.* Zagreb: Institut de Musicologie, 1971.

——. "Science on music and values in music." *Journal of Aesthetics and Art Criticism,* 28(1):71–77, 1969.

Supičić, Ivo, et al. "Sociology in music: Results and perspectives of current research," in *Report of the Tenth Congress of the International Musicological Society,* Ljubljana, 1967, Dragotin Cvetko, ed. Kassel: Bärenreiter, Ljubljana: University of Ljubljana, 1970, pp. 405–423.

Szwed, John F. "Paul E. Hall: A Newfoundland song-maker and his community of song," in *Folksongs and Their Makers,* Henry G. Glassie, Edward D. Ives, and John F. Szwed. Bowling Green: Bowling Green University Popular Press, 1970, pp. 147–169.

——. "Musical adaptation among Afro-Americans." *Journal of American Folklore,* 82(324):112–121, 1969.

——. "Negro music: Urban renewal," in *Our Living Traditions: An Introduction to American Folklore,* Tristram Potter Coffin, ed. New York: Basic Books, 1968.

——. "Musical style and racial conflict." *Phylon,* 27(4):358–366, 1966.

Szweykowski, Zygmunt M. "Tradition and popular elements in Polish music of the Baroque era." *Musical Quarterly,* 56(1):99–115, 1970.

Taylor, Gene Fred. "Culturally Transcendent Factors in Musical Perception." Ph.D. Thesis (Music), Florida State University, 1969.

Thieme, Darius L. "Ethnomusicology—The discipline and its objective." *Musart,* 18(2): 14–15, 38–40, 1965.

Thurman, Howard. *Deep River: Reflections on the Religious Insight of the Negro Spirituals,* 1955. Reprint. Port Washington, N.Y.: Kennikat Press, 1969.

Underhill, Ruth Murray. *Singing for Power: The Song Magic of the Papago Indians of Southern Arizona,* 1938. Reprint. Berkeley: University of California Press, 1968.

Upadhyaya, Hari S. "Mother-daughter relationship patterns in the Hindu joint family: A study based upon the analysis of the Bhojpuri folksongs of India." *Folklore* (London), 79:217–226, 1968.

Variakojis, Danguole Jurate. "Concepts of Secular and Sacred among the White Mountain Apache as Illustrated by Musical Practice." Ph.D. Thesis (Anthropology), Indiana University, 1968.

Vetterl, Karel. *K Sociologii Hudebniho Rozhlasu, Musikologie I.* Brno, 1938.

Vig, Rudolf. *Indian Folk Music Ethnomusicology: Comparative Study of Indian Folk Music and the Music of European Gypsies by Recording Indian Folk Music on Tape.* Budapest: Hungarian Academy of Sciences, 1968.

Vučković, Vojislav. "Hudba jako propagační prostředek." *Klič,* 3, 1932–1933.

Wachsmann, Klaus P. "Recent trends in ethnomusicology." *Proceedings of the Royal Musical Association,* 85:65–80, 1958–1959.

———. "The sociology of recording in Africa south of the Sahara." *African Music*, **2**(2): 77–79, 1959.

Waterman, Richard A. "Music in Australian aboriginal culture—Some sociological and psychological implications." *Music Therapy*, 5:40–49, 1956.

Watson, Thomas William. "A Study of Musical Attitudes and Their Relationship to Environment among Rural Socio-economically Deprived Students in Central Oklahoma." D. Mus. Ed. Thesis, University of Oklahoma, 1968.

Weber, Marianne. *Max Weber: Ein Lebensbild*. Tübingen: Mohr, 1925.

Weber, Max. *The Rational and Social Foundations of Music*, (1921). Trans. and ed. by Don Martindale, Johannes Riedel, and Gertrude Neuwirth. Carbondale: Southern Illinois University Press, 1958.

———. *Die Rationalen und Soziologischen Grundlagen der Musik*. Munich: Drei Masken Verlag, 1921.

Werner, Eric. *From Generation to Generation: Studies in Jewish Music Tradition*. New York: American Conference of Cantors, 1968.

Westby, David Leroy. "The Social Organization of a Symphony Orchestra, with Special Attention to the Informal Associations of Symphony Members." M.A. Thesis (Sociology), Minnesota, 1957.

White, Harrison C., and Cynthia A. White. *Canvases and Careers: Institutional Change in the French Painting World*. New York: Wiley, 1965.

Whiteside, Dale R. "Traditions and directions in the music of Vietnam." *Daily Egyptian* (Carbondale, Southern Illinois University, pp. 6–7, 9, February 6, 1971.

Wilson, John S. *Jazz: The Transition Years, 1940–1960*. New York: Appleton-Century-Crofts, 1966.

Wilson, Robert N. *The Arts in Society*. Englewood Cliffs, N.J.: Prentice-Hall, 1964.

———. *Man made Plain: The Poet in Contemporary Society*. Cleveland Howard Allen, 1958.

Winçkel, Fritz. "Aspects of information theory in relation to comparative music studies," in *Artistic Values in Traditional Music: Proceedings of a Conference, July 14 to 16, 1965*, Peter Crossley-Holland, ed. Berlin: International Institute for Comparative Music Studies and Documentation, 1966, pp. 124–127.

Winick, Charles. "The use of drugs by jazz musicians." *Social Problems*, 7(3):240–253, 1959–1960.

Wiora, Walter. "Ethnomusicology and the history of music." *Studia Musicologica*, 7: 187–193, 1965.

Wolff, Kurt H. *The Sociology of Georg Simmel*. Glencoe: Free Press, 1950.

Wylie, Floyd E. M., Jr. "An Investigation of Some Aspects of Creativity of Jazz Musicians." Ph.D. Thesis (Psychology), Wayne State University, 1968.

Yablonsky, Lewis. *The Hippie Trip*. New York: Pegasus, 1968.

Yamaguchi, Osamu. "The Music of Palau: An Ethnomusicological Study of the Classical Tradition." M.A. Thesis (Music), University of Hawaii, Honolulu, 1967.

Yasser, J. A. *A Theory of Evolving Tonality*. New York: American Library of Musicology, 1932.

Zemp, Hugo. *Musique Dan: La musique dans la pensée et la vie sociale d'une société africaine*. The Hague: Mouton, 1971.

BIBLIOGRAPHIC UPDATE (1972–1988)
MAJOR THEMES AND VARIATIONS

GENERAL SOCIOLOGY

Becker, Howard S. *Art Worlds*, Berkeley, Calif.: University of California Press, 1982. xiv + 392p.

Blacking, John. Book Review of K. Peter Etzkorn, *Music and Society*. *Ethnomusicology*, 20(1):143–45, 1976.

Blaukopf, Kurt. "Max Weber und die Musiksoziologie," in *Rudolf Haase Festschrift*, Werner Schulze, ed. Eisenstadt: Elfriede Rötzer Verlag, 1980. 13–23p.

Blaukopf, Kurt. *Musik im Wandel der Gesellschaft: Grundzüge der Musiksoziologie*, München: R. Piper & Co. Verlag, 1982. 383p.

Blaukopf, Kurt. "Towards a theory of 'cultural barriers'," in *Contributions to the Sociology of the Arts*, Ivan Vitanyi, ed. ISA Research Committee 37. Sofia: Research Institute for Culture, 1983, pp. 123–27.

Blomster, Wes V. "Sociology of music: Adorno and beyond." *Telos*, 28(Summer):81–112, 1976. [Adorno, Blaukopf, and Silbermann are contrasted and placed into the context of critically surveyed, largely German literature.]

Bontinck, Irmgard. "Mass media and new types of youth music. Methodological and terminological problems." *International Review of the Aesthetics and Sociology of Music*, VI(1):47–56, 1975.

Bontinck, Irmgard. "Die Massenmedien als Herausforderung für die Musiksoziologie," *Massenmedien, Musikpolitik und Musikerziehung*, Elena Ostleitner, Ed. Wien: Verlag des Verbandes der wissenschaftlichen Gesellschaften österreichs, 1987, pp. 11–23. 337p. [Schriftenreihe Musik und Gesellshaft, 20.]

Bourdieu, Pierre. *Distinction: A Social Critique of the Judgement of Taste*. Cambridge: Harvard University Press, 1984. xiv + 613p.

Braun, Joachim. "Aspekte der Musiksoziologie in Israel," in *Hamburger Jahrbuch*, Band 9, n.d., pp. 85–103.

Brook, Barry S., Edward O.D. Downes, and Sherman Van Solkema (Eds.) *Perspectives in Musicology*, New York: W.W. Norton and Co., Inc., 1972. xviii + 365p. [Collection of authoritative essays reflecting state of the field.]

Burger, Peter. "The institution of 'art' as a category in the sociology of literature." *Cultural Critique*, 2(Winter):5–33, 1985–1986.

Burton, Barbara. "A cultural study of music: Suggestions for a contemporary framework." *Critical Social Research* (UK), 1(2):67–85, 1985.

Dasilva, Fabio B., Anthony Blasi, and David R. Dees. *The Sociology of Music*, Notre Dame, Ind.: University of Notre Dame Press, 1984. viii + 186p.

Dasilva, Fabio B., and David R. Dees. "The social realms of music." *Revue Internationale de Sociologie* (Italy), 12(1–2): 35–51, 1976. [Husserl's methodological strategies are investigated for applicability to music.]

de Arce, Daniel Mendoza. "Alfred Schütz on music and society." *The Annals of Phenomenological Sociology*, 1:47–55, 1976. [Schütz's writings are culled for their impact on sociology of music.]

de Persia, Jorge. "Notas sobre la historia de la musica y la sociedad." *Revista Internacional de Sociologia* (Spain), 39(Oct.–Dec.):523–540, 1981.

Destreri, Luigi Del Grosso. "Max Weber e la sociologia della musica." *Studi di Sociologie* (Italy), 20(1):55–62, 1982.

Destreri, Luigi Del Grosso. *La Sociologia, La Musica e le Musiche*. Milano: Unicopli, 1988. 130p. [History of sociology of music with detailed discussion of Comte, Spencer, Simmel, Weber, Michels, Sorokin, Honigsheim, Silbermann, Blaukopf, and Adorno.]

Durga, S.A.K. *A New Approach to Indian Musicological Methodology, an Ethnomusicological Perspective*, Ph.D. Thesis, Wesleyan University, 1984. 238p.

Etzkorn, K. Peter. *Music and Society: The Later Writings of Paul Honigsheim* (edited, with additional material and bibliographies). New York: John Wiley & Sons, Inc., 1973. xxii + 327p.

Etzkorn, K. Peter. Book Review of Walter Wawrzy, "Walter Benjamins Kunsttheorie: Kritik einer Rezeption." Contemporary Sociology, 3:336, 1974.

Etzkorn, K. Peter. "Manufacturing music." *Society*, 14(1):19–23, 1976. [Musical differentiation in urban society corresponds to social differentiation.]

Etzkorn, K. Peter. "On the sociological potential of the sociology of the arts: Introductory comments." *Revue Internationale de Sociologie*, XII:16–19, 1976.

Etzkorn, K. Peter. "On the sociology of musical practice and social groups." *International Social Science Journal*, 34(4): 555–569, 1982.

Etzkorn, K. Peter. "Publications and their influence on the development of ethnomusicology." *Yearbook for Traditional Music*, 20:43–50, 1988. [A sociology of knowledge study of the discipline of ethnomusicology.]

Federico, Ronald. Book Review of K. Peter Etzkorn, ed., *Music and Society: The Later Writings of Paul Honigsheim. Social Forces*, 53(4):656–657, 1975.

Feher, Ferenc. "Negative philosophy of music—Positive results." *New German Critique*, 4(Winter):99–111, 1975. [Adorno and Lukacs jointly reject the notion of "collective creativity" and admire the autonomous individual in the totality of art.]

Freedman, Alex S. "Big bands and groups: Towards a sociology of musical innovation." *Quarterly Journal of Ideology*, 6(2):5–17, 1982.

Frow, John. "Adorno and metaphor: Adorno and the sociology of art." *CLIO*, 12(1):57–65, 1982.

Harrison, Frank Ll. "American musicology and the European tradition." in *Musicology*, Frank Ll. Harrison, Mantle Hood and Claude V. Palisca. Englewood Cliffs, New Jersey: Prentice-Hall, Inc., 1963. xii+337p. pp. 1–85.

Haselauer, Elisabeth. *Handbuch der Musiksoziologie*, Wien: Herman Böhlaus Nachf., 1980. 232p.

Hatch, D. J., and D. R.Watson. "Hearing the blues: An essay in the sociology of music." *Acta Sociologica* (Norway), 17(2):162–178, 1974. [Listeners' ability to hear varies with their 'musical competence.']

Hauser, Arnold. *The Sociology of Art*. Trans. by Kenneth J. Northcott. Chicago: The University of Chicago Press, 1982. xxi+776p.

Hennion, Antoine. "La sociologie de la musique: Structures et analyses locales." *L'Année Sociologigue*, 34:379–390, 1984.

Hesbacher, Peter. Book Review of K. Peter Etzkorn, *Music and Society: The Later Writings of Paul Honigsheim*. *Contemporary Sociology: A Journal of Reviews*, IV(2):110–111, 1975.

Kaden, Christian. *Musiksoziologie*, Wilhelmshaven: Heinrichshofen Verlag, 1985. 475p.

Kalekin-Fishman, Devorah. "From the perspective of sound: Towards an explication of the social construction of meaning." *Sociologia Internationalis* (FRG), 24(2):171–195, 1986.

Kamerman, Jack B., and Rosanne Martorella. (Eds.) *Performers and Performances: The Social Organization of Artistic Work* (contributors: Howard S. Becker, Joseph Bensman, Robert Faulkner, and Stephen Couch). New York: Praeger Publishers, 1983. xiii+303p.

Karbusicky, Vladimir. "Ein Ende der System-Aesthetiken? Zum Widerspiegelungsmodell der Musik in Lukacs 'ästhetik'." *Kölner Zeitschrift für Soziologie und Sozialpsychologie*, Special Issue (17):68–92, 1974. [Lukac's Marxism, lip service to Leninism, and possibly revisionist tendencies are placed into the context of other aesthetic systems.]

Karbusicky, Vladimir. *Empirische Musiksoziologie*. Wiesbaden: Breitkopf & Härtel, 1975, 490p.

Käsler, Dirk. (Ed.) *Max Weber: Sein Werk und Seine Wirkung*. München: Nymphenburger Verlagshandlung, 1972. 367pp. (Nymphenburger Texte zur Wissenschaft, Modelluniversität 3.)

Keller, Marcello Sorce. "Sociology of music and ethnomusicology: Two disciplines in competition." *JGE: The Journal of General Education*, 38(3):167–181, 1986. [Different historical roots, rather than subject matter, have kept the disciplines from cooperating more closely.]

Klausmeier, Friedrich. *Die Lust, Sich Musikalisch Auszudrücken*. Reinbeck: Rowolt Verlag, 1978. 318p.

Klausmeier, Friedrich. *Musikalische Interpretationen Zur Entwicklung Einer Methode*, Fragmente als Beiträge zur Musiksoziologie herausgegeben von Elisabeth Haselauer. Wien: Doblinger, 1980. 56p.

Kneif, Tibor. *Politische Musik*, Wien: Doblinger Verlag, 1977. 60p.

Layton, Robert. *The Anthropology of Art*. New York: Columbia University Press, 1981. x+227p.

Levy, Ernst. *Des Rapports entre la Musique et la Société.* Neuchâtel: La Bacconière, 1979. 66p.

Ling, Jan. "The sociology of music." *Canadian University Music Review,* 5:3–16, 1984.

Ling, Jan. (Organizer) *Musiksociologiskkonferens 1988.* Göteborg: Musikvetenskapliga Av-delningen Musikhögskolan, 1988. [Invitational papers on the role of sociology as a scientific tool in public policy affecting musical dissemination]

Malhotra, Valerie Ann. "Weber's concept of rationalization and the electronic revolution in Western classical music." *Qualitative Sociology,* 1(3):100–120, 1979. [Weber's expectation of the continued restriction of musical expressiveness as a result of technological rationalization is called into question by the empirical breadth of electronic music.]

Malhotra, Valerie Ann. "Adorno and Schutz: Towards a dialectical phenomenology of music," in *Contribution to the Sociology of the Arts,* [Ivan Vitanyi, ed.] ISA Research Committee 37. Sofia: 1983, [pp. 233–241.]

Marcus, Judith, and Zoltan Tar. (Eds.) *Foundations of the Frankfurt School of Social Research.* New Brunswick, NJ: Transaction, 1984. 440p.

Mark, Desmond. "John H. Mueller und sein Beitrag zur Musiksoziologie." *International Review of the Aesthetics and Sociology of Music,* VII(2):312–317, 1976.

Mark, Desmond (Ed.) *Stock-Taking of Musical Life. Sociography and Music Education. Report on a Seminar,* ISME Edition Number One. Wien-München: Doblinger, 1981.

Mark, Desmond. "Pop and folk as a going concern for sociological research." *International Review of the Aesthetics and Sociology of Music,* 14(1):93–98, 1983.

Mendoza de Arce, Daniel. "The concept of musical meaning in some modern sociological theories." *Revue Internationale de Sociologie* (Italy), 12(1–2):19–34, 1976. [Positivist sociology of music and other schools of thought are reviewed concerning the location of 'meaning' in musical communication.]

Menger, Pierre-Michel, *Le Paradoxe du Musicien: Le Compositeur, le Mélomane et l'état dans la Société Contemporaine,* Paris: Harmoniques Flammarion, 1983. 396p. [Sociological inquiry into changes in musical life in France since 1945.]

Morgenstern, Dan, Charles Nanry, and David A. Cayer (Eds.) *Annual Review of Jazz Studies I.* New Brunswick, N.J.: Transaction, 1982. 178p.

Morgenstern, Dan, Charles Nanry, and David A. Cayer (Eds.) *Annual Review of Jazz Studies II.* New Brunswick, N.J.: Transaction, 1983. 224p.

Morgenstern, Dan, Charles Nanry, and David A. Cayer (Eds.) *Annual Review of Jazz Studies III.* New Brunswick, N.J.: Transaction, 1984. 256p.

Morgenstern, Dan, Charles Nanry, and David A. Cayer (Eds.) *Annual Review of Jazz Studies IV.* New Brunswick, N.J.: Transaction, 1987. 224p.

Murvar, Vatro (Ed.) *Theory of Liberty, Legitimacy and Power: New Directions in the Intellectual and Scientific Legacy of Max Weber* (contributors: Thomas Burger, Edith E. Graber, K. Peter Etzkorn, David C. Yu, and others). London: Routledge & Kegan Paul, 1985. xii + 264p.

Nattiez, Jean-Jacques. "Sur les relations entre sociologie et sémiologie musicales." *International Review of the Aesthetics and Sociology of Music,* V(1):61–77, 1974.

Nketia, J. H. Kwabena. "African music and Western praxis: A review of Western perspectives on African musicology." *Revue Canadienne des Études Africaines,* 20(1):36–56, 1986.

Ostleitner, Elena (Ed.) *Massenmedien, Musikpolitik und Musikerziehung.*Wien:Verlag des Verbundes der Wissenschaftlichen Gesellschaften Österreichs, 1987, 337p. Series Musik und Gesellschaft.

Ridgeway, Cecilia L. "Affective interaction as a determinant of musical involvement." *The Sociological Quarterly,* 17(3):414–428, 1976. [Music listeners are more likely to adapt to complex social situations than nonlisteners.]

Rummenhöller, Peter. *Einführung in die Musiksoziologie.* Wilhelmshaven: Heinrichshofen, 1978. 280p.

Rupel, Dimitrij (Ed.) *Alienation and Participation in Culture.* Ljubliana: University Edvard Kardelj, 1985. 163p.

Serravezza, Antonio. (Ed.) *La Sociologia della Musica.* Torino:Edizioni di Torino, 1980. 316p.

Shepherd, John C. "Music and social control: An essay on the sociology of musical knowledge." *Catalyst* (Canada), 13(Spring):1–54, 1979. [Capitalist society has unconsciously used serious music to preserve the 'asocial' status of the musical establishment. The artistic elements of popular music are ignored by the establishment.]

Shepherd, John C., and Graham Vulliamy. "A comparative sociology of school knowledge." *British Journal of Sociology of Education,* 4(1):3–18, 1983.

Shepherd, John. "Music consumption and cultural self-identities: Some theoretical and methodological reflections." *Media, Culture and Society,* 8:305–330, 1986.

Siegmund-Schultze, Walther. "Musik und Klassenkampf." *Wissenschaftliche Zeitschrift der Martin Luther Universität Halle-Wittenberg,* Gessellschafts-Sprachwissenschaftliche Reihe, 23(4):27–35, 1974. [Class struggle impacts on music production and consumption.]

Silbermann, Alphons. *Empirische Kunstsoziologie. Eine Einführung mit kommentierter Bibliographie.* Stuttgart: F. Enke, 1973.

Silbermann, Alphons. "Massenkommunikation," in *Handbuch der empirischen Sozialforschung,* René König. ed. dtv Wissenschaftliche Reihe. Stuttgart: Ferdinand Enke Verlag, 1977, pp. 146–278. xii + 310p.

Silbermann, Alphons. "Soziologie der Künste," in *Handbuch Empirischer Sozialforschung,* René König, ed. Stuttgart: Ferdinand Enke, 1979, pp. 117–345. x + 378p.

Silbermann, Alphons. "What questions does the empirical sociology of music attempt to answer." *International Social Science Journal,* 34(4):571–581, 1982.

Silbermann, Alphons. *Empirische Kunstsoziologie.* Stuttgart: B.G. Teubner, 1986. 206p.

Silbermann, Alphons, and Paul Röhrig (Eds.) *Kultur, Volksbildung und Gesellschaft: Paul Honigsheim zum Gedenken Seines 100. Geburtstages. Beiträge zum Werk, Ausgewählte Texte und ein Verzeichnis der Schriften von Paul Honigsheim.* Frankfurt-Bern-New York: Peter Lang, 1987. 204p.

Sochor, Arnold N. *Die Entwichlung der Musiksoziologie in der Sovietunion. Eine Musiksoziologische Untersuchung.* Köln, Arno Volk Verlag. 1973. 197p.

Supicic, Ivo. *Music in Society: A Guide to the Sociology of Music.* Stuyvesant, N.Y.: Pendragon Press, 1987. xiv + 488p.

Wade, Bonnie C. "Fixity and flexibility: From musical structure to cultural structure." *Anthropologia* (Canada), 18(1):15–26, 1976. [Analysis of North-Indian music is employed to define 'culture.']

Wilson, Robert N. Book Review of K. Peter Etzkorn, *Music and Society: The Later Writings of Paul Honigsheim. American Journal of Sociology*, (September):448–449, 1975.

Wilson, Robert N. *Experiencing Creativity: On the Social Psychology of Art*. New Brunswick, N.J.: Transaction, 1986. 179p.

Yinger, J. Milton, *Countercultures: The Promise and Peril of a World Turned Upside Down*. New York: The Free Press, 1982. xi + 371p.

Ziff, Paul. "Art and Sociobiology." *Mind* (UK), 90:505–520, 1981.

Zimmerman, Carle C. Book Review of K. Peter Etzkorn, *Music and Society: The Later Writings of Paul Honigsheim. Social Science*, 172–175, 1975.

SOCIOLOGY OF AESTHETICS

Byrd, Donald. "Music without aesthetics: How some nonmusical forces and institutions influence change in black music." *The Black Scholar*, 9(10):2–5, 1978. [Economics and commercial dimensions of record production need to be considered when dealing with black music.]

DeNora, Tia. "How is extra-musical meaning possible? Music as a place and space for 'work'." *Sociological Theory*, 4(1):84–94.

Faltin, Peter. "Die Bedeutung von Musik als Ergebnis soziokultureller Prozesse." *Die Musikforschung*, XXVI(4):435–445, 1973.

Ferguson, Linda. "Tape composition: An art in search of its metaphysics." *Journal of Aesthetics and Art Criticism*, 42(1):17–27, 1983. [Fundamental distinctions between the ontology of different types of musical reproduction are drawn. A basic paper!]

Greenfeld, Liah, "The role of the public in the success of artistic styles." *Arch. Europ. Sociol.*, XXV:83–98, 1984.

Hosokawa, Shushei. "Technique/technology and reproduction in music," in *The Semiotic Web '85. An International Yearbook,* Thomas A. Sebeok and Jean Umiker-Sebeok, eds. Berlin: Mouton de Gruyter, 1987, pp. 536–555. [Production of music is contrasted to *re-production*. Reproduced music demands an aesthetic of its own.]

Jopling, Carol F. (Ed.) *Art and Aesthetics in Primitive Societies: A Critical Anthology*. New York: E.P. Dutton, 1971. xx + 427p.

Karbusicky, Vladimir. "Zeichen und Musik." *Zeitschrift für Semiotik*, 9(3–4):227–249, 1987.

Karbusicky, Vladimir. "The index sign in music." *Semiotica, 66(1–3):23–35, 1987.*

Kaufman, Mitchell Lewis. *Technology and Expressiveness in Recorded Classical Music: A Case Study in Recent Western Art and Culture*. Ph.D. Thesis, Fordham University, 1982. 320p.

Kolleritsch, Otto. *Adorno und die Musik*. Studien zur Wertungsforschung. Wien: Universal Edition, 1979. 240p.

Leppert, Richard, and Susan McClary (Eds.) *Music and Society: The Politics of Composition, Performance and Reception*. Cambridge: Cambridge University Press, 1987. xx + 202p. [A collection of essays by noted sociologists on the subjects of musical autonomy and new media.]

Lissa, Zofia. "Einige kritische Bemerkungen zur Ingardenschen Theorie des musikalischen Werkes," in *Neue Aufsätze zur Musikästhetik, Zofia Lissa. Wilhelmshaven: Heinrichshofen, 1975, pp. 127–207.*

Lissa, Zofia, *Neue Aufsätze zur Musikästhetik*. Wilhelmshaven: Heinrichshofen Verlag, 1975. xii + 261p. [Taschenbücher zur Musikwissenschaft, vol. 38.]

Lowenthal, Leo. *Literature and the Image of Man*. New Brunswick, N.J.: Transaction, 1986. 352p. [Vol. #2 of Communication in Society.]

Lowenthal, Leo. *Judaism in the German Mind and other Essays on Adorno, Horkheimer and Benjamin*. New Brunswick, N.J.: Transaction, 1988. 328p. [Vol 4 of Communication in Society.]

Loza, Steven Joseph. *The Musical Life of the Mexican/Chicano People in Los Angeles, 1945– 1985: A Study in Maintenance, Change, and Adaptation*. Ph.D. Dissertation, University of California, Los Angeles, 1985. 629p.

Menger, Pierre-Michel. "L'Oreille speculative. Consommation et perception de la musique contemporaine." *Revue Francaise de Sociologie*, 27(3):445–479, 1986.

Mowitt, John. "The sound of music in the era of its electronic reproducibility," in Richard Leppert and Susan McClary, Eds. *Music and Society: The Politics of Composition, Performance and Reception*. Cambridge: Cambridge University Press, 1987, pp. 173–197. xx + 202p. [Adorno and Benjamin are examined for insights on how to deal with the history of contemporary music "where the fetish of noise reduction has gone hand in hand with the aggressive marketing of distortion boosters."]

Nehring, Neil Robert. *The Destructive Character: Walter Benjamin and a Situationist Approach to English Literature and Pop Music Since the 1930s*. Ph.D. Thesis, The University of Michigan, 1985. 366p.

Otten, Charlotte M. (Ed.) *Anthropology and Art: Readings in Cross-Cultural Aesthetics*. Garden City, N.Y.: The Natural History Press, 1971. [American Museum Sourcebooks in Anthropology.]

Schwadron, Abraham A. "Philosophy in music education: State of the research." *Bulletin Council for Research in Music Education*, 34(Fall):41–53, 1973. [Survey of educational literature 1957–1972.]

Schwadron, Abraham A. "Philosophy and aesthetics in music education: A critique of the research." *Bulletin of the Council for Research in Music Education*, 79(Summer):11–32, 1984. [An Update of the 1973 study with recommendations for future research and scholarly emphases.]

Shelton, Roosevelt Orinthal. *The Relationship Between Formal and Informal Music Educational Patterns of Black College Students' Verbal Response to Musical Excerpts from Diverse Stylistic Traditions*. Ph.D. Thesis, The University of Alabama, 1986. 182p.

Smudits, Alfred. "Die Wiederkehr des Körpers in der Musik als Ergebnis neuer Produktionsmittel der elektronischen Medien." *Österreichische Zeitschrift für Soziologie*, 11(4):7–23, 1986.

Stebbins, Robert A. "Creating high culture: The American amateur classical musician." *Journal of American Culture*, 1(3):616–631, 1978. [Relationships among musical amateurs, professionals, and their audiences form the basis for groups of devotees of high culture.]

Thrasher, Alan Robert. *Foundations of Chinese Music: A Study of Ethics and Aesthetics*. Ph.D. Thesis, Wesleyan University, 1980. 256p.

Wolf, Janet. "Foreword: The Ideology of Autonomous Art," in *Music and Society: The Politics of Composition, Performance and Reception*, Richard Leppert and Susan McClary, eds. Cambridge: Cambridge University Press, 1987, pp. 1–12. xx + 202p. ["The ideology of autonomy still rules in the study of music."]

MEDIA AND MUSIC

Anderson, Bruce, Peter Hesbacher, K. Peter Etzkorn, and R. Serge Denisoff. "Hit record trends, 1940–1977." *Journal of Communication,* 30(2):31–43, 1980.

Anderson, Robert T., and Enda M. Mitchell. "The politics of music in Nepal." *Anthropological Quarterly,* 51(4):247–259, 1978. [Acculturation to Western music varies by stratification within Nepal society; through governmental policy discourages exposure, young elites are in contact and may influence others.]

Aufderheide, Pat. "Music videos: The Look of the sound." *Journal of Communication,* 36(1):57–78, 1986.

Bachmann, Claus-Henning. "Rundfunk, neue Musik, Publikum; Fragen und Versäumnisse." *Schweizerische Musikzeitung,* 5:253–260, 1977.

Ball-Rokeach, Sandra J., and Muriel G. Cantor (Eds.) *Media, Audience, and Social Structure.* Beverly Hills, Calif.: Sage Publications, Inc., 1986. 400p.

Bennett, H. Stith. *On Becoming a Rock Musician.* Amherst: The University of Massachusetts Press, 1980. xiv + 258p.

Bennett, H. Stith, and Jeff Ferrell. "Music videos and epistemic socialization." *Youth and Society,* 18(4):344–362, 1987.

Berger, Arthur Asa (Ed.) *Television and Society.* New Brunswick, N.J.: Transaction, 1987. 282p.

Berland, Jody Dee. *Cultural Repercussions: The Social Production of Music Broadcasting in Canada.* Ph.D. Thesis, York University (Canada), 1986.

Birnbaum, Alfred (Interviewer). "Hard dreams/soft nightmares: Akira Asada und Shuhei Hosokawa," in *Clip, Klapp, Bum: Von der Visuellen Musik zum Musikvideo,* Veruschka Body and Peter Weibel, eds. Köln: DuMont Buchverlag, 1987, pp. 264–272.

Blaukopf, Kurt (Ed.) *The Phonogram in Cultural Communication.* Wien-New York: Springer Verlag, 1982. 183p.

Blaukopf, Kurt. "L'Utilisation secondaire de la musique dans les medias." *Études de Radio-Télévision* (Belgium), 35(November):45–54, 1985.

Blomster, Wes V. "Electronic music." *Telos,* 32(Summer):65–78, 1977. [Electronic music is composed/created for "reproduction."]

Bontinck, Irmgard (Ed.) *New Patterns of Musical Behaviour of the Young Generation in Industrial Societies.* Wien: Universal Edition, 1974. 240p.

Bontinck, Irmgard, Desmond Mark, Elena Ostleitner, and Alfred Smudits. *Die Laqe der Komponisten in Österreich* (project director Kurt Blaukopf.) Wien: Landeskulturkonferenz, 1984. 457p.

Burton, Thomas L. "Rock music and social change, 1953–1978." *Loisir et Société* (Canada), 8(2):665–683, 1985.

Buxton, David. "Rock music, the star-system and the rise of consumerism." *Telos,* 57(Fall):93–106, 1983.

Campbell, Murray. *The Musician's Guide to Acoustics.* J. M. Dent & Sons, 1987.

Chase, Anthony. "Toward a legal theory of popular culture." *Wisconsin Law Review,* 3:527–569, 1986.

Denisoff, R. Serge. *Solid Gold: The Popular Record Industry.* New Brunswick, N.J.: Transaction, 1975. Reissue 1981. 504p.

Denisoff, R. Serge. *Tarnished Gold: The Record Industry Revisited.* New Brunswick, N.J.: Transaction, 1986. 503p.

Denisoff, R. Serge. *Inside MTV.* New Brunswick, N.J.: Transaction, 1987. 224p.

Destreri, Luigi Del Grosso. *Televisione e Stratificazione Sociale. Materiali di Studio.* Trento: Cooperative Libraria Univ., 1976. 137p.

Etzkorn, K. Peter. "Über soziale und musikalische Eigenschaften: Aspekte der Statusdimensionen kreativer Musiker." *Kölner Zeitschrift für Soziologie und Sozialpsychologie,* Special Issue (17):93–109, 1974. [Electronification and mass production of music has introduced systematic adaptations to exposure and forms of musical expression.]

Etzkorn, K. Peter. "Contemporary mediated music: Challenge to music education." Paper presented at the ISME Seminar *Changes in Professional Profiles of Music Educators Prompted by Technological Innovation,* Byron Bay, NSW, Australia, July 11–13, 1988. [Loudspeaker music is extensively and unwittingly used by music educators as if they were marketing agents for multinational music conglomorates.]

Finscher, Ludwig. *Studien zur Geschichte des Streichquartetts.* Kassel: Bärenreiter Verlag, 1974. 301p.

Frick, Ulrich. "Rockmusik als Ware." *Österreichische Zeitschrift für Soziologie,* 8(4):164–173, 1983.

Heister, Hanns-Werner, et al. *Segmente der Unterhaltungsindustrie.* Frankfurt am Main: Suhrkamp, 1974. *Edition Suhrkamp 651.*

Hosokawa, Shushei. "Fascinating banality of the hit parade." *One Two Three Four: A Rock 'n' Roll Quarterly,* (Winter):66–73, 1987.

Hosokawa, Shushei. "The Walkman effect." *Popular Music,* (4):165–179, 1984.

Jost, Ekkehard. *Sozialpsychologische Faktoren der Popmusik-Rezeption,* Mainz: B. Schott, 1976. 99p.

Karbusicky, Vladimir. "Die musikalische Masse," in *Die Produktive Distanz: Beiträge zum Verhältnis von Masse und Elite.* Hamburg: Marketing Journal, n.d., pp. 3–12.

Kealy, Edward R. "From craft to art: The case of sound mixers and popular music." *Sociology of Work and Occupations,* 6(1):3–29, 1979. [Technological changes in the recording studio are connected with changes in the social organization of unions and corporate controls.]

Lampman, Richard Alan. *The Idea of a Democratic Culture: The Evolution of Popular Music from 1955 to 1975.* Ph.D. Thesis, Purdue University, 1980. 255p.

Lewis, George H. "The meaning's in the music and the music's in me: Popular music as symbolic communication." *Theory, Culture & Society* (UK), 1(3):133–141, 1983.

Lull, James (Ed.) *Popular Music and Communication.* Newbury Park, Calif.: Sage Publications, Inc., 1987. 268p. [Covers popular music with emphasis on how school experience influence peer formation and media consumption.]

Martorella, Rosanne. *The Sociology of Opera.* South Hadley, Mass.: J.F. Bergin Publishers, Inc., 1982. xi+228p.

Peterson, Richard A., and David G. Berger. "Cycles in symbol production: The case of popular music." *American Sociological Review,* 40(2):158–173, 1975. [Five popular music 'markets' are identified by market concentration between 1948 and 1973. Increases in concentration and decreases in consumer satisfaction are shown to be followed by brief spurts of intense innovation.]

Peterson, Richard A., and John Ryan. "Success, failure, and anomie in arts and crafts work: Breaking into commercial country music songwriting." *Research in the Sociology of Work*, 2(301–323)1983.

Rösing, Helmut. "Thesen zur Funktionsnivellierung massenmedial dargebotener Musik," in *Symposium Musik und Massenmedien*, Helmut Rösing. ed. München: 1978, pp. 95–104.

Saramaki, Martii, and Jukka Haarma. *The International Music Industry*. Helsinki: Finnish Broadcast Industry, Planning Research, 1979.

Sherman, Barry L., and Joseph R. Dominick. "Violence and sex in music videos: TV and rock 'n' roll." *Journal of Communication*, 36(1):79–93, 1986.

Silbermann, Alphons (Ed.) *Die Rolle der Elektronischen Medien in der Entwicklung der Kümste*. Frankfurt am Main: Verlag Peter Lang, 1987.

Smudits, Alfred (Ed.) *New Media: A Challenge to Cultural Policies. Report on a Research Project Undertaken by MEDICACULT*. Vienna: Verband der Wissenschaftlichen Gesellschaften Österreichs, 1987.

Snow, Robert P. "Youth, rock 'n roll, and electronic media." *Youth and Society*, 18(4):326–343, 1987.

Stigberg, David Kenneth. *Urban Musical Culture in Mexico: Professional Musicianship and Media in the Musical Life of Contemporary Veracruz*. Ph.D. Thesis, University of Illinois at Urbana-Champaign, 1980. 408p.

Stroh, Wolfgang Martin. *Zur Soziologie der Elektronischen Musik*. Zürich: Amadeus Verlag, 1975. 200p.

Sun, Se-Wen, and James Lull. "The adolescent audience for music videos and why they watch." *Journal of Communication*. 36(1):115–125, 1986.

Tetzlaff, David J. "MTV and the politics of postmodern pop." *Journal of Communication Inquiry*, 10(1):80–91, 1986.

Vignolle, Jean-Pierre. "Mixing genres and reaching the public: The production of popular music." *Social Science Information* (Netherlands), 19(1):79–105, 1980.

Waite, Bradley M. *Popular Music Videos: A Content Analysis and Social-Developmental Investigation of their Effects on Gender Orientation and Attitudes*. Ph.D. Thesis, Kent State University, 1987. 193p. [Twenty-three most popular music videos of 1985 were categorized into "sexist," "nonsexist," and "neutral." Overall, however, males were portrayed as more dominant, females as sexually suggestive, deferent, and harm avoidant. Fifth and ninth grade and college students were shown these videos under controlled conditions. Results indicate that viewing videos with differing content did not change pre- and post-test measures on masculinity, femininity, and attitudes toward women.]

Wallis, Roger, and Krister Malm. *Big Sounds from Small Peoples: The Music Industry in Small Countries*. London: Constable & Co, Ltd., 1984. xv + 419p.

White, Robert George, Jr. *Martin Block and WNEW: The Rise of the Recorded Music Radio Format, 1934–1954*. Ph.D. Thesis, Bowling Green State University, 1981. 186p.

EDUCATION AND AGE GROUPS

Adler, Thomas Albert. *The Acquisition of a Traditional Competence: Folk-Musical and Folk-Cultural Learning among Bluegrass Banjo Players*. Ph.D. Thesis, Indiana University, 1980. 641p.

Ayres, Barbara. "Effects of Infant Carrying Practices on Rhythm in Music." *Ethos,* 1(4):387–404, 1973. [Based on human relations area files, correlations between child-rearing practices (close body contact with infants) and dominant rhythmic patterns in social groups are found to be statistically significant.]

Blaukopf, Kurt. *Neue Musikalische Verhaltungsweisen der Jugend.* Mainz: B. Schott's Söhne, 1974. 72p. Musikpädagogik, Forschung und Lehre, vol. 5.

Bontinck, Irmgard. "The impact of electronic media on adolescents, their everyday experience, their learning orientations and leisure time activities." *Communications,* 12(1):21–30, 1986.

Booth, Gregory David. *The Oral Tradition in Transition: Implications for Music Education from a Study of North Indian Tabla Transmission.* Ph.D. Thesis, Kent State University, 1986. 614p.

Bresler, Liora. *The Role of the Computer in a Music Theory Classroom: Integration, Barriers, and Learning.* Ph.D. Thesis, Stanford University, 1987. 234p.

Card, Caroline Elizabeth. *Tuareg Music and Social Identity* (Algeria, Niger). Ph.D. Thesis, Indiana University, 1982. 258p.

Chabrier, Jean-Claude. "Problèmes contemporaines du musicien et de la musique dans le monde arabe orientale, selon l'école de Bagdad." *Ethnospychologie* (France), 32(1):37–67, 1977. [Changes in education of performers and audience are reviewed along with the contributions of outstanding scholar/performers in reinvigorating Arab music.]

Chapman, Antony J., and Alan R. William. "Prestige effects and aesthetic experiences: Adolescents' reactions to music." *The British Journal of Social and Clinical Psychology,* 15(1):61–72, 1976. [Salomon Ash's hypothesis is validated that prestige effects in aesthetic evaluations are mediated by perceptual reorganizations and altered understandings of stimuli.]

Choate, Robert A. "The Symposium: An Introduction." *Music Educators Journal,* 54(3):49–79, 1967. [Contains text of MENC's "Tanglewood Declaration."]

Christenson, Peter G., and Peter DeBenedittis. "'Eavesdropping' on the FM band: Children's use of radio." *Journal of Communication, 36(2):27–38, 1986.*

Dees, David R., and Vera Hernon. "Soundtracking everyday life: The use of music in redefining situations." *Sociological Inquiry,* 48(2):133–141, 1978. [College students are found to identify specific social situations with types of music.]

Fraser, Wilmot Alfred. *Jazzology: A Study of the Tradition in Which Jazz Musicians Learn to Improvise.* Ph.D. Thesis, University of Pennsylvania, 1983. 266p.

Frissell, Susan. *A Historical Study of the Implications of Black Music and Its Relationships to the Selected Aspect of Social, Cultural, and Educational Experiences of Black Americans: 1955–1980.* Ph.D. Thesis, Loyola University of Chicago, 1985. 358p.

Frith, Simon. *Sound Effects: Youth, Leisure, and the Politics of Rock 'N' Roll,* New York, NY: Pantheon Books, 1981. vii + 294p.

Garrison, Virginia Hope. *Traditional and Non-Traditional Teaching and Learning Practices in Folk Music: An Ethnographic Field Study of Cape Breton Fiddling.* Ph.D. Thesis, The University of Wisconsin-Madison, 1985. 390p.

Gibson, Barbara L. *Young Children's Response to Interpretation in Music and Speech.* Ph.D. Thesis, The University of Connecticut, 1986. 103p.

Gold, Brian D. "Self-Image of Punk Rock and Nonpunk Rock Juvenile Delinquents." *Adolescence,* 22(Fall):535–544, 1987.

Gross, Robert Wenzel. *A Comparison of Active Experience and Lecture-Discussion Methodology as Means for Developing Musical Knowledge, Musical Discrimination, and Musical Preference within an Electronic Music Course at the High School Level.* D.Ed. Thesis, Harvard University, 1984. 160p.

Hamilton, Gail P. *The Roles of Pet and Music Therapy in Providing Sensory Stimulation to Institutionalized Elderly Persons.* D.S.W. Thesis, University of Pennsylvania, 1985. 250p.

Kaplan, Max. "An Approach to Leisure Studies—Origins and Influences." *Loisir et Société* (Canada), 3(2):219–234, 1980.

Kellman, Rudolf Hubert. *The Development of a Music Education Program for Older Adults Suitable for Use in Senior Citizen Centers, Retirement Homes, or other Sites.* Ed.D. Thesis, New York University, 1984. 237p.

Kingsbury, Henry Ovington. *Music as a Cultural System: Structure and Process in an American Conservatory.* Ph.D. Thesis, Indiana University, 1984. 334p.

LaVoie, Joseph C., and Betty R. Collins. "Effect of youth culture music on high school students' academic performance." *Journal of Youth and Adolescence*, 4(1):57–65, 1975. [In a controlled study, students listening to rock music while studying retained less information than non-listeners.]

Miller, Linda Bryant. *Music in Early Childhood: Naturalistic Observation of Young Children's Musical Behaviors.* Ph.D. Thesis, University of Kansas, 1983. 171p.

Patchen, Jeffrey H. *The Relationships among Current Musical Activity Level and Selected Musical and Demographic Variables within an Elderly Population.* D.Mus.Ed. Thesis, Indiana University, 1986. 168p.

Shepherd, John C. "Conflict in patterns of socialization: The role of the classroom music teacher." *La Revue Canadienne de Sociologie et d'Anthropologie*, 20(1):23–43, 1983.

Smith, David Scott, *Preferences for Differentiated Frequency Loudness Levels in Older Adult Music Listening.* Ph.D. Thesis, The Florida State University, 1987. 295p.

Tatum, Marielon Elaine. *A Descriptive Analysis of the Status of Music Programs in Selected Retirement Residences and Senior Citizens' Centers in the Southeastern United States.* D.Mus.Ed. Thesis, Indiana University, 1985. 250p.

Trinka, Jill Leslie. *The Performance Style of American Folksongs on School Music Series and Non-School Music Series Recordings: A Comparative Analysis of Selected Factors.* Ph.D. Thesis, The University of Texas at Austin, 1987. 442p. [Recordings produced for school music series are judged to be less representative of performance aspects of folk music than regular commercial releases.]

Weissman, Judy Anne. *Meeting Selected Needs and Treatment Goals of Aged Individuals in Long-Term Care Facilities through the Therapeutic Use of Music Activities.* Ph.D. Thesis, New York University, 1981. 212p.

MUSIC AND COMMUNITIES

Adegbite, Ademola Moses. *Oriki: A Study in Yoruba Musical and Social Perception.* Ph.D. Thesis, University of Pittsburgh, 1978. 249p.

Albrecht, Theodore John. *German Singing Societies in Texas.* Ph.D. Thesis, North Texas State University, 1975. 501p.

Armstrong, Edward G. "Country music sex songs: An ethnomusicological account." *Journal of Sex Research*, 22(3):370–378, 1986.

Arom, Simha. "Un ethnomusicologue chez les Pygmées." *La Recherche* (France), 12(June):768–773, 1981.

Avorgbedor, Daniel Kodzo. *Modes of Musical Continuity among the Anlo Ewe of Accra: A Study in Urban Ethnomusicology.* Ph.D. Thesis, Indiana University, 1986. 362p.

Bailey, Olive Jean. *The Influence of Ernst Krenek on the Musical Culture of the Twin Cities.* Ph.D. Thesis, University of Minnesota, 1980. 573p.

Bjorn, Lars. "The mass society and group action theories of cultural production: The case of stylistic innovation in jazz." *Social Forces*, 60(2):377–394, 1981.

Blaukopf, Kurt, Irmgard Bontinck, Harald Gardos, and Desmond Mark. *Kultur von Unten. Innovationen und Barrieren in Österreich.* Wien: Löcker Verlag, 1983.

Blumenthal, Fred A. *The German Romantic Movement in St. Louis.* Ph.D. Thesis, Washington University, 1983. 258p.

Bontinck-Küffel, Irmgard. Special Series of *Musik und Bildung.* "Die Instrumentenwahl in der volkstümlichen Musizierpraxis der Großstadt unter Berücksichtigung der Geige." *Forschung in der Musikerziehung*, 5/6, 1971.

Botstein, Leon. *Music and Its Public: Habits of Listening and the Crisis of Musical Modernism in Vienna, 1870–1914.* Ph.D. Thesis, Harvard University, 1984. 1544p.

Brevan, Bruno. "Vie musicale et société parisienne de 1774 à 1799." *Ethnopsychologie* (France), 34(1):109–147, 1979. [Pre- and post-revolutionary Parisian musical conditions (opera, court and church music, free masonry, public concerts, etc. are reviewed concerning creation, diffusion, and reception of musical compositions in this period deemed critical to the development of modern French music.]

Brevan, Bruno. *Les Changements de la Vie Musicale Parisienne de 1774 à 1799.* Paris: Presses Universitaires de France, 1980.

Burnim, Mellonee Victoria. *The Black Gospel Music Tradition: Symbol of Ethnicity.* Ph.D. Thesis, Indiana University, 1980. 327p.

Cahn, Geoffrey Stephen. *Weimar Culture and Society as Seen through American Eyes: Weimar Music—The View from America.* Ph.D. Thesis, St. John's University, 1982. 493p.

Carter, Ann L. "Black music—More than meets the ear." *The Black Scholar*, 9(10):6–10, 1978. [Lyrics are necessary ingredients to gain understanding of black music.]

Catlin, Ann Ruth. *Variability and Change in Three Karnataka Kriti-s: A Study of South Indian Classical Music.* Ph.D. Thesis, Brown University: 1980, 332p.

Correa de Azavedo, Luiz Heitor. "The musician in Brazilian society, past and present." *International Social Science Journal*, 34(4):667–682, 1982.

Cwi, David, and Katherine Lyall. *Economic Impact of Arts and Cultural Institutions: A Model for Assessment and a Case Study in Baltimore: A Report.* Washington: National Endowment for the Arts, 1977. v+92p. [Research Division Report No. 6.]

Danuser, Hermann, Dietrich Kämper, and Paul Terse Eds. *Amerikanische Musik seit Charles Ives.* Laaber: Laaber-Verlag, 1987. 439p. [A collection of historical briefs and biographic information on U.S. composers along with information on music industry and general social conditions.]

Disharoon, Richard Alan. *A History of Municipal Music in Baltimore, 1914–1947.* Ph.D. Thesis, University of Maryland, 1980. 386p.

Drum, Gary Richard. *The Message in the Music: A Content Analysis of Contemporary Christian and Southern Gospel Song Lyrics.* Ph.D. Thesis, The University of Tennessee, 1987. 229p. [Contemporary Christian music (gospel messages set to a rock beat) from the 1986 top ten chart of *Contemporary Christian Music and Singing News* was found to be almost devoid of doctrinal content. The finding negated the hypothesis that contemporary Christian lyrics would reflect an evangelical-pentacostal-charismatic doctrine and that country gospel songs would reflect a Calvinist, fundamentalist perspective.]

El-Shawan, Salwa Aziz. *Al-Musika Al-'Arabiyyah: A Category of Urban Music in Cairo, Egypt, 1927–1977.* Ph.D. Thesis, Columbia University, 1981. 349p.

Fogal, Robert Edwin. *Traditional Music and the Middle Class: A Case Study of Mercedes, Province of Buenos Aires, Argentina.* Ph.D. Thesis, Indiana University, 1981. 378p.

Fohrbeck, Karla, and Andreas Johannes Wiesand. *Der Künstler-Report: Musikschaffende, Darsteller/Realisatoren, Bildende Künstler/Designer.* München-Wien: Carl Hanser Verlag, 1975.

Fulie, Linda Kiyo. *Matsuri-Bayashi of Tokyo: The Role of Supporting Organizations in Traditional Music.* Ph.D. Thesis, Columbia University, 1986. 325p.

Gülke, Peter. "Edition Peters: 175 Jahre Musikverlag in Leipzig." *Musik und Gesellschaft,* xxv(12):749–752, 1975.

Hamm, Charles E., Bruno Nettl, and Ronald Byrnside. *Contemporary Music and Music Cultures.* Englewood Cliffs, N.J.: Prentice-Hall, 1975. 270p.

Hansell, Kathleen Kuzmick. *Opera and Ballet at the Regio Ducal Teatro of Milan, 1771–1776: A Musical and Social History.* Ph.D. Thesis, University of California, Berkeley, 1980. 1161p.

Hanson, Alice Marie. *The Social and Economic Context of Music in Vienna from 1815 to 1830.* Ph.D. Thesis, University of Illinois at Urbana-Champaign, 1980. 397p.

Hasbany, Richard. "The musical goes ironic: The evolution of genres." *Journal of American Culture,* 1(1):120–136, 1978. [History of American "musical" as a sequence of genres.]

Heister, Hanns-Werner. *Das Konzert: Theorie einer Kulturform,* Wilhelmshaven: Heinrichshofen, 1983. (Taschenbücher zur Musikwissenschaft: 87–88, 2 vols.) [Historical and sociological analysis of symphony concerts.]

Husch, Jerri Ann. *Music of the Workplace: A Study of Muzak Culture.* Ph.D. Thesis, University of Massachusetts, 1984. 197p.

Jackson, Irene Viola. *Afro-American Gospel; Music and Its Social Setting with Special Attention to Roberta Martin.* Ph.D. Thesis, Wesleyan University, 1974. 361p.

Johnstone, Thomas F. "Eskimo Music: A Comparative Survey." *Anthropologica* (Canada), 17(2):217–232, 1975. [Summarizes studies of Eskimo music from 1911–1975.]

Joshi, O. P. "The Changing Social Structure of Music in India." *International Social Science Journal,* 34(4):625–637, 1982.

Keeling, Richard Hamilton. *Songs of the Brush Dance and their Basis in Oral-Expressive Magic: Music and Culture of the Yurok, Hupa and Karok Indians of Northwestern California.* Ph.D. Thesis, University of California, Los Angeles, 1982. 605p.

Keldany-Mohr, Irmgard. *"Unterhaltungsmusik" als Soziokulturelles Phänomen des 19. Jahrhunderts.* Regensburg: Gustav Bosse Verlag, 1977. 143 p.

Kleeman, Janice Ellen. *The Origins and Stylistic Development of Polish-American Polka Music.* Ph.D. Thesis, University of California, Berkeley, 1982. 370p.

Kwiatkowska, Barbara Jolante. *The Present State of Musical Culture among the Diequeno Indians from San Diego County Reservations.* Ph.D. Thesis, University of California, Los Angeles, 1981. 345p.

Lee, Dorothy Sara. *Music Performance and the Negotiation of Identity in Eastern Viti Levu, Fiji.* Ph.D. Thesis, Indiana University, 1984. 261p.

Lomax, Alan. *Folk Song Style and Culture.* New Brunswick, N.J.: Transaction, 1978. 384p.

Lowry, W. McNeil (Ed.) *The Performing Arts and American Society.* Englewood Cliffs, N.J.: Prentice-Hall, Inc., 1987. (*The American Assembly, Columbia University.*)

Lynn, Kwaku Eddie. *American Afrikan Music: A Study of Musical Change.* Ph.D. Thesis, University of California, Los Angeles, 1987. 247p.

Mark, Desmond. *Zur Bestandaufnahme des Wiener Orchesterrepertoires. Ein Soziographischer Versuch nach der Methode von John H. Mueller.* Wien: Universal Edition, 1979.

McCue, George (Ed.) *Music in American Society 1776–1976: From Puritan Hymn to Synthesizer.* (contributors: K. Peter Etzkorn, Charlotte J. Frisbie, Joseph C. Hickerson, and William Schuman.) New Brunswick, N.J.: Transaction, 1977. 201p.

Moore, Julia Virginia. *Beethoven and Musical Economics.* Ph.D. Thesis, University of Illinois at Urbana-Champaign, 1987. 656p.

Morato, Maria-Eugenia Brighenti. *Ma Io Sono Brasiliano: An Ethnographic Study of the Ethnicity and the Vernacular Expressive Culture of Italian Immigrants in the City of Sao Paulo, Brazil.* Ph.D. Thesis, University of Illinois at Urbana-Champaign, 1987. 243p.

Myrvik, Donald Arthur. *Musical and Social Interaction for Composers and Performers: Differences between 'Source' Music and the 1950 Avant Garde.* Ph.D. Thesis, University of Minnesota, 1975. 259p.

Nanry, Charles. *American Music: From Storyville to Woodstock.* New Brunswick, N.J.: Transaction, 1972. 304p.

Nketia, J. H. Kwabena. *The Music of Africa.* New York: W. W. Norton, 1974. × +278p.

Nketia, J. H. Kwabena. "Interaction through music: The dynamics of music-making in African societies." *International Social Science Journal,* 34(4):639–656, 1982.

Nyabongo, Ada Naomi. *Peasant Music Ensembles in Poland: A Culture History.* Ph.D. Thesis, University of Washington, 1986. 983p.

Osterlund, David Conrad. *The Anuak Tribe of South Western Ethiopia: A Study of Its Music within the Context of Its Sociocultural Setting.* Ph.D. Thesis, University of Illinois at Urbana-Champaign, 1978. 532p.

Pena, Manuel Heriberto. *The Emergence of Texas-Mexican 'Conjunto' Music, 1935–1960: An Interpretative History.* Ph.D. Thesis, The University of Texas at Austin, 1981. 323p.

Peterson, Richard A., and Paul Di Maggio. "From region to class, the changing Locus of country music: A test of the massification hypothesis." *Social Forces,* 53(3):497–506, 1975. [Changing audiences for country music illustrate the fluidity of social boundaries of taste. Authors question the view that social classes have distinct cultures and suggest that musical styles may represent convenient indicators of emerging classes.]

Qureshi, Regula Burckhardt. *Qawwali: Sound, Context and Meaning in Indo-Muslim Sufi Music.* Ph.D. Thesis, University of Alberta (Canada), 1981. 513p.

Riggins, Stephen Harold. *Institutional Change in Nineteenth-Century French Music.* Ph.D. Thesis, The University of Toronto (Canada), 1980.

Rumble, John Woodruff. *Fred Rose and the Development of the Nashville Music Industry, 1942–1954.* Ph.D. Thesis, Vanderbilt University, 1980. 434p.

Salem, Mahmoud. *Organizational Survival: The Case of the Seattle Opera Company.* New York: Praeger Books, 1976.

Shanet, Howard. *Philharmonic: A History of New York's Orchestra.* Garden City: Doubleday and Co., 1975. 788p.

Shepherd, John, Phil Virden, Graham Vulliamy, and Trevor Wishart. *Whose Music? A Sociology of Musical Languages.* New Brunswick, N.J.: Transaction, 1980. 300p.

Singer, Roberta Louise. *My Music Is Who I Am and What I Do: Latin Popular Music and Identity in New York City.* Ph.D. Thesis, Indiana University, 1982. 265p.

Slawek, Stephen Matthew. *Kirtan: A Study of the Sonic Manifestations of the Divine in the Popular Hindu Culture of Banaras.* Ph.D. Thesis, University of Illinois at Urbana-Champaign, 1986. 458p.

Sluder, Claude K. *Music in New Harmony, Indiana, 1825–1865: A Study of the Music and Musical Activities of Robert Owen's Community of Equality (1825–1827) and its Cultural Afterglow (1827–1865).* Ph.D. Thesis, Indiana University, 1987. 478p.

Stebbins, Robert A. "Music among friends: The social networks of amateur musicians." *Revue Internationale de Sociologie* (Italy), 12(1–2):52–73, 1976. [200 biographic records form the basis of six derived types of social support networks (orchestral, administrative, organizer, instrumental, performance, expert)]

Stebbins, Robert A. "Classical music amateurs: A definitional study." *Humboldt Journal of Social Relations,* 5(2):78–103, 1978. [Musical amateurs are 'marginal people' of leisure.]

Such, David Glen. *Music, Metaphor and Values among Avant-Garde Jazz Musicians Living in New York City.* Ph.D. Thesis, University of California, Los Angeles, 1985. 317p.

Survilla, Thomas Richard. *Folksong in Zillertal.* Ph.D. Thesis, University of California, Los Angeles, 1986. 324p.

Sweet, Jill Drayson. *Tewa Ceremonial Performances: The Effects of Tourism on an Ancient Pueblo Indian Dance and Music Tradition.* Ph.D. Thesis, The University of New Mexico, 1981. 244p.

Titon, Jeff Todd (General Ed.) *Worlds of Music: An Introduction to the Music of the World's Peoples.* (contributors: James T. Koetting, David P. McAllester, David B. Reck, and Mark Slobin). New York: Schirmer Books, 1984. xviii + 325p.

Turino, Thomas Robert. *Power Relations, Identity and Musical Choice: Music in a Peruvian Altiplano Village and among Its Migrants in the Metropolis.* Ph.D. Thesis, The University of Texas at Austin, 1978. 706p.

Van Khe, Tran. "The status of the traditional musician in Asia." *International Social Science Journal,* 34(4):701–719, 1982.

Vetter, Roger R. *Music for the 'Lap of the World': Gamelan Performance, Performers, and Repertoire in the Kraton Yogyarkarta.* Ph.D. Thesis, The University of Wisconsin-Madison, 1986. 649p.

Vitanyi, Ivan, and Maria Sagi. "Rediscovery and re-animation of folk-art in modern industrial societies." *International Social Science Journal,* 35(1):201–211, 1983.

Waterman, Christopher Alan. *Juju: The Historical Development, Socioeconomic Organization, and Communicative Functions of a West African Popular Music* (Yoruba). Ph.D. Thesis, University of Illinois at Urbana-Champaign, 1986. 458p.

Wheaton, Jack William. *The Technological and Sociological Influences on Jazz as an Art Form in America.* Ph.D. Thesis, University of Northern Colorado, 1976. 347p.

Wright, Judith Lucy. *A Uses and Gratifications Approach to Marketing the Arts: An Audience Survey for the Concert and Chamber Music Series at the University of Kansas.* Ph.D. Thesis, University of Kansas, 1986. 144p.

Yeh, Nora. *Nanquan Music in Taiwan: A Little Known Classical Tradition.* Ph.D. Thesis, University of California, Los Angeles, 1985. 481p.

AUTHOR INDEX

SUBJECT INDEX